Love the Great Outdoors?

When getting away means getting off the beaten path, visit **AAA.com/campgrounds** or **AAA.com/maps** for:

△ Thousands of places to camp across the U.S. and Canada

△ Complete mapping and travel information to plan your adventure

Look for locations with the trusted mark of approval.

Inspected & Approved

Idaho, Montana & Wyoming

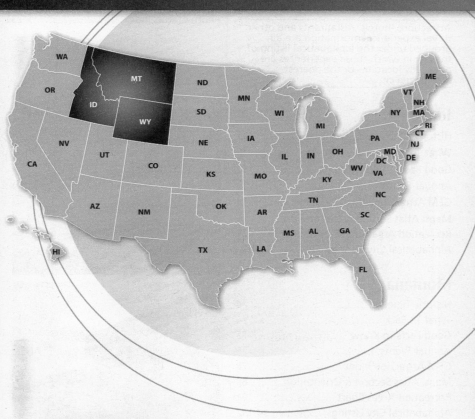

Published by AAA Publishing
1000 AAA Drive, Heathrow, FL 32746-5063
Copyright AAA 2018, All rights reserved

Advertising Rate and Circulation Information: (407) 444-8280

Printed in the USA by Quad/Graphics

This book is printed on paper certified by third-party standards for sustainably managed forestry and production.

Printed on recyclable paper.
Please recycle whenever possible.

Stock #4611

CONTENTS

Get more travel information at AAA.com/travelguides and AAA.com/traveltips

Attractions, hotels, restaurants and other travel experience information are all grouped under the alphabetical listing of the city in which those experiences are physically located—or the nearest recognized city.

Featured Information

Idaho

Montana

Wyoming

free to
rock the boat

TripAssist travel insurance allows you to go with the flow. It can free you up to make the most of your vacation. Nothing will hold you back knowing that you and your travel plans are safe.

Talk to your AAA Travel Agent today for more information.

Using Your Guide

AAA TourBook guides are packed with travel insights, maps and listings of places to stay, play, eat and save. For more listings, more details and online booking, visit **AAA.com/travelguides**.

Helping You Make the Connection

Look for this symbol ✔ throughout the guides for direct links to related content.

A to Z City Listings

Cities and places are listed alphabetically within each state or province. Attractions, hotels and restaurants are listed once — under the city in which they are physically located.

Cities that are considered part of a larger destination city or area have an expanded city header. The header identifies the larger region and cross-references pages that contain shared trip planning resources:

- Destination map – outline map of the cities that comprise a destination city or area
- Attraction spotting map – regional street map marked with attraction locations
- Hotel/restaurant spotting map and index – regional street map numbered with hotel and restaurant locations identified in an accompanying index

Cities that are not considered part of a larger destination city or area but have a significant number of listings may have these resources within the individual city section:

- Attraction spotting map
- Hotel/restaurant spotting map and index

Location Abbreviations

Directions are from the center of town unless otherwise specified, using these highway abbreviations:

Bus. Rte.=business route

CR=county road

FM=farm to market

FR=forest road

Hwy.=Canadian highway

I=interstate highway

LR=legislative route

R.R.=rural route

SR/PR=state or provincial route

US=federal highway

About Listed Establishments

AAA/CAA Inspected & Approved hotels and restaurants are listed on the basis of merit alone after careful evaluation and approval by full-time, professionally trained AAA inspectors. An establishment's decision to advertise in the TourBook guide has no bearing on its evaluation or rating; nor does inclusion of advertising imply AAA endorsement of products and services.

Information in this guide was believed accurate at the time of publication. However, since changes inevitably occur between annual editions, please contact your AAA travel professional, visit **AAA.com/travelguides** or download the free AAA Mobile app to confirm prices and schedules.

Attraction Listing Icons

SAVE AAA Discounts & Rewards® member discount

▸ Electric vehicle charging station on premises. Domestic station information provided by the U.S. Department of Energy. Canadian station information provided by Plug'n Drive Ontario.

GT Guided Tours available

⛰ Camping facilities

🍴 Food on premises

✗ Recreational activities

🐾 Pet friendly (Call for restrictions/fees.)

🎋 Picnicking allowed

In select cities only:

🚇 Mass transit station within 1 mile. Icon is followed by station name and AAA/CAA designated station number within listing.

◈ AAA/CAA travel experts may designate an attraction of exceptional interest and quality as a AAA GEM — a *Great Experience for Members®*. See GEM Attraction Index (listed on CONTENTS page) for a complete list of locations.

Consult the online travel guides at **AAA.com/travelguides** or visit AAA Mobile for additional things to do if you have time.

Hotel Listing Icons

May be preceded by CALL and/or SOME UNITS.

Member Information:

SAVE Member rates: discounted standard room rate or lowest public rate available at time of booking for dates of stay.

6 USING YOUR GUIDE

ECO Eco-certified by government or private organization.

EV Electric vehicle charging station on premises. Domestic station information provided by the U.S. Department of Energy. Canadian station information provided by Plug'n Drive Ontario.

⊠ Smoke-free premises

In select cities only:

🚇 Mass transit station within 1 mile. Icon is followed by station name and AAA/CAA designated station number within listing.

Services:

✈ Airport transportation
🐾 Pet friendly (Call for restrictions/fees.)
🍴 Restaurant on premises
🍴+ Restaurant off premises
🍽 Room service for 2 or more meals
🍸 Full bar
🧒 Child care
BIZ Business center
♿ Accessible features (Call property for available services and amenities.)

Activities:

🎰 Full-service casino
🏊 Pool
💪 Health club or exercise room on premises

In-Room Amenities:

HS High-speed Internet service
$HS High-speed Internet service (Call property for fees.)
🛜 Wireless Internet service
$🛜 Wireless Internet service (Call property for fees.)
🚫🛜 No wireless Internet service
🎬 Pay movies
🧊 Refrigerator
🍱 Microwave
☕ Coffeemaker
🌡 No air conditioning
📺 No TV
☎ No telephones

Restaurant Listing Icons

SAVE AAA Discounts & Rewards® member discount

ECO Eco-certified by government or private organization.

EV Electric vehicle charging station on premises. Domestic station information provided by the U.S. Department of Energy. Canadian station information provided by Plug'n Drive Ontario.

🌡 No air conditioning
♿ Accessible features (Call property for available services and amenities.)
⧄ Designated smoking section
B Breakfast
L Lunch
D Dinner
24 Open 24 hours
LATE Open after 11 p.m.
🐾 Pet friendly (Call for restrictions/fees.)

In select cities only:

🚇 Mass transit station within 1 mile. Icon is followed by station name and AAA/CAA designated station number within listing.

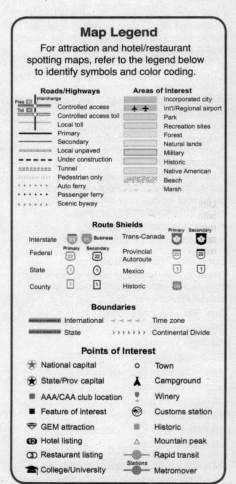

Map Legend

For attraction and hotel/restaurant spotting maps, refer to the legend below to identify symbols and color coding.

Roads/Highways
Interchange
Free — Controlled access
Toll — Controlled access toll
Local toll
Primary
Secondary
Local unpaved
Under construction
Tunnel
Pedestrian only
Auto ferry
Passenger ferry
Scenic byway

Areas of Interest
Incorporated city
Int'l/Regional airport
Park
Recreation sites
Forest
Natural lands
Military
Historic
Native American
Beach
Marsh

Route Shields

	Primary	Secondary
Interstate	95	95 Business
Federal	Primary 22	Secondary 22
State	1	1
County	1	1

Trans-Canada — Primary / Secondary
Provincial Autoroute — 22 / 22
Mexico — 1 / 1
Historic — 66

Boundaries
International
State
Time zone
Continental Divide

Points of Interest

★ National capital	○	Town
✦ State/Prov capital	人	Campground
■ AAA/CAA club location	♟	Winery
■ Feature of interest	⊛	Customs station
▽ GEM attraction	■	Historic
12 Hotel listing	△	Mountain peak
3 Restaurant listing	— Rapid transit
🎓 College/University	Stations — Metromover

Understanding the Diamond Ratings

Hotel and restaurant evaluations are unscheduled to ensure our professionally trained inspectors encounter the same experience members do.

- When an establishment is Diamond Rated, it means members can expect a good fit with their needs. The inspector assigns a rating that indicates the type of experience to expect.
- While establishments at high levels must offer increasingly complex personalized services, establishments at every level are subject to the same basic requirements for cleanliness, comfort and hospitality. Learn more at **AAA.com/diamonds**.

Hotels	Restaurants
Budget-oriented, offering basic comfort and hospitality.	Simple, economical food, often quick-serve, in a functional environment.
Affordable, with modestly enhanced facilities, décor and amenities.	Familiar food, often cooked to order, served in casual surroundings.
Distinguished, multifaceted with enhanced physical attributes, amenities and guest comforts.	Trendy cuisine, skillfully prepared and served, with expanded beverage options, in an enhanced setting.

Refined, stylish with upscale physical attributes, extensive amenities and high degree of hospitality, service and attention to detail.	Distinctive fine-dining. Creative preparations, skillfully served, often with wine steward, amid upscale ambience.

Ultimate luxury, sophistication and comfort with extraordinary physical attributes, meticulous personalized service, extensive amenities and impeccable standards of excellence.	Leading-edge cuisine of the finest ingredients, uniquely prepared by an acclaimed chef, served by expert service staff led by maître d' in extraordinary surroundings.

Guest Safety

Inspectors view a sampling of rooms during evaluations and, therefore, AAA/CAA cannot guarantee the presence of working locks and operational fire safety equipment in every guest unit.

Contacting AAA/CAA About the TourBook Guide

Tell us what you think about the content and format of the TourBook guide or about your experience at a listed hotel, restaurant or attraction. If your visit to an attraction, hotel or restaurant listed by AAA/CAA doesn't meet your expectations, please tell us about it **during your visit or within 30 days**. Be sure to save your receipts and other documentation for reference. Or, maybe you'd like to recommend a place you visited and would like AAA inspectors to consider.

Use the easy online form at **AAA.com/MemberFeedback** to send us the details.

Alternatively, you can email your comments to: memberrelations@national.aaa.com or submit them via postal mail to: AAA Member Comments, 1000 AAA Dr., Box 61, Heathrow, FL 32746.

Sawtooth Mountains

Idaho

Visit Idaho and you'll need an oxygen mask; the scenery is that breathtaking. From the serrated granite peaks of the Sawtooth Mountains at the state's core to the towering Seven Devils flanking Hells Canyon, Idaho features some of the country's most stunning high-altitude panoramas. And if the views don't steal your breath away, the thin air at these lofty elevations just might.

Fortunately, there's no better place to deeply inhale than within the state's numerous unspoiled wilderness areas. Clean air and peaceful solitude attract urbanites from around the country seeking refuge from pollution and stress. They come to places like the Selway-Bitterroot Wilderness or Craters of the Moon National Monument and Preserve.

Expel that fresh air in a shout of triumph as you conquer exhilarating white water along the Snake, Selway or Salmon rivers. Whoop

Hells Canyon National Recreation Area

with excitement while flying down a powder-covered slope in Sun Valley or on Schweitzer Mountain. Scream with delight at the discovery of a star garnet near Coeur d'Alene, the only place outside of India you can find one and just one reason Idaho's nickname—the Gem State—is appropriate.

The Call of the Wild West

Idaho remains one of the country's most isolated and rugged regions. To early explorers and entrepreneurs—from Meriwether Lewis and William Clark to adventurous traders and prospectors—the territory was practically impenetrable. But with a determination undaunted come Hells Canyon or high water, they journeyed west. Follow their lead, and you, too, will be struck by this land's power to inspire.

Idaho counts plenty of contemporary dreamers and doers on its dossier. The memorial marking one of Ernest Hemingway's favorite fly-fishing spots is half-hidden near a shady stream in Sun Valley's outskirts. And astronaut Alan Shepard and his crew trained for a lunar landing at the aptly named Craters of the Moon National Monument and Preserve, an eerie volcanic landscape outside Arco.

As you shop and stroll in the resort towns of Ketchum and Hailey, keep a covert eye out for famous faces; a who's who of movie stars and Olympic athletes lives here part time. Still, Idaho's allure sways more than celebrities. The state is home to one of the world's largest concentrations of nesting hawks, falcons, owls and other raptors; spy on some of these magnificent birds at Boise's World Center for Birds of Prey.

Not For Your Eyes Only

So, what *is* all the fuss about? Mountains, mostly. Three of Idaho's borders wear crowns topping 9,000 feet. From Bruneau River Canyon's Goliath-like stone shoulders to the Precambrian pillars of City of Rocks National Reserve, grandiose mountain scenery dominates this state.

Not that less rugged diversions are lacking. State capital Boise offers a fine orchestra and opera. Coeur d'Alene reinforces its resort image with a fun theme park and a golf course featuring one offshore green. In Sandpoint, the focal point is a city bridge-turned-popular downtown market.

But it's the outdoors that beckon. Here you can watch the slow, mesmerizing spiral of a golden eagle poised on a canyon-channeled thermal of mountain air, or paddle through a fast, furious white-water spin cycle with a boatful of cohorts. The offerings are as vast as the mountains.

Recreation

An abundance of publicly held land and wilderness area is set aside in scenic Idaho—all the better for play in any season.

Thousands of miles of groomed trails—as well as millions of acres of forest land and backcountry—provide fast snowmobiling fun in the chilly winter air. Best bets include Clearwater, Idaho Panhandle and Nez Perce national forests.

For downhill skiing, Bogus Basin, 16 miles north of Boise; Silver Mountain, south of Kellogg; and Sun Valley will satisfy your need for speed. If you prefer cross-country skiing or snowshoeing, outfitters plan overnight treks through the Boulder, Pioneer, Sawtooth and Teton mountains. Skiers of moderate ability enjoy Fish Creek Meadows and Lolo Pass in Nez Perce National Forest; the scenic trails in Farragut State Park; and the paths winding throughout Sawtooth National Recreation Area.

Idaho's waterways provide thrills of their own. Class III and IV rapids, with names like Split Rock and Whiplash, may explain how the Salmon got its nickname as the "River of No Return." Rafting and kayaking also are wild and woolly on the Middle Fork of the Salmon and the Owyhee, Payette and Lochsa rivers, the last of which is a Nez Perce Indian word for "rough water." Jet boats zip along the Snake River through Hells Canyon.

Want to take it slowly? Go canoeing between the cliffs rising around the Snake River at Hagerman Fossil Beds National Monument in Hagerman, or watch eagles, ospreys and mink as you enjoy a leisurely float trip down the placid Boise River.

Dories and drift boats take anglers to favorite fishing waters on the Clearwater, Salmon and Snake rivers, where hardy steelhead thrive. Meanwhile, the upper St. Joe River is a haven for cutthroat.

Anglers find the northern lakes no less exciting. Coeur d'Alene, Pend Oreille and Priest lakes teem with chinook and kokanee salmon, Kamloops trout and northern pike.

Equestrian activities abound in the Grand Tetons and near Coeur d'Alene, Sun Valley and Yellowstone, while ridgelines across such ranges as the Bitterroot, Cougar and Salmon afford outstanding panoramas for mountain bikers.

Climbing expeditions tackle Slick Rock, near McCall; City of Rocks National Reserve, near Almo; and the state's highest peak, Mount Borah. For a less rugged experience, go hiking or backpacking or make your way up mountains around McCall and Sun Valley on a llama. Only pack trains and hikers penetrate the unspoiled terrain of the Frank Church-River of No Return, Sawtooth and Selway-Bitterroot wilderness areas, which blanket more than 2 million acres.

Go fly fishing in Sun Valley

Historic Timeline

1805	Meriwether Lewis and William Clark explore what is now Idaho.
1860	Mormons establish Franklin, the first permanent white settlement in Idaho.
1874	The railroad first reaches Idaho at Franklin.
1890	Idaho becomes the 43rd state.
1951	An Atomic Energy Commission testing station near Idaho Falls first uses fission to generate electricity.
1968	Engineers complete three dams to harness the power of the Snake River.
1983	An earthquake registering 7.3 on the Richter scale shakes central Idaho.
1988	Congress establishes Hagerman Fossil Beds National Monument and the City of Rocks National Reserve.
1995	Idaho native Picabo Street becomes the first American to win a World Cup season title in a speed event.
1999	University of Idaho graduate Jeffrey S. Ashby pilots the space shuttle *Columbia*.
2009	Native American Larry EchoHawk, a former Idaho attorney general, becomes head of the U.S. Bureau of Indian Affairs.

What To Pack

Temperature Averages Maximum/Minimum	JANUARY	FEBRUARY	MARCH	APRIL	MAY	JUNE	JULY	AUGUST	SEPTEMBER	OCTOBER	NOVEMBER	DECEMBER
Boise	36/21	42/26	52/31	62/37	71/45	79/51	90/59	88/57	78/49	65/40	48/30	39/25
Idaho Falls	28/3	33/8	42/18	58/29	68/38	76/44	88/50	86/47	75/38	62/28	43/17	33/9
Lewiston	38/24	44/28	53/33	63/39	71/46	78/52	90/58	88/56	78/49	64/40	48/32	42/28
Pocatello	32/13	37/18	46/26	60/33	69/41	78/48	90/55	87/53	77/44	64/34	45/25	36/19
Salmon	28/9	37/15	50/25	60/32	69/40	78/46	87/51	86/48	75/40	60/30	41/21	29/11
Sandpoint	32/19	38/23	46/28	56/34	65/41	72/47	80/50	80/49	70/41	56/33	40/28	32/21

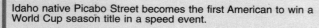

From the records of The Weather Channel Interactive, Inc.

Good Facts To Know

ABOUT THE STATE

POPULATION: 1,567,582.

AREA: 83,569 square miles; ranks 14th.

CAPITAL: Boise.

HIGHEST POINT: 12,662 ft., Borah Peak.

LOWEST POINT: 710 ft., Snake River at Lewiston.

TIME ZONE(S): Mountain/Pacific. DST.

GAMBLING

MINIMUM AGE FOR GAMBLING: 18 (for lotto/scratch-off tickets).

REGULATIONS

TEEN DRIVING LAWS: No more than one passenger under age 17 (excluding family members) is permitted for the first 6 months. Driving is not permitted daily dusk-dawn. The minimum age for an unrestricted driver's license is 16. Phone (208) 334-8000 for more information about Idaho driver's license regulations.

SEAT BELT/CHILD RESTRAINT LAWS: Seat belts are required for driver and all passengers ages 7 and older. Children under age 7 are required to be in a child restraint. AAA recommends the use of seat belts and appropriate child restraints for the driver and all passengers.

CELLPHONE RESTRICTIONS: Text messaging while driving is prohibited for all drivers.

HELMETS FOR MOTORCYCLISTS: Required for riders under 18.

RADAR DETECTORS: Permitted. Prohibited for use by commercial vehicles.

MOVE OVER LAW: Driver is required to slow to below posted speed limit and vacate lane nearest stopped police, fire and rescue vehicles using audible or flashing signals. The law also includes tow trucks.

FIREARMS LAWS: Vary by state and/or county. Contact Idaho Attorney General's Office, 700 W. Jefferson St., Suite 210, P.O. Box 83720, Boise ID 83720-0010; phone (208) 334-2400.

HOLIDAYS

HOLIDAYS: Jan. 1 ▪ Martin Luther King Jr. Day, Jan. (3rd Mon.) ▪ Washington's Birthday/Presidents Day, Feb. (3rd Mon.) ▪ Memorial Day, May (last Mon.) ▪ July 4 ▪ Labor Day, Sept. (1st Mon.) ▪ Columbus Day, Oct. (2nd Mon.) ▪ Veterans Day, Nov. 11 ▪ Thanksgiving, Nov. (4th Thurs.) ▪ Christmas, Dec. 25.

MONEY

TAXES: Idaho's statewide sales tax is 6 percent. There is a 2 percent Travel & Convention Tax on lodgings, with local options to levy up to an additional 5 percent.

VISITOR INFORMATION

INFORMATION CENTERS: State welcome centers that provide details about state attractions, accommodations, historic sites, parks and events as well as road and ski reports are at Fruitland I-84E, Milepost 1 ▪ 6 miles south of Malad City on I-15N ▪ and along I-90E at Post Falls.

FURTHER INFORMATION FOR VISITORS:

Idaho Department of Commerce—Tourism Division
700 W. State St.
Boise, ID 83720
(208) 334-2470
(800) 847-4843

NATIONAL FOREST INFORMATION:

U.S. Forest Service, Idaho Panhandle National Forests
3815 Schreiber Way
Coeur d'Alene, ID 83815-8363
(208) 765-7233
(877) 444-6777 (reservations)

USDA Forest Service, Ogden Ranger District
507 25th St., Suite 103
Ogden, UT 84401
(801) 625-5112

FISHING AND HUNTING REGULATIONS:

Idaho Department of Fish and Game
600 S. Walnut St.
Boise, ID 83712
(208) 334-3700

RECREATION INFORMATION:

Idaho State Department of Parks and Recreation
5657 Warm Springs Ave.
Boise, ID 83716
(208) 334-4199

Idaho Annual Events

Please call ahead to confirm event details.

 Visit **AAA.com/travelguides/events** to find
AAA-listed events for every day of the year

WINTER

Dec. - Famous Idaho Potato Bowl / Boise
208-424-1011
- Holiday Pops / Nampa
208-344-7849
- Yuletide Celebration and Lighting
Festival / Wallace / 208-753-7151
Jan. - Winter Carnival / McCall
208-634-7631
Feb. - Lionel Hampton Jazz Festival
Moscow / 208-885-6765
- Pierce Winter Festival / Pierce
208-464-1057

SPRING

Mar. - St. Patrick's Day Parade / Coeur
d'Alene / 208-415-0116
- Chrome in the Dome Car and Bike
Show / Pocatello / 208-282-3605
- Boise Flower & Garden Show / Boise
503-335-3336
Apr. - Gene Harris Jazz Festival / Boise
208-426-1711
- Dogwood Festival of the Lewis-Clark
Valley / Lewiston / 208-743-3531
- Salmon River Jet Boat Races
Riggins / 208-628-3320
May - Sun Valley Wellness Festival / Sun
Valley / 208-726-2777
- Lost in the 50s / Sandpoint
208-263-9321
- Riggins Rodeo and Parade / Riggins
208-628-4084

SUMMER

June - Meridian Dairy Days / Meridian
208-318-3981
July - Sidewalk Art Festival / Idaho
Falls / 208-523-1010
- Snake River Stampede / Nampa
208-466-8497
- Idaho International SummerFest
Rexburg / 888-463-6880
Aug. - The Festival at Sandpoint / Sandpoint
208-263-6858
- Huckleberry Heritage Festival
Wallace / 208-290-7183
- Caldwell Night Rodeo / Caldwell
208-459-7493

FALL

Sept. - Idaho State Draft Horse and Mule
International Show / Sandpoint
208-263-8414
- Eastern Idaho State Fair / Blackfoot
208-785-2480
Oct. - Sun Valley Jazz & Music Festival
Sun Valley / 208-726-3423
- Fall Harvest Festival / Boise
208-343-8649
- Trailing of the Sheep / Ketchum
800-634-3347
Nov. - Winter Garden aGlow at the Idaho
Botanical Garden / Boise
208-343-8649
- Kootenai Health Foundation Festival
of Trees / Coeur
d'Alene / 208-625-4433
- Boise Holiday Parade / Boise
208-433-5675

For complete hotel, dining and attraction listings: AAA.com/travelguides

Spirit of Boise Balloon Classic

Craters of the Moon National Monument and Preserve

Explore bike trails in Sandpoint

Shoshone Falls, Twin Falls

Elk in Yellowstone National Park

Index: Great Experience for Members

AAA editor's picks of exceptional note

Hells Canyon National
Recreation Area

Craters of the Moon
National Monument
and Preserve

Silverwood

The Museum of Idaho

See Orientation map on p. 20 for corresponding grid coordinates, if applicable.
*Indicates the GEM is temporarily closed.

STAY CONNECTED

TO ALL THE THINGS
MEMBERSHIP CAN DO FOR YOU

- member discounts around you
- cheapest gas nearby
- Diamond Rated hotels and restaurants
- travel information and reservations
- roadside assistance

Download today. Connect every day.
AAA.com/mobile | CAA.ca/mobile

Idaho
Atlas Section

ROADS/HIGHWAYS

- INTERSTATE
- CONTROLLED ACCESS
- CONTROLLED ACCESS TOLL
- TOLL ROAD
- PRIMARY DIVIDED
- PRIMARY UNDIVIDED
- SECONDARY DIVIDED
- SECONDARY UNDIVIDED
- LOCAL DIVIDED
- LOCAL UNDIVIDED
- UNPAVED ROAD
- UNDER CONSTRUCTION
- TUNNEL
- PEDESTRIAN ONLY
- AUTO FERRY
- PASSENGER FERRY
- SCENIC BYWAY
- DISTANCE BETWEEN MARKERS
- EXIT NUMBER-FREE/TOLL
- INTERCHANGE FULL/PARTIAL
- WELCOME/INFORMATION CENTER
- REST AREA/ SERVICE CENTER

BOUNDARIES

- INTERNATIONAL
- STATE
- COUNTY
- TIME ZONE
- CONTINENTAL DIVIDE

ROAD SHIELDS

- INTERSTATE/BUSINESS
- U.S./STATE/COUNTY
- FOREST/INDIAN
- TRANS- CANADA
- PROVINCIAL AUTOROUTE/ KING'S HIGHWAY
- MEXICO
- HISTORIC ROUTE 66
- VT 41 REFERENCE PAGE INDICATOR

AREAS OF INTEREST

- INDIAN
- MILITARY
- PARK
- FOREST
- GRASSLANDS
- HISTORIC
- INT'L/REGIONAL AIRPORT
- INCORPORATED CITY

POINTS OF INTEREST

- TOWN
- NATIONAL CAPITAL
- STATE/PROVINCIAL CAPITAL
- AAA/CAA CLUB LOCATION
- FEATURE OF INTEREST
- COLLEGE/UNIVERSITY
- CUSTOMS STATION
- HISTORIC
- LIGHTHOUSE
- MONUMENT/MEMORIAL
- STATE/PROVINCIAL PARK
- NATIONAL WILDLIFE REFUGE
- SKI AREA
- SPORTS COMPLEX
- DAM

CITIES/TOWNS are color-coded by size, showing where to find AAA Inspected and Approved lodgings or restaurants listed in the AAA TourBook guides and on AAA.com:

- ● Red - major destinations and capitals; many listings
- ● Black - destinations; some listings
- ● Grey - no listings

IDAHO

ER020-1S

Use these detailed driving maps to plan your stops and find your way. For complete route planning, purchase the latest AAA Road Atlas at participating AAA/CAA offices, and use the free online TripTik Travel Planner at AAA.com/maps

Atlas
ROAD
2019

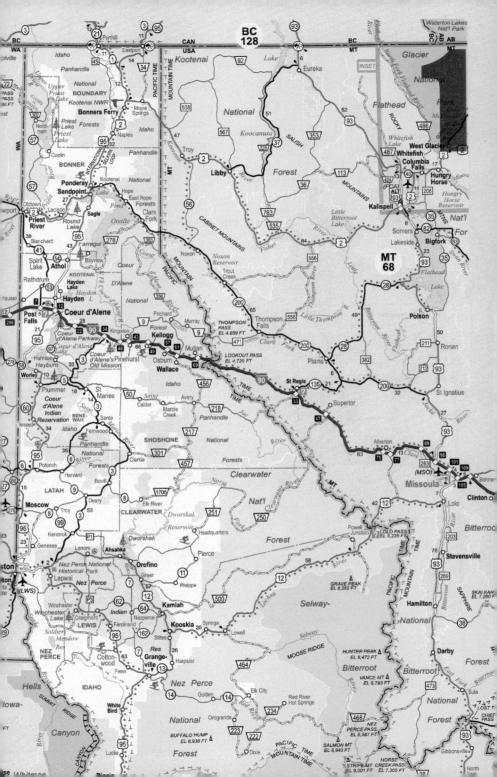

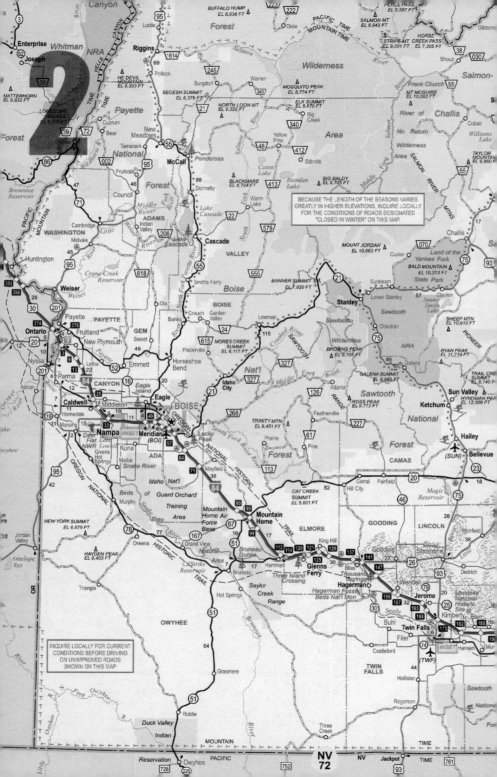

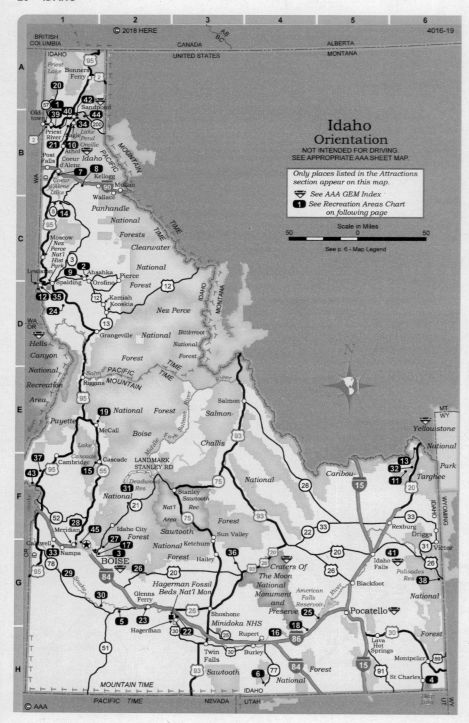

© 2018 HERE

4016-19

BRITISH
COLUMBIA

CANADA
UNITED STATES

ALBERTA
MONTANA

IDAHO

Idaho
Orientation
NOT INTENDED FOR DRIVING.
SEE APPROPRIATE AAA SHEET MAP.

Only places listed in the Attractions
section appear on this map.

See AAA GEM Index

1 See Recreation Areas Chart
on following page

Scale in Miles
50   0   50

See p. 6 - Map Legend

PACIFIC

MOUNTAIN

TIME

MOUNTAIN TIME

PACIFIC TIME

NEVADA   UTAH

IDAHO

© AAA

Recreation Areas Chart

The map location numerals in column 2 show an area's location on the preceding map.

Find thousands of places to camp at AAA.com/campgrounds

	MAP LOCATION	CAMPING	PICNICKING	HIKING TRAILS	BOATING	BOAT RAMP	BOAT RENTAL	FISHING	SWIMMING	PET FRIENDLY	BICYCLE TRAILS	WINTER SPORTS	VISITOR CENTER	LODGE/CABINS	FOOD SERVICE
NATIONAL FORESTS *(See place listings.)*															
Boise (E-2) 2,612,000 acres. South-central Idaho.		●	●	●	●	●		●	●	●		●		●	
Caribou-Targhee (F-5) 3,000,000 acres. Southeastern Idaho.		●	●	●	●	●	●	●	●	●		●		●	
Clearwater (C-2) 1.8 million acres. Northeastern Idaho.		●	●	●	●	●		●	●	●		●		●	
Idaho Panhandle (B-1) 2,495,517 acres. Northern Idaho.		●	●	●	●	●		●	●	●		●		●	
Nez Perce (D-2) 2,223,594 acres. North-central Idaho.		●	●	●	●	●		●	●	●		●		●	
Payette (E-1) 2,307,897 acres. West-central Idaho.		●	●	●	●	●		●	●	●		●		●	●
Salmon-Challis (E-3) 4,300,000 acres. East-central Idaho.		●	●	●	●	●		●	●	●		●		●	
Sawtooth (F-3) 2,101,422 acres. South-central Idaho. Horse rental.		●	●	●	●	●		●	●	●		●		●	
NATIONAL RECREATION AREAS *(See place listings.)*															
Hells Canyon (D-1) 652,977 acres in northeastern Oregon and western Idaho. Horse rental.		●	●	●				●		●		●		●	
Sawtooth (F-3) 756,000 acres in south-central Idaho.		●	●	●	●	●	●	●	●	●	●	●	●	●	●
ARMY CORPS OF ENGINEERS															
Albeni Cove (A-1) 20 acres 1 mi. e. of Oldtown on a county road. Water skiing.	❶	●	●	●	●	●		●	●	●	●				
Dworshak Reservoir (C-1) 19,823 acres 7 mi. n. of Orofino. Bird-watching, water skiing.	❷	●	●	●	●	●	●	●	●	●			●		
Lucky Peak Lake (G-2) 237 acres 9 mi. s.e. of Boise on SR 21. Water skiing.	❸	●	●	●	●	●	●	●	●	●					●
STATE															
Bear Lake (H-6) 966 acres just e. of St. Charles on E. Shore Rd. Snowmobiling, water skiing.	❹	●			●	●		●	●		●	●			●
Bruneau Dunes (G-2) 4,800 acres 5 mi. n. of Bruneau on SR 51/78, then 2 mi. e. on SR 78. Equestrian trails, sand dunes. No motorized boats.	❺	●	●	●				●	●	●	●	●	●		
Castle Rocks (H-4) 1,440 acres 2 mi. n. of Almo on Elba-Almo Rd., then 1.4 mi. w. on 2800 S. (Big Cove Ranch Rd.). Bird-watching, horseback riding, rock climbing, snowshoeing.	❻	●	●	●						●	●	●	●	●	
Coeur d'Alene Parkway (B-1) 34 acres e. of Coeur d'Alene off I-90 exit 15 on Coeur d'Alene Lake Dr.	❼		●	●	●	●		●		●	●				
Coeur d'Alene's Old Mission (B-1) 18 acres 11 mi. w. off I-90 exit 39. Historic.	❽		●	●	●	●		●		●	●				
Dworshak (C-1) 850 acres 26 mi. n.w. of Orofino.	❾	●	●	●	●	●		●	●	●				●	
Farragut (B-1) 4,000 acres 4.9 mi. e. of Athol on SR 54. Historic. Cross-country skiing, snowmobiling. Museum.	❿	●	●	●	●	●		●	●	●	●	●	●		
Harriman (F-6) 11,000 acres 9 mi. s. of Island Park via US 20 at 3489 Green Canyon Rd. Bird-watching, boating (no motors), cross-country skiing, mountain biking, snowshoeing; horse rental, wildlife viewing.	⓫		●	●	●	●		●			●	●	●	●	●
Hells Gate (D-1) 360 acres 4 mi. s. of Lewiston off Snake River Ave. Water skiing. Interpretive centers.	⓬	●	●	●	●	●		●	●	●	●		●		●
Henrys Lake (F-6) 586 acres 15 mi. w. of West Yellowstone off US 20. Bird-watching, canoeing, kayaking, water skiing.	⓭	●	●	●	●	●		●	●	●				●	
Heyburn (C-1) 8,076 acres 5 mi. e. of Plummer on SR 5. Canoeing, cross-country skiing, horseback riding, ice fishing, water skiing.	⓮	●	●	●	●	●	●	●	●	●	●	●	●	●	●
Lake Cascade (F-1) 4,450 acres just n.w. of Cascade. Bird-watching, cross-country skiing, ice fishing, snowmobiling; horse-shoe play.	⓯	●	●	●	●	●		●	●	●	●	●	●		●
Lake Walcott (H-4) 65 acres 11 mi. n.e. of Rupert off SR 24.	⓰	●		●	●	●		●	●	●			●		●
Lucky Peak (G-2) 240 acres 10 mi. s.e. of Boise off SR 21. Marina; boat moorage.	⓱		●	●	●	●		●	●	●	●				●
Massacre Rocks (G-4) 990 acres 10 mi. s.w. of American Falls off I-86. Historic. Canoeing, disc golf, kayaking.	⓲	●	●	●	●			●		●	●	●			

Recreation Areas Chart

The map location numerals in column 2 show an area's location on the preceding map.

 Find thousands of places to camp at AAA.com/campgrounds

	MAP LOCATION	CAMPING	PICNICKING	HIKING TRAILS	BOATING	BOAT RAMP	BOAT RENTAL	FISHING	SWIMMING	PET FRIENDLY	BICYCLE TRAILS	WINTER SPORTS	VISITOR CENTER	LODGE/CABINS	FOOD SERVICE
Ponderosa (E-2) 1,515 acres 2 mi. n.e. of McCall via Park St. and Thompson Ave. at 1920 N. Davis Ave. Canoeing, cross-country skiing, snowshoeing.	19	•	•	•	•	•	•	•	•	•	•	•	•	•	
Priest Lake (A-1) 755 acres 11 mi. n. of Coolin. Cross-country skiing, ice fishing, snowmobiling.	20	•	•	•	•	•		•	•	•		•	•	•	•
Round Lake (B-1) 142 acres 10 mi. s. of Sandpoint off US 95 on Dufort Rd. Cross-country skiing, ice fishing, ice-skating, sledding, snowshoeing. No motorized boats.	21	•	•	•	•	•	•	•	•	•		•	•	•	
Thousand Springs (H-3) 1,500 acres .2 mi. s. off I-84 exit 147, then .2 mi. w. following signs to the welcome kiosk at Malad Gorge. Canoeing, kayaking, horseback riding.	22		•	•				•	•	•			•	•	
Three Island Crossing (G-2) 513 acres 1 mi. w. of Glenns Ferry via S. Commercial St. and W. Madison Ave. Historic.	23	•	•	•				•		•		•	•	•	
Winchester Lake (D-1) 418 acres .25 mi. s. of Winchester on US 95 Bus. Rte. Cross-country skiing, ice fishing, ice-skating, sledding. No motorized boats (except with electric motors).	24	•	•	•	•	•	•	•	•	•		•	•	•	
OTHER															
American Falls Reservoir (G-4) 59,893 acres .2 mi. n. of American Falls on I-15. Historic.	25	•	•	•	•	•		•	•	•	•		•		•
Anderson Ranch Reservoir (G-2) 5,000 acres 30 mi. n.e. of Mountain Home on SR 20 and FR 61.	26	•	•	•	•	•	•	•	•	•		•			
Arrowrock Reservoir (F-2) 4,000 acres 16 mi. e. of Boise on SR 21 and FR 268.	27	•	•	•	•	•		•	•	•		•			
Black Canyon Reservoir (F-1) 2,364 acres 8 mi. n.e. of Emmett on SR 52.	28	•	•	•	•	•		•	•	•					
Celebration Park (G-1) 84 acres 8.1 mi. s. of Melba at 6530 Hot Spot Ln. Historic. Scenic. Bird-watching, horseback riding; interpretive programs.	29	•	•	•	•	•		•		•	•	•	•		
C.J. Strike Reservoir (G-2) 7,500 acres n.w. of Bruneau via SR 78.	30	•	•	•	•	•		•	•	•	•				
Deadwood Reservoir (F-2) 3,000 acres 34 mi. n.e. of Garden Valley on FR 555.	31	•	•	•	•	•		•	•	•		•			
Island Park Reservoir (F-6) 7,800 acres 27 mi. n. of Ashton off US 20. Snowmobiling.	32	•	•	•				•	•				•	•	•
Lake Lowell (G-1) 10,587 acres 8 mi. s. of Caldwell via 10th Ave. or SR 55. Bird-watching; water skiing.	33		•	•				•	•	•	•	•			
Lake Pend Oreille (B-1) 94,600 acres s. and e. of Sandpoint.	34	•	•	•	•	•	•	•	•	•	•		•	•	•
Lake Waha (D-1) 180 acres 18 mi. s.e. of Lewiston on Thain Rd.	35		•	•	•	•	•	•	•				•		
Little Wood River Reservoir (G-3) 976 acres 11 mi. n. of Carey on access road.	36	•	•	•				•	•	•					
Mann Creek Reservoir (F-1) 280 acres 9 mi. n. of Weiser on US 95. Water skiing.	37	•	•	•	•	•	•	•	•	•					
Palisades Reservoir (G-6) 27,845 acres 50 mi. s.e. of Idaho Falls on US 26.	38	•	•	•		•	•	•	•	•		•			•
Priest River (B-1) 20 acres .5 mi. e. of Priest River off US 2. Bird-watching; water skiing.	39	•	•	•	•	•		•	•	•	•	•			
Riley Creek (B-1) 45 acres 1 mi. s. of US 2 at Laclede on Riley Creek Rd. Water skiing.	40	•	•	•	•	•		•	•	•	•	•			
Ririe Reservoir (G-6) 6,069 acres 20 mi. n.e. of Idaho Falls on US 26.	41	•	•	•	•	•		•	•	•		•			
Springy Point (A-1) 13 acres 3.2 mi. w. of US 95 at Sandpoint on Lakeshore Dr. Water skiing.	42	•	•	•				•	•	•	•	•			
Steck Park (F-1) 20 mi. n.w. of Weiser via SR 70 on the Snake River.	43	•	•		•	•	•	•	•		•	•			
Trestle Creek (B-1) 2 acres n.w. of Hope on SR 200. Water skiing.	44		•		•	•		•	•	•					
Veterans Memorial (F-1) 80 acres on SR 44 at 36th St. in Boise. Bird-watching. Playground. No motorized boats.	45		•	•	•			•	•	•	•	•			

AAA Life Insurance Company

MAKE LIFE A PRIORITY

PUT A PLAN IN PLACE FOR THE FUTURE WITH LIFE INSURANCE

You insure your automobile, your home, and your most valuable possessions.

But have you taken the steps to help protect your most precious asset:
Your life and the lives of those most important to you?

AAA Life Insurance Company offers you additional peace of mind.

▼ **Term Life**   ▼ **Permanent Life**   ▼ **Annuities**

Get a FREE Quote Today! Visit AAALife.com

AHSAHKA (C-1) elev. 1,001'

DWORSHAK DAM VISITOR CENTER 1842 Viewpoint Rd., is 3 mi. e. on SR 7, following signs, on the North Fork of the Clearwater River. The visitor center overlooks the 717-foot dam, one of the highest straight-axis concrete gravity dams in North America. Behind the dam, Dworshak Reservoir *(see Recreation Areas Chart)* extends 54 miles into wild, rugged timberland.

Interpretive displays are available. Audiovisual presentations are shown in the theater upon request. **Hours:** Visitor center daily 8:30-4:30, Memorial Day weekend-Labor Day; Mon.-Fri. 8:30-4:30, rest of year. Ninety-minute guided tours are available daily at 9, 11:30 and 2:30, Memorial Day weekend-Labor Day. Closed winter holidays and Christmas-Jan. 1. Phone ahead to confirm schedule. **Cost:** Free. **Phone:** (208) 476-1255. GT

DWORSHAK NATIONAL FISH HATCHERY, s.e. on SR 7 at the confluence of the North Fork and Main Stem Clearwater rivers, just below Dworshak Dam. About 2.1 million steelhead trout, 1.5 million Chinook salmon and 400,000 coho salmon are raised in environmentally controlled ponds. The best time to see the adult steelhead is November through April; the returning salmon brood stock July through October.

Displays, a viewing balcony above the spawning room and 126 outdoor ponds are on-site. A self-guiding tour is available. **Time:** Allow 30 minutes minimum. **Hours:** Grounds daily dawn-dusk. Main building daily 7-3:30; hatchery building closed major holidays. **Cost:** Free. **Phone:** (208) 476-4591.

ATHOL (B-1) pop. 692, elev. 2,391'
• Hotels p. 24

In a region rich with timber, Athol developed around a sawmill established at the turn of the 20th century. The town is in a popular summer recreation area centered on Lake Pend Oreille.

SILVERWOOD 3 mi. s. of Athol on US 95. One of the Northwest's largest theme parks, Silverwood covers 221 acres and offers more than 70 rides, slides, shows and attractions. Aftershock is a 191-foot-tall steel roller coaster that travels forward and backward through a cobra loop at speeds exceeding 65 mph. SpinCycle is a 104-foot-tall thrill ride that swings upside down like a giant pendulum with riders strapped into a cylinder on the other end that spins 360 degrees.

Other rides include two wooden coasters: the 55-mph Timber Terror and Tremors, which reaches speeds of 63 mph during a 103-foot drop; the 140-foot-tall Panic Plunge drop tower; the Thunder Canyon white-water ride and a 1915 steam-powered train. Garfield's Summer Camp has 10 family-friendly rides for kids. The park also has dozens of traditional amusement rides. Entertainment includes a magic show, a staged train robbery, and appearances by Garfield and Odie.

Time: Allow 6 hours minimum. **Hours:** Open daily, late May-Labor Day; Sat.-Sun., early-late May and day after Labor Day-late Sept. Hours vary for special events; phone ahead. **Cost:** One-day pass $48; $25 (ages 3-7 and 65+). One-day pass after 5 p.m. $25. Two-day pass $76; $38 (ages 3-7 and 65+). All passes include Boulder Beach Water Park when open. **Parking:** $5. **Phone:** (208) 683-3400.

Boulder Beach Water Park 2 mi. s. on US 95 at Silverwood to 27843 N. US 95. Rides include two gigantic wave pools, four tube slides, three high-velocity body slides, two family raft rides, a lazy river and two play areas for children. **Time:** Allow 4 hours minimum. **Hours:** Opens daily at 11, early June-Labor Day. Closing times vary; phone ahead. **Cost:** (includes Silverwood) $48; $25 (ages 3-7 and 65+). Discounted admission is offered after 5 p.m. **Parking:** $5. **Phone:** (208) 683-3400.

LOG SPIRIT BED & BREAKFAST   (208)683-4722

Bed & Breakfast
$140-$200

Address: 31328 N Tiara Ln 83801 **Location:** US 95, just e on SR 54 to Howard Rd, 1.8 mi n, then 0.5 mi e. **Facility:** The grounds of this log B&B offers a small bridge with a waterfall, gardens and small farm animals. Rooms and bathrooms are large with wood floors and luxurious bedding. 6 units. 2 stories (no elevator), interior corridors. **Parking:** winter plug-ins. **Activities:** trails. **Guest Services:** coin laundry. **Featured Amenity: full hot breakfast.**

BITTERROOT NATIONAL FOREST—See
Montana p. 99

BLACKFOOT (G-5) pop. 11,899, elev. 4,497'

At the northern end of the Snake River Valley, land is key. In the 19th century the fertile lava soil helped establish Blackfoot as an important agricultural center, with the russet potato eventually becoming the town's main crop. Visit the Idaho Potato Museum *(see attraction listing)* to learn why Blackfoot is known as the "Potato Capital of the World," then head next door to Depot Park for a self-guiding walking tour past antique potato harvesting devices. Remnants of the past also are exhibited at Veterans Park, which features army tanks and other military equipment.

Stemming from Blackfoot's agricultural roots, the Eastern Idaho State Fair attracts tens of thousands of revelers with livestock shows as well as mouthwatering foodstuffs—from Indian tacos to (what else?) loaded baked potatoes. The weeklong end-of-summer party takes place around Labor Day. Watch a bull riding competition or marvel over fine equestrian specimens; browse antiques and charming quilt displays; or sniff out the best recipes for such tasty bites as hash browns, brownies and peanut butter cookies.

Although residents have been tapping Blackfoot's natural resources since the late 1880s, the area still boasts striking, untouched terrain. You'll discover year-round recreational opportunities in and around town. In warm weather, you can hike, fish or get drenched white-water rafting at Wolverine Canyon, about 19 miles northeast. When temperatures drop there are still plenty of outdoor activities to enjoy, including cross-country skiing and snowmobiling.

Wildlife viewing is popular throughout the region. Blackfoot River Canyon—home to golden eagles, prairie falcons, red-tailed hawks and great horned owls—is especially breathtaking. In summer swimmers and boaters crowd 55-acre Jensen Lake at Jensen Grove; nearby you'll find such man-made recreational features as a skate park and a 2-mile paved walking path. Abutting Jensen Lake's northern bank at 3115 Teeples Dr. is the 18-hole Blackfoot Golf Course; phone (208) 785-9960.

Greater Blackfoot Area Chamber of Commerce: 130 N.W. Main St., P.O. Box 801, Blackfoot, ID 83221. **Phone:** (208) 785-0510.

IDAHO POTATO MUSEUM, 130 N.W. Main St., presents a variety of exhibits related to the potato, including antique machinery and tools, gunnysack clothing and, at 24 by 14 inches, the "Guinness World Records" world's largest potato crisp. Each visitor is offered a free potato product. Videos about the potato industry and production processes are shown. Phone for special tour arrangements. . RV parking is available in the north parking lot. **Time:** Allow 1 hour minimum. **Hours:** Mon.-Sat. 9:30-5, Sept.-May; Mon.-Sat. 9:30-7, June-Aug. Closed Thanksgiving and Dec. 25-Jan. 2. **Cost:** $4; $3.50 (military with ID and ages 60+); $2 (ages 5-12); $3 Group Rate for groups of 15 or more. **Phone:** (208) 785-2517.

BEST WESTERN BLACKFOOT INN   (208)785-4144

Hotel
$100-$135

 Best Western. AAA Benefit: Members save up to 15% and earn bonus points!

Address: 750 Jensen Grove Dr 83221 **Location:** I-15 exit 93, 0.3 mi e to Parkway Dr, then 0.4 mi n. **Facility:** 60 units. 2 stories (no elevator), interior corridors. **Parking:** winter plug-ins. **Terms:** cancellation fee imposed. **Pool:** heated indoor. **Activities:** hot tub. **Guest Services:** coin laundry.

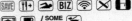

SUPER 8 BY WYNDHAM BLACKFOOT   (208)785-9333
Hotel. **Address:** 1279 Parkway Dr 83221

WHERE TO EAT

TOMMY VAUGHN'S GRILL   208/785-6400
American. Casual Dining. **Address:** 850 Jensen Grove Dr 83221

BOISE (G-1) pop. 205,671, elev. 2,739'
• Hotels p. 32 • Restaurants p. 35
• Hotels & Restaurants map & index p. 29

The woods lining the Boise River were a welcome sight for French-Canadian trappers who were grateful to reach a forest again after trudging across the territory's semiarid plain. As a result, they named the area *Boisé*, meaning "wooded." The city, however, was not founded until 1863, a year after the gold rush reached the Boise Basin.

"The City of Trees," Boise is Idaho's capital and largest metropolitan area. The first sessions of the territorial government were held during 1863 in Lewiston, then moved to this population center the following year. The new territorial capital was the center of commerce and culture for miners and traders from nearby mountain boomtowns. Built in 1863, the O'Farrell Cabin on Fort Street is one of the city's oldest buildings.

The quality of life, low cost of living and liberal tax advantages as well as the city's role as state capital and transportation hub, account for Boise's steady economic growth. Many national and multinational firms have their headquarters in Boise, and light industry flourishes. The city also is the home of Boise State University *(see attraction listing),* where the Broncos play football on the blue field of Albertsons Stadium from early September to early December; the Famous Idaho Potato Bowl takes place at the stadium after football season ends. In addition, the Boise Philharmonic plays in the university's Velma V. Morrison Center for the Performing Arts. Entertaining audiences since 1998, the Gene Harris Jazz Festival takes place at the college in April.

Boise is the southwest terminus of SR 21, the Ponderosa Pine Scenic Route. The route passes through part of Sawtooth National Forest before ending in Stanley; depending on weather conditions, portions of SR 21 may be closed in winter.

Protected from unduly harsh winter weather by the Owyhee Mountains, the capital enjoys year-round opportunities for leisure and recreation. Ann Morrison Park, 153 acres between Americana and Capital boulevards, offers picnicking, playgrounds, ball fields and tennis courts as well as the Spirit of Boise Balloon Classic, held in August.

A novel way to reach Ann Morrison Park is by floating down the Boise River on a rental raft or inner tube from Barber Park, which is on the southeast edge of town; at the junction of Warm Springs Avenue and SR 21 turn onto Eckert to reach the park. Rentals are available daily mid-June through Labor Day, river flows permitting; a return shuttle bus is available. Phone (208) 577-4584.

Kathryn Albertson Park is a 41-acre downtown wildlife sanctuary across Americana Boulevard from Ann Morrison Park. Paved footpaths meander past gazebos, ponds and fountains while offering glimpses of waterfowl and other wildlife. The park also provides nearby access to the Boise Greenbelt, a 25-mile path following the Boise River. A favorite

(See map & index p. 29.)

place to walk, jog, skate or ride a bicycle, the greenbelt connects 12 area parks.

The Idaho Shakespeare Festival presents five plays in repertory from the last weekend in May through September at an outdoor amphitheater at 5657 Warm Springs Ave.; phone (208) 336-9221.

Once used as a Native American lookout, Table Rock rises 1,100 feet above the valley east of Boise. Its flat summit, surmounted by an illuminated cross that can be seen for miles, affords a view of the city and a pioneer route south of the river.

In the 1921 St. Paul Baptist Church building at 508 Julia Davis Dr. in Julia Davis Park, the Idaho Black History Museum presents changing educational exhibits about the history and culture of African-Americans in Idaho; phone (208) 789-2164.

To the southeast, 12 miles south of Kuna, the Morley Nelson Snake River Birds of Prey National Conservation Area provides a 600,000-acre haven for two dozen species of raptors. The area represents one of the world's densest concentrations of birds of prey; phone (208) 384-3300.

Boise Convention & Visitors Bureau: 1101 W. Front St., Suite 100, Boise, ID 83702. **Phone:** (208) 344-7777 or (800) 635-5240.

Self-guiding tours: A map showcasing downtown Boise's public art displays and historical points of interest is available from information kiosks at 8th and Idaho streets, 8th and Broad streets and the city hall front entrance.

Shopping: Boise Factory Outlets, I-84 exit Gowen Road, offers such factory stores as Eddie Bauer, Levi's Outlet and Reebok. Boise Towne Square Mall, Milwaukee and Franklin streets, features Dillard's, JCPenney, Kohl's, Macy's, Nordstrom Rack and Sears. Downtown shopping includes BoDo (short for Boise Downtown), a former late-1890s warehouse district at 8th and Front streets; Hyde Park on N. 13th Street; and Old Boise Historic District on Main Street between Capitol and 4th streets. The 85 vendors comprising the gift shop at the State Capitol (see attraction listing) specialize in items made in Idaho, including jewelry that uses semi-precious stones from the state.

BASQUE MUSEUM AND CULTURAL CENTER, 611 Grove St., on the Basque block, celebrates the legacy of the Basques and is the only museum in the country dedicated to the ethnic group. Permanent and temporary exhibits focus on the history and culture of these modern people with ancient roots. Basque traditions are further depicted through a cultural center and a restored Basque boarding house.

Time: Allow 30 minutes minimum. **Hours:** Tues.-Fri. 10-6, Sat. 11-4, 1st Tues. in June-Labor Day; Tues.-Fri. 10-4, Sat. 11-3, rest of year. Guided tours of Cyrus Jacobs Uberuaga Boarding House depart Tues.-Fri. at 11:30, 1, 3 and 4:30; Sat. at 11:30, 1 and 2:30, Jun.-Aug; and Sat. at 12 and 1:30, rest of

year. Closed major holidays. **Cost:** $5; $4 (ages 65+ and students with ID); $3 (ages 6-12). **Phone:** (208) 343-2671. GT

BOISE STATE UNIVERSITY, 1910 University Dr. along the Boise River, is the state's largest institution of higher learning, with more than 200 fields of study in seven colleges. Established in 1932, the university has approximately 22,000 students enrolled in graduate and undergraduate programs.

Highlights of the campus include the Velma V. Morrison Center for the Performing Arts. Bronco Stadium is noted for its blue artificial turf. **Hours:** Public tours of the university are offered Mon.-Fri. at 10 and 1, during the academic year; at 10, in summer. **Cost:** Free. Reservations are recommended. **Phone:** (208) 426-1156.

BOISE TROLLEY TOURS departs from Joe's Crab Shack restaurant, 2288 N. Garden St., on the riverfront. The tour, aboard a replica open-air trolley car, includes a 75-minute historical narration covering downtown Boise, the State Capitol and other government buildings, Harrison Boulevard and Warm Springs-area mansions, Hyde Park and the Old Idaho Penitentiary State Historic Site. **Time:** Allow 1 hour minimum. **Hours:** Historical tours depart Mon.-Fri. at 11 a.m., Sat.-Sun. at 2 p.m., May-Sept. Halloween tours depart daily at 8 p.m. in Oct.; phone ahead to confirm. Holiday Lights tours nightly, early Dec.-late Dec.; departs from Evergreen Business Mall. **Cost:** $20; $18 (ages 65+, military and students with ID); $10 (ages 3-12); $5 (ages 0-2). Reservations are recommended. **Phone:** (208) 433-0849.

GEM SAVE **DISCOVERY CENTER OF IDAHO,** 131 W. Myrtle St., is a hands-on museum with more than 160 exhibits relating to science, math and technology. Visitors can use the Whisper Dish exhibit to carry on a quiet conversation across the room; squeeze clay with 24,000 pounds of force at the Make a Rock exhibit; generate electricity using the Pedal Generator; and experiment with electric arcs at the Electric Flame exhibit.

Other displays designed to encourage interaction with natural science phenomena include Touch the Spring, Disappearing Glass Rods, Pedaling Legs and Air Brake. In-house featured exhibits rotate approximately every six months.

Time: Allow 1 hour minimum. **Hours:** Mon.-Sat. 10-5, Sun. noon-5. Closed Jan. 1, Easter, Thanksgiving and Christmas. **Cost:** $12; $11 (ages 65+ and military with ID); $10 (ages 2-17). **Phone:** (208) 343-9895.

SAVE **IDAHO BOTANICAL GARDEN,** 1.5 mi. e. on Warm Springs Ave. from Broadway, then n. to 2355 N. Penitentiary Rd., offers 14 specialty gardens on 33 acres of the former Idaho Penitentiary. The sandstone walls provide a historic backdrop for theme gardens, garden art and a labyrinth. The Lewis and Clark Native Plant Garden features a

(See map & index p. 29.)

bronze likeness of Sacagawea and has examples of period plants catalogued by the explorers; it also offers views of Treasure Valley.

Time: Allow 1 hour minimum. **Hours:** Mon.-Sun. 9-7, mid-Mar. to early Nov.; Mon.-Fri. 9-5 rest of year. **Cost:** $7; $5 (ages 5-12 and 65+). **Phone:** (208) 343-8649.

THE IDAHO MILITARY HISTORY MUSEUM is at 4692 W. Harvard St. Weapons, photographs, artifacts, military guidons and small arms chronicle the participation of various Idaho military units in conflicts ranging from the Civil War to current events including items from the Philippine Insurrection, Operation Iraqi Freedom and Operation Enduring Freedom. Armored vehicles and aircraft are displayed outdoors. **Time:** Allow 1 hour minimum. **Hours:** Tues.-Sat. noon-4. Closed major holidays. **Cost:** Donations. **Phone:** (208) 272-4841.

JULIA DAVIS PARK, with entrances on Capitol Blvd. or Third St. off Myrtle St., contains within its 89-acre expanse the Boise Art Museum; the Idaho State Museum; the Idaho Black History Museum; Zoo Boise; and the Discovery Center of Idaho, which offers hands-on exhibits *(see attraction listing p. 26)*. A lagoon, a rose garden, a playground, a tennis complex, the R.A. and Annette Bloch Cancer Survivor Plaza and a band shell are within the park; a portion of the Boise River Greenbelt runs through the park as well. **Hours:** Daily dawn-midnight; hours may be extended for events at Boise State University. **Cost:** Free. **Phone:** (208) 608-7600.

SAVE **Boise Art Museum,** 670 Julia Davis Dr. at the Julia Davis Park entrance, displays more than 15 changing art exhibitions annually. **Time:** Allow 1 hour minimum. **Hours:** Tues.-Sat. 10-5 (also first Thurs. of the month 5-8), Sun. noon-5. Closed Jan. 1, Easter, Thanksgiving, the day after Thanksgiving and Christmas. **Cost:** $6; $4 (ages 62+ and military with ID); $3 (students in grades 1-12 and college students with ID); donations (first Thurs. of the month). **Phone:** (208) 345-8330.

Idaho State Museum, 610 Julia Davis Dr., provides an overview of the state's history. Displays include a 19th-century saloon as well as artifacts of early Idaho. . **Hours:** Mon.-Sat. 10-5, Sun. noon-5. Closed major holidays. Phone ahead to confirm schedule. **Cost:** $10; $8 (ages 65+, students and retired military with ID); $5 (ages 6-12). **Phone:** (208) 334-2120.

Zoo Boise, .5 mi. s. off Capitol Blvd. in Julia Davis Park, has more than 300 animals from around the world, including Amur tigers, zebras, snow leopards, Magellanic penguins, lions, giraffes and red pandas. Small Animal Kingdom spotlights animals and plants indigenous to islands, deserts and rainforests. Conservation Action Stations feature seasonal activities including giraffe feeding, a sloth bear encounter, a zoo farm and a conservation cruise. **Hours:** Daily 9-5, June-Aug.; 10-5, rest of year. Closed Jan. 1,

Thanksgiving and Christmas. **Cost:** May-Sept. $10; $8 (ages 62+); $7 (ages 3-11). Rest of year $7; $4.50 (ages 62+); $4.25 (ages 3-11). Carousel $1. Giraffe and sloth bear encounter $3. Conservation cruise $1. Prices may vary. **Phone:** (208) 608-7760. 🍽

MORRISON KNUDSEN NATURE CENTER is 2.5 mi. off I-84 exit 54 (Broadway Ave.); cross the Boise River, turn e. onto Park Blvd. then head .5 mi. e. to 600 S. Walnut St., following signs. This 4.5-acre area features a sampling of Idaho's ecosystems. Walking trails pass a mountain stream with logjams and waterfalls, a wetlands pond and a high desert plain with sagebrush and lava rock. Along the way are plants and wildlife indigenous to each area. Windows along the stream walk offer "face-to-fish" viewing opportunities and lessons on stream ecology.

The visitor center features exhibits and offers educational programs. **Time:** Allow 1 hour minimum. **Hours:** Outdoor area daily dawn-dusk. Visitor center Tues.-Fri. 9-5, Sat.-Sun. 11-5. **Cost:** Free. **Phone:** (208) 334-2225.

SAVE **OLD IDAHO PENITENTIARY STATE HISTORIC SITE,** 1.5 mi. e. of Broadway and Warm Springs Ave. at 2445 Old Penitentiary Rd., was used 1872-1973 as Idaho's state penitentiary. Additions to the complex were constructed by prisoners with sandstone they quarried and cut. Exhibits include historical weapons and vehicles; an explanation of the history of tattoos; and a video presentation recalling prison history, notorious inmates and conditions of prison life.

Guided tours are offered on weekends and during summer months. Visitors should wear comfortable shoes and dress for an outdoor experience. Picnicking is permitted outside the prison walls. **Time:** Allow 2 hours minimum. **Hours:** Daily 10-5, Memorial Day-Labor Day; noon-5, rest of year. Last admission 45 minutes before closing. Closed major holidays. Phone ahead to confirm schedule. **Cost:** $6; $4 (ages 60+); $3 (ages 6-12). **Phone:** (208) 334-2844.

STATE CAPITOL, bordered by Jefferson, W. State, 6th and 8th sts., is Boise's most treasured public building. The Idaho sandstone exterior base is carved to resemble logs—a tribute to pioneer cabins. Vermont and Georgian marble and handcrafted scagliola (imitation marble) dominate the bright interior spaces of all four floors of the rotunda.

Begun in 1905, the five-part neoclassical building that motorists see while approaching from Capitol Boulevard was finished in 1920. A restored 5-foottall statue of a golden eagle sits atop the Capitol dome 208 feet above street level. **Hours:** Mon.-Fri. 6-6 (also 6-10 p.m., during legislative sessions), Sat.-Sun. 9-5. **Cost:** Free. **Phone:** (208) 332-1000 during legislative sessions, (208) 332-1012 in the interim between sessions or (800) 626-0471. GT

(See map & index p. 29.)

SAVE **WORLD CENTER FOR BIRDS OF PREY** is 7 mi. s. at 5668 W. Flying Hawk Ln.; take I-84 exit 50 to S. Cole Rd., then s. 6 mi. and w. on Flying Hawk Ln. to the top of the hill. The world headquarters of the Peregrine Fund—an organization dedicated to the conservation of birds of prey—includes a 7,200-square-foot interpretive center. Exhibits about wildlife, biology and ecology are featured, and live birds, such as falcons, California condors and eagles, can be seen. Outdoor flight demonstrations are offered Friday through Sunday in October. Docents are available to answer questions and to lead tours of the interpretive center.

Hours: Tues.-Sun. 10-5, Mar.-Oct.; Tues.-Sun. 10-4, rest of year. Last admission 45 minutes before closing. Closed major holidays. **Cost:** $7; $6 (ages 62+); $5 (ages 4-16). **Phone:** (208) 362-8687.

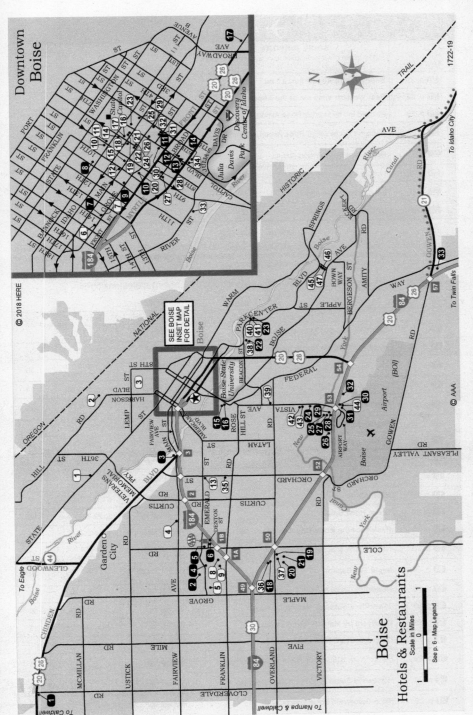

Downtown Boise

© 2018 HERE

Boise

Hotels & Restaurants

Scale in Miles

See p. 6 - Map Legend

1722-19

✈ Airport Hotels

Map Page	BOISE AIRPORT (Maximum driving distance from airport: 1.0 mi)	Diamond Rated	Rate Range	Page
30 p. 29	Best Western Airport Inn, 0.5 mi	◈◈	$90-$120 SAVE	32
31 p. 29	Best Western Vista Inn at the Airport, 0.5 mi	◈◈	$85-$139 SAVE	33
28 p. 29	Fairfield Inn by Marriott Boise Airport, 0.9 mi	◈◈◈	$80-$237	33
29 p. 29	Hampton Inn by Hilton Boise Airport, 0.8 mi	◈◈◈	Rates not provided	33
27 p. 29	Holiday Inn Boise Airport, 0.8 mi	◈◈◈	Rates not provided	33
25 p. 29	Holiday Inn Express & Suites Boise Airport, 1.0 mi	◈◈◈	$129-$259	33
32 p. 29	Inn America Boise Airport, 0.7 mi	◈◈	Rates not provided	34
24 p. 29	La Quinta Inn & Suites Boise Airport, 1.0 mi	◈◈	$79-$149	34

Boise

This index helps you "spot" where approved hotels and restaurants are located on the corresponding detailed maps. Hotel daily rate range is for comparison only. Restaurant price range is a combination of lunch and/or dinner. Turn to the listing page for more information and consult display ads for special promotions.

 For more details, rates and reservations: AAA.com/travelguides/hotels

BOISE

Map Page	Hotels	Diamond Rated	Rate Range	Page
1 p. 29	SpringHill Suites by Marriott Boise/Eagle	◈◈◈	$84-$224	35
2 p. 29	**Hyatt Place Boise Towne Square** *(See ad p. 34.)*	◈◈◈	$99-$229 SAVE	34
3 p. 29	The Riverside Hotel	◈◈◈	Rates not provided	35
4 p. 29	La Quinta Inn & Suites Boise Towne Square	◈◈◈	$74-$159	34
5 p. 29	Candlewood Suites Boise Towne Square	◈◈◈	Rates not provided	33
6 p. 29	Residence Inn by Marriott Boise West	◈◈◈	$88-$248	35
7 p. 29	Modern Hotel and Bar	◈◈	$128-$140	34
8 p. 29	**Hyatt Place Boise Downtown**	◈◈◈	$99-$329 SAVE	34
9 p. 29	Safari Inn Downtown	◈◈	Rates not provided	35
10 p. 29	**Hotel 43**	◈◈◈	$139-$539 SAVE	33
11 p. 29	**Grove Hotel Boise**	◈◈◈◈	$129-$349 SAVE	33
12 p. 29	**Residence Inn Boise City Center**	◈◈◈	$114-$365 SAVE	35
13 p. 29	Hampton Inn & Suites Boise/Downtown	◈◈◈	Rates not provided	33
14 p. 29	**Inn at 500 Capitol**	◈◈◈◈	Rates not provided SAVE	34
15 p. 29	Residence Inn by Marriott Downtown-University	◈◈◈	$88-$296	35
16 p. 29	TownePlace Suites by Marriott Downtown	◈◈◈	$98-$282	35
17 p. 29	**Courtyard by Marriott Boise Downtown**	◈◈◈	$94-$362 SAVE	33
18 p. 29	**Oxford Suites Boise Spectrum**	◈◈◈	$89 SAVE	34
19 p. 29	Hampton Inn & Suites by Hilton Boise Spectrum	◈◈◈	Rates not provided	33
20 p. 29	Homewood Suites by Hilton Boise Spectrum	◈◈◈	Rates not provided	33
21 p. 29	Hilton Garden Inn Boise Spectrum	◈◈◈	Rates not provided	33

BOISE (cont'd)

Map Page	Hotels (cont'd)	Diamond Rated	Rate Range	Page
22 p. 29	Holiday Inn Express Boise University Area	◆◆◆	Rates not provided	33
23 p. 29	SpringHill Suites by Marriott Boise Parkcenter	◆◆◆	$77-$249	35
24 p. 29	La Quinta Inn & Suites Boise Airport	◆◆	$79-$149	34
25 p. 29	Holiday Inn Express & Suites Boise Airport	◆◆◆	$129-$259	33
26 p. 29	Comfort Inn & Suites Boise Airport	◆◆◆	$109-$149	33
27 p. 29	Holiday Inn Boise Airport	◆◆◆	Rates not provided	33
28 p. 29	Fairfield Inn by Marriott Boise Airport	◆◆◆	$80-$237	33
29 p. 29	Hampton Inn by Hilton Boise Airport	◆◆◆	Rates not provided	33
30 p. 29	**Best Western Airport Inn**	◆◆	$90-$120 [SAVE]	32
31 p. 29	**Best Western Vista Inn at the Airport**	◆◆	$85-$139 [SAVE]	33
32 p. 29	Inn America Boise Airport	◆◆	Rates not provided	34
33 p. 29	**Best Western Northwest Lodge**	◆◆◆	$109-$209 [SAVE]	32

Map Page	Restaurants	Diamond Rated	Cuisine	Price Range	Page
1 p. 29	Flying Pie Pizzaria State St	◆	Pizza	$7-$29	35
2 p. 29	Highlands Hollow Brewhouse	◆◆	American	$7-$17	36
3 p. 29	Java Hyde Park	◆	Breakfast Sandwiches	$6-$9	36
4 p. 29	Flying Pie Pizzaria Fairview	◆	Pizza	$7-$29	35
5 p. 29	Edge Brewing Company	◆◆	American	$10-$22	35
6 p. 29	Big City Coffee & Cafe	◆	Breakfast Sandwiches	$5-$12	35
7 p. 29	Modern Hotel Bar & Restaurant	◆◆	American	$10-$20	36
8 p. 29	The Cheesecake Factory	◆◆◆	International	$11-$30	35
9 p. 29	Cafe Ole Restaurant & Cantina	◆◆	Mexican	$10-$20	35
10 p. 29	Yen Ching	◆◆	Regional Chinese	$8-$18	36
11 p. 29	10 Barrel Brewing Company	◆◆	American	$12-$21	35
12 p. 29	Asiago's Restaurant & Winebar	◆◆◆	Italian	$7-$25	35
13 p. 29	Tango's Subs & Empanadas	◆	Argentine	$4-$7	36
14 p. 29	Zeppole Downtown	◆	Breads/Pastries Deli	$5-$8	36
15 p. 29	Bombay Grill	◆◆	Indian	$9-$20	35
16 p. 29	Bittercreek Alehouse	◆◆	Pacific Northwest	$9-$25	35
17 p. 29	Red Feather Lounge	◆◆	New American	$8-$25	36
18 p. 29	FORK Restaurant	◆◆◆	New American	$9-$32	35
19 p. 29	Mai Thai Modern Asian Cuisine	◆◆◆	Thai	$8-$30	36
20 p. 29	Chandlers Steakhouse	◆◆◆	Steak Seafood	$29-$75	35
21 p. 29	Moon's Kitchen	◆	American	$7-$12	36
22 p. 29	Flatbread Neapolitan Pizzeria Downtown	◆◆	Pizza Sandwiches	$8-$17	35
23 p. 29	Boise Fry Company	◆	Specialty Burgers	$6-$12	35
24 p. 29	Piper Pub & Grill	◆◆	Scottish	$10-$19	36

Map Page	Restaurants (cont'd)	Diamond Rated	Cuisine	Price Range	Page
㉕ p. 29	Java Downtown	◆	Breakfast Sandwiches	$5-$9	36
㉖ p. 29	Goldy's Breakfast Bistro	◆◆	Breakfast Sandwiches	$8-$13	35
㉗ p. 29	Bonefish Grill	◆◆◆	Seafood	$10-$29	35
㉘ p. 29	Happy Fish Sushi & Martini Bar	◆◆	Sushi	$11-$21	36
㉙ p. 29	Reef	◆◆	Polynesian	$10-$27	36
㉚ p. 29	Emilio's at Grove Hotel Boise	◆◆◆	American	$12-$38	35
㉛ p. 29	Bardenay Restaurant & Distillery	◆◆	American	$10-$25	35
㉜ p. 29	Leku Ona	◆◆	Basque	$7-$28	36
㉝ p. 29	Cottonwood Grille	◆◆◆	Regional American	$10-$39	35
㉞ p. 29	Richard's Boise	◆◆◆	Regional Italian	$10-$42	36
㉟ p. 29	Luciano's Italian Restaurant	◆◆	Italian	$11-$28	36
㊱ p. 29	Tucanos Brazilian Grill	◆◆	Brazilian	$15-$23	36
㊲ p. 29	Legends Sports Pub & Grill	◆◆	American	$7-$19	36
㊳ p. 29	La Tapatia Mexican Restaurant	◆◆	Mexican	$8-$18	36
㊴ p. 29	Cucina di Paolo	◆◆	Italian	$9-$11	35
㊵ p. 29	The Griddle Parkcenter	◆◆	American	$6-$14	35
㊶ p. 29	Mazzah Mediterranean Grill Parkcenter	◆	Mediterranean	$5-$14	36
㊷ p. 29	Willowcreek Grill	◆◆	American	$9-$22	36
㊸ p. 29	RAW Sushi	◆◆	Sushi	$8-$23	36
㊹ p. 29	Kopper Kitchen Pub & Grill	◆◆	American	$9-$22	36
㊺ p. 29	Bier:Thirty Bottle & Bistro Bown Crossing	◆	German	$9-$12	35
㊻ p. 29	Tavern at Bown Crossing	◆◆	Steak Sushi	$10-$45	36
㊼ p. 29	Flatbread Neapolitan Pizzeria Bown Crossing	◆◆	Pizza Sandwiches	$12-$15	35

BEST WESTERN AIRPORT INN   (208)384-5000 ㉚

◆◆
Motel
$90-$120

AAA Benefit: Members save up to 15% and earn bonus points!

Address: 2660 Airport Way 83705 **Location:** I-84 exit 53 (Vista Ave), just se. **Facility:** 50 units. 2 stories (no elevator), exterior corridors. **Terms:** cancellation fee imposed. **Pool:** heated outdoor. **Guest Services:** coin laundry. **Featured Amenity:** continental breakfast.

BEST WESTERN NORTHWEST LODGE
(208)287-2300 ㉝

◆◆◆
Hotel
$109-$209

AAA Benefit: Members save up to 15% and earn bonus points!

Address: 6989 S Federal Way 83716 **Location:** I-84 exit 57 (Gowen Rd/Idaho City), just e, then just s. **Facility:** 69 units. 3 stories, interior corridors. **Terms:** cancellation fee imposed. **Pool:** heated indoor. **Activities:** hot tub, exercise room. **Guest Services:** valet and coin laundry.

/ SOME UNITS 🐕

(See map & index p. 29.)

BEST WESTERN VISTA INN AT THE AIRPORT
(208)336-8100 **31**

♥♥♥ ◆
Motel
$85-$139

 Best Western. **AAA Benefit:** Members save up to 15% and earn bonus points!

Address: 2645 Airport Way 83705 **Location:** I-84 exit 53 (Vista Ave), just s. **Facility:** 85 units. 2 stories (no elevator), interior/exterior corridors. **Terms:** check-in 4 pm, cancellation fee imposed. **Pool:** heated indoor. **Activities:** hot tub, exercise room. **Guest Services:** valet and coin laundry. **Featured Amenity:** breakfast buffet.

[SAVE] [✈] [†|†] [➔] [♨] [BIZ] [📶]

[✕] [🚻] [▣] / SOME UNITS [HS]

CANDLEWOOD SUITES BOISE TOWNE SQUARE
208/322-4300 **5**

♥♥♥♥ Extended Stay Hotel. **Address:** 700 N Cole Rd 83704

COMFORT INN & SUITES BOISE AIRPORT
(208)342-1075 **26**

♥♥♥ Contemporary Hotel. **Address:** 3625 W Elder St 83705

COURTYARD BY MARRIOTT BOISE DOWNTOWN
(208)331-2700 **17**

♥♥♥♥
Contemporary Hotel
$94-$362

COURTYARD **AAA Benefit:** Members save 5% or more!

Address: 222 S Broadway Ave 83702 **Location:** I-84 exit 54 (Broadway Ave), 3 mi n. **Facility:** 163 units. 4 stories, interior corridors. **Terms:** cancellation fee imposed. **Dining:** 11 restaurants. **Pool:** heated indoor. **Activities:** hot tub, exercise room. **Guest Services:** valet and coin laundry, boarding pass kiosk.

[SAVE] [✈] [†|†] [Y] [CALL] [♿] [➔]

[♨] [BIZ] [HS] [📶] [✕] [🚻] [▣]

/ SOME UNITS [▣]

FAIRFIELD INN BY MARRIOTT BOISE AIRPORT
(208)331-5656 **28**

♥♥♥♥ Contemporary Hotel. **Address:** 3300 S Shoshone St 83705

AAA Benefit: Members save 5% or more!

GROVE HOTEL BOISE
(208)333-8000 **11**

♥♥♥ ♥♥♥
Boutique Hotel
$129-$349

Address: 245 S Capitol Blvd 83702 **Location:** At Front St and S Capitol Blvd; downtown. Connected to Century Link Arena. **Facility:** This impressive highrise hotel has a strikingly sophisticated lobby featuring nightly live piano music. Guest rooms are beautifully appointed with a large desk and multiple upscale bedding accents. 250 units. 16 stories, interior corridors. **Parking:** on-site (fee) and valet. **Terms:** cancellation fee imposed. **Dining:** Emilio's at Grove Hotel Boise, see separate listing, entertainment. **Pool:** heated indoor. **Activities:** sauna, hot tub, health club, spa. **Guest Services:** valet laundry.

[SAVE] [✈] [†|†] [➔] [Y] [CALL] [♿] [➔] [♨] [BIZ] [📶]

[✕] [📷] [🚻] [▣]

HAMPTON INN & SUITES BOISE/DOWNTOWN
208/331-1900 **13**

♥♥◆♥ Contemporary Hotel. **Address:** 495 S Capitol Blvd 83702

AAA Benefit: Members save 5% or more!

HAMPTON INN & SUITES BY HILTON BOISE SPECTRUM
208/323-2500 **19**

♥♥◆♥ Hotel. **Address:** 7499 W Overland Rd 83709

AAA Benefit: Members save 5% or more!

HAMPTON INN BY HILTON BOISE AIRPORT
208/331-5600 **29**

♥♥◆♥ Hotel. **Address:** 3270 S Shoshone St 83705

AAA Benefit: Members save 5% or more!

HILTON GARDEN INN BOISE SPECTRUM
208/376-1000 **21**

♥♥◆♥ Contemporary Hotel. **Address:** 7699 W Spectrum Way 83709

AAA Benefit: Members save 5% or more!

HOLIDAY INN BOISE AIRPORT
208/344-7444 **27**

♥♥◆♥ Contemporary Hotel. **Address:** 2970 W Elder St 83705

HOLIDAY INN EXPRESS & SUITES BOISE AIRPORT
(208)342-4322 **25**

♥♥◆♥ Contemporary Hotel. **Address:** 3050 S Shoshone St 83705

HOLIDAY INN EXPRESS BOISE UNIVERSITY AREA
208/345-2002 **22**

♥♥◆♥ Hotel. **Address:** 475 W Parkcenter Blvd 83706

HOMEWOOD SUITES BY HILTON BOISE SPECTRUM
208/375-8500 **20**

♥♥◆♥ Extended Stay Contemporary Hotel. **Address:** 7957 W Spectrum Way 83709

AAA Benefit: Members save 5% or more!

HOTEL 43
(208)342-4622 **10**

♥♥♥
Boutique Contemporary Hotel
$139-$539

Address: 981 W Grove St 83702 **Location:** At 10th and W Grove sts; downtown. **Facility:** This hotel is on the 43rd parallel in the 43rd state and boasts artfully designed guest rooms offering a variety of city views and a distinctive décor style throughout. 112 units. 6 stories, interior corridors. **Parking:** on-site (fee) and valet. **Terms:** check-in 4 pm, cancellation fee imposed. **Dining:** Chandlers Steakhouse, see separate listing. **Activities:** exercise room. **Guest Services:** valet laundry, boarding pass kiosk.

[SAVE] [✈] [†|†] [Y] [CALL] [♿] [♨]

[📶] [✕] [🐾] [▣]

/ SOME UNITS [🚻] [▣]

(See map & index p. 29.)

HYATT PLACE BOISE DOWNTOWN   (208)991-5275 **8**

Contemporary Hotel
$99-$329

HYATT PLACE·

AAA Benefit: Members save 5% or more!

Address: 1024 W Bannock St 83702 **Location:** Jct N 11th and W Bannock sts; downtown. **Facility:** 150 units. 5 stories, interior corridors. **Parking:** on-site (fee) and street. **Pool:** heated outdoor. **Activities:** hot tub, exercise room. **Guest Services:** valet and coin laundry. **Featured Amenity: breakfast buffet.**

HYATT PLACE BOISE TOWNE SQUARE
(208)375-1200 **2**

Hotel
$99-$229

HYATT PLACE·

AAA Benefit: Members save 5% or more!

Address: 925 N Milwaukee St 83704 **Location:** I-84 exit 49 (Franklin St), just w, then 0.5 mi n. Located in a residential area. **Facility:** 127 units. 4 stories, interior corridors. **Amenities:** safes. **Pool:** heated indoor. **Activities:** exercise room. **Guest Services:** valet laundry, area transportation. **Featured Amenity: breakfast buffet.** *(See ad this page.)*

INN AMERICA BOISE AIRPORT   208/389-9800 **32**
◈◈ Hotel. **Address:** 2275 Airport Way 83705

INN AT 500 CAPITOL   208/227-0500 **14**

Boutique Hotel
Rates not provided

Address: 500 Capitol Blvd 83702 **Location:** At Capitol Blvd and Myrtle St; downtown. **Facility:** Set amid restaurants, specialty retailers and nightlife, this hotel's vibrant guest rooms include a gas fireplace and luxurious bedding; some offer a terrace or balcony with mountain or city views. 110 units. 6 stories, interior corridors. **Parking:** valet only. **Amenities:** safes. **Dining:** Richard's Boise, see separate listing. **Activities:** bicycles, exercise room. **Guest Services:** valet laundry, area transportation.

LA QUINTA INN & SUITES BOISE AIRPORT
(208)388-0800 **24**
◈◈◈ Hotel. **Address:** 2613 S Vista Ave 83705

LA QUINTA INN & SUITES BOISE TOWNE SQUARE
(208)378-7000 **4**
◈◈◈ Hotel. **Address:** 7965 W Emerald St 83704

MODERN HOTEL AND BAR   (208)424-8244 **7**
◈◈ Boutique Motel. **Address:** 1314 W Grove St 83702

OXFORD SUITES BOISE SPECTRUM
(208)322-8000 **18**

Hotel
$89

Address: 1426 S Entertainment Ave 83709 **Location:** I-84 exit 50A, just s to Spectrum Way, just w, then just n. **Facility:** 132 units, some efficiencies. 4 stories, interior corridors. **Terms:** check-in 4 pm, 2-14 night minimum stay - seasonal and/or weekends, 30 day cancellation notice-fee imposed, resort fee. **Pool:** heated indoor. **Activities:** sauna, hot tub, steamroom, exercise room. **Guest Services:** valet and coin laundry. **Featured Amenity: breakfast buffet.**

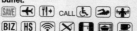

▼ See AAA listing this page ▼

(See map & index p. 29.)

RESIDENCE INN BOISE CITY CENTER
(208)424-9999 **12**

Extended Stay Contemporary Hotel
$114-$365

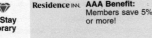
Residence INN. **AAA Benefit:** Members save 5% or more!

Address: 400 S Capitol Blvd 83702 **Location:** I-84 exit 53 (Vista Ave), 3.2 mi n, at Capitol Blvd and Broad St; downtown. **Facility:** 185 units, some two bedrooms, efficiencies and kitchens. 10 stories, interior corridors. **Parking:** on-site (fee). **Terms:** check-in 4 pm, cancellation fee imposed. **Pool:** heated indoor. **Activities:** hot tub, picnic facilities, exercise room. **Guest Services:** valet and coin laundry. **Featured Amenity: full hot breakfast.**

RESIDENCE INN BY MARRIOTT BOISE WEST
(208)385-9000 **6**

Extended Stay Hotel. **Address:** 7303 W Denton St 83704

AAA Benefit: Members save 5% or more!

RESIDENCE INN BY MARRIOTT DOWNTOWN-UNIVERSITY
(208)344-1200 **15**

Extended Stay Hotel. **Address:** 1401 S Lusk Pl 83706

AAA Benefit: Members save 5% or more!

THE RIVERSIDE HOTEL
208/343-1871 **3**
Hotel. **Address:** 2900 W Chinden Blvd 83714

SAFARI INN DOWNTOWN
208/344-6556 **9**
Hotel. **Address:** 1070 Grove St 83702

SPRINGHILL SUITES BY MARRIOTT BOISE/EAGLE
(208)939-8266 **1**

Hotel. **Address:** 6325 N Cloverdale Rd 83713

AAA Benefit: Members save 5% or more!

SPRINGHILL SUITES BY MARRIOTT BOISE PARKCENTER
(208)342-1044 **23**

Contemporary Hotel. **Address:** 424 E Parkcenter Blvd 83706

AAA Benefit: Members save 5% or more!

TOWNEPLACE SUITES BY MARRIOTT DOWNTOWN
(208)429-8881 **16**

Extended Stay Hotel. **Address:** 1455 S Capitol Blvd 83706

AAA Benefit: Members save 5% or more!

WHERE TO EAT

10 BARREL BREWING COMPANY
208/344-5870 **11**
American. Brewpub. **Address:** 826 W Bannock St 83702

ASIAGO'S RESTAURANT & WINEBAR
208/336-5552 **12**
Italian. Casual Dining. **Address:** 1002 Main St 83701

BARDENAY RESTAURANT & DISTILLERY
208/426-0538 **31**
American. Casual Dining. **Address:** 610 Grove St 83702

BIER:THIRTY BOTTLE & BISTRO BOWN CROSSING
208/342-1916 **45**
German. Quick Serve. **Address:** 3073 S Bown Way 83706

BIG CITY COFFEE & CAFE
208/345-3145 **6**
Breakfast Sandwiches. Quick Serve. **Address:** 1416 W Grove St 83702

BITTERCREEK ALEHOUSE
208/345-1813 **16**
Pacific Northwest. Gastropub. **Address:** 246 N 8th St 83702

BOISE FRY COMPANY
208/949-7523 **23**
Specialty Burgers. Quick Serve. **Address:** 204 N Capitol Blvd 83702

BOMBAY GRILL
208/345-7888 **15**
Indian. Casual Dining. **Address:** 928 W Main St 83702

BONEFISH GRILL
208/433-1234 **27**
Seafood. Fine Dining. **Address:** 855 W Broad St 83702

CAFE OLE RESTAURANT & CANTINA
208/322-0222 **9**
Mexican. Casual Dining. **Address:** 210 N Milwaukee Rd 83704

CHANDLERS STEAKHOUSE
208/383-4300 **20**
Steak Seafood. Fine Dining. **Address:** 981 W Grove St 83702

THE CHEESECAKE FACTORY
208/377-4466 **8**
International. Casual Dining. **Address:** 330 N Milwaukee St 83704

COTTONWOOD GRILLE
208/333-9800 **33**
Regional American. Fine Dining. **Address:** 913 W River St 83702

CUCINA DI PAOLO
208/345-7150 **39**
Italian. Quick Serve. **Address:** 1504 S Vista Ave 83702

EDGE BREWING COMPANY
208/995-2979 **5**
American. Brewpub. **Address:** 525 Steelhead Way 83704

EMILIO'S AT GROVE HOTEL BOISE
208/333-8002 **30**
American. Fine Dining. **Address:** 245 S Capitol Blvd 83702

FLATBREAD NEAPOLITAN PIZZERIA BOWN CROSSING
208/343-4177 **47**
Pizza Sandwiches. Casual Dining. **Address:** 3139 S Bown Way 83706

FLATBREAD NEAPOLITAN PIZZERIA DOWNTOWN
208/287-4757 **22**
Pizza Sandwiches. Casual Dining. **Address:** 800 W Main St, Suite 230 83702

FLYING PIE PIZZARIA FAIRVIEW
208/345-0000 **4**
Pizza. Quick Serve. **Address:** 6508 Fairview Ave 83704

FLYING PIE PIZZARIA STATE ST
208/384-0000 **1**
Pizza. Quick Serve. **Address:** 4320 W State St 83703

FORK RESTAURANT
208/287-1700 **18**
New American. Casual Dining. **Address:** 199 N 8th St 83702

GOLDY'S BREAKFAST BISTRO
208/345-4100 **26**
Breakfast Sandwiches. Casual Dining. **Address:** 108 S Capitol Blvd 83702

GOODWOOD BARBECUE COMPANY
208/658-7173
Barbecue. Casual Dining. **Address:** 7849 W Spectrum St 83709

THE GRIDDLE PARKCENTER
208/297-7615 **40**
American. Casual Dining. **Address:** 404 E Parkcenter Blvd #200 83706

(See map & index p. 29.)

HAPPY FISH SUSHI & MARTINI BAR   208/343-4810   (28)
♥♥ Sushi. Casual Dining. **Address:** 855 Broad St, Suite 250 83702

HIGHLANDS HOLLOW BREWHOUSE   208/343-6820   (2)
♥♥ American. Brewpub. **Address:** 2455 Harrison Hollow Ln 83702

JAVA DOWNTOWN   208/345-0777   (25)
♥ Breakfast Sandwiches. Quick Serve. **Address:** 223 N 6th St 83702

JAVA HYDE PARK   208/345-4777   (3)
♥ Breakfast Sandwiches. Quick Serve. **Address:** 1612 N 13th St 83702

KOPPER KITCHEN PUB & GRILL   208/344-4271   (44)
♥♥ American. Casual Dining. **Address:** 2661 Airport Way 83705

LA TAPATIA MEXICAN RESTAURANT   208/343-6403   (38)
♥♥ Mexican. Casual Dining. **Address:** 401 E Parkcenter Blvd 83706

LEGENDS SPORTS PUB & GRILL   208/377-1819   (37)
♥♥ American. Sports Bar. **Address:** 7609 W Overland Rd, Suite 100 83709

LEKU ONA   208/345-6665   (32)
♥♥ Basque. Casual Dining. **Address:** 117 S 6th St 83702

LUCIANO'S ITALIAN RESTAURANT   208/577-6415   (35)
♥♥ Italian. Casual Dining. **Address:** 11 N Orchard St 83706

MAI THAI MODERN ASIAN CUISINE   208/344-8424   (19)
♥♥♥ Thai. Casual Dining. **Address:** 750 W Idaho St 83702

MAZZAH MEDITERRANEAN GRILL PARKCENTER
208/333-2223   (41)
♥ Mediterranean. Quick Serve. **Address:** 404 E Parkcenter Blvd, #250 83706

MCGRATH'S FISH HOUSE   208/375-6300
♥♥ Seafood. Casual Dining. **Address:** 1749 S Cole Rd 83709

MODERN HOTEL BAR & RESTAURANT   208/424-8244   (7)
♥♥ American. Casual Dining. **Address:** 1314 W Grove Ave 83702

MOON'S KITCHEN   208/385-0472   (21)
♥ American. Casual Dining. **Address:** 712 W Idaho St 83702

PIPER PUB & GRILL   208/343-2444   (24)
♥♥ Scottish. Casual Dining. **Address:** 150 N 8th St, Suite 200 83702

RAM RESTAURANT & BREWERY   208/345-2929
♥♥ American. Casual Dining. **Address:** 709 E Park Blvd 83712

RAW SUSHI   208/343-0270   (43)
♥♥ Sushi. Casual Dining. **Address:** 2273 S Vista Ave 83705

RED FEATHER LOUNGE   208/429-6340   (17)
♥♥ New American. Casual Dining. **Address:** 246 N 8th St 83702

REEF   208/287-9200   (29)
♥♥ Polynesian. Casual Dining. **Address:** 105 S 6th St 83702

RICHARD'S BOISE   208/472-1463   (34)
♥♥♥ Regional Italian. Fine Dining. **Address:** 501 S Capitol Blvd 83702

SMOKY MOUNTAIN PIZZERIA GRILL   208/387-2727
♥♥ Italian. Casual Dining. **Address:** 1805 W State St 83702

SMOKY MOUNTAIN PIZZERIA GRILL   208/429-0011
♥♥ Italian. Casual Dining. **Address:** 415 E Parkcenter Blvd 83706

TANGO'S SUBS & EMPANADAS   208/322-3090   (13)
♥ Argentine. Quick Serve. **Address:** 701 N Orchard St 83706

TAVERN AT BOWN CROSSING   208/345-2277   (46)
♥♥ Steak Sushi. Casual Dining. **Address:** 3111 S Bown Way 83706

TUCANOS BRAZILIAN GRILL   208/343-4300   (36)
♥♥ Brazilian. Casual Dining. **Address:** 1388 S Entertainment Ave 83709

WILLOWCREEK GRILL   208/343-5544   (42)
♥♥ American. Casual Dining. **Address:** 2273 S Vista Ave, Suite 150 83705

YEN CHING   208/384-0384   (10)
♥♥ Regional Chinese. Casual Dining. **Address:** 305 N 9th St 83702

ZEPPOLE DOWNTOWN   208/345-2149   (14)
♥ Breads/Pastries Deli. Quick Serve. **Address:** 217 N 8th St 83702

BOISE NATIONAL FOREST (E-2)

> Elevations in the forest range from 2,860 ft. at Lucky Peak Reservoir to 10,751 ft. at Thomason Peak. Refer to AAA maps for additional elevation information.

In south-central Idaho, lakes, abandoned mines and ghost towns amid ponderosa pine and Douglas fir dot the 2,612,000 acres of mountainous terrain that make up the Boise National Forest. Large areas of the forest serve as summer range for big game. Black bears, wolves, mountain goats, bighorn sheep, mule deer and elk inhabit the woods. Upland game birds including chukars, sage grouse, Hungarian partridges and turkeys roam the backcountry. Salmon, trout and bass thrive in the cold, clear rivers, streams and reservoirs.

Deep canyons, rugged peaks exceeding 9,000 feet and high meadows offer an abundance of recreation opportunities year-round. Cross-country skiing and snowmobiling are popular during the winter. The forest offers more than 900 miles of hiking trails.

Scenic drives wind through the canyons and along the edge of the Sawtooth Wilderness; only trails enter the Frank Church-River of No Return Wilderness in the northeast section. Lake Cascade recreation facilities include camping; phone for more information about special facilities and amenities.

Additional information can be obtained from the Boise National Forest Visitor Center, 1387 S. Vinnell Way, Boise, ID 83709; phone (208) 373-4100, (208) 373-4039 or (208) 373-4007. *See Recreation Areas Chart.*

BONNERS FERRY (A-1) pop. 2,543, elev. 1,773'

Although trappers David Thompson and Finan McDonald were drawn to the banks of the Kootenai

River and established a fur trading post in 1808, it was not until 1864 that a permanent settlement was founded. It was in that year that E.L. Bonner's ferry replaced the canoes of Native Americans, who the previous year had carried gold miners rushing to the Canadian Wild Horse lode.

Trapping and river transportation no longer dominate the commerce of Bonners Ferry; today the town, 25 miles south of Canada, maintains a resource-oriented economy of lumbering and farming.

The mountainous terrain of northern Idaho and the gorge cut by the Kootenai River make the Bonners Ferry region popular for its beauty. Katka View Point, 9 miles east on CR 24, provides a view of the Kootenai Valley, the Selkirk Mountains and the proposed Selkirk Crest National Wilderness area. Another popular and easy-to-reach spot to enjoy mountain scenery is near the junction of US 95 and SR 1.

Greater Bonners Ferry Visitor Center: 6373 Bonner St., Bonners Ferry, ID 83805. **Phone:** (208) 267-5922.

BEST WESTERN PLUS KOOTENAI RIVER INN CASINO & SPA
(208)267-8511

Hotel
$159-$399

Best Western PLUS

AAA Benefit: Members save up to 15% and earn bonus points!

Address: 7169 Plaza St 83805 **Location:** On US 95; City Center. **Facility:** This hotel is located right off the freeway for easy access. Some of the rooms offer balconies with great views while others feature a hot tub or fireplace. 103 units. 3 stories, interior corridors. **Terms:** check-in 4 pm, cancellation fee imposed. **Amenities:** safes. **Pool:** heated indoor. **Activities:** hot tub, game room, exercise room, spa. **Guest Services:** coin laundry. **Featured Amenity:** full hot breakfast.

BONNERS FERRY LOG INN
208/267-3986

Motel
Rates not provided

Address: 43 Tobe Way 83805 **Location:** 2.5 mi n on US 95. **Facility:** 22 units. 1 story, exterior corridors. **Parking:** winter plug-ins. **Activities:** hot tub. **Guest Services:** complimentary laundry. **Featured Amenity:** continental breakfast.

NORTHSIDE SCHOOL BED & BREAKFAST
208/267-1826

Historic Boutique Bed & Breakfast. **Address:** 6497 Comanche St 83805

WHERE TO EAT

MUGSY'S TAVERN AND GRILL   208/267-8059
American. Casual Dining. **Address:** 7161 Main St 83805

BURLEY (H-4) pop. 10,345, elev. 4,165'

Hydroplanes, super stock and other powerful racing craft churn up Burley's Snake River waterfront during the month of June, when such national speedboat championships as the Idaho Regatta take place.

BEST WESTERN PLUS BURLEY INN & CONVENTION CENTER
(208)678-3501

Hotel
$89-$199

Best Western PLUS

AAA Benefit: Members save up to 15% and earn bonus points!

Address: 800 N Overland Ave 83318 **Location:** I-84 exit 208, just s. **Facility:** 124 units. 2 stories, interior/exterior corridors. **Parking:** winter plug-ins. **Terms:** cancellation fee imposed. **Pool:** heated outdoor. **Activities:** hot tub, exercise room. **Guest Services:** valet and coin laundry. **Featured Amenity:** full hot breakfast.

FAIRFIELD INN & SUITES BY MARRIOTT BURLEY
(208)677-5000

Hotel
$85-$197

Fairfield

AAA Benefit: Members save 5% or more!

Address: 230 W 7th St N 83318 **Location:** I-84 exit 208, just sw. **Facility:** 81 units. 3 stories, interior corridors. **Parking:** winter plug-ins. **Terms:** cancellation fee imposed. **Pool:** heated indoor. **Activities:** hot tub, picnic facilities, exercise room. **Guest Services:** valet and coin laundry. **Featured Amenity:** full hot breakfast.

WHERE TO EAT

STEVO'S   208/679-3887
American. Casual Dining. **Address:** 290 S 600 W 83336

CALDWELL (F-1) pop. 46,237, elev. 2,367'
• Hotels p. 38 • Restaurants p. 38

On the Boise River, Caldwell was established in the late 19th century. The community, which began as a construction camp for the Oregon Short Line Railroad, is now associated with the processing and distribution of farm products. Boone Science Hall, near the corner of 20th and Fillmore streets on the 800-student College of Idaho campus, houses the Orma J. Smith Museum of Natural History, the Evans Gem and Mineral Collection and the Whittenberger Planetarium; phone (208) 459-5011.

Caldwell Chamber of Commerce: 704 Blaine St., Caldwell, ID 83606. **Phone:** (208) 459-7493.

WINERIES
• **Ste. Chapelle Winery** is 8 mi. s.w. on SR 55, then .5 mi. e., following signs. **Hours:** Mon.-Sat. 10-5

(also Thurs.-Sat. 5-6 p.m.), Sun. noon-5, May-Oct.; Sun.-Fri. noon-5, Sat. 10-5, rest of year. Closed Easter, Thanksgiving and Christmas. **Phone:** (208) 453-7843. [GT]

BEST WESTERN PLUS CALDWELL INN & SUITES
(208)454-7225

Hotel
$92-$158

AAA Benefit: Members save up to 15% and earn bonus points!

Address: 908 Specht Ave 83605 **Location:** I-84 exit 29, just s. **Facility:** 81 units. 3 stories, interior corridors. **Terms:** cancellation fee imposed. **Pool:** heated indoor. **Activities:** hot tub, picnic facilities, exercise room. **Guest Services:** coin laundry.

WILD ROSE MANOR BED & BREAKFAST   (208)454-3331
▼▼▼ Bed & Breakfast. **Address:** 5800 Oasis Rd 83607

WHERE TO EAT

MR. V'S FAMILY RESTAURANT   208/454-9778
▼▼ American. Casual Dining. **Address:** 407 N 10th Ave 83605

CAMBRIDGE (F-1) pop. 328, elev. 2,739'

CAMBRIDGE MUSEUM, jct. US 95 and SR 71, provides information about area heritage, from the arrival of the first settlers in 1869 through the 1930s. Displays focus on geology, farming, Native American life and the community's pioneer days. A blacksmith shop and a replica schoolroom with historical items can be seen. A reproduction of a mine entrance features illustrations demonstrating dynamiting techniques.

A genealogy library is available by appointment. **Time:** Allow 30 minutes minimum. **Hours:** Museum Wed.-Sat. 10-4, June-Aug. Phone ahead to confirm schedule. **Cost:** Donations. **Phone:** (208) 257-3485.

RECREATIONAL ACTIVITIES
White-water Rafting

• **Hughes River Expeditions** departs from various locations depending on trip. **Hours:** Schedule varies; phone ahead. **Phone:** (208) 257-3477 or (800) 262-1882.

• **ROW Adventures** departs from the Frontier Motel at 240 S. Superior St. **Hours:** Snake River trips are offered May-Sept. Schedule varies; phone ahead. **Phone:** (208) 765-0841 or (800) 451-6034.

CARIBOU-TARGHEE NATIONAL FOREST (F-5)

Elevations in the forest range from 4,700 ft. at Curlew Campground to 12,197 ft. at Diamond Peak. Refer to AAA maps for additional elevation information.

In southeast Idaho extending into Wyoming and Utah, Caribou-Targhee National Forest covers more than 3 million acres. The Caribou unit is noted for rugged scenery marked by towering mountain ranges and beautiful valleys. Drives along the Snake River and through the many canyons provide scenic vistas. A few traces of the ghost towns of Keenan and Caribou City recall the gold rush days.

Named for Tygee, a Bannock Indian chief, the Targhee section is in the Lemhi, Beaverhead, Teton, Centennial, Palisades and Caribou ranges and extends in a semicircle around the headwaters of Henry's Fork of the Snake River. The Continental Divide forms most of the northern boundary; Yellowstone and Grand Teton national parks make up most of the eastern border. Canyons, high peaks and desert add to the picturesque scenery.

Minnetonka Cave in St. Charles Canyon is one of two accessible caves and features interesting geological formations. Ice never melts in Paris Cave, a small, undeveloped cave in nearby Paris Canyon.

Water is abundant throughout the Targhee. Big Springs, one of the largest springs in the United States, is reached by SR 59 from US 20 at Macks Inn. It issues from the base of a high plateau at a constant 52 F and is the headwaters of Henry's Fork, which is the north fork of the Snake River.

A 3- to 5-hour canoe/float trip can be taken along a 5-mile national recreation water trail just below Big Springs. Moose, trumpeter swans, ospreys and bald eagles can often be seen. Further down Henry's Fork, boaters must portage around several sections of dangerous water between Macks Inn and Ashton.

Upper and Lower Mesa falls are east of US 20 and north of Ashton on Mesa Falls Scenic Byway. The Upper Mesa Falls is 114 feet high; the Lower Mesa Falls is 65 to 70 feet high.

Trout fishing is excellent, most notably at Palisades Reservoir, Henry's Lake, Island Park Reservoir, Henry's Fork and South Fork of the Snake River.

Winter sports activity areas near Ashton, Driggs, Heise, Island Park, Montpelier and Pocatello contain miles of groomed snowmobile and cross-country skiing trails as well as downhill ski resorts. More than 1,100 miles of hiking, horse and mountain bike trails provide a variety of summer backcountry experiences.

Camping is available from Memorial Day weekend to Labor Day (weather permitting). Fees for developed camping areas range from $10 to $36 at single-family campgrounds, depending on the level of service at each facility. Group camping facilities also are available. Phone (877) 444-6777 for campsite reservations.

Brochures are available at the visitor center, 425 N. Capitol Ave. in Idaho Falls, open year-round. For more information contact the Forest Supervisor's Office, Caribou-Targhee National Forest, 1405 Hollipark Dr., Idaho Falls, ID 83401; phone (208) 524-7500. *See Recreation Areas Chart.*

CASCADE (F-2) pop. 939, elev. 4,760'

Though logging has historically been an important industry for Cascade, tourism has increasingly contributed to the local economy. The town is a jumping-off point for travel to millions of acres of mountainous backcountry and wilderness, where snowmobiling and Nordic skiing are popular cold weather pursuits.

In addition, the community is located in Long Valley near the southern end of Lake Cascade, a 30,000-acre reservoir formed in 1948. Boating, sailing, kayaking, water skiing and some of the state's best perch fishing can be enjoyed on the body of water, and in winter, ice fishing is added to the long list of recreational activities. Lake Cascade State Park, 4,450 acres off SR 55, offers camping facilities and six boat ramps *(see Recreation Areas Chart).*

Cascade Chamber of Commerce: P.O. Box 571, Cascade, ID 83611. **Phone:** (208) 382-3833.

THE ASHLEY INN   (208)382-5621
▼◆▼ Boutique Hotel. **Address:** 500 N Main St 83611

CHALLIS NATIONAL FOREST—See
Salmon-Challis National Forest p. 63

CLEARWATER NATIONAL FOREST (C-2)

Elevations in the forest range from 1,200 ft. to 8,820 ft. at Ranger Peak. Refer to AAA maps for additional elevation information.

In the northeastern part of the state, large stands of tall trees and many miles of clear, fast-running streams and rivers characterize the rugged, mountainous Clearwater National Forest. Scenic Lewis and Clark Highway (US 12) runs a few miles south of but roughly parallel to the Lolo Trail, the Native American route across the Bitterroots to buffalo-hunting country.

A portion of the Selway-Bitterroot Wilderness, the second largest wilderness area in the continental United States, makes up part of Clearwater's 1.8 million acres. US 12 follows the rugged Lochsa Wild and Scenic River, where kayak and raft enthusiasts challenge the stream's white water. Recreation information is available at ranger stations in Kooskia, Orofino, Potlatch and Powell.

Lolo Pass Visitors Center, along US 12 at the crest of the Bitterroots on the Idaho-Montana border, and the restored Lochsa Historical Ranger Station, halfway between Powell and Kooskia on US 12, are open Memorial Day weekend through late September. For further information, contact the North

Fork Ranger's Office, 12730 US 12, Orofino, ID 83544; phone (208) 476-8267. *See Recreation Areas Chart.*

COEUR D'ALENE (B-1) pop. 44,137, elev. 2,157'
• Hotels p. 40 • Restaurants p. 40

The largest city in northern Idaho takes its name from the local tribe of Native Americans. French trappers dubbed them Coeur d'Alene (CORE-dah-LANE), meaning "heart of the awl," a vernacular phrase describing them as shrewd traders.

Gen. William Tecumseh Sherman established an Army post in 1878 at the point where the Spokane River drains Lake Coeur d'Alene. Fort Sherman became the nucleus of a settlement that was named for the lake. The 1880s mining boom in the Silver Valley brought prosperity, as Coeur d'Alene became an important shipping point. For a period it was the busiest steamboat port west of the Mississippi River. By 1900 boats were carrying tourists on excursion cruises.

North Idaho College now occupies the old fort site, and Fort Sherman Chapel survives at the corner of Hubbard Street and Woodland Drive. The community college has an enrollment of 4,600; phone (208) 769-3300.

Idaho's "Lake City" remains a popular resort. In summer the city's beaches, parks and docks throng with outdoor enthusiasts. Boating, houseboating, swimming, water skiing, parasailing and fishing are popular activities.

Downtown on the shores of Lake Coeur d'Alene is forested Tubbs Hill, a 120-acre preserve featuring trails to secluded coves and beaches, and to the summit for panoramic views. Also along the waterfront, The Coeur d'Alene Resort Golf Course is a par 71 distinguished by its floating, 15,000-square-foot island green; phone (208) 667-4653 or (800) 935-6283.

What is said to be the world's longest floating boardwalk runs 3,300 feet from Independence Point in City Park to the foot of Third Street, around The Coeur d'Alene Resort. The park offers a large public beach as well as a playground designed after Fort Sherman. Here, walkers, bicyclists and skaters also find access to the North Idaho Centennial Trail. The paved pathway extends 24 miles from Higgens Point, east of Coeur d'Alene, west to the Idaho/Washington border, where it connects with Spokane's Centennial Trail.

Coeur d'Alene Visitor Bureau: 105 N. 1st St., Suite 100, Coeur d'Alene, ID 83814. **Phone:** (208) 664-3194 or (877) 782-9232.

Shopping: Downtown Coeur d'Alene, along Sherman Avenue, is home to a number of art galleries and retail outlets offering clothing, custom jewelry and housewares. Silver Lake Mall, 3.5 miles north on US 95, offers JCPenney, Macy's and Sears. Antiques can be found at Coeur d'Alene Antique Mall, 408 Haycraft, and at Government Way Antique Mall, 3650 N. Government Way.

HUMAN RIGHTS EDUCATION INSTITUTE is at 414 West Fort Grounds Dr. in the historic 1902 Spokane & Inland Empire Electric Railway substation building in the northeast corner of Coeur d'Alene City Park. The cultural organization educates and raises awareness about various human rights issues; its exhibit galleries host changing displays that support these goals. The Peace Lives Here Gallery showcases artwork illustrating human rights principles and responsibilities. Interactive activities for children are offered.

Time: Allow 30 minutes minimum. **Hours:** Mon.-Fri. 10-5. Closed major holidays. Phone ahead to confirm schedule. **Cost:** Free. **Phone:** (208) 292-2359. GT

LAKE COEUR D'ALENE is s. of town. Once called one of the five most beautiful lakes in the world by *National Geographic,* it is surrounded by mountains and a lush forest. Twenty-five miles long, it averages 2.5 miles in width and has a 135-mile-long shoreline. It has one of the nation's largest populations of osprey, and bald eagles can be seen diving into the lake to catch salmon in winter. Power boating, sailing and fishing are popular summer sports.

LAKE COEUR D'ALENE CRUISES departs from the Coeur d'Alene city dock at Independence Point. A 90-minute, narrated lake cruise provides glimpses of wildlife and local scenery. Brunch, sunset, full-day and themed cruises also are available. **Time:** Allow 2 hours minimum. **Hours:** Narrated lake cruises depart daily, late Apr.-late Oct. Departure times vary; phone ahead. **Cost:** $24.75; $22.75 (ages 55+); $16.75 (ages 6-17). **Phone:** (208) 765-4000, ext. 21.

SILVERWOOD—see Athol p. 24.

RECREATIONAL ACTIVITIES
White-water Rafting
- **ROW Adventures** offers trips on the Grande Ronde, Owyhee and Snake rivers from various departure points. **Hours:** Trips are offered mid-May to mid-Sept. Schedule varies; phone ahead. **Phone:** (208) 765-0841 or (800) 451-6034.

BAYMONT INN & SUITES COEUR D'ALENE   (208)667-6777
Hotel. **Address:** 2209 E Sherman Ave 83814

BEST WESTERN PLUS COEUR D'ALENE INN
(208)765-3200

Hotel
$94-$259

Best Western PLUS. **AAA Benefit:** Members save up to 15% and earn bonus points!

Address: 506 W Appleway Ave 83814 **Location:** I-90 exit 12, just nw. **Facility:** 122 units. 2 stories, interior corridors. **Parking:** winter plug-ins. **Terms:** check-in 4 pm, cancellation fee imposed. **Pool:** heated indoor. **Activities:** hot tub, exercise room. **Guest Services:** valet and coin laundry, area transportation. **Featured Amenity:** breakfast buffet.

THE COEUR D'ALENE RESORT   208/209-5026
Resort Hotel. **Address:** 115 S 2nd St 83814

DAYS INN-COEUR D'ALENE   (208)667-8668
Hotel. **Address:** 2200 Northwest Blvd 83814

FAIRBRIDGE INN   208/765-3011
Hotel. **Address:** 330 W Appleway Ave 83814

HAMPTON INN & SUITES BY HILTON COEUR D'ALENE
208/769-7900
Hotel. **Address:** 1500 Riverstone Dr 83814   **AAA Benefit:** Members save 5% or more!

HOLIDAY INN EXPRESS HOTEL & SUITES COEUR D'ALENE
208/667-3100
Hotel. **Address:** 2300 W Seltice Way 83814

JAPAN HOUSE SUITES   (208)667-0600
Hotel. **Address:** 2113 E Sherman Ave 83814

LA QUINTA INN & SUITES COEUR D'ALENE   (208)665-9000
Hotel. **Address:** 333 Ironwood Dr 83814

QUALITY INN & SUITES COEUR D'ALENE   (208)765-5500
Hotel. **Address:** 280 W Appleway Ave 83814

RAMADA INN COEUR D'ALENE   (208)664-1649
Hotel. **Address:** 2303 N 4th St 83814

RESORT CITY INN   (208)676-1225

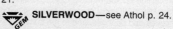

Motel
$75-$249

Address: 621 Sherman Ave 83814 **Location:** I-90 exit 11 (Northwest Blvd), 2.5 mi e via Northwest Blvd and Sherman Ave; downtown. **Facility:** 18 units, some efficiencies. 2 stories (no elevator), exterior corridors. **Terms:** 3 day cancellation notice.

THE ROOSEVELT INN AND SPA   208/765-5200
Historic Bed & Breakfast. **Address:** 105 E Wallace Ave 83814

SPRINGHILL SUITES BY MARRIOTT COEUR D'ALENE
(208)667-2212
Hotel. **Address:** 2250 W Seltice Way 83814   **AAA Benefit:** Members save 5% or more!

WHERE TO EAT

ANTHONY'S AT COEUR D'ALENE   208/664-4665
American. Casual Dining. **Address:** 1926 W Riverstone Dr 83815

BARDENAY   208/765-1540
American. Gastropub. **Address:** 1710 W Riverstone Dr 83814

BEVERLY'S   208/765-4000
Pacific Rim. Fine Dining. **Address:** 115 S 2nd St 83814

THE BREAKFAST NOOK   208/667-1699
American. Casual Dining. **Address:** 1719 N 4th St 83814

THE CEDARS FLOATING RESTAURANT   208/664-2922
Steak Seafood. Casual Dining. **Address:** 1 Marina Dr 83814

COSMIC COWBOY GRILL   208/277-0000
🍷 American. Casual Dining. **Address:** 412 W Haycraft Ave
83815

CRICKET'S RESTAURANT & OYSTER BAR   208/765-1990
🍷🍷 American. Casual Dining. **Address:** 424 Sherman Ave
83814

MELTZ EXTREME GRILLED CHEESE   208/664-1717
🍷 Sandwiches. Quick Serve. **Address:** 1735 W Kathleen Ave
83815

MOON TIME   208/667-2331
🍷🍷 American. Casual Dining. **Address:** 1602 Sherman Ave,
Suite 116 83814

THE OLYMPIA   208/666-9495
🍷🍷 Greek. Casual Dining. **Address:** 301 E Lakeside Ave
83814

PHILLY EXPRESS   208/916-7131
🍷 Sandwiches. Quick Serve. **Address:** 1500 Northwest Blvd
83815

THAI BAMBOO   208/667-5300
🍷🍷 Thai. Casual Dining. **Address:** 2010 N 4th St 83814

TOMATO STREET   208/667-5000
🍷🍷 Italian. Casual Dining. **Address:** 221 W Appleway Ave
83814

TONY'S ON THE LAKE   208/667-9885
🍷🍷🍷 Italian. Casual Dining. **Address:** 6823 Coeur d'Alene
Lake Dr 83814

TOP OF CHINA BUFFET   208/676-8888
🍷 Chinese. Casual Dining. **Address:** 757 W Appleway Ave
83814

THE WINE CELLAR   208/664-9463
🍷🍷 International. Casual Dining. **Address:** 317 E Sherman
Ave 83814

◆GEM CRATERS OF THE MOON NATIONAL MONUMENT AND PRESERVE (G-4)

Eighteen miles west of Arco via US 20/26/93, Craters of the Moon National Monument and Preserve is at the base of the Pioneer Mountains.

This 1,100-square-mile area contains more basaltic volcanic features than any other area of its size in the continental United States. Lava rivers once flooded the surrounding countryside, leaving vast lava fields covered by cinder cones with large central vents that were thought by early observers to resemble the craters on the moon. The volcanic activity dates back about 15,000 years, with the last eruptions occurring about 2,000 years ago.

The area's variety of surface patterns and formations is typical of the world's other basaltic lava sites. Visitors should be cautious of sharp lava formations.

A 7-mile loop drive, open from April through November, leads past the monument's main points of interest and takes about 30 minutes to complete. The view from the summit of Inferno Cone takes in the cinder cone chain along the Great Rift, a weakened zone of fissures in the Earth's crust. In winter, when the snow is sufficiently deep, the loop road is closed to vehicular traffic and is groomed for cross-country skiing and snowshoeing.

The cones formed when fountains of molten, gas-charged rock shot into the air. The frothy lava then cooled and hardened into cinders that fell around the vent, producing symmetrical cones. Numerous lava bombs, ejected blobs of less frothy lava that range from an inch to several feet in diameter, are scattered over the slopes. Big Cinder, 700 feet high, is one of the world's largest purely basaltic cinder cones.

Nearby is the Big Craters-Spatter Cone Area. These cones formed when clots of pasty lava stuck together as they fell back to Earth. A trail leads from the drive to the Cave Area, a series of lava tubes that range up to 40 feet in diameter and hundreds of feet in length. The largest is 830-foot Indian Tunnel; Boy Scout Cave has a floor of ice, even in summer. Some of the tubes can be explored; wear sturdy shoes and carry a flashlight. Permits are required and are available at the visitor center.

Other trails lead to Devil's Orchard, cinder fields scattered with fragments of a crater wall, and the Tree Mold Area, where lava slowly enveloped a group of living trees.

More than 700 species of plants and many different species of animals live in this seemingly desolate terrain. In early summer, wildflowers burst into bloom on the cinder fields and slopes of the cones.

Note: Off-road vehicles may be needed on some undeveloped dirt roads. Inquire about road conditions in advance.

A visitor center and campground-picnic area are near the entrance. Guided walks and evening programs are provided during summer months; phone for schedule. The entrance fee is $20 (per private vehicle); $15 (per motorcycle); $10 (per bicycle or per person on foot); free (ages 0-15).

ROBERT LIMBERT VISITOR CENTER is at the start of the 7-mi. loop drive. Exhibits explain the geology, plants, animals and history of the monument. **Hours:** Daily 8-6, Memorial Day-Labor Day; 8-4:30, rest of year. Closed winter holidays. **Phone:** (208) 527-1300.

DRIGGS (F-6) pop. 1,660, elev. 6,109'
- Hotels p. 42 • Restaurants p. 42
- Hotels & Restaurants map & index p. 195
- Part of Jackson Hole Including Grand Teton National Park area — see map p. 193

Settled by Mormon pioneers in 1889, Driggs is the main trading center for the Teton Valley. The town center is an eclectic mix of Old West and contemporary, with specialty shops, art galleries, pubs, eateries and outdoor outfitters. Teton Valley Museum, 137 SR 33N, offers a glimpse into the area's history; phone (208) 354-6000.

If you're the outdoorsy type, embark on a horseback riding, hunting, mountain biking or skiing expedition. And if you can handle heights, why not check out the town from a hot air balloon? You can experience the oldest successful human-carrying flight technology during the Teton Valley Balloon Rally, a 4-day event held in early July.

(See map & index p. 195.)

Teton Valley Chamber of Commerce: 57 S. Main St., P.O. Box 250, Driggs, ID 83422. **Phone:** (208) 354-2500.

Teton Geotourism Center: 60 S. Main St., P.O. Box 1562, Driggs, ID, 83422. **Phone:** (208) 354-2607.

SUPER 8 TETON WEST   (208)354-8888   **39**

Hotel
$65-$118

Address: 1361 N Hwy 33 83422 **Location:** SR 33, 1.4 mi n of downtown. **Facility:** 46 units, some efficiencies. 2 stories (no elevator), interior corridors. **Parking:** winter plug-ins. **Pool:** heated indoor. **Activities:** hot tub. **Guest Services:** coin laundry. **Featured Amenity: continental breakfast.**

TETON VALLEY CABINS   208/354-8153   **41**
🔹 Cabin. **Address:** 1 Mountain Vista Dr 83422

TETON WEST MOTEL   208/354-2363   **40**

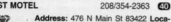
Motel
Rates not provided

Address: 476 N Main St 83422 **Location:** SR 33, 0.5 mi n of downtown. **Facility:** 38 units. 2 stories (no elevator), interior corridors. **Pool:** heated indoor. **Activities:** hot tub. **Guest Services:** coin laundry. **Featured Amenity: full hot breakfast.**

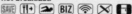

WHERE TO EAT

AGAVE MEXICAN RESTAURANT   208/354-2003   **51**
🔹🔹 Mexican. Casual Dining. **Address:** 310 N Main St 83422

BIG HOLE BAGEL & BISTRO   208/354-2245   **52**
🔹 Breakfast Deli. Casual Dining. **Address:** 285 N Main St 83422

FORAGE BISTRO & LOUNGE   208/354-2858   **54**
🔹🔹🔹 Regional American. Casual Dining. **Address:** 285 E Little Ave, Suite A 83422

PROVISIONS LOCAL KITCHEN   208/354-2333   **55**
🔹🔹 American. Casual Dining. **Address:** 95 S Main St 83422

SEOUL RESTAURANT - KOREAN CUISINE & SUSHI
                              208/354-1234   **50**
🔹🔹 Korean Sushi. Casual Dining. **Address:** 528 Valley Center Dr, Suite 4 83422

TETON THAI   208/787-8424   **53**
🔹🔹 Thai. Casual Dining. **Address:** 18 N Main St 83422

EAGLE pop. 19,908

HILTON GARDEN INN BOISE-EAGLE   208/938-9600
🔹🔹🔹 Hotel. **Address:** 145 E Riverside Dr 83616

AAA Benefit:
Members save 5%
or more!

WHERE TO EAT

BARDENAY RESTAURANT & DISTILLERY EAGLE
                              208/938-5093
🔹🔹 International. Casual Dining. **Address:** 155 E Riverside Dr 83616

THE GRIDDLE EAGLE   208/939-9070
🔹🔹 American. Casual Dining. **Address:** 177 Eagle River St 83616

REMBRANDT'S COFFEE HOUSE   208/938-1564
🔹 Coffee/Tea Breads/Pastries. Quick Serve. **Address:** 93 S Eagle Rd 83616

SMOKY MOUNTAIN PIZZERIA GRILL   208/939-0212
🔹🔹 Italian. Casual Dining. **Address:** 34 E State St 83616

GLENNS FERRY (G-2) pop. 1,319, elev. 2,560'

Off I-84 on the Snake River, the community traces its beginnings to a ferry crossing established here in 1869. Housed in a former school building built in 1909, the Glenns Ferry Historical Museum exhibits artifacts that depict area history; for more information phone the Glenns Ferry City Hall at (208) 366-7418.

FUDGE FACTORY GRILL & ICE CREAM   208/366-7687
🔹🔹 Sandwiches Desserts. Quick Serve. **Address:** 160 S Commercial St 83623

GRANGEVILLE (D-1) pop. 3,141, elev. 3,323'

A boomtown in gold rush days, Grangeville is a light industry and agricultural center and the largest town on the fertile Camas Prairie, one of the leading wheat-producing areas in the country. The prairie takes its name from *camassia esculenta,* an onion-like bulb common in the area and favored by the Nez Perce Indians. Today it is a site for an archeological excavation for mammoth bones.

A life-size replica of the giant mammoth unearthed in 1995 at nearby Tolo Lake, 6 miles west of town, can be seen in Eimers Park on US 95 at Pine Street. Grangeville also is an outfitting point for wilderness and float trips.

South of Grangeville US 95 descends 3,000 feet to the Salmon River Canyon via the White Bird Grade. This 7-mile section of the highway bypasses the dozens of switchbacks and hairpin curves of the original route, which can be seen to the east. White Bird Battlefield, a designated site of Nez Perce National Historical Park *(see place listing p. 56),* is about 16 miles south on US 95.

Grangeville Chamber of Commerce: US 95 at N. Pine, P.O. Box 212, Grangeville, ID 83530. **Phone:** (208) 983-0460.

Self-guiding tours: A trail guide of White Bird Battlefield is available at the chamber of commerce and at the Nez Perce National Forest office in Grangeville.

GATEWAY INN

208/983-2500

Motel
Rates not provided

Address: 700 W Main St 83530 **Location:** Jct US 95 and SR 13. **Facility:** 30 units, some efficiencies. 2 stories (no elevator), exterior corridors. **Parking:** winter plug-ins. **Pool:** heated outdoor. **Guest Services:** coin laundry. **Featured Amenity:** continental breakfast.

WHERE TO EAT

CREMA CAFE
208/983-0490

Coffee/Tea Breads/Pastries. Quick Serve. **Address:** 111 N College St 83530

HILLTOP CAFE
208/983-1724

American. Casual Dining. **Address:** 500 E Main St 83530

SEASONS RESTAURANT
208/983-4203

American. Casual Dining. **Address:** 124 W Main St 83530

HAGERMAN (G-3) pop. 872, elev. 2,959'

THOUSAND SPRINGS STATE PARK is .2 mi. s. off I-84 exit 147, then .2 mi. w., following signs to the welcome kiosk at Malad Gorge. The highlight of this multi-unit state park are aquifer-fed springs that gush in beautiful cascades from the sides of Snake River Canyon. The springs are believed to be the re-appearance of Lost River, which vanishes into the lava fields near Arco.

Park headquarters is at the Malad Gorge unit, where markers indicate points of interest along a 3.5-mile loop road. From a footbridge visitors can see the bottom of a 250-foot-deep gorge where a waterfall plunges into Devil's Washbowl. Part of the Oregon Trail, volcanic collapse features and underground springs also can be viewed.

Wildlife can be seen throughout the state park, which also encompasses the Niagara Springs unit, featuring 350-foot-high sheer basalt cliffs; the historic Kelton Trail, boasting pioneer wagon ruts; the Ritter Island unit, host to September's Thousand Springs Festival of the Arts; the Billingsley Creek unit, offering an indoor equestrian arena; and the Earl M. Hardy Box Canyon Springs Nature Preserve. *See Recreation Areas Chart.*

Time: Allow 45 minutes minimum. **Hours:** Park open daily 7:30-4 Memorial Day-Labor Day. Ritter Island unit open Thurs.-Mon. 10-3, Memorial Day-Labor Day. **Cost:** $5 (per private vehicle). **Phone:** (208) 837-4505.

Get the scoop from AAA inspectors:

AAA.com/travelguides/restaurants

HAGERMAN VALLEY INN

(208)837-6196

Motel
$72-$120

Address: 661 Frog's Landing 83332 **Location:** South end of town on US 30. **Facility:** 16 units. 2 stories (no elevator), exterior corridors. **Terms:** cancellation fee imposed. **Dining:** Snake River Grill, see separate listing.

WHERE TO EAT

SNAKE RIVER GRILL
208/837-6227

American. Casual Dining. **Address:** 611 Frog's Landing 83332

HAGERMAN FOSSIL BEDS NATIONAL MONUMENT (G-2)

The monument is 4 mi. s. on US 30, then 3 mi. w. on Bell Rapids Rd., following signs. The 3.4-million-year-old fossil beds, one of the continent's best Pliocene freshwater fish and small-mammal fossil sites, have yielded more than 220 plant and animal species, including complete skeletons of the Hagerman horse. A 10.5-mile auto route provides insights into area geology and geography and access to the Upper Salmon Falls Dam, the Snake River Overlook, the 3-mile trailhead for the Emigrant Trail and the Oregon Trail Overlook.

HAGERMAN FOSSIL BEDS NATIONAL MONUMENT VISITOR CENTER is at 221 N. State St., directly across US 30 from the high school. With exhibits of fossils, a discovery center, an orientation movie, auto tour brochures and trail maps, the center is a good place to stop for information before touring the monument, as access to some trails and overlooks may be restricted. **Hours:** Daily 9-5, Memorial Day-Labor Day; Thurs.-Mon. 9-5, rest of year. Closed major holidays. Phone ahead to confirm schedule. **Cost:** Free. **Phone:** (208) 933-4105.

HAILEY (G-3) pop. 7,960, elev. 5,330'
• Hotels p. 44 • Restaurants p. 44

Hailey, laid out in the spring of 1881 by John Hailey, was the center of a rich mining district in its early days. An early Northwest pioneer, Hailey had previously taken part in the Boise Basin Gold Rush in 1862 and had established a name for himself as the owner of a stage and freight line. Fortunes in gold, silver and lead were extracted from mines with such names as Black Cinder, Star, Hope, Climax, Democrat and Big Camas until the mining boom played out in the late 1890s.

On May 7, 1883, Hailey residents witnessed the driving of the last spike of the Wood River branch of the Oregon Short Line. In October of that year the Idaho Territory's first telephone exchange went into use at Hailey. Hailey also was the first to have an electric light plant.

Passing through the community are the Big Wood River and a system of paved recreational trails. Surrounded by Sawtooth National Recreation Area *(see place listing p. 64)*, Hailey offers a variety of outdoor activities, including hiking, bicycling and cross-country skiing.

Hailey Chamber of Commerce/Welcome Center: 781 Main St. S., P.O. Box 100, Hailey, ID 83333. **Phone:** (208) 788-3484.

Self-guiding tours: Brochures describing a self-guiding walking tour of Hailey's historic area are available at the chamber of commerce.

AIRPORT INN HAILEY	208/788-2477

Motel. **Address:** 820 4th Ave S 83333

AMERICINN LODGE & SUITES HAILEY	(208)788-7950

Hotel. **Address:** 51 Cobblestone Ln 83333

WOOD RIVER INN & SUITES	(208)578-0600

Hotel. **Address:** 601 N Main St 83333

WHERE TO EAT

CK'S REAL FOOD	208-788-1223

Natural/Organic. Fine Dining. **Address:** 320 Main St S 83333

POWER HOUSE PUB & BIKE SHOP	208-788-9184

American. Gastropub. **Address:** 502 N Main St 83333

RED SHOE BAR & GRILL	208-788-5048

American. Casual Dining. **Address:** 107 S Main St 83333

SHORTY'S DINER	208-578-1293

American. Casual Dining. **Address:** 126 S Main St 83333

ZOU 75 ASIAN & SUSHI BAR & GRILL	208-788-3310

Asian. Casual Dining. **Address:** 416 N Main St 83333

HELLS CANYON NATIONAL RECREATION AREA (D-1)

Hells Canyon National Recreation Area is reached via SRs 82 and 86 in northeastern Oregon and US 95 in western Idaho. The 652,977-acre area straddles the Snake River Canyon and encompasses parts of national forests in both states.

Confined within steep, eroded black basalt walls, the surging Snake River has carved North America's deepest river gorge, measuring 7,913 feet from He Devil Mountain to Granite Creek below. White-water rapids alternating with deep pools characterize this 72-mile free-flowing portion of the Snake River as it races north to meet the Columbia River.

The varied elevations of Hells Canyon support mixed plant communities sheltering such wildlife as bears, bobcats, bighorn sheep, cougars, elk, mule deer, mountain goats and many smaller birds, mammals and reptiles. Sturgeon, reputedly growing up to 11 feet long, inhabit the Snake River, sharing it with bass, catfish, salmon, steelhead trout and rainbow trout.

From the desertlike canyon floor to the alpine lakes of the Seven Devils region, the area presents a variety of recreational opportunities, including boating, float trips and backpacking. From Pittsburg Landing, the Kirkwood Historic Ranch and Museum, once the home of Idaho governor and U.S. senator Len B. Jordan, is accessible by powerboat, float boat or pack trail.

The Rapid River originates in the Seven Devils Mountains and eventually joins the Little Salmon River. The forks of the Rapid River provide quality water for raising chinook salmon and, therefore, house the Rapid River Fish Hatchery.

The 214,944-acre Hells Canyon Wilderness, with its extensive trail system, protects a large portion of the canyon along the Oregon-Idaho border. If you plan to fish the lakes and the Snake River shoreline, you must acquire the appropriate state licenses *(see Good Facts To Know)*; both Oregon and Idaho licenses are valid for boat fishing on the river.

Scenic Hells Canyon All American Road/SR 86 is a series of routes to and through the Hells Canyon National Recreation Area. **On the Oregon side** the best route is a two-lane paved loop that originates in Baker City. From Baker City follow SR 86 to Richland for approximately 41 miles. From Richland continue on SR 86 north for 11 miles to Halfway. From Halfway follow SR 86 for 20 miles to Oxbow. Nine miles north off Halfway, SR 86 will intersect with FR 39N. Take FR 39N through the heart of the Wallowa Mountains, high mountain country and through the town of Joseph to Enterprise. One mile west of Enterprise on SR 82 is the Wallowa Mountain Visitor Center. Continue along SR 82 west for approximately 64 miles to arrive back on I-84 at La Grande. The highest elevation portions of FR 39 are closed in winter. The entire loop will take approximately 5 hours.

Another possible route from the Oregon side to the recreation area is via SR 82 to Enterprise and Joseph. From Joseph it is possible to go to Hat Point, a 6,982-foot ridge overlooking Hells Canyon, via Imnaha. The route to Hat Point, open summer through early fall, follows FR 4240, a gravel, narrow road with steep grades.

Another route from Imnaha, FR 3955, parallels the Imnaha River as it meanders through rims and benches similar to those along the Snake River. This route connects with the Wallowa Mountain Loop (FR 39), which leads back to Joseph or Halfway. FR 3955 and FR 39 are maintained for cars and trailers. FR 39 can be followed east to FR 3965, which leads to the Hells Canyon overlook. With an elevation of 6,000 feet, the overlook provides a spectacular view of the Wallowa Mountains in Oregon and Idaho. These roads are closed in winter.

Buckhorn Springs, a scenic area overlooking the Imnaha drainage, can be reached from FR 46 off SR 3, a mostly gravel logging road.

For maps and brochures of different drives contact the Visit Baker Chamber of Commerce and Visitors Bureau, 490 Campbell St., Baker City, OR 97814; phone (541) 523-5855.

On the Idaho side there are two routes to the canyon. From Cambridge, SR 71 runs 29 miles northwest to Oxbow, Ore., crossing the Snake River near Brownlee Dam. It crosses back into Idaho at Oxbow, then follows the river north to Hells Canyon Dam. The total distance is about 55 miles. The other access point is Pittsburg Landing, 17 miles west of US 95 at White Bird via gravel FR 493. The drive from White Bird to Hells Canyon takes about 45 minutes.

Note: The majority of the Idaho side of the canyon is in the Mountain Time Zone; White Bird, Idaho, and the Oregon side of the canyon observe Pacific Time. It is advisable to check with the Hells Canyon National Recreation Area regarding road conditions and construction. Some roads are gravel and caution should be exercised. Phone (541) 426-5546.

More than 30 outfitters provide float and jet boat trips down the Snake River from Hells Canyon Dam and jet boat trips upstream from Lewiston and White Bird, Idaho, and from Asotin and Clarkston, Wash. For a list of local outfitters contact the Supervisor, Hells Canyon National Recreation Area, 2535 Riverside Dr., Clarkston, WA 99403; phone (509) 758-0616, or (509) 758-0270 for powerboat reservations. *See Recreation Areas Chart.*

Visit Lewis Clark Valley: 847 Port Way, Clarkston, WA 99403. **Phone:** (509) 758-7489 or (877) 774-7248.

BEAMERS HELLS CANYON TOURS departs from the Beamers Tour Dock behind the Quality Inn at 700 Port Dr. in Clarkston, Wash. This tour company offers jet boat excursions through Hells Canyon—North America's deepest river gorge. The full-day tour provides opportunities to view three mountain ranges, three states and five rivers. Half-day tours and other excursions also are available. **Hours:** Trips offered daily, May-Sept.; Sat.-Sun. only, Mar.-Apr. and in Oct. Departure times vary; phone ahead. **Cost:** Full-day tour $219; $10 (ages 0-8 with paid adult). Half-day trip $139; free (ages 0-8 with paid adult). Reservations are required. **Phone:** (509) 758-4800 or (800) 522-6966. GT ⑪

HELLS CANYON ADVENTURES is on SR 86 (All American Rd.), 1 mi. n. of Hells Canyon Dam and 23 mi. n. of Oxbow, Ore. Two-hour jet boat tours depart at 10 and at 2. Full-day jet boat tours depart at 10, traveling through the deepest part of Hells Canyon, navigating the largest rapids and visiting the Kirkwood Historical Ranch. Overnight jet boat adventures, 1- and 2-day rafting trips and fishing charters on the Snake River also are available.

Hours: Tours depart daily May-Sept. Inquire about off-season tours. Departure times vary. **Cost:** Granite Creek Tour $85; $60 (ages 3-11). Wild Sheep Tour $60-$75; $35-$37.50 (ages 3-11). Kirkwood $177; $88 (ages 5-11). A fuel surcharge may apply; phone ahead for more information. Reservations are recommended. **Phone:** (541) 785-3352 or (800) 422-3568.

KILLGORE ADVENTURES checks in guests at its office, 1 mi. s. on Old Hwy. 95 in White Bird, Idaho. The 65-mile, round-trip Wild River Tour through Class II to V rapids on the Snake River navigates the deepest and most rugged section of Hells Canyon, passing alongside Seven Devils Mountains en route to the dam. Other tours are available.

Time: Allow 6 hours minimum. **Hours:** Departures require a minimum of six people. Trips depart daily, Mar.-Oct. **Cost:** (includes a meal) $189; $110 (ages 0-12). Prices may vary. A shuttle to the departure point at Pittsburgh Landing marina, 17 mi. s.w. on a gravel road, is offered for a fee, or private vehicle parking is available at the marina. Reservations are required. **Phone:** (208) 839-2255 or (800) 469-8757.

IDAHO CITY (F-2) pop. 485, elev. 4,000'

Soon after gold was discovered in the Boise Basin in 1862, Idaho City became one of the largest cities in the Pacific Northwest. By 1865 it was home to some 7,000 gold seekers; nearly one quarter were Chinese. At its peak the basin was home to 15,000-20,000 miners. The mining district around Idaho City, including nearby Placerville and Centerville, was one of the largest sources of gold ever discovered.

More than 20 pioneer buildings from the 1860s and miles of dredge workings are still visible. The First Masonic Hall, built in 1865 to house Idaho's first Grand Lodge of Masons, displays Masonic items. Idaho City was the site of the territory's first prison, a portion of which has been restored. Guided town walking tours are available from the Boise Basin Museum by appointment; there is a $30 minimum per group.

Boise National Forest *(see place listing p. 36)* surrounds the town. Idaho City lies on scenic SR 21, also known as the Ponderosa Pine Scenic Route. SR 21 heads northeast through Sawtooth National Forest *(see place listing p. 64)* and ends in Stanley.

Idaho City Chamber of Commerce: 100 Main St., P.O. Box 507, Idaho City, ID 83631.

GOLD MINE EATERY & SPIRITS   208/392-2233
🍷🍷 American. Casual Dining. **Address:** 3867 SR 21 83631

IDAHO FALLS (G-5) pop. 56,813, elev. 4,742'
• Hotels p. 46 • Restaurants p. 47

Although it lies miles from the silver and gold lodes discovered in the region during the mid-1800s, Idaho Falls owes its formation to these riches. The settlement—originally called Taylor's Crossing—was established about 1860 along one of the few fording points on the upper Snake River. J.M. Taylor's ferry attracted many miners en route to Montana from Salt Lake City.

As the veins of precious metal diminished, transients and disillusioned residents abandoned the area. The few remaining settlers, faced with either adopting a new livelihood or adding the community to the growing list of Western ghost towns, dug channels to irrigate the arid land. Soon the town flourished along with the newly established agriculture'. The irrigation system that saved the town now provides water to more than 1 million acres of farmland.

Tautphaus Park has sports facilities, picnic grounds, amusement rides and a zoo *(see attraction listing)*. Sandy Downs, 2 miles south of 17th Street on St. Clair Road, is the site of various recreational activities.

Greater Idaho Falls Chamber of Commerce & Visitors Center: 365 River Pkwy., Idaho Falls, ID 83402. **Phone:** (208) 523-1010 or (866) 365-6943.

THE IDAHO FALLS ZOO AT TAUTPHAUS PARK is at Rogers St. and Carnival Way. More than 250 animals of over 100 species reside in Idaho's largest zoo in regional habitats representing North and South America, Africa, Asia, Australia and New Guinea. Come Meet a Zookeeper shows are scheduled daily in summer. Also popular is the Penguin Interaction Program in which participants meet a zookeeper, interact with the birds and learn about the fascinating lives of African penguins. A children's zoo is also on-site.

Time: Allow 1 hour minimum. **Hours:** Daily 9-6, Memorial Day weekend-Labor Day; 9-5, mid-Apr. through day before Memorial Day weekend and day after Labor Day-early Oct. Penguin Interaction Program is offered Thurs.-Sun. at 11, late May-early Oct. Phone ahead to confirm schedule. **Cost:** $7.50; $6 (ages 62+); $4.50 (ages 4-12). Penguin Interaction Program $30; $20 (ages 4-12). Prices may vary; phone ahead. Reservations for the Penguin Interaction Program are required. **Phone:** (208) 612-8552.

THE MUSEUM OF IDAHO is off I-15 exit 118 (Broadway) at 200 N. Eastern Ave. It features such exhibits as Race for Atomic Power, which documents important milestones in the history of nuclear energy that occurred in southeastern Idaho; Lewis and Clark in Idaho; a children's discovery room; and Eagle Rock USA, a replica of the 19th-century community that later became Idaho Falls.

Temporary exhibitions also are offered. **Time:** Allow 1 hour minimum. **Hours:** Mon. and Fri. 10-8, Tues.-Thurs. and Sat 10-6, Sun. 1-5. Closed Jan. 1, Thanksgiving and Christmas. Phone ahead to confirm schedule. **Cost:** $12; $11 (ages 62+); $10 (ages 4-17 and college student with ID); $42 (family); $37 (family, Mon. 5-8 p.m.). Prices may vary. **Phone:** (208) 522-1400.

BEST WESTERN DRIFTWOOD INN   (208)523-2242

Motel
$69-$229

AAA Benefit: Members save up to 15% and earn bonus points!

Address: 575 River Pkwy 83402 **Location:** Waterfront. I-15 exit 118 (Broadway), 0.5 mi e, then 0.3 mi n. **Facility:** 75 units, some efficiencies and kitchens. 2 stories (no elevator), exterior corridors. **Parking:** winter plug-ins. **Terms:** cancellation fee imposed. **Pool:** heated outdoor. **Activities:** hot tub, bicycles, trails, exercise room. **Guest Services:** valet and coin laundry, boarding pass kiosk.

BEST WESTERN PLUS COTTONTREE INN IDAHO FALLS   (208)523-6000

Hotel
$89-$229

AAA Benefit: Members save up to 15% and earn bonus points!

Address: 900 Lindsay Blvd 83402 **Location:** I-15 exit 119, just e. Near the Idaho Falls River Walk. **Facility:** 94 units. 3 stories, interior corridors. **Parking:** winter plug-ins. **Terms:** cancellation fee imposed. **Pool:** heated indoor. **Activities:** hot tub, trails, exercise room. **Guest Services:** valet and coin laundry.

CANDLEWOOD SUITES IDAHO FALLS   208/525-9800
Extended Stay Hotel. **Address:** 665 Pancheri Dr 83402

FAIRFIELD INN & SUITES BY MARRIOTT IDAHO FALLS   (208)552-7378
Contemporary Hotel. **Address:** 1293 W Broadway St 83402

AAA Benefit: Members save 5% or more!

HAMPTON INN BY HILTON IDAHO FALLS-AIRPORT   208/523-1400
Hotel. **Address:** 645 Lindsay Blvd 83402

AAA Benefit: Members save 5% or more!

HAMPTON INN BY HILTON IDAHO FALLS AT THE MALL   208/529-9800
Hotel. **Address:** 2500 Channing Way 83404

AAA Benefit: Members save 5% or more!

HILTON GARDEN INN IDAHO FALLS   208/522-9500
Hotel. **Address:** 700 Lindsay Blvd 83402

AAA Benefit: Members save 5% or more!

HOLIDAY INN EXPRESS & SUITES   208/542-9800
Hotel. **Address:** 2270 Channing Way 83404

HOME2 SUITES BY HILTON IDAHO FALLS   208/529-0400

▼▼▼ Extended Stay Contemporary Hotel. **Address:** 1160 Whitewater Dr 83402

AAA Benefit: Members save 5% or more!

LA QUINTA INN & SUITES IDAHO FALLS   208/552-2500

▼▼▼ Hotel. **Address:** 2501 S 25th St E 83404

RESIDENCE INN BY MARRIOTT IDAHO FALLS   (208)542-0000

▼▼▼ Extended Stay Hotel. **Address:** 635 W Broadway 83402

AAA Benefit: Members save 5% or more!

SLEEP INN & SUITES IDAHO FALLS   (208)821-3647

Hotel
$84-$169

Address: 3200 Outlet Blvd 83402 **Location:** I-15 exit 116, just w. **Facility:** 75 units. 3 stories, interior corridors. **Parking:** winter plug-ins. **Amenities:** safes. **Pool:** heated indoor. **Activities:** exercise room. **Guest Services:** valet and coin laundry, area transportation. **Featured Amenity: full hot breakfast.**

SPRINGHILL SUITES BY MARRIOTT IDAHO FALLS
(208)552-7000

▼▼▼ Contemporary Hotel. **Address:** 665 Riverwalk Dr 83402

AAA Benefit: Members save 5% or more!

WHERE TO EAT

BLUE HASHI   208/525-2583
▼▼ Japanese. Casual Dining. **Address:** 2894 S 25th E 83401

THE CELT IRISH PUB & GRILL   208/881-5128
▼▼ Irish. Casual Dining. **Address:** 398 W Broadway St 83402

CHEF SHANE'S PERSPECTIVE   208/932-2727
▼▼ American. Casual Dining. **Address:** 3192 S 25th E 83404

COPPER RILL RESTAURANT   208/529-5800
▼▼ American. Casual Dining. **Address:** 415 River Pkwy 83402

DIXIE'S DINER   208/542-1950
▼▼ Comfort Food. Casual Dining. **Address:** 2150 Channing Way 83404

JAKERS BAR & GRILL   208/524-5240
▼▼ Steak Seafood. Casual Dining. **Address:** 851 Lindsay Blvd 83402

JALISCO'S MEXICAN RESTAURANT   208/612-0102
▼▼ Mexican. Casual Dining. **Address:** 325 River Pkwy 83401

LA VANILLA BEAN PATISSERIE   208/881-5176
▼ Breads/Pastries Sandwiches. Quick Serve. **Address:** 489 Park Ave 83402

SANDPIPER   208/524-3344
▼▼ American. Casual Dining. **Address:** 750 Lindsay Blvd 83402

THE SNAKEBITE RESTAURANT   208/525-2522
▼▼ American. Casual Dining. **Address:** 401 Park Ave 83402

SNOW EAGLE BREWING & GRILL   208/557-0455
▼▼ American. Brewpub. **Address:** 455 River Pkwy 83402

STOCKMAN'S RESTAURANT   208/552-6500
▼▼ Seafood Steak. Casual Dining. **Address:** 1175 Pier View Dr 83402

IDAHO PANHANDLE NATIONAL FORESTS (B-1)

Elevations in the forests range from 2,060 ft. at Lake Pend Oreille to 7,705 ft. at Northwest Peak. Refer to AAA maps for additional elevation information.

In northern Idaho and adjoining parts of Montana and Washington, the many-segmented Idaho Panhandle National Forests have rugged peaks, canyons and valleys. The approximately 2.5-million-acre area includes the former St. Joe, Kaniksu and Coeur d'Alene national forests.

Of particular interest are the stands of old-growth cedars at Hanna Flats and Roosevelt Grove near Priest Lake, the Settlers Grove of Ancient Cedars near Prichard and the Hobo Cedar Grove near Clarkia. Among the nearly 400 species of wildlife are wolves and grizzly bears.

Fishing is available at Priest Lake, Lake Coeur d'Alene and Lake Pend Oreille; nature trails traverse these areas. Float trips are popular on the Coeur d'Alene, St. Joe and Priest rivers. Winter sports areas are off SR 6 between St. Maries and Moscow, at Lookout Pass just off I-90 on the Idaho-Montana border and at 4th of July Pass off I-90.

Information is available at the headquarters in Coeur d'Alene and at ranger stations at Avery, Bonners Ferry, Priest River, St. Maries, Sandpoint and Smelterville. For additional information contact the Forest Supervisor's Office, Idaho Panhandle National Forests, 3815 Schreiber Way, Coeur d'Alene, ID 83815-8363; phone (208) 765-7223. *See Recreation Areas Chart.*

JEROME pop. 10,890
• Restaurants p. 48

BEST WESTERN SAWTOOTH INN & SUITES
(208)324-9200

Hotel
$94-$189

 Best Western.

AAA Benefit: Members save up to 15% and earn bonus points!

Address: 2653 S Lincoln Ave 83338 **Location:** I-84 exit 168, just n. Located in a commercial area. **Facility:** 67 units. 2 stories (no elevator), interior corridors. **Parking:** winter plug-ins. **Terms:** check-in 4 pm. **Pool:** heated indoor. **Activities:** hot tub. **Guest Services:** valet and coin laundry. **Featured Amenity: full hot breakfast.**

COMFORT INN & SUITES TWIN FALLS/JEROME
(208)644-1200

▼▼▼ Hotel. **Address:** 379 Crossroads Point Blvd 83338

WHERE TO EAT

BURNT LEMON GRILL   208/324-8800
▼ Sandwiches Burgers. Quick Serve. **Address:** 306 S Lincoln Ave 83338

KAMIAH (D-2) pop. 1,295, elev. 1,196'

Meriwether Lewis and William Clark camped on the north bank of the Clearwater River just north of Kamiah (KAM-ee-eye) in the spring of 1806 on their homeward journey. Today a sawmill occupies the site of their monthlong encampment.

A pasture about a half mile northwest of Kamiah is supposedly the location of the mission that Asa and Sarah Smith started in 1839. They stayed only 2 years, and their work in this area was not resumed until 30 years later.

The 1871 First Presbyterian Church is said to be the oldest Native American church in continuous use in Idaho. The Northwest Passage Scenic Byway (US 12) also passes through town. It's considered one of the top 10 motorcycle roads in the nation.

Kamiah Chamber of Commerce: 518 Main St., P.O. Box 1124, Kamiah, ID 83536. **Phone:** (208) 935-2290.

HEARTHSTONE ELEGANT LODGE   208/935-1492
▼▼▼
Bed & Breakfast
Rates not provided

Address: 3250 Hwy 12 at Milepost 64 83536 **Location:** On SR 12, 2.2 mi w of center; MM 64. **Facility:** Spacious, artistically appointed guest rooms have fine linens on canopied king-size beds with beautiful antique headboards, vaulted ceilings, fireplaces and a covered deck entrance with skylights. 5 units, some cottages. 1-2 stories (no elevator), exterior corridors. **Parking:** winter plug-ins. **Terms:** check-in 4 pm. **Activities:** limited beach access, massage. **Featured Amenity: continental breakfast.**

SAVE CALL ⬇ 🛜 ✕ 🔋 🖥
/ SOME UNITS 🐾

WHERE TO EAT

HEARTHSTONE BAKERY & TEA HOUSE   208/935-1912
▼▼ Breakfast Sandwiches. Casual Dining. **Address:** 502 Main St 83536

HUB BAR & GRILL   208/935-2211
▼▼ American. Casual Dining. **Address:** 406 Main St 83536

KAMIAH HOTEL BAR AND GRLL   208/935-0545
▼▼ Steak Sandwiches. Casual Dining. **Address:** 501 4th St 83536

KELLOGG (B-1) pop. 2,120, elev. 2,305'

Kellogg, the Silver Valley's largest town, celebrates its heritage as a longtime mining community. The Coeur d'Alene mining district has yielded more than a billion dollars in silver, lead, gold and zinc; the Lucky Friday and Galena Mine are a couple of the largest mines that still operate. The Shoshone County Mining and Smelting Museum, also known as The Staff House Museum chronicles the colorful history of Silver Valley. The Sunshine

Miners Memorial, off I-90 exit 54, commemorates the 1972 mine fire that claimed 91 lives. It was one of the nation's worst metal and nonmetal mine disasters.

The Kellogg area also is known for outdoor recreation, particularly its biking trails, which range from easy to "What was I thinking?" Accessible here is the Trail of the Coeur d'Alenes, a 72-mile paved path that runs from the Montana border to the Washington state line. Hardy cyclists also can take their bikes up the Silver Mountain Gondola to enjoy 40 miles of trails, including some that descend 3,000 feet.

Historic Silver Valley Chamber of Commerce: 10 Station Ave., Kellogg, ID 83837. **Phone:** (208) 784-0821.

RECREATIONAL ACTIVITIES
Skiing

- **Silver Mountain Resort** is off I-90 exit 49 at 610 Bunker Ave. Other activities are offered. **Hours:** Winter activities are available Thurs.-Mon. 9-4, late Nov. to mid-Apr. Schedule varies during holiday weeks; phone ahead. **Phone:** (208) 783-1111 or (800) 204-6428.

FAIRBRIDGE INN & SUITES   (208)783-1234
▼▼ Hotel. **Address:** 601 Bunker Ave 83837

MORNING STAR LODGE   208/783-0202
▼▼▼ Resort Condominium. **Address:** 602 Bunker Ave 83837

KETCHUM (G-3) pop. 2,689, elev. 5,821'

In the late 19th century Ketchum sprang up almost overnight as a shipping and smelting center for the remote mountain mines surrounding the Wood River Valley. Ores and supplies were transported by the giant ore wagons of the Horace Lewis Fast Freight Line. These relics of the area's past are displayed in the Ore Wagon Museum on East Avenue next to City Hall and once again appear on the streets during the Wagon Days Celebration Labor Day weekend. The history and culture of Wood River Valley's sheep industry is spotlighted in October during the ▼ Trailing of the Sheep festival. The Ketchum Cemetery includes the grave of Ernest Hemingway.

As the gateway to the Sun Valley *(see place listing p. 65)* resort area and the Sawtooth National Recreation Area *(see place listing p. 64)*, the town offers an abundance of activities year-round. Such outdoor recreational activities as swimming, mountain biking and bicycling, hiking, horseback riding, cross-country skiing, snowshoeing and camping are foremost among Ketchum's attractions. For the spectator Ketchum offers some 30 art galleries and the nexStage Theatre, where local theater companies perform year-round. For theater information phone (208) 726-4857.

Sun Valley Visitors Center: 491 Sun Valley Rd., Ketchum ID 83340. **Phone:** (208) 726-3423 or (800) 634-3347.

Self-guiding tours: The Sun Valley Museum of History, 1st Street and Washington Avenue, has a booklet about the history of Ketchum that includes a walking tour through the downtown area; phone (208) 726-8118.

Shopping: Downtown Ketchum offers more than 70 shops and restaurants offering everything from antiques and books to children's toys and specialty gifts.

RECREATIONAL ACTIVITIES
Horseback Riding
- **Galena Stage Stop Corrals-Trail Rides** is 24 mi. n. on SR 75. Other activities are offered. **Hours:** Horseback riding trips daily 9-5, mid-June through Labor Day. **Phone:** (208) 726-1735.

BEST WESTERN PLUS KENTWOOD LODGE
(208)726-4114

Hotel
$110-$490

Best Western PLUS
AAA Benefit: Members save up to 15% and earn bonus points!

Address: 180 S Main St 83340 **Location:** On SR 75; at Main and Rivers sts. **Facility:** 57 units, some efficiencies. 3 stories, interior corridors. **Parking:** winter plug-ins. **Terms:** 7 day cancellation notice-fee imposed. **Pool:** heated indoor. **Activities:** hot tub, trails, exercise room. **Guest Services:** valet and coin laundry.

BEST WESTERN TYROLEAN LODGE
(208)726-5336

Hotel
$129-$259

Best Western.
AAA Benefit: Members save up to 15% and earn bonus points!

Address: 260 Cottonwood St 83340 **Location:** Just s of center to Rivers St, w to 2nd Ave, s to Cottonwood St, then just w. **Facility:** 52 units. 3 stories (no elevator), interior corridors. **Parking:** winter plug-ins. **Terms:** 4 night minimum stay - seasonal, 3 day cancellation notice-fee imposed. **Pool:** heated outdoor. **Activities:** sauna, hot tub, game room, trails, exercise room. **Guest Services:** coin laundry.

LIMELIGHT HOTEL KETCHUM
(208)726-0888

Boutique Contemporary Hotel
$215-$525

Address: 151 S Main St 83340 **Location:** At Main (SR 75) and 1st sts; downtown. **Facility:** This stylish, trendy hotel provides mega-seating arrangements in the lobby. Enjoy the underground parking, upscale bedding, 50-inch flat-panel HDTVs and luxury personal care products. 102 units, some two bedrooms, three bedrooms, kitchens and condominiums. 5 stories, interior corridors. **Parking:** on-site (fee); winter plug-ins. **Terms:** check-in 4 pm, 30 day cancellation notice, resort fee. **Amenities:** safes. **Dining:** entertainment. **Pool:** heated outdoor. **Activities:** hot tub, recreation programs in season, bicycles, game room, trails, exercise room, massage. **Guest Services:** valet and coin laundry, area transportation. **Featured Amenity:** continental breakfast.

WHERE TO EAT

CRISTINA'S RESTAURANT & BAKERY — 208/726-4499
European. Casual Dining. **Address:** 520 2nd St E 83340

DESPO'S, MEXICAN WITH ALTITUDE — 208/726-3068
Mexican. Casual Dining. **Address:** 211 4th St E 83340

ENOTECA RESTAURANT AND WINE BAR — 208/928-6280
Small Plates Pizza. Fine Dining. **Address:** 300 Main St N 83340

GLOBUS RESTAURANT WINE & SPIRITS — 208/726-1301
Asian. Fine Dining. **Address:** 131 Washington Ave 83340

JAVA ON FOURTH — 208/726-2882
Sandwiches Breads/Pastries. Quick Serve. **Address:** 191 4th St 83340

KETCHUM GRILL — 208/726-4660
New American. Fine Dining. **Address:** 520 East Ave N 83340

THE KNEADERY — 208/726-9462
American. Casual Dining. **Address:** 260 Leadville Ave 83340

MICHEL'S CHRISTIANIA RESTAURANT & OLYMPIC BAR — 208/726-3388
French. Fine Dining. **Address:** 303 N Walnut Ave 83340

PIONEER SALOON — 208/726-3139
Steak Seafood. Casual Dining. **Address:** 320 N Main St 83340

RICKSHAW — 208/726-8481
Asian. Casual Dining. **Address:** 460 N Washington Ave 83340

SAWTOOTH CLUB — 208/726-5233
American. Casual Dining. **Address:** 231 N Main St 83340

SMOKY MOUNTAIN PIZZERIA GRILL — 208/622-5625
Italian. Casual Dining. **Address:** 200 Sun Valley Rd 83340

TOWN SQUARE TAVERN — 208/726-6969
Mediterranean. Fine Dining. **Address:** 360 East Ave N 83340

VINTAGE RESTAURANT — 208/726-9595
American. Fine Dining. **Address:** 231 Leadville Ave N 83340

KOOTENAI NATIONAL FOREST—See
Montana p. 127

LAPWAI (D-1) pop. 1,137, elev. 891'

Lapwai (LAP-way) is the site of the first military fort in Idaho, built in 1862 to prevent clashes between pioneers and Native Americans in the area. The U.S. Army occupied the fort until 1884. Some of the old buildings around the parade ground are still in use. The Old Fort Lapwai Cemetery is located on the ridge just south of the fort.

LAVA HOT SPRINGS (H-5) pop. 407, elev. 5,151'

Lava Hot Springs was named for the mineral springs that boil out of lava rocks at the base of massive cliffs along the Portneuf River. Geologists believe that the pools have remained at the same temperature—110 F—for 50 million years. Lava Hot Springs is a popular health and pleasure resort offering hiking, bicycling, tubing, ziplining and swimming.

For centuries the Shoshone and Bannock Indians regarded the springs as a neutral site. But the tribes camp was disrupted during the 19th century when the springs were discovered by Oregon-bound travelers and Utah pioneers who founded a settlement called Dempsey. By 1902 the Native Americans had ceded their rights to the springs, selling the land to the U.S. government, which in turn gave the area to the state.

Southeast Idaho High Country Tourism: P.O. Box 669, Lava Hot Springs, ID 83246. **Phone:** (208) 776-5221 or (888) 201-1063.

IDAHO WORLD FAMOUS HOT POOLS AND OLYMPIC SWIMMING COMPLEX, on US 30E, is a state-owned facility that consists of hot mineral pools on the end of town and outdoor Olympic-size swimming pools with slides and diving boards as well as an indoor aquatic center and kiddie cove on the west end. The Sunken Gardens bloom on terraces that cling to the walls of an extinct volcano. Snowmobiling and skiing, subject to local weather conditions, are possible on the surrounding mountains.

Hours: Mineral baths daily 8 a.m.-11 p.m., May-Sept.; Sun.-Thurs. 9 a.m.-10 p.m., Fri.-Sat. 9 a.m.-11 p.m., rest of year. Swimming pool daily noon-8, mid-May through Labor Day. Indoor swimming pool and kiddie cove open year-round with limited hours. Closed Thanksgiving and Christmas. Phone ahead to confirm schedule.

Cost: Mineral bath Fri.-Sun. and holidays $8; $7.50 (ages 3-11 and 60+); $2 (ages 0-2). Mineral bath Mon.-Thurs. $6; $5.50 (ages 3-11 and 60+); $2 (ages 0-2). Swimming pool Fri.-Sun. and holidays $10; $9 (ages 3-11); $2 (ages 0-2). Swimming pool Mon.-Thurs. $7.50; $7 (ages 3-11); $2 (ages 0-2). A combination mineral bath and swimming pool all-day pass is available, as are discounted family rates on Wed. **Phone:** (208) 776-5221 or (800) 423-8597.

LIONS GATE MANOR BED & BREAKFAST   208/776-5118
♦♦♦ Bed & Breakfast. **Address:** 10376 S Dempsey Creek Rd 83246

WHERE TO EAT

78 MAIN STREET GRILL   208/776-5106
♦♦ American. Casual Dining. **Address:** 78 E Main St 83246

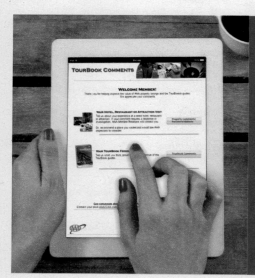

LEWISTON (D-1) pop. 31,894, elev. 738'

At the confluence of the Clearwater and Snake rivers, Lewiston is on a site where Meriwether Lewis and William Clark camped in 1805 and again in 1806. Following the discovery of gold nearby, the settlement became a supply point for mining camps and, subsequently, the state's first territorial capital 1863-65.

Large quantities of grain and other cargo are shipped from Lewiston, known as "Idaho's Seaport," by barge 465 miles down the Snake and Columbia rivers to the Pacific. Boats reach the port by passing through locks at eight dams.

In April the city celebrates the arrival of spring with the Dogwood Festival of the Lewis-Clark Valley. Lewiston lies on an especially scenic section of US 95 that extends north to Plummer and south to Banks. North of the city US 95 climbs 2,000 feet to the top of Lewiston Hill, where a viewpoint overlooks the valley. The original road up the hill, known as the Spiral Highway for its 64 curves, opened in 1917. The old road is still open but was replaced in 1979 by the long, easier grade of the new alignment.

Shopping: Lewiston Center Mall, 1 mile south of US 12 via 18th or 21st streets, features JCPenney and Macy's.

FAIRBRIDGE INN & SUITES   208/746-3311
◈◈ Hotel. **Address:** 1325 Main St 83501

HAMPTON INN BY HILTON - LEWISTON   208/743-9004
◈◈◈ Hotel. **Address:** 2701 Nez Perce Dr 83501

AAA Benefit:
Members save 5% or more!

HOLIDAY INN EXPRESS   208/750-1600
◈◈◈
Hotel
Rates not provided

Address: 2425 Nez Perce Dr 83501 **Location:** 1.2 mi s on US 12 from jct US 95, 1.2 mi s on 21st St, just e. **Facility:** 100 units. 3 stories, interior corridors. **Pool:** heated indoor. **Activities:** hot tub, exercise room. **Guest Services:** valet and coin laundry, area transportation. **Featured Amenity:** breakfast buffet.

WHERE TO EAT

MAIN STREET GRILL   208/746-2440
◈◈ American. Casual Dining. **Address:** 625 Main St 83501

MYSTIC CAFE   208/743-1811
◈◈ American. Casual Dining. **Address:** 1303 Main St 83501

WAFFLES N' MORE   208/743-5189
◈◈ Breakfast Sandwiches. Casual Dining. **Address:** 1421 Main St 83501

WAYBACK CAFE   208/743-2396
◈◈ American. Casual Dining. **Address:** 2138 13th Ave 83501

ZANY GRAZE 208/746-8131
 American. Casual Dining. **Address:** 2004 19th Ave 83501

MCCALL (E-1) pop. 2,991, elev. 5,025'

At the southern end of beautiful Payette Lake, McCall is a year-round recreational resort with a municipal airport. Fishing, boating, water skiing, horseback riding, white-water rafting, golf, camping and hunting are available. Skiing, snowboarding, snowshoeing and snowmobiling are popular winter sports. Manchester Ice and Event Centre is open year-round for indoor ice-skating and curling.

Firefighting facilities at the Forest Service's Smokejumper Headquarters feature smokejumping equipment, a fire retardant mixing plant and communications services. Tours are offered twice daily; phone (208) 634-0378.

McCall lies on an especially scenic section of SR 55, also called the Payette River Scenic Byway. The highway heads north, merges with US 95 and continues toward Coeur d'Alene. The southern terminus of the route is Boise.

McCall Area Chamber of Commerce and Visitors Bureau: 301 E. Lake St., P.O. Box 350, McCall, ID 83638. **Phone:** (208) 634-7631 or (800) 260-5130.

PONDEROSA STATE PARK is 1.5 mi. n.e. at 1920 N. Davis Ave. Embracing most of a 1,000-acre peninsula on the shores of Payette Lake, the park is named for its old-growth forest of ponderosa pines, some upwards of 150 feet tall. More than 12 miles of trails lead hikers and mountain bikers through the diverse landscape, which ranges from dense woods and sagebrush flats to marsh and lakeside cliffs.

Osprey Cliff, accessible by road and trail, offers stunning views 300 feet above the lake. Along Payette Lake's western bank, the Warren Wagon Road leads to the 500-acre North Beach Unit. A sandy beach and popular canoeing route along 4 miles of the North Fork Payette River is also part of the park, about eight miles north of McCall.

On Saturdays in summer, junior ranger and evening programs are offered. Winter activities include snowshoeing on 3 miles of trails and Nordic skiing on more than 12 miles of groomed trails. Cabins are open year-round. *See Recreation Areas Chart.* **Time:** Allow 1 hour minimum. **Hours:** Park open daily dawn-dusk. Visitor center open daily 9-9, Memorial Day weekend-Labor Day; Tues.-Sat. 10-4, rest of year. **Cost:** Day-use fee $5 (per private vehicle). Camping $12-49 per night. Cabins $75-165

🔗 **For complete hotel, dining and attraction listings: AAA.com/travelguides**

per night. **Phone:** (208) 634-2164.

BEST WESTERN PLUS MCCALL LODGE & SUITES
(208)634-2230

Hotel
$150-$330

BW Best Western PLUS.

AAA Benefit: Members save up to 15% and earn bonus points!

Address: 211 S 3rd St 83638 **Location:** 1 mi s of downtown on SR 55. **Facility:** 66 units, some efficiencies. 3 stories, interior corridors. **Parking:** winter plug-ins. **Terms:** cancellation fee imposed. **Pool:** heated indoor. **Activities:** sauna, hot tub, exercise room. **Guest Services:** coin laundry. **Featured Amenity:** full hot breakfast.

HOLIDAY INN EXPRESS & SUITES 208/634-4700
 Hotel. **Address:** 210 N 3rd St 83638

SHORE LODGE
(208)634-2244

Resort Hotel
$169-$319

Address: 501 W Lake St 83638 **Location:** Waterfront. 1 mi w of downtown; on SR 55. On Payette Lake. **Facility:** Spring, summer, fall or winter, the picture-perfect postcard views of Payette Lake is spellbinding. This hotel offers ample amenities for everyone, whether staying overnight or for an extended stay. 77 units. 3 stories, interior corridors. **Parking:** on-site and valet, winter plug-ins. **Terms:** 2-3 night minimum stay - seasonal and/or weekends, 30 day cancellation notice-fee imposed, resort fee. **Amenities:** safes. **Dining:** 3 restaurants, also, The Narrows Steakhouse, see separate listing. **Pool:** heated outdoor. **Activities:** hot tub, limited beach access, marina, regulation golf, recreation programs in summer, bicycles, game room, exercise room, spa. **Guest Services:** area transportation.

WHERE TO EAT

BISTRO 45 WINE BAR & CAFE 208/634-4515
American. Quick Serve. **Address:** 1101 N 3rd St 83638

LARDO'S GRILL & SALOON 208/634-8191
American. Casual Dining. **Address:** 600 W Lake St 83638

MY FATHER'S PLACE 208/634-4401
Burgers. Quick Serve. **Address:** 901 N 3rd St 83638

THE NARROWS STEAKHOUSE 208/634-2244
(fyi) American. Fine Dining. Under major renovation, call for details. Last rated: **Address:** 501 W Lake St 83638

MCCALL PANCAKE HOUSE AND CHRISTMAS & SPECIALTY SHOPS 208/634-5849
American. Casual Dining. **Address:** 209 N 3rd St 83638

PUEBLO LINDO MEXICAN RESTAURANT 208/634-2270
Mexican. Casual Dining. **Address:** 1007 W Lake St 83638

RUPERT'S AT HOTEL MCCALL 208/634-8108
American. Fine Dining. **Address:** 1101 N 3rd St 83638

SALMON RIVER BREWERY 208/634-4772
American. Casual Dining. **Address:** 411 Railroad Ave 83638

SOUTHSIDE GRILL　　208/634-2128
♥♥ Mexican. Casual Dining. **Address:** 339 Deinhard Ln 83638

STEAMERS STEAK & SEAFOOD RESTAURANT　208/634-1411
♥♥ Steak Seafood. Casual Dining. **Address:** 308 E Lake St 83638

THE SUSHI BAR　　208/634-7874
♥♥ Asian Sushi. Casual Dining. **Address:** 414 Railroad Ave 83638

MERIDIAN　(G-1) pop. 75,092, elev. 2,600'

SAVE **ROARING SPRINGS WATERPARK** is off I-84 exit 44, then w. at 400 W. Overland Rd. The water park features more than 20 attractions, including the Corkscrew Cavern, Cliffhanger, two family raft rides, a wave pool, an endless river, tube slides, a bowl slide, a four-lane racing slide and a children's play area. The adjacent Wahooz Family Fun Zone offers miniature golf, laser tag, go-karts, bumper boats, an arcade and a 24-lane bowling center.

Time: Allow 4 hours minimum. **Hours:** Water park daily 11-8, June-Aug.; Sat.-Sun. 11-7, mid-May through May 31 and Sept. 1 to mid-Sept. Wahooz Family Fun Zone daily 10-10, June-Aug.; 11-9, rest of year. Phone ahead to confirm schedule. **Cost:** Water park $30.99; $25.99 (ages 55+ and under 48 inches tall). Water park after 3 p.m. $23.99. Wahooz Family Fun Zone prices vary. **Phone:** (208) 884-8842 for water park, or (208) 898-0900 for Wahooz Family Fun Zone. 🍴

BEST WESTERN PLUS MERIDIAN　　(208)887-7888

Hotel
$99-$159

Best Western PLUS
AAA Benefit:
Members save up to 15% and earn bonus points!

Address: 1019 S Progress Ave 83642 **Location:** I-84 exit 44 (Meridian/Kuna), just ne. **Facility:** 61 units. 2 stories, interior corridors. **Parking:** winter plug-ins. **Terms:** cancellation fee imposed. **Pool:** heated indoor. **Activities:** hot tub, exercise room. **Guest Services:** valet and coin laundry.

/ SOME UNITS

CANDLEWOOD SUITES BOISE WEST-MERIDIAN　208/888-5121
♥♥♥ Extended Stay Hotel. **Address:** 1855 S Silverstone Way 83642

COUNTRY INN & SUITES BY RADISSON - BOISE WEST AT MERIDIAN　208/639-3300

Hotel
Rates not provided

Address: 3355 E Pine Ave 83642 **Location:** I-84 exit 46 (Eagle Rd), 0.8 mi n, then just e. **Facility:** 82 units. 4 stories, interior corridors. **Pool:** heated indoor. **Activities:** hot tub, exercise room. **Guest Services:** valet and coin laundry. **Featured Amenity:** breakfast buffet.

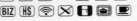

COURTYARD BY MARRIOTT BOISE WEST/MERIDIAN
(208)888-0800
♥♥♥ Contemporary Hotel. **Address:** 1789 S Eagle Rd 83642
AAA Benefit: Members save 5% or more!

HAMPTON INN & SUITES BY HILTON MERIDIAN/BOISE WEST
208/887-3600
♥♥♥ Hotel. **Address:** 875 S Allen St 83642
AAA Benefit: Members save 5% or more!

HOLIDAY INN EXPRESS & SUITES BOISE WEST/MERIDIAN
208/288-2060
♥♥♥ Hotel. **Address:** 2610 E Freeway Dr 83642

LA QUINTA INN & SUITES MERIDIAN/BOISE WEST
(208)288-2100
♥♥♥ Hotel. **Address:** 800 S Allen St 83642

MY PLACE HOTEL BOISE/MERIDIAN　208/898-0009
♥♥ Extended Stay Hotel. **Address:** 3050 E Jewel St 83642

TOWNEPLACE SUITES BY MARRIOTT BOISE WEST/MERIDIAN　(208)884-8550

♥♥♥
Extended Stay Hotel
$95-$326

TOWNEPLACE SUITES MARRIOTT
AAA Benefit: Members save 5% or more!

Address: 1415 S Eagle Rd 83642 **Location:** I-84 exit 46 (Eagle Rd), just sw. **Facility:** 100 efficiencies, some two bedrooms and kitchens. 4 stories, interior corridors. **Terms:** check-in 4 pm, cancellation fee imposed. **Pool:** heated indoor. **Activities:** hot tub, picnic facilities, exercise room. **Guest Services:** valet and coin laundry. **Featured Amenity:** full hot breakfast.

TRU BY HILTON MERIDIAN BOISE/WEST　208/519-3535
♥♥ Contemporary Hotel. **Address:** 1401 S Eagle Rd 83642
Members save 5% or more!

WHERE TO EAT

EPI'S BASQUE RESTAURANT　　208/884-0142
♥♥ Basque. Casual Dining. **Address:** 1115 N Main St 83642

FLATBREAD NEAPOLITAN PIZZERIA　　208/288-0969
♥♥ Italian. Casual Dining. **Address:** 830 N Main St, Suite A 83642

GINO'S ITALIAN RISTORANTE　　208/887-7710
♥♥ Southern Italian. Casual Dining. **Address:** 3015 W McMillan Rd, #108 83646

GOODWOOD BARBECUE COMPANY　　208/884-1021
♥♥ Barbecue. Casual Dining. **Address:** 1140 N Eagle Rd 83642

THE GRIDDLE　　208/288-1848
♥♥ American. Casual Dining. **Address:** 2310 E Overland Rd, Suite 130 83642

KAHOOTZ STEAK & ALE HOUSE　　208/895-9861
♥♥ American. Casual Dining. **Address:** 1603 N Main St 83642

LOUIE'S PIZZA & ITALIAN RESTAURANT　　208/884-5200
♥♥ Italian. Casual Dining. **Address:** 2500 E Fairview Ave 83642

RAM RESTAURANT & BREWERY   208/888-0314
⬦⬦ American. Casual Dining. **Address:** 3272 E Pine St
83642

RUDY'S PUB & GRILL   208/884-4453
⬦⬦ American. Sports Bar. **Address:** 2310 E Overland Rd,
Suite 150 83642

SA-WAD-DEE THAI RESTAURANT   208/884-0701
⬦⬦ Thai. Casual Dining. **Address:** 1890 E Fairview Ave
83642

SMOKY MOUNTAIN PIZZERIA GRILL   208/884-1067
⬦⬦ Italian. Casual Dining. **Address:** 980 E Fairview Ave
83642

MINIDOKA NATIONAL HISTORIC SITE
(G-3)

Minidoka, the site of a relocation camp used for
the detainment of Japanese persons living in the
United States after the attack on Pearl Harbor, is
northeast of Twin Falls via US 93 and SR 25; from
the intersection of I-84 and US 93, head 5 miles
north on US 93, 9.5 miles east on SR 25 to the Hunt
Road exit, then 2.2 miles east on Hunt Road.

President Franklin D. Roosevelt ordered the
opening of 10 such facilities in February 1942, dis-
placing more than 110,000 people of Japanese an-
cestry until 1945.

Most of the 600 buildings at the 33,000-acre
camp were removed. The current 300-acre site features interpretive signs as well as remains of an
entry guard station, a waiting room, a root cellar, an
ornamental rock garden and a 1.6-mile crushed rock
walking trail. Those who died after leaving the camp
to serve in the U.S. military during World War II are
commemorated on plaques. More than 900 names
of Minidoka residents are listed on the Honor Roll at
the entrance to the site.

Note: A visitor center is planned for the site, but
until then, exhibits about Minidoka and maps are
available at the visitor center at Herrmann House
(296 S. 1400 E., Jerome); phone (208) 933-4169.
There is a small gravel parking lot. The historic site
is open daily dawn to dusk. Admission is free.

MONTPELIER (H-6) pop. 2,597, elev. 5,934'

Montpelier, one of the state's oldest towns, is at
the junction of US 89 and US 30N, the historic Old
Oregon Trail. Brigham Young established a Mormon
community and named the town for the capital of his
home state, Vermont. In 1896 Butch Cassidy re-
lieved the Bank of Montpelier of $7,000. Bear Lake
resort is about 17 miles south on US 89.

[SAVE] **NATIONAL OREGON/CALIFORNIA TRAIL
CENTER** is at jct. US 30 and US 89 at 320 N.
4th St. This living-history center, which sits directly
on the site of the historic Clover Creek Encampment
on the Oregon Trail, depicts the pioneers' journey
across the continent. A wagon master guides visitors

through the experience of riding the trail in a covered wagon courtesy of a computer simulation. Displays and artifacts about the history of the Bear
Lake valley and the railroad era can be seen in the
Rails and Trails Museum. A variety of quilts is on display May to mid-October.

Time: Allow 30 minutes minimum. **Hours:** Mon.-
Sat. 9-5; Sun. 9-3, May 15-Oct. 15; Tues.-Thurs.
10-2 by appointment, rest of year. **Cost:** $12.50;
$11.50 (ages 60+); $9.50 (ages 8-17); $5.50 (ages
4-7). **Phone:** (208) 847-3800. [GT]

CLOVER CREEK INN   (208)847-1782
⬦⬦⬦
Motel
$75-$130

Address: 243 N 4th St 83254 **Location:**
On US 30, just n of jct US 89. **Facility:**
63 units. 2 stories (no elevator), exterior
corridors. **Parking:** winter plug-ins. **Activities:** hot tub, exercise room. **Guest
Services:** coin laundry. **Featured Amenity: full hot breakfast.**

[SAVE] [⊻] [✚] [BIZ] [HS] [📶] [🔌]
[▢] [▱] / SOME UNITS [🐾]

MOSCOW (C-1) pop. 23,800, elev. 2,574'

Moscow (MOSS-co) lies on an especially scenic
section of US 95, which heads north toward Coeur
d'Alene and south to Banks. The area to the west is
rolling, fertile Palouse country where black volcanic
ash soil, ample rainfall and warm autumn temperatures combine to produce bountiful crops of lentils,
dry peas, canola, wheat and barley.

Home to the University of Idaho, Moscow is a
quintessential college town with an emerging arts
community. The annual arts scene includes February's ⬦ Lionel Hampton Jazz Festival; the Idaho
Repertory Theatre; and the Moscow Renaissance
Fair, which is held the first weekend in May.

Moscow Chamber of Commerce: 411 S. Main St.,
Moscow, ID 83843. **Phone:** (208) 882-1800.

BEST WESTERN PLUS UNIVERSITY INN   (208)882-0550
⬦⬦⬦
Hotel
$109-$299

[BW] Best
Western
PLUS.

AAA Benefit:
Members save up to
15% and earn bonus
points!

Address: 1516 W Pullman Rd 83843
Location: Jct US 95, 1 mi w on SR 8.
Adjacent to University of Idaho. **Facility:**
173 units. 2 stories, interior corridors.
Parking: winter plug-ins. **Terms:**
check-in 4 pm, cancellation fee imposed,
resort fee. **Pool:** heated indoor. **Activities:** sauna, hot tub, bicycles, exercise
room. **Guest Services:** valet and coin
laundry, area transportation.

[SAVE] [↤] [🍴] [⊻] [CALL] [🛗] [✈] [✚] [BIZ] [📶] [✕]
[🔌] [▢] [▱] / SOME UNITS [🐾] [HS]

FAIRFIELD INN & SUITES BY MARRIOTT MOSCOW
                                           (208)882-4600
⬦⬦⬦ Hotel. **Address:** 1000 W
Pullman Rd 83843

AAA Benefit:
Members save 5%
or more!

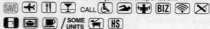

LA QUINTA INN & SUITES MOSCOW   (208)882-5365
♦♦♦♦ Hotel. **Address:** 185 Warbonnet Dr 83843

THE MONARCH MOTEL   208/882-2581
♦♦ Boutique Motel. **Address:** 120 W 6th St 83843

WHERE TO EAT

BLOOM   208/882-4279
♦♦ Breakfast Sandwiches. Casual Dining. **Address:** 403 S
Main St 83843

THE BREAKFAST CLUB   208/882-6481
♦♦ Breakfast Sandwiches. Casual Dining. **Address:** 501 S
Main St 83843

LA CASA LOPEZ   208/883-0536
♦♦ Mexican. Casual Dining. **Address:** 415 S Main St 83843

MAIALINA PIZZERIA NAPOLETANA   208/882-2694
♦♦♦ Italian. Casual Dining. **Address:** 602 S Main St 83843

NECTAR RESTAURANT & WINE   208/882-5914
♦♦♦ New American. Casual Dining. **Address:** 105 W 6th St
83843

SANGRIA GRILLE   208/882-2693
♦♦♦♦ Peruvian. Casual Dining. **Address:** 2124 W Pullman
Hwy 83843

SMOKY MOUNTAIN PIZZERIA GRILL   208/892-8000
♦♦ Italian. Casual Dining. **Address:** 1838 W Pullman Rd
83843

TAPPED - TAPHOUSE & KITCHEN   208/596-4422
♦♦ American. Casual Dining. **Address:** 210 S Main St 83843

MOUNTAIN HOME pop. 14,206

BEST WESTERN FOOTHILLS INN   (208)587-8477

♦♦♦
Motel
$99-$169

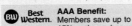

BW Best Western. **AAA Benefit:**
Members save up to
15% and earn bonus
points!

Address: 1080 Hwy 20 83647 **Location:** I-84 exit 95, just n. **Facility:** 77
units, some kitchens. 2 stories (no elevator), exterior corridors. **Pool:** heated
outdoor. **Activities:** hot tub, picnic facilities, exercise room. **Guest Services:**
valet and coin laundry.

HAMPTON INN & SUITES MOUNTAIN HOME   208/587-7300
♦♦♦ Contemporary Hotel. **Address:** 3175 NE Foothills Ave 83647

AAA Benefit:
Members save 5%
or more!

MOUNTAIN HOME INN   208/587-9743
♦♦♦ Hotel. **Address:** 1180 Hwy 20 83647

MULLAN (B-2) pop. 692, elev. 3,277'

Silver Valley's easternmost mining town was established in 1885 and named for John Mullan, an Army captain credited with blazing a 624-mile road across Montana, Idaho and Washington in the early 1860s. The Lucky Friday Mine, dating back to 1899, still produces silver.

Mullan nestles below Lookout Pass in the Bitterroot Mountains, a popular year-round recreation

area for skiing, snowboarding, hiking and mountain biking. The paved Trail of the Coeur d'Alenes follows a former Union Pacific railway path 72 miles west from Mullan to Plummer; phone (208) 682-3814 for additional information. With 10 tunnels and seven trestles, the gravel, 15-mile Route of the Hiawatha runs south of Lookout Pass along another repurposed railroad right-of-way. Shuttles are available at trailheads from late May to late September; phone (208) 744-1301 or (208) 245-2531.

RECREATIONAL ACTIVITIES
Skiing and Snowboarding
• **SAVE** **Lookout Pass Ski and Recreation Area** is 12 mi. e. on I-90, Exit O. Other activities are offered, including mountain biking (late May-late Sept.). **Hours:** Season begins in late Nov. Winter activities are available Thurs.-Mon. 9-4, early-late Dec.; daily 9-4, late Dec.-early Jan.; Wed.-Mon. 9-4, Jan.-Feb. (also Sat.-Sun. from 8:30); Thurs.-Mon. 9-4, Mar.-April (also Sat.-Sun. from 8:30). **Phone:** (208) 744-1301.

NAMPA (G-1) pop. 81,557, elev. 2,492'
• Hotels p. 56 • Restaurants p. 56

Col. W.H. Dewey moved his fortune during the 1890s to Nampa, an agricultural hamlet just north of the Great Basin Desert. Dewey brought prosperity to Nampa by attracting several railway branches and constructing the Dewey Palace hotel, which was a town landmark for several decades until it was damaged by fire and torn down. Nampa's name comes from Nampuh, or "Bigfoot," a Shoshone chief who was so large that his feet were supposedly 17 inches long.

Nampa is a central location from which to explore southwestern Idaho's natural wonders and historical sites. Givens Hot Springs is 17 miles south on SR 45, then 8 miles west on SR 78 on the south side of the Snake River. There are steam baths, an indoor natural hot-water pool and a picnic area.

Silver City and DeLamar, high in the Owyhee Mountains, can be reached by taking SR 45 south to Walter's Ferry, then turning east on SR 78 4.5 miles past Murphy. The towns, at one time thriving mining communities in one of the greatest silver-producing areas in the nation, are on a rough gravel and earth road. DeLamar has been abandoned.

Nampa Chamber of Commerce: 315 11th Ave. S., Nampa, ID 83651. **Phone:** (208) 466-4641.

SAVE **WARHAWK AIR MUSEUM** is at 201 Municipal Dr. next to Nampa Municipal Airport. The museum features restored and flyable aircraft from World War II, including a Curtiss P-40E Kittyhawk, a P-51 Mustang, a Curtiss P-40N Warhawk and a 1940 Navy N3N biplane trainer. Other World War II items displayed are a restored 1940 DeSoto staff car, period poster art, trench art, uniforms and home-front memorabilia.

Time: Allow 2 hours minimum. **Hours:** Tues.-Sat. 10-5, Sun. 11-4. Closed Jan. 1, Easter, Mother's

Day, July 4, Thanksgiving and Christmas. Phone ahead to confirm schedule. **Cost:** $12; $10 (ages 65+ and military with ID); $5 (ages 5-12). **Phone:** (208) 465-6446.

BEST WESTERN PLUS PEPPERTREE NAMPA CIVIC CENTER   (208)936-2222

Contemporary Hotel
$99-$399

Best Western PLUS **AAA Benefit:** Members save up to 15% and earn bonus points!

Address: 205 3rd St S 83651 **Location:** I-84 exit 35 (Northside Blvd), 1 mi s. **Facility:** 82 units. 4 stories, interior corridors. **Parking:** winter plug-ins. **Terms:** check-in 4 pm. **Pool:** heated indoor. **Activities:** hot tub, exercise room. **Guest Services:** valet and coin laundry.

FAIRFIELD INN & SUITES BY MARRIOTT BOISE-NAMPA   (208)467-5888

Hotel
$107-$251

Fairfield **AAA Benefit:** Members save 5% or more!

Address: 16150 N Merchant Way 83687 **Location:** I-84 exit 33B westbound; exit 33 eastbound, just e. Located in a commercial area. **Facility:** 88 units. 3 stories, interior corridors. **Terms:** cancellation fee imposed. **Pool:** heated indoor. **Activities:** hot tub, exercise room. **Guest Services:** valet and coin laundry. **Featured Amenity:** breakfast buffet.

HAMPTON INN & SUITES BOISE-NAMPA AT IDAHO CENTER   208/442-0036

Hotel. **Address:** 5750 E Franklin Rd 83687

AAA Benefit: Members save 5% or more!

HOLIDAY INN EXPRESS & SUITES NAMPA   (208)466-4045

Hotel. **Address:** 4104 E Flamingo Ave 83687

HOLIDAY INN NAMPA   208/468-0944

Contemporary Hotel. **Address:** 16245 N Merchant Way 83687

WHERE TO EAT

BRICK 29 BISTRO   208/468-0029
American. Casual Dining. **Address:** 320 11th Ave S, Suite 101 83651

THE EGG FACTORY   208/466-2728
Breakfast Sandwiches. Casual Dining. **Address:** 820 Caldwell Blvd 83651

JALAPENO'S BAR & GRILL   208/442-6355
Mexican. Casual Dining. **Address:** 1921 Caldwell Blvd 83651

MESSENGER PIZZA & BREWERY   541/461-0081
Sandwiches Pizza. Quick Serve. **Address:** 1224 1st St S 83651

SMOKY MOUNTAIN PIZZERIA GRILL   208/461-7333
Italian. Casual Dining. **Address:** 2007 N Cassia St 83651

NEZ PERCE NATIONAL FOREST (D-2)

> Elevations in the forest range from 1,350 ft. in Hells Canyon to 9,393 ft. at Devil's Peak. Refer to AAA maps for additional elevation information.

In the north-central part of the state, Nez Perce National Forest was named for the Nez Perce Indians, whose ancestral lands once included this rugged area of 2,223,594 acres. The forest contains the Gospel-Hump Wilderness and portions of the Selway-Bitterroot Wilderness, Frank Church-River of No Return Wilderness, Hells Canyon Wilderness and Hells Canyon National Recreation Area *(see place listing p. 44)*. Portions of the forest are close to parts of Nez Perce National Historical Park *(see place listing)*.

More than 150 miles of the Rapid, Salmon and Selway rivers and the Middle Fork of the Clearwater River are classified as wild and scenic rivers. Elk, moose, deer, cougars, mountain goats, bighorn sheep and bears inhabit the forest, while steelhead trout, white sturgeon and small-mouth bass can be found in the rivers and streams.

The historic Magruder Corridor Road (FR 468) is open to forest visitors July through October. The primitive road, rough but passable to two-wheel-drive, high-clearance vehicles, begins at the Red River Ranger Station and ends in Darby, Mont. The wilderness areas adjoining the route together form the largest tract of roadless land in the U.S. outside Alaska. Other roads, many unpaved, lead to such mining ghost towns as Dixie, Florence and Orogrande.

Ranger stations are located in Elk City, Grangeville, White Bird and near Kooskia. For information contact the Grangeville Office, Nez Perce National Forest, 104 Airport Rd., Grangeville, ID 83530; phone (208) 983-1950. *See Recreation Areas Chart.*

NEZ PERCE NATIONAL HISTORICAL PARK (C-1)

Encompassing 38 sites scattered across 12,000 square miles of north-central Idaho as well as 10 sites in Oregon, Washington and Montana, each part of Nez Perce National Historical Park reflects a portion of the history and culture of the Nez Perce Indians and their relationships with white explorers, missionaries, miners, settlers and soldiers.

Some sites are scenic views, some are geologic formations and others contain historic places and buildings. They include the Lolo Trail, Native American battlefields and former campsites of Meriwether Lewis and William Clark.

For thousands of years the Nez Perce lived in the valleys of the Clearwater and Snake rivers and their tributaries. Their first documented meeting with white settlers in Nez Perce territory took place in

September 1805, when the Lewis and Clark expedition encountered them, and the Indians gave supplies and assistance. In 1855 the Nez Perce reluctantly signed a treaty setting aside their ancestral home as a reservation.

A new treaty was negotiated in 1863 with some of the Nez Perce bands after gold was discovered within the reservation; this treaty reduced the reservation to one-tenth of its original size.

The first major battle of the Nez Perce War was on June 17, 1877, near White Bird. The U.S. Army pursued the bands of Nez Perce who had not signed the 1863 treaty across the Nez Perce Trail to Montana. After many battles the Nez Perce surrendered only 40 miles from the Canadian border. They were exiled for 8 years to Oklahoma Territory; the survivors eventually returned to the Pacific Northwest. Today the Nez Perce National Historic Trail parallels much of the original 1877 route. A brochure for a self-guiding walking tour of White Bird Battlefield is available.

The Weippe (WEE-ipe) Prairie, 18 miles east of US 12 on SR 11, is part of Nez Perce National Historical Park. The Idaho section of the Nez Perce Trail and Pass climbs through 150 miles of rough terrain east of Weippe as it ascends the 5,187-foot Lolo Pass through the Bitterroot Mountains.

The park's headquarters and visitor center are in Spalding. Also see Grangeville, Kamiah, Lapwai, Nez Perce National Forest and Orofino.

Spalding Visitor Center open daily 8-5, Memorial Day weekend-Labor Day; 8-4:30, mid-Mar. through day before Memorial Day weekend and day after Labor Day to mid-Nov.; 9-4, rest of year. Closed Jan. 1, Thanksgiving and Christmas. Free. Phone (208) 843-7009.

Heart of the Monster is 2 mi. e. of Kamiah on US 12. This volcanic rock formation is the place of creation in Nez Perce mythology. Folklore says that in the prehuman years, a monster was devouring the animals. Coyote, the chief animal, slew the monster, cut him into pieces and scattered these bits to the winds. Where each bit landed, a new Native American tribe arose. The Nez Perce tribe came from blood from the monster's heart. East Kamiah is a designated site of Nez Perce National Historical Park *(see place listing p. 56).* An interpretive display is available. **Hours:** Daily dawn-dusk. **Phone:** (208) 843-7009.

NEZ PERCE NATIONAL HISTORICAL PARK VISITOR CENTER, 39063 US 95, contains exhibits and audiovisual programs about Nez Perce culture. Area history also is chronicled. A park brochure is available for a self-guiding driving tour of the 38 sites that make up the park. **Hours:** Daily 9-5, Memorial Day-day before Labor Day; 8:30-4, Labor Day-day before Memorial Day. Ranger-led programs are offered daily, Memorial Day-Labor Day. Closed Jan. 1, Thanksgiving and Christmas. **Cost:** Free. **Phone:** (208) 843-7009.

SPALDING SITE, part of the Nez Perce National Historical Park at 39063 US 95, is the location of the second mission built by the Rev. Henry H. Spalding and his wife in 1838. The Presbyterian mission included the territory's first printing press, sawmill and gristmill, and it contains the first Indian Agency office. The Spaldings are buried at Spalding Cemetery, an active Nez Perce cemetery. **Time:** Allow 30 minutes minimum.

Weis Rockshelter is in Nez Perce National Historical Park, 8 mi. s. of Cottonwood, 7 miles w. of US 95. Archeological excavations of this cliff recess have revealed almost continuous human occupation between 5500 B.C. and A.D. 1400. The niche near the Salmon River is thought to be the first shelter for the Nez Perce more than 8,000 years ago. **Hours:** Daily dawn-dusk. **Cost:** Free. **Phone:** (208) 843-7009 for Nez Perce National Historic Park Spalding Visitor Center.

OLDTOWN (B-1) pop. 184, elev. 2,180'

Oldtown is separated from Newport, Wash., by State Avenue and is the site of the original settlement from which the two towns evolved.

Greater Newport Area Chamber of Commerce: 325 W. 4th St., P.O. Box 2006, Newport, WA 99156. **Phone:** (509) 447-5812.

OROFINO (C-1) pop. 3,142, elev. 1,027'
• Hotels p. 58 • Restaurants p. 58

In 1805 members of Meriwether Lewis' and William Clark's expedition passed near the present site of Orofino on their way west. The first gold miners swarmed into the area 60 years later from California, and soon Idaho's first permanent settlements began to take shape. Orofino is on the Nez Perce Indian Reservation, and the Clearwater River runs through the town's boundaries. The Clearwater National Forest *(see place listing p. 39)* and Nez Perce National Forest *(see place listing p. 56)* are nearby.

Orofino's economy relies on lumbering, farming and government employment. A long growing season, ample precipitation and fertile soil contribute to the prosperity of this agricultural community. Northwest of Orofino, near Ahsahka *(see place listing p. 24),* is the Dworshak National Fish Hatchery and Dworshak Dam and Reservoir.

Orofino Chamber of Commerce: 125 Johnson Ave., Suite 7, P.O. Box 2346, Orofino, ID 83544. **Phone:** (208) 476-4335.

BEST WESTERN LODGE AT RIVER'S EDGE
(208)476-9999

Hotel
$139-$159

Best Western.

AAA Benefit: Members save up to 15% and earn bonus points!

Address: 615 Main St 83544 **Location:** Waterfront. US 12, 0.3 mi e to Main St, 0.3 mi s. **Facility:** 49 units. 3 stories, interior corridors. **Parking:** winter plug-ins. **Terms:** check-in 4 pm, cancellation fee imposed, resort fee. **Amenities:** *Some:* safes. **Pool:** heated indoor. **Activities:** hot tub, fishing, exercise room. **Guest Services:** coin laundry.

HELGESON PLACE HOTEL & SUITES   208/476-5729
Extended Stay Hotel. **Address:** 125 Johnson Ave 83544

KONKOLVILLE MOTEL   208/476-5584
Motel. **Address:** 2600 Michigan Ave 83544

WHERE TO EAT

AUGIE'S DELI   208/476-5450
Deli Sandwiches. Quick Serve. **Address:** 202 Johnson Ave 83544

DINING ON THE EDGE   208/476-7805
American. Casual Dining. **Address:** 625 Main St 83544

FIESTA EN JALISCO   208/476-7506
Mexican. Casual Dining. **Address:** 207 Johnson Ave 83544

NORTHFORK CAFE OROFINO/AHSAHKA   208/476-0868
Burgers Sandwiches. Casual Dining. **Address:** 56 Northfork Dr 83520

PAYETTE NATIONAL FOREST (E-1)

Elevations in the forest range from 1,464 ft. in Hells Canyon to 9,545 ft. at Mormon Mountain. Refer to AAA maps for additional elevation information.

Bounded by the Snake and Salmon rivers and the Middle Fork of the Salmon River in the west-central part of the state, Payette National Forest contains 2,307,897 acres ranging in elevation from 1,400 to 9,000 feet above sea level. More than 1,800 miles of both motorized and non-motorized trails include Lava Ridge National Recreation Trail and Sheep Rock Nature Trail. The forest's remote rivers and mountains offer exceptional fishing, hiking, hunting, climbing and boating opportunities during summer and fall months.

Winter sports include alpine skiing at Brundage Mountain Resort and the smaller Payette Lakes Ski Hill as well as cross-country skiing and snowmobiling in many other areas. Thousands of burned forest acres continue to regenerate as part of the natural cycle after major fires in 1994, 2000 and 2007.

A small portion of the Hells Canyon Wilderness and Hells Canyon National Recreation Area *(see place listing p. 44)* and a large portion of the Frank Church-River of No Return Wilderness are within the forest. These primitive mountainous areas overlap several national forests and contain extensive non-motorized trail networks. For more information, contact Payette National Forest, 501 N. Mission St., McCall, ID 83638; phone (208) 634-0700. *See Recreation Areas Chart.*

PIERCE (C-2) pop. 508, elev. 3,094'

Gold was found here in 1860, triggering a rush of some 6,000 prospectors, many of whom were Chinese. In 1861 the rough mining camp became seat of Shoshone County and the first established town in what was to become Idaho Territory 3 years later. After mining played out in the 1880s, Pierce re-emerged as a forest products center in the 1900s. Its population peaked at over 1,200 in 1970.

Idaho's oldest government building, a courthouse built in 1862, still stands 1 block east of SR 11 on Court Street. It became a private residence after the county seat was moved to Murray in 1885. The J. Howard Bradbury Memorial Logging Museum, 103 S. Main St., has historical photographs, indoor and outdoor displays of mining and logging relics, and a 1920 log cabin; phone (208) 464-2677. An interpretive pavilion, on SR 11 at the north end of town, features 15 panels describing the history of the area.

Pierce is on the Gold Rush Historic Byway, a 43-mile route following SR 11 from Greer up to Weippe and Pierce and ending at Headquarters. Numerous roadside plaques describe points of interest along the byway.

POCATELLO (G-5) pop. 54,255, elev. 4,365'
• Restaurants p. 60

Originally part of the Fort Hall Indian Reservation, Pocatello is named for a 19th-century Shoshone chief who granted the Utah & Northern a right-of-way for a Salt Lake City-to-Butte railroad line. The subsequent arrival in 1882 of the Union Pacific Railway, which linked the Midwest and Pacific Northwest, spawned a makeshift community—a congregation of tents at the meeting of the two lines—that was first called Pocatello Junction.

Pocatello maintains its position as one of the region's leading industrial, distribution and transportation centers. Education also is a principal concern; Idaho State University, with more than 17,000 students, is one of the state's leading 4-year institutions. The school's state-of-the-art L.E. and Thelma E. Stephens Performing Arts Center, 1002 Sam Nixon Ave., entertains lovers of music, dance and theater; phone (208) 282-3595.

The town is the northern terminus of an especially scenic section of I-15, which heads south into Utah. Just off Main Street visitors can see the exterior of the Union Pacific Depot, a three-story passenger station designed in the late 1800s. Train passengers of the era stayed overnight across the street at the historic Yellowstone Hotel.

Visit Pocatello: 324 S. Main, Pocatello, ID 83204. **Phone:** (208) 479-7659.

DON ASLETT MUSEUM OF CLEAN is at 711 S. 2nd Ave. This five-story green building, a renovated 20th-century brick warehouse, is filled with captivating themed displays that relate the history of cleaning. More than 5,000 items are exhibited, including art, appliances, tools and live cleaning plants. How-to videos, such as "How to Clean Your Bathroom in 3.5 Minutes," offer quick and easy cleaning tips to visitors. The three-story Kids' Cleaning World teaches children about cleanliness and responsibility and features mops, buckets and other supplies for wee ones to try out. **Time:** Allow 1 hour, 30 minutes minimum. **Hours:** Tues.-Sat. 10-5. Closed Jan. 1, Thanksgiving and Christmas. Phone ahead to confirm schedule. **Cost:** $6; $5 (ages 3-15); $20 (family, two adults and three children). **Phone:** (208) 236-6906. GT

IDAHO MUSEUM OF NATURAL HISTORY is located at 698 E. Dillon St. on the Idaho State University campus. Exhibits change frequently and among the permanent displays are Giants of the Snake River Plain, which features ice age mammals and a natural history garden. The Discovery Room allows children hands-on encounters with fossils and other specimens.

Hours: Tues.-Fri. 10-6, Sat. 9-5, Sun. noon-5, Apr.-Aug; Tues.-Fri noon-6, Sat. 9-5, Sun. noon-5, rest of year. Closed major holidays. **Cost:** $7; $5 (ages 60+); $3 (ages 4-17). **Phone:** (208) 282-3317.

ROSS PARK is between 2nd and 5th aves. With such amenities as a skate park and horseshoe and volleyball areas on-site, a variety of recreational activities can be enjoyed. The community park also comprises a museum, a re-created historical trading post and a zoo. In addition its stellar aquatic complex offers a 50-meter swimming pool, a waterslide, a lazy river and an interactive wading area.

Time: Allow 1 hour minimum. **Hours:** Park open daily dawn-dusk. Aquatic complex open daily noon-8, Memorial Day weekend-Labor Day (weather permitting). Phone ahead to confirm schedule. **Cost:** Park admission free. Aquatic complex (excludes waterslide) $6; $5 (ages 7-17); $4 (ages 60+); $2 (ages 1-6). Half-price admission Mon. and Wed. 5-8 p.m. Aquatic complex unlimited waterslide pass $3. **Phone:** (208) 234-0472.

Bannock County Historical Museum is off I-15 exit 67, then 1 mi. n. on N. 5th Ave. (US 30/91) to 3000 Alvord Loop in Upper Ross Park. The museum contains Native American and railroad displays, a restored stagecoach, a 1916 La France fire truck and a history/donor mural wall. Other displays include a Victorian parlor, a Japanese shrine, a country store, an early dental office and antique printing presses. **Hours:** Mon.-Sat. 10-6, Sun. 1-5, Memorial Day weekend-Labor Day; Tues.-Sat. 10-4, rest of year. Closed major holidays. **Cost:** Memorial Day weekend-Labor Day (includes Fort Hall Replica

and Pocatello Junction) $6; $5 (ages 60+, fire, military and police); $3 (ages 6-17). Rest of year (museum only) $5; $4 (ages 60+, fire, military and police); $3 (ages 6-17). **Phone:** (208) 233-0434.

Fort Hall Replica, off I-15 exit 67, then 1 mi. n. on N. 5th Ave. (US 30/91) to 3000 Avenue of the Chiefs in Upper Ross Park, re-creates the fur-trading post that operated nearby 1834-64. Original Hudson's Bay Co. plans were used to create the full-scale replica.

Time: Allow 1 hour minimum. **Hours:** Mon.-Sat. 10-6, Sun. 1-5, Memorial Day weekend-Labor Day. Tue.-Sat. 10-4 in May and Sep., weather permitting. Closed major holidays. Phone ahead to confirm schedule. **Cost:** (includes Bannock County Historical Museum and Pocatello Junction) $6; $5 (ages 60+, and fire, military and police); $3 (ages 6-17). **Phone:** (208) 233-0434.

Zoo Idaho, 2900 S. 2nd Ave. in the lower level of Ross Park, features native North American wildlife including elk, bison, grizzly and black bears, bighorn sheep, cougars, eagles, owls, pronghorn, mountain lions and waterfowl in 25 acres of natural habitats. Children can play in a 900-square-foot tree house or a 30-foot tipi. **Time:** Allow 1 hour minimum. **Hours:** Mon.-Thurs. 10-5, Fri.-Sun. 10-6, June 1-Labor Day; daily 10-5 in May; Sat.-Sun. 10-4 in Apr. and day after Labor Day-Oct. 31. **Cost:** $5.75; $4.50 (ages 60+); $3.75 (ages 3-11). **Phone:** (208) 234-6196 or (208) 234-6264.

LA QUINTA INN & SUITES POCATELLO   (208)234-7500
ₚₚₚ Hotel. **Address:** 1440 Bench Rd 83201

QUALITY INN POCATELLO   (208)237-8155

Hotel
$60-$115

Address: 1333 Bench Rd 83201 **Location:** I-15 exit 71, just e. **Facility:** 52 units. 2 stories (no elevator), interior corridors. **Amenities:** safes. **Pool:** heated indoor. **Activities:** hot tub. **Guest Services:** valet laundry. **Featured Amenity:** breakfast buffet.

TOWNEPLACE SUITES BY MARRIOTT POCATELLO
(208)478-7000
ₚₚₚ Extended Stay Hotel. **Address:** 2376 Via Caporatti Dr 83201

AAA Benefit:
Members save 5% or more!

WHERE TO EAT

BRIDGE STEAKHOUSE   208/234-7000
ₚ New American. Casual Dining. **Address:** 230 W Bonneville St 83204

BUDDY'S ITALIAN RESTAUANT   208/233-1172
ₚₚ Italian. Casual Dining. **Address:** 626 E Lewis St 83201

BUTTERBURR'S RESTAURANT   208/232-3296
ₚₚ American. Casual Dining. **Address:** 917 Yellowstone St 83201

CAFE TUSCANO   208/233-7702
ₚₚ Italian. Casual Dining. **Address:** 2231 E Center St 83201

EL HERRADERO   208/233-6747
ₚₚ Mexican. Casual Dining. **Address:** 123 Jefferson Ave 83201

JAKERS BAR & GRILL   208/478-2000
ₚₚ Steak Seafood. Casual Dining. **Address:** 2365 Via Caporatti Dr 83201

PORTNEUF VALLEY BREWING   970/232-1644
ₚ American. Brewpub. **Address:** 615 S 1st Ave 83201

THE SANDPIPER   208/233-1000
ₚₚ Seafood Steak. Casual Dining. **Address:** 1400 Bench Rd 83201

PONDERAY pop. 1,137

DAYS INN SANDPOINT   (208)263-1222
ₚₚ Hotel. **Address:** 363 Bonner Mall Way 83852

FAIRBRIDGE INN & SUITES SANDPOINT   (208)263-2210
ₚₚ Hotel. **Address:** 476841 Hwy 95 N 83852

HOLIDAY INN EXPRESS & SUITES   208/255-4500
ₚₚₚ Hotel. **Address:** 477326 Hwy 95 N 83852

HOTEL RUBY PONDERAY   (208)263-5383
ₚₚ Hotel. **Address:** 477255 Hwy 95 N 83852

WHERE TO EAT

FIESTA BONITA   208/263-6174
ₚₚ Mexican. Casual Dining. **Address:** 700 Kootenai Cut Off Rd 83852

SWEET LOU'S   208/263-1381
ₚₚ Barbecue. Gastropub. **Address:** 477272 Hwy 95 N 83852

POST FALLS (B-1) pop. 27,574, elev. 2,169'

On the Spokane River at the Washington-Idaho state line, Post Falls was founded in the late 1800s by Frederick Post when he harnessed the falls to generate power for his sawmill.

Stateline Speedway, off I-90 exit 2 at 1349 N. Beck Rd., features stock car racing Wednesdays and Saturdays from mid-April through September; phone (208) 773-5019.

Post Falls/Coeur d'Alene Visitor Center: 201 E. Fourth Ave., Post Falls, ID 83854. **Phone:** (208) 773-5016 or (800) 292-2553.

FALLS PARK, off I-90 Spokane St. exit, 2 blks. s. on Spokane St., then 1.5 blks. w. to 305 W. 4th St., offers visitors picturesque views of Post Falls and the gorge. The best viewing is during spring runoff. Children also can fish in a stocked pond and enjoy the playground. Trails lead to nearby Treaty Rock Historic Site *(see attraction listing)*, which marks the location of Post Falls' founding. **Hours:** Daily dawn-dusk (weather permitting). **Cost:** Free. **Phone:** (208) 773-0539.

Q'EMILN PARK AND TRAILS is off I-90 exit 5, .9 mi. s. on Spokane St., then .2 mi. w. on Parkway Dr. Twelve connected trails wind along the south bank of the Spokane River. The pathways lead to historic sites, abandoned homesteads, mining camps, logging areas and scenic spots above and below Post Falls Dam. The park is known for its rock climbing, with opportunities that appeal to all skill levels. A boat launch, picnic areas and seasonal community events are offered. Swimming is permitted in designated areas. **Time:** Allow 1 hour minimum. **Hours:** Daily dawn-dusk. **Cost:** Free. **Parking:** Memorial Day weekend-Labor Day $8 (cars); $10 (boats). **Phone:** (208) 773-0539.

TREATY ROCK HISTORIC SITE, jct. 7th and Compton sts., commemorates the spot where Coeur d'Alene Indian Chief Andrew Seltice transferred land to Frederick Post, the founder of Post Falls. A trail with interpretive signage features Native American petroglyphs and paintings. **Time:** Allow 30 minutes minimum. **Hours:** Daily dawn-dusk. **Cost:** Free. **Phone:** (208) 773-0539.

RED LION TEMPLIN'S HOTEL ON THE RIVER - POST FALLS
208/773-1611
ₚₚₚ Hotel. **Address:** 414 E 1st Ave 83854

SLEEP INN   (208)777-9394
ₚₚ Hotel. **Address:** 157 S Pleasant View Rd 83854

WHERE TO EAT

BIG BEAR DELI   208/457-8465
ₚ Deli. Quick Serve. **Address:** 700 E 8th Ave 83854

FAMOUS WILLIES BARBECUE   208/773-0000
American. Casual Dining. **Address:** 107 E 7th Ave 83854

FLEUR DE SEL   208/777-7600
French. Fine Dining. **Address:** 4365 Inverness Dr 83854

FU-KI JAPANESE STEAKHOUSE   208/457-7077
Japanese. Casual Dining. **Address:** 1500 E Seltice Way 83854

OLD EUROPEAN RESTAURANT   208/777-2017
European Breakfast. Casual Dining. **Address:** 1710 E Schneidmiller Ave 83854

TIMBER GASTRO PUB   208/262-9593
American. Gastropub. **Address:** 1610 E Schneidmiller Ave 83854

THE WHITE HOUSE GRILL   208/777-9672
Mediterranean. Casual Dining. **Address:** 712 N Spokane St 83854

PRIEST RIVER (B-1) pop. 1,751, elev. 2,082'

Priest River, at the junction of the Pend Oreille and Priest rivers and 30 miles south of Priest Lake via SR 57, is the gateway to the Idaho Panhandle National Forests *(see place listing p. 47)*. The Priest River Museum and Timber Education Center contains historical displays. The city hosts Priest River Timber Days in July and Oktoberfest in late September.

Priest River Chamber of Commerce: 119 Main St., Suite 102, P.O. Box 929, Priest River, ID 83856. **Phone:** (208) 448-2721.

EAGLE'S NEST MOTEL   (208)448-2000
Motel. **Address:** 5678 Hwy 2 83856

REXBURG (F-6) pop. 25,484, elev. 4,861'

In the late 1870s many miners heading into Montana in search of gold stopped along the west side of the Snake River and claimed land under the Homestead Act of 1862. Many of these first homesteaders were Mormons. In 1883 another influx of settlers drove their sleighs to the banks of the Snake River and established the present town site of Rexburg.

In June 1976 the nearby Teton Dam collapsed, sending 8 billion gallons of flood water into the valley below. To see the site, travel 20 miles northeast on SR 33.

Rexburg plays host to the Idaho International SummerFest in July. The Centennial Carousel, which took 5 years to restore, is in Porter Park. Located at 2nd West 2nd South in downtown Rexburg, the park offers picnic tables; a playground; and recreational facilities for volleyball, tennis and basketball.

Rexburg Area Chamber of Commerce: 127 E. Main St., Suite 2, Rexburg, ID 83440. **Phone:** (208) 356-5700.

YELLOWSTONE BEAR WORLD is 7 mi. s. on US 20. From the comfort of your automobile, you'll experience up-close encounters with black and grizzly bears at this drive-through wildlife park. Elk, deer and timber wolves also roam the 120-acre grounds.

Guided curator tours and bottle-feeding tours are available. **Time:** Allow 1 hour minimum. **Hours:** Daily 9-6, Memorial Day weekend-Labor Day; 9-5, early May-day before Memorial Day weekend and day after Labor Day to mid-Oct. **Cost:** $16.95; $15.95 (ages 65+); $10.95 (ages 3-10); $74.95 (family, per private vehicle with up to seven people). Prices may vary; phone ahead. **Phone:** (208) 359-9688.

AMERICINN LODGE & SUITES REXBURG   (208)356-5333
Hotel. **Address:** 1098 Golden Beauty Dr 83440

HAMPTON INN & SUITES BY HILTON REXBURG
                                           208/497-0424
Contemporary Hotel. **Address:** 1195 S Yellowstone Hwy 83440

AAA Benefit:
Members save 5%
or more!

QUALITY INN REXBURG   (208)359-1311

Hotel
$89-$179

Address: 885 W Main St 83440 **Location:** US 20 exit 333 (Salmon), just e. **Facility:** 52 units. 2 stories (no elevator), interior corridors. **Parking:** winter plugins. **Pool:** heated indoor. **Activities:** hot tub. **Guest Services:** coin laundry. **Featured Amenity:** breakfast buffet.

SPRINGHILL SUITES BY MARRIOTT REXBURG
                                           (208)356-3003
Hotel. **Address:** 1177 S Yellowstone Hwy 83440

AAA Benefit:
Members save 5%
or more!

WHERE TO EAT

DA PINEAPPLE GRILL   208/356-4398
Hawaiian Sushi. Casual Dining. **Address:** 383 S 2nd W 83440

FRESCO KITCHEN & GRILL   208/497-0480
American. Casual Dining. **Address:** 1181 S Yellowstone Hwy 83440

RIGGINS (E-1) pop. 419, elev. 1,800'
• Hotels p. 62 • Restaurants p. 62

Riggins, where the Little Salmon pours into the main Salmon River, is a starting point for a drive north along US 95 through the scenic gorge of the Salmon River. The town is considered a white-water capital and features opportunities for white-water rafting, boating and fishing.

East of town lies the wilderness of the Payette National Forest *(see place listing p. 58)*. To the west rise the 9,000-foot Seven Devils Mountains, which form a semicircle above the Snake River's chasm, Hells Canyon; some 30 alpine lakes are clustered around the peaks. To the south is the Rapid River Fish Hatchery, one of the Northwest's most successful chinook salmon-breeding operations.

Salmon River Chamber of Commerce: P.O. Box 289, Riggins, ID 83549. **Phone:** (208) 628-3320.

RECREATIONAL ACTIVITIES
White-water Rafting

- **Salmon River Challenge** is at 121 N. Main St. Rafting trips over Class III rapids, inflatable kayaking and fishing trips are offered on the Salmon River near Riggins. **Hours:** Rafting trips available May 15-Oct. 1. Half-day trips depart daily 8:30 and noon; Full-day trips at 8:30. Multi-day camping/rafting trips available July 1-Aug. 31. **Cost:** Half-day: Adult, $69 (8:30-noon), ($79 noon-4); Youth (5-17) $59 (8:30-noon), $69 (noon-4). Full-day: Adult, $99; Youth (5-17) $79. Multi-day: $399. **Phone:** (208) 717-2007.

PINEHURST RESORT CABINS & RV   208/628-3323
🍷 Cabin. **Address:** 5604 Hwy 95 83654

SALMON RAPIDS LODGE   208/628-2743
🍷🍷 Hotel. **Address:** 1010 S Main St 83549

WHERE TO EAT

RIVER ROCK CAFE   208/628-3434
🍷🍷 American. Casual Dining. **Address:** 1149 S Main St 83549

SEVEN DEVILS STEAKHOUSE & SALOON   208/628-3558
🍷🍷 American. Casual Dining. **Address:** 312 Main St 83549

TWO RIVERS COFFEE ROASTERS   208/628-9222
🍷 Coffee/Tea Deli. Quick Serve. **Address:** 616 S Main St 83549

RUPERT (H-4) pop. 5,554, elev. 4,158'

Rupert was platted by the Bureau of Reclamation, which accounts for its business district being built around a square that is now a public park. Irrigation from dam projects on the Snake River has transformed the surrounding area from semiarid land to one of Idaho's principal agricultural areas. Potatoes and sugar beets are important crops.

Camping, picnicking, birding, hiking and other recreational opportunities are available in nearby Lake Walcott State Park. *See Recreation Areas Chart.*

SAGLE (B-1) elev. 2,149'

BIRD AVIATION MUSEUM AND INVENTION CENTER is 12 mi. e. of US 95 on Sagle Rd., following signs to 325 Bird Ranch Rd. The museum hangar exhibits six mint-condition aircraft (1927-72) and motor vehicles from the same period. Additional displays include military uniforms, models, artwork and items from NASA.

The Imagination Room honors inventors who perfected products ranging from Kitty Litter and Barbie dolls to microprocessors and the artificial heart. An upstairs gallery displays a respiratory ventilator and an Anti-"G" Suit used by high-altitude pilots, both invented by museum co-founder Dr. Forrest Bird.

Time: Allow 1 hour minimum. **Hours:** Mon.-Sat. 8-4, Memorial Day-Labor Day; Mon.-Fri. 8-4, rest of year. Closed Jan. 1, Easter, Thanksgiving, Christmas and Dec. 31. **Cost:** Donations. **Phone:** (208) 255-4321. 🍴

THE LODGE AT SANDPOINT   208/263-2211
🍷🍷🍷 Hotel. **Address:** 41 Lakeshore Dr 83860

WHERE TO EAT

FORTY-ONE SOUTH   208/265-2000
🍷🍷🍷 American. Fine Dining. **Address:** 41 Lakeshore Dr 83860

ST. CHARLES (H-6) pop. 131, elev. 5,944'

This small town near the northwest corner of Bear Lake was the birthplace of Gutzon Borglum (1867-1941), the artist and sculptor who carved the Mount Rushmore National Memorial in South Dakota.

Bear Lake straddles the Idaho-Utah border south and east of St. Charles. Known as the "Caribbean of the Rockies" for its turquoise hue, the result of soluble microscopic carbonates suspended in the water, the 120-square-mile lake is popular with fishermen seeking cutthroat trout, sculpin and whitefish. In winter anglers use nets to catch the Bonneville cisco, a species of fish endemic to the lake.

Bear Lake National Wildlife Refuge, a 19,000 acre tract of wetlands north of Bear Lake, provides habitat for migratory birds and small mammals. Bear Lake State Park *(see Recreation Areas Chart)*, just e. of St. Charles at 5637 E. Shore Rd., has two units. The North Beach unit has a boat launch and a 2-mile-long shorefront; the East Beach unit, with its 1.5-mile-long beach, offers a campground. Phone (208) 945-2325.

SALMON (E-4) pop. 3,112, elev. 4,040'

Once the winter campsite of fur trappers, including Jim Bridger and Kit Carson, Salmon is at the fork of the Salmon and Lemhi rivers near the edge of the Salmon Valley, a prosperous livestock and mining area. Permanent settlement of this region began with the discovery of gold in 1866. The town is a favorite starting point for pack trips into the Frank Church-River of No Return Wilderness and for float trips down the Salmon River and its wildest branch, the Middle Fork.

Salmon lies on a scenic section of US 93, which heads north to the Montana border and southwest toward Sawtooth National Forest *(see place listing p. 64).*

Visit Salmon Valley: 803 Monroe St., Salmon ID, 83467. **Phone:** (208) 756-1505.

SACAJAWEA INTERPRETIVE, CULTURAL AND EDUCATIONAL CENTER, 1 mi. e. on SR 28 (Main St.), is in the Lemhi River Valley, the homeland of the Agaidika Shoshone and Sacajawea (Sacagawea). The 71-acre park commemorates Sacajawea's role in the Lewis and Clark expedition and features an interpretive center with exhibits, demonstrations, outdoor art pieces and a 1-mile interpretive trail with a tipi and fishing weir exhibits.

Time: Allow 1 hour minimum. **Hours:** Trails daily dawn-dusk. Interpretive center Mon.-Sat. 9-5, Sun. 12:30-5, Memorial Day-Labor Day; by appointment, rest of year. **Cost:** $5; $12 (family). **Phone:** (208) 756-1188. 🏕

STAGECOACH INN   208/756-2919
▼▼ Hotel. **Address:** 201 Riverfront Dr (US 93 N) 83467

WHERE TO EAT

BERTRAM'S SALMON VALLEY BREWERY & RESTAURANT
                                            208/756-3391
▼▼ American. Casual Dining. **Address:** 101 S Andrews St 83467

JUNKYARD BISTRO   208/756-2466
▼▼ American. Casual Dining. **Address:** 405 Main St 83467

SHADY NOOK RESTAURANT   208/756-4182

▼▼	**AAA Inspector Notes:** Experience the lovely atmosphere at this local landmark restaurant. Menu items include a variety of juicy charbroiled steaks, Alaskan king crab legs, steamer clams and mussels, killer nachos, popular snack baskets and specialty burgers. Enjoy watching the
American Casual Dining	
$10-$28	

Salmon River while dining on the patio during the summer. Nightly specials and desserts made locally are sure to delight. **Features:** full bar, patio dining, happy hour. **Reservations:** suggested, in summer. **Address:** 501 Riverfront Dr (US 93 N) 83467 **Location:** Jct US 93 and SR 28, just n. 🄳

SALMON-CHALLIS NATIONAL FOREST
(E-3)

Elevations in the forest range from 2,200 ft. in the lower canyon of the Salmon River to 12,662 ft. at Borah Peak. Refer to AAA maps for additional elevation information.

From the headwaters of the Salmon River, down the Lost River, Pahsimeroi and Lemhi Mountain Ranges, to the western slope of the Continental Divide, the Salmon-Challis National Forest covers 4.3 million acres. Over 300,000 acres are in the Frank Church-River of No Return Wilderness (see Payette National Forest p. 58).

The historic Lewis and Clark Trail passes through part of the forest, where several monuments to the explorers have been erected. The Custer Motorway Loop and Salmon River Road provide glimpses of historic mining towns and native wildlife.

Because of swift currents the Salmon River west of Salmon is known as the "River of No Return."

Now, however, it is possible to navigate this river upstream via jet boats. Boat trips down the river can be arranged in Salmon (see place listing).

More than 2,800 miles of trail stripe the forest floor. Hiking season is generally between April and October; hunting, fishing, camping and wildlife viewing also are excellent.

The section of the river between Corn Creek and Riggins can be traveled by kayaks, jet boats or rubber rafts. Skiing is available nearby on the Idaho-Montana border at Lost Trail Pass. For more information write the Salmon-Challis National Forest Headquarters, 1206 S. Challis St., Salmon, ID 83467; phone (208) 756-5100. See Recreation Areas Chart.

SANDPOINT (B-1) pop. 7,365, elev. 2,086'
• Hotels p. 64 • Restaurants p. 64

Sandpoint, at the north end of Lake Pend Oreille, is a year-round resort town and artists' community that offers a wide variety of land- and water-based recreational opportunities. Park facilities at City Beach, west of First Avenue via Bridge Street, include beaches, two marinas, a boat launch and a pedestrian bridge over Sand Creek that links the park with downtown. Lake Pend Oreille Cruises offers a variety of tours; phone (208) 255-5253.

One of the West's great railroad towns, Sandpoint is known as "The Funnel" for the major rail lines that converge here. More than 50 trains a day draw rail fans to the city. A brochure "A Rail Fan's Guide to Sandpoint, Idaho" is available from the chamber of commerce.

Greater Sandpoint Chamber of Commerce: 1202 Fifth Ave., P.O. Box 928, Sandpoint, ID 83864. **Phone:** (208) 263-2161 or (800) 800-2106.

Shopping: One of downtown Sandpoint's focal points is the Cedar Street Bridge Public Market. Formerly a city bridge over Sand Creek, this renovated two-level structure is patterned after the famed Ponte Vecchio bridge in Florence, Italy, and contains two levels of restaurants and shops.

INTERNATIONAL SELKIRK LOOP is a 280-mile National Scenic Byway in northern Idaho, northeastern Washington and adjoining British Columbia. Starting at Sandpoint the 89-mile Idaho segment follows US 2 west to the Washington border at Oldtown. North from Sandpoint the byway takes US 2/95 to Bonners Ferry, then US 95 and SR 1 to the Canadian border at Porthill.

West from Sandpoint the loop follows the Pend Oreille (pond-ah-RAY) River, which drains Lake Pend Oreille. Several recreation sites offer access to the river, and there are numerous roadside pull-outs. At Priest River, SR 57 runs 30 miles north to jewel-like Priest Lake, a paradise for kayaking, canoeing and fishing set amid cedars and pines in the heart of the Selkirks. Public campgrounds and lodging options are numerous.

North of Sandpoint the route runs along the Purcell Trench, a long, narrow trough between the Selkirk, Cabinet and Purcell Mountains. The trench is a natural funnel for migratory birds. Between Bonners Ferry and Priest Lake, the Selkirks are a rugged wilderness with peaks in excess of 7,000 feet. The Kootenai National Wildlife Refuge, 5 miles west of Bonners Ferry, offers a 4-mile auto-tour route and numerous hiking trails.

Chambers of commerce and visitor centers along the loop provide maps and information. Visitors also can order a free copy of the visitor travel guide online or write to International Selkirk Loop, P.O. Box 920, Bonners Ferry, ID 83805. **Phone:** (208) 267-0822 or (888) 823-2626.

BEST WESTERN EDGEWATER RESORT   (208)263-3194

Hotel
$109-$299

AAA Benefit: Members save up to 15% and earn bonus points!

Address: 56 Bridge St 83864 **Location:** Just e of US 95; downtown. **Facility:** 54 units. 2-3 stories (no elevator), interior corridors. **Terms:** cancellation fee imposed. **Dining:** Trinity at City Beach, see separate listing. **Pool:** heated indoor. **Activities:** sauna, hot tub, limited beach access, boat dock, fishing, exercise room.

LA QUINTA INN SANDPOINT   (208)263-9581
Hotel. **Address:** 415 Cedar St 83864

QUALITY INN BY CHOICE HOTELS - SANDPOINT
                                          (208)263-2111
Hotel. **Address:** 807 N 5th Ave 83864

SELKIRK LODGE AT SCHWEITZER MOUNTAIN RESORT
                                          208/265-0257
Resort Condominium. **Address:** 10000 Schweitzer Mountain Rd 83864

WHITE PINE LODGE AT SCHWEITZER MOUNTAIN RESORT
                                          208/265-0257
Condominium. **Address:** 145 Village Ln 83864

WHERE TO EAT

HYDRA STEAKHOUSE   208/263-7123
American. Casual Dining. **Address:** 115 Lake St 83864

IVANO'S RISTORANTE & CAFFE   208/263-0211
Regional Italian. Fine Dining. **Address:** 102 S 1st Ave 83864

JALAPENOS   208/263-2995
Mexican. Casual Dining. **Address:** 314 N 2nd Ave 83864

PIE HUT SANDWICH SHOP   208/265-2208
Desserts. Quick Serve. **Address:** 502 Church St 83864

TRINITY AT CITY BEACH   208/255-7558
American. Casual Dining. **Address:** 58 Bridge St 83864

SAWTOOTH NATIONAL FOREST (F-3)

Elevations in the forest range from 4,514 ft. at Rock Creek Drain to 12,009 ft. at Hyndman Peak. Refer to AAA maps for additional elevation information.

In south-central Idaho, the Sawtooth National Forest embraces approximately 2.1 million acres. Offering a wide range of recreational opportunities and spectacular scenery, the forest consists of a northern division containing the Sawtooth National Recreation Area and a southern division along the Nevada and Utah borders.

Adjacent to Sun Valley *(see place listing p. 65)*, the northern division is bisected by the Sawtooth Scenic Byway (SR 75) and provides hundreds of miles of hiking and horseback-riding trails in the Smoky, Pioneer, Sawtooth, Boulder and White Cloud mountains. The Baumgartner Nature Trail, near Baumgartner Campground in the Fairfield District, is a popular hiking area.

The southern division contains the Rock Creek Canyon, Howell Canyon, Black Pine, Raft River and Sublett areas. Alpine and cross-country skiing as well as snowmobiling are available in areas near Twin Falls *(see place listing p. 66)*, Burley *(see place listing p. 37)*, Fairfield and Sun Valley *(see place listing p. 65)*.

Information about campgrounds and recreational opportunities is available at the forest supervisor's office in Twin Falls and the district ranger stations. For further information write Sawtooth National Forest, 2647 Kimberly Rd. E., Twin Falls, ID 83301; phone (208) 737-3200. *See Recreation Areas Chart.*

SAWTOOTH NATIONAL RECREATION AREA (F-3)

In south-central Idaho, the Sawtooth National Recreation Area comprises 756,000 acres of the northern division of the Sawtooth National Forest. The recreation area features three mountain ranges of peaks exceeding 11,000 feet, deep forests and high mountain lakes. The recreation area includes the Sawtooth Wilderness, the White Cloud-Boulder Mountains, portions of the Smokey Mountains, the Salmon River and five major lakes. The backcountry has 750 miles of hiking trails and more than 300 lakes.

Nature trails in the forest include the Fishhook Creek Nature Trail, adjacent to Redfish Lake Visitor Center, and the Wood River Adventure Trail, bordering the Wood River Campground.

The Stanley Ranger Station is open Mon.-Fri. 8:30-4:30. A visitor center on the northern shore of Redfish Lake, 5 miles south of Stanley on SR 75, is open daily 10-5, mid-June to mid-Sept. The North Fork visitor center and national recreation area headquarters is open Mon.-Fri. 8:30-5 (also Sat., Memorial Day-late Dec.).

A free audio tour explaining the area's history and features can be borrowed at the Sawtooth National

Recreation Area headquarters, Stanley Ranger Station or the Ketchum Ranger District. For more information write Sawtooth National Recreation Headquarters, 5 North Fork Canyon Rd., Ketchum, ID 83340; phone (208) 727-5000 for headquarters, (208) 774-3000 for the Stanley Ranger Station or (208) 774-3376 for the Redfish Lake Visitors Center. *See Recreation Areas Chart.*

SHOSHONE (G-3) pop. 1,461, elev. 3,968'

Shoshone, in an irrigated farming belt and sheep-raising area, was settled in 1882. Many buildings, including the Community Methodist Church at Apple and C streets, are made from local dark, porous lava rock.

SPALDING (D-1) elev. 840'

Catholic, Protestant and Mormon missionaries occupied much of central Idaho during the mid- and late 1800s in an attempt to convert the Native Americans. Spalding, now within the boundaries of the Nez Perce National Historical Park *(see place listing p. 56)*, is named for the Rev. Henry H. Spalding, who built a mission near the present town of Lapwai in 1836.

Two years later he moved the mission 2 miles north to the Clearwater River, where the headquarters of the Nez Perce National Historical Park is today.

Several geologic formations near Spalding have significance in Nez Perce tradition. Coyote's Fishnet, about 4 miles west, is a formation on the bluffs of the Clearwater River's south shore. A talus slope known as The Bear is high on the north side of the river. Ant and Yellowjacket is a rock arch 1.5 miles west off US 12 just before its junction with US 95.

Idaho's first homestead, the Craig Donation Land Claim, is about 8 miles south along US 95. In 1840 mountain man William Craig settled on 630 acres given to him by the Nez Perce. He is buried in the nearby town of Jacques. St. Joseph's Mission, 4 miles south of Jacques in the village of Slickpoo, was dedicated in 1874 and was the first Catholic church in Nez Perce country.

STANLEY (F-3) pop. 63, elev. 6,260'

On the Salmon River (the "River of No Return"), Stanley is within the Sawtooth National Recreation Area *(see place listing p. 64)*, Sawtooth Valley and the spectacular Sawtooth Basin. Most float trips on the Middle Fork of the Salmon River and the main Salmon River are outfitted at this site. The town lies on two exceptionally scenic highways, SRs 21 and 75.

The Ponderosa Pine Scenic Byway (SR 21) passes through part of the Sawtooth National Forest *(see place listing p. 64)* and ends in Boise; motorists should check for possible temporary closures due to snow. The northeastern segment of SR 75, the Salmon River Scenic Byway, passes through the Sawtooth National Recreation Area and then merges with US 93. The southeastern segment of SR 75, the Sawtooth Scenic Byway, heads south toward Twin Falls and Sun Valley.

Stanley-Sawtooth Chamber of Commerce: P.O. Box 8, Stanley, ID 83278. **Phone:** (208) 774-3411 or (800) 878-7950.

RECREATIONAL ACTIVITIES

Horseback Riding

- **Redfish Lake Corrals-Trail Rides** is off SR 21. **Hours:** Trips are offered daily 9-3, Memorial Day to mid-Sept. **Phone:** (208) 774-3311.

White-water Rafting

- **The River Company** is at 1150 Eva Falls Ave. Other activities are offered. **Hours:** Day rafting trips are offered mid-May to early Sept. Schedule varies; phone ahead. **Phone:** (208) 788-5775 or (800) 398-0346.

- **ROW Adventures** offers trips on the Middle Fork of the Salmon River. Other activities are offered. **Hours:** One- to 6-day rafting trips are offered mid-May to mid-Sept. Schedule varies; phone ahead. **Phone:** (208) 765-0841 or (800) 451-6034.

POT BELLY CAFE   208/774-2202
🍴 American. Casual Dining. **Address:** 12655 SR 21 83278

STANLEY BAKING CO. & CAFE   208/774-6573
🍴🍴 Sandwiches Soup. Casual Dining. **Address:** 250 Wall St 83278

SUN VALLEY (F-3) pop. 1,406, elev. 5,926'
• Hotels p. 66 • Restaurants p. 66

Sun Valley got its start in 1935 when Union Pacific Railroad Chairman Averell Harriman hired Austrian Count Felix Shaffgotsch to find the most scenic snow spot in the country for a huge ski resort. Passing up places that would become Aspen, Jackson Hole and Mount Hood, Shaffgotsch chose Sun Valley. Soon stars from all across the country came to ski down Dollar Mountain (chairlifts were not installed on 9,150-foot-tall Bald Mountain until Sun Valley's fourth operating season) and hobnob in the huge lodge Harriman built. Gary Cooper and Clark Gable were frequent visitors; novelist Ernest Hemingway spent his last years in the area, and a memorial to him stands alongside Trail Creek.

Today nearly a quarter-million persons visit the area, which somehow still manages to maintain an uncrowded, non-tourist atmosphere. Sun Valley, along with the neighboring town of Ketchum *(see place listing p. 48)*, offers heated outdoor pools, saunas and indoor and outdoor ice-skating rinks. The list of local summer activities includes golf, tennis, swimming, white-water rafting, camping, bicycling, hiking, horseback riding, skeet shooting, trapshooting, fishing, mountaineering and kayaking. Offering respite from the great outdoors, The Sun Valley Pavilion, 1 Sun Valley Rd., hosts the Sun Valley Summer Symphony for 3 weeks in July and August. Admission is free; phone (208) 622-2135 for the pavilion, (208) 622-5607 for the symphony, or (888) 622-2108 for the schedule.

Winter brings sleigh rides, snowmobiling and ice-skating as well as downhill, cross-country and helicopter skiing. Saturday nights are reserved for hockey games in winter and professional ice shows in summer. Skiing begins on Thanksgiving.

SUN VALLEY LODGE & SUN VALLEY INN

(208)622-4111

Resort Hotel
$159-$2400

Address: 1 Sun Valley Rd 83353 **Location:** 1.2 mi ne of Main St (SR 75) and Sun Valley Rd. **Facility:** On manicured grounds with a swan pond at the entrance, this property's lobby overlooks a world-renowned ice skating rink. Elegant guest rooms and spa-quality bathrooms make this a must-see resort. 420 units, some two bedrooms, three bedrooms, kitchens, cottages and condominiums. 1-4 stories, interior corridors. **Parking:** on-site and valet. **Terms:** check-in 4 pm, 30 day cancellation notice-fee imposed, resort fee. **Amenities:** Some: safes. **Dining:** 7 restaurants, also, Gretchen's, see separate listing, entertainment. **Pool:** heated outdoor. **Activities:** sauna, hot tub, regulation golf, tennis, downhill & cross country skiing, snowboarding, sledding, ice skating, recreation programs, bicycles, playground, game room, trails, exercise room, spa. **Guest Services:** valet and coin laundry, area transportation.

[icons]

WHERE TO EAT

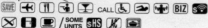

GRETCHEN'S	208/622-4111

New American Fine Dining
$11-$42

AAA Inspector Notes: Named after the first American to win an Olympic gold medal for alpine skiing, this restaurant features a selection of game, pasta dishes, seafood and freshly baked desserts. Maple-braised pork belly or Dungeness crab with fried green tomatoes make wonderful starter plates. Seasonal entrée recommendations include filet mignon, wild salmon with sweet corn flan or rack of lamb in fig and mint jus. **Features:** full bar, patio dining. **Address:** 1 Sun Valley Rd 83353 **Location:** 1.2 mi ne of Main St (SR 75) and Sun Valley Rd; in Sun Valley Lodge & Sun Valley Inn. **Parking:** on-site and valet. [B] [L] [D] CALL [icon]

Local ingredients create dining at its flavorable best.

SWAN VALLEY pop. 204

• Part of Jackson Hole Including Grand Teton National Park area — see map p. 193

SNAKE RIVER ROADHOUSE 208/483-2000
American. Casual Dining. **Address:** 2998 Swan Valley Hwy 83449

TARGHEE NATIONAL FOREST—See
Caribou-Targhee National Forest p. 38

TWIN FALLS (H-3) pop. 44,125, elev. 3,745'

• Restaurants p. 68

Twin Falls is in the center of 500,000 acres of prime farmland irrigated by the waters of the Snake River. Since the turn of the 20th century, the "Magic Valley" area has been known as one of the nation's most prolific crop-producing regions. Twin Falls also is on the edge of the Snake River Canyon, which was gouged out some 30,000 years ago by the Great Bonneville Flood.

From Bliss, the 67.8-mile Thousand Springs Scenic Byway runs southeast, following US 30 through Hagerman *(see place listing p. 43)*, Buhl and Twin Falls, and SR 50 north to the junction of I-84; a spur road (US 93) juts due north from Twin Falls to I-84. Cascading from the sides of Snake River Canyon, the lovely natural springs are fed by the Snake River Plain Aquifer, one of the world's largest groundwater systems. The scenic byway affords access to the five units of Thousand Springs State Park *(see attraction listing p. 43)* as well as three hot mineral pools: Banbury Hot Springs, 10 miles west of Buhl, Miracle Hot Springs, 9 miles south of Hagerman, and Thousand Springs Resort, 5 miles south of Hagerman.

Just northeast of Twin Falls, the white waters of the Snake River plunge more than 212 feet at Shoshone Falls, known as the "Niagara of the West." The best time to view the falls is late April through early June, since irrigation waters are retained upstream during the summer months. **Note:** During drought, the falls may be dry; phone the chamber at (208) 733-3974 to check the status.

Twin Falls Area Chamber of Commerce: 2015 Neilsen Point Pl., Suite 100, Twin Falls, ID 83301. **Phone:** (208) 733-3974 or (866) 894-6325. *(See ad p. 67.)*

[SAVE] **THE HERRETT CENTER FOR ARTS & SCIENCE,** on the north side of the College of Southern Idaho campus, contains artifacts from pre-Columbian civilizations of the Western Hemisphere. The center features contemporary art, a mammoth skeleton and changing exhibits. Visitors can see educational and entertainment shows in a planetarium. The observatory has a research-grade 24-inch telescope. A rain forest exhibit is home to live reptiles and features interactive displays.

Time: Allow 30 minutes minimum. **Hours:** Museum Tues.-Fri. 9:30-4:30 (also Tues. and Fri. 4:30-9), Sat. 1-9. Planetarium and observatory show times vary; phone for schedule. Closed major holidays. **Cost:** Museum and galleries free. Planetarium $6; $5 (ages 60+); $4 (ages 2-18). **Phone:** (208) 732-6655.

BEST WESTERN PLUS TWIN FALLS HOTEL

(208)736-8000

Hotel
$89-$169

AAA Benefit: Members save up to 15% and earn bonus points!

Address: 1377 Blue Lakes Blvd N 83301 **Location:** I-84 exit 173, 4 mi s on US 93. **Facility:** 120 units. 3 stories, interior corridors. **Pool:** heated indoor. **Activities:** hot tub, exercise room. **Guest Services:** coin laundry.

YOUR GUIDE TO SOUTHERN IDAHO'S NATURAL

WONDERS

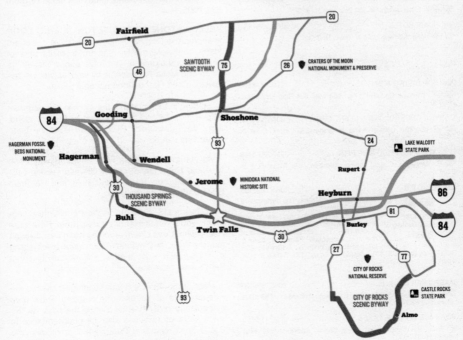

Fairfield

20

20

SAWTOOTH
SCENIC BYWAY

75

26

CRATERS OF THE MOON
NATIONAL MONUMENT & PRESERVE

46

84

Gooding

Shoshone

24

LAKE WALCOTT
STATE PARK

HAGERMAN FOSSIL
BEDS NATIONAL
MONUMENT

Hagerman

Wendell

93

Rupert

Jerome

MINIDOKA NATIONAL
HISTORIC SITE

Heyburn

86

30

THOUSAND SPRINGS
SCENIC BYWAY

81

Buhl

Twin Falls

30

Burley

84

27

77

City OF ROCKS
NATIONAL RESERVE

CASTLE ROCKS
STATE PARK

93

CITY OF ROCKS
SCENIC BYWAY

Almo

THIS IS AUTHENTIC IDAHO.
VISITSOUTHIDAHO.COM

FAIRFIELD INN & SUITES BY MARRIOTT (208)734-8444

♦♦♦
Hotel
$75-$307

Fairfield

AAA Benefit: Members save 5% or more!

Address: 1788 Washington St N 83301 **Location:** I-84 exit 173, 3 mi s to Pole Line Rd, 1 mi w, then just n. **Facility:** 92 units. 3 stories, interior corridors. **Terms:** cancellation fee imposed. **Pool:** heated indoor. **Activities:** hot tub, trails, exercise room. **Guest Services:** valet and coin laundry, boarding pass kiosk. **Featured Amenity: breakfast buffet.**

SAVE CALL ♿ 🏊 🛏 BIZ HS

📶 ✖ 🗄 🖥 💻

HAMPTON INN BY HILTON TWIN FALLS   208/734-2233
♦♦♦ Hotel. **Address:** 1658 Fillmore St N 83301

AAA Benefit: Members save 5% or more!

HILTON GARDEN INN   208/733-8500
♦♦♦ Hotel. **Address:** 1741 Harrison St N 83301

AAA Benefit: Members save 5% or more!

HOLIDAY INN EXPRESS & SUITES TWIN FALLS
208/732-6001
♦♦♦ Hotel. **Address:** 1554 Fillmore St N 83301

LA QUINTA INN & SUITES   (208)736-9600
♦♦♦ Hotel. **Address:** 539 Pole Line Rd 83301

MY PLACE HOTEL   (208)733-0999
♦♦ Hotel. **Address:** 440 N Haven Dr 83301

WHERE TO EAT

ANCHOR BISTRO & BAR   208/733-6566
♦♦ American. Casual Dining. **Address:** 334 Blue Lakes Blvd N 83301

CANYON CREST DINING & EVENT CENTER   208/733-9392
♦♦ American. Casual Dining. **Address:** 330 Canyon Crest Dr 83301

ELEVATION 486 FOOD & SPIRITS   208/737-0486
♦♦ American. Casual Dining. **Address:** 195 River Vista Pl 83301

IDAHO JOE'S   208/734-9403

♦♦
American
Casual Dining
$5-$14

AAA Inspector Notes: The atmosphere is rustic at this local favorite. In addition to generous portions and satisfying breakfasts, there are many fruit and cream pies. The Navajo taco is one of the house specials. **Features:** beer & wine, Sunday brunch. **Address:** 598 Blue Lakes Blvd N 83301 **Location:** I-84 exit 173, 5 mi s; in Lynwood Shopping Center. B L D

JAKERS BAR & GRILL   208/733-8400
♦♦♦ Seafood Steak. Casual Dining. **Address:** 1598 Blue Lakes Blvd 83301

JAVA CAFE ON BLUE LAKES   208/733-9555
♦ Breakfast Sandwiches. Quick Serve. **Address:** 228 Blue Lakes Blvd N 83301

LA CASITA MEXICAN RESTAURANT   208/734-7974
♦♦ Mexican. Casual Dining. **Address:** 111 S Park Ave W 83301

LA FIESTA MEXICAN RESTAURANT   208/734-0685
♦♦ Mexican. Casual Dining. **Address:** 1288 Blue Lakes Blvd 83301

SCOOTERS CHILLIN' N GRILLIN' SPORTS BAR 208/969-9940
♦♦ American. Casual Dining. **Address:** 137 2nd Ave N 83301

SLICE PIZZA   208/595-2777
♦♦ Pizza. Casual Dining. **Address:** 132 Main Ave N 83301

TWIN FALLS SANDWICH COMPANY   208/734-8372
♦ Deli Coffee/Tea. Quick Serve. **Address:** 128 Main Ave N 83301

WOK'N GRILL RESTAURANT   208/734-6898
♦♦ Chinese. Casual Dining. **Address:** 1188 Blue Lakes Blvd N 83301

VICTOR (G-6) pop. 1,928, elev. 6,214'
• Hotels & Restaurants map & index p. 195
• Part of Jackson Hole Including Grand Teton National Park area — see map p. 193

BAGLEY'S TETON MOUNTAIN RANCH is at 2655 West 8000 South (Cedron Rd.). The ranch offers tours featuring up-close encounters with elk and buffalo herds. Stops are afforded for photos. Horseback riding trips of various lengths from 1 hour to overnight trail rides also are available.

Time: Allow 1 hour, 30 minutes minimum. **Hours:** Tours Mon.-Sat. 9-5, June-Sept. **Cost:** Tour $10; free (ages 0-3). Prices vary for other tours. Reservations are required. **Phone:** (208) 787-9005 or (866) 787-9005.

YELLOWSTONE-GRAND TETON SCENIC LOOP is an approximately 263-mile scenic drive in eastern Idaho, northwestern Wyoming and a small portion of south-central Montana. The route encompasses the Teton and Mesa Falls scenic byways as well as Yellowstone and Grand Teton national parks.

Starting in Victor, Idaho, the 47-mile first segment follows SRs 33 and 32 northwest to Ashton, Idaho, along the Teton Scenic Byway, from which the Teton Mountains can be viewed to the east.

As you take the Mesa Falls Scenic Byway north to Island Park, Idaho, on the 35-mile second segment, you'll pass Upper Mesa Falls and Harriman State Park, both to the west.

Following US 20 north on the 28-mile third segment, you'll reach Henry's Lake State Park (see Recreation Areas Chart) and then head east through touristy West Yellowstone, Mont. (see place listing p. 138), which is situated at Yellowstone National Park's west entrance (hence the name).

Most of the 98-mile fourth segment traverses the western side of Yellowstone National Park (see place listing p. 214). After exiting the park via the south entrance (which is also the north entrance to Grand Teton National Park), you'll drive over the Continental Divide, through pine and fir forests and past Jackson Lake. Recreational opportunities abound at Jackson Lake and throughout Grand Teton National Park (see place listing p. 180).

(See map & index p. 195.)

The 30-mile fifth segment begins at the Moran junction. US 26/191, with the Tetons on the northern side and pastures with buffalo and elk on the southern side, has numerous pull-offs with informational plaques. The route passes the National Elk Refuge, where you can observe elk from boardwalks and decks, and then enters Jackson Hole.

On the 25-mile final segment of the trip, you'll head back to Victor via SR 33, which winds through Caribou-Targhee National Forest *(see place listing p. 38)* over dramatic mountains with hairpin turns.

Note: Mesa Falls Scenic Byway is closed from mid-November to late April; take US 20 toward Island Park as an alternate route. The road between Yellowstone National Park's west and south entrances also is closed from mid-November to late April. **Phone:** (208) 354-2607 (Teton Geotourism Center).

KNOTTY PINE SUPPER CLUB   208/787-2866 ⑤⑧

▼▼ American. Casual Dining. **Address:** 58 S Main St 83455

WALLACE (B-2) pop. 784, elev. 2,744'
• Hotels p. 70 • Restaurants p. 70

The center of a great lead- and silver-mining region, Wallace is at the junction of four major canyons, three of which lead to important active mining districts. This region claims several of the world's largest and deepest silver mines; some of the mines founded in the late 1800s have 200 miles of tunnels.

Among the historic buildings still standing in town are the railroad depot with its original Chinese bricks; the Smokehouse Building, which was once the courthouse; and the Rossi Building with its Queen Anne-style turret. The turret is a characteristic architectural feature seen on most of the corner buildings throughout the historic district.

Pulaski Trail, 1 mile south, features interpretive signs describing the 1910 fire that consumed 3 million acres and is said to be one of the largest fires in U.S. history.

At the east end of Wallace, SR 4 leads north from I-90 exit 62 into Burke Canyon, one of the district's historic mining areas. The 7-mile road passes tailings, abandoned mines, derelict buildings and the once bustling towns of Gem and Burke. The latter town, in a narrow canyon, was renowned for the 150-room Tiger Hotel, which was not only built over a creek, but also had a rail line tunneling through its center and a street running under its west end; the hotel was razed in 1964.

Area back roads attract all-terrain vehicle enthusiasts in summer and snowmobilers in winter.

Historic Wallace Chamber of Commerce Visitor Center: 10 River St., Wallace, ID 83873. **Phone:** (208) 753-7151.

Self-guiding tours: A brochure describing driving and walking tours of the mining and historic districts is available at the visitor center.

NORTHERN PACIFIC RAILROAD DEPOT MUSEUM, 219 Sixth St., occupies a restored station that was built in 1901 and operated until 1980. Exhibits include a re-creation of an early 1900s railroad depot as well as photographs and railway relics recalling the history of the Coeur d'Alene Mining District. Changing exhibits also are featured. **Time:** Allow 30 minutes minimum. **Hours:** Daily 9-5, Apr.-Oct.; by appointment rest of year. **Cost:** $3.50; $8 (family). **Phone:** (208) 752-0111.

SIERRA SILVER MINE TOUR, at 509 Cedar St., takes visitors into an underground mine where they can view exhibits, equipment in operation and techniques used in hard-rock silver mining. Retired miners conduct the 75-minute guided tour, which includes a ride through town aboard a vintage-style trolley and anecdotes about the mining days.

Time: Allow 1 hour, 30 minutes minimum. **Hours:** Mine tours depart every 30 minutes daily 10-4, June-Aug.; 10-2 in May and Sept. **Cost:** Mine tour $15; $13 (ages 60+); $8.50 (ages 4-16); $48 (family, two adults and children). Trolley ride only $6. **Phone:** (208) 752-5151.

SIXTH STREET MELODRAMA is at 212 Sixth St. Audience participation is encouraged each summer during a family-style melodrama that reflects the area's mining background. The play, staged in the 1899 Lux Building, is followed by the Kelly's Alley Revue, during which visitors can enjoy old-fashioned music and humor. Other plays and musicals also are produced during the rest of the year; phone for schedule and rates.

Time: Allow 2 hours minimum. **Hours:** Summer performances are given Wed.-Sat. at 7 p.m., Sun. at 2, early July-late Aug. **Cost:** $10. **Phone:** (208) 752-8871 or (877) 749-8478.

THE WALLACE INN

208/752-1252

Hotel
Rates not provided

Address: 100 Front St 83873 **Location:** I-90 exit 61 (Business Rt 90), just se. **Facility:** 63 units. 2 stories (no elevator), interior corridors. **Parking:** winter plug-ins. **Terms:** check-in 4 pm. **Pool:** heated indoor. **Activities:** sauna, hot tub, steamroom, exercise room.

WHERE TO EAT

1313 CLUB

208/752-9391

American
Casual Dining
$6-$23

AAA Inspector Notes: This historic mining town's classic old-time bar and grill has eclectic décor heavy on taxidermists' mounts and collectible items. The menu here has offerings such as salads, wraps, burgers, sandwiches, steaks and a variety of appetizers. As an unexpected treat you will also find quesadillas, nachos and burritos. Try the chicken enchiladas—you may be pleasantly surprised. **Features:** full bar, patio dining, happy hour. **Address:** 608 Bank St 83873 **Location:** Downtown. **Parking:** street only.

B L D

THE BROOKS RESTAURANT

208/752-8171

American. Casual Dining. **Address:** 500 Cedar St 83873

WORLEY pop. 257, elev. 2,650'

COEUR D'ALENE CASINO RESORT HOTEL

(208)769-2600

Resort Hotel
$100-$190

Address: 37914 S Nukwalqw Rd 83876 **Location:** On US 95, 3 mi n. **Facility:** Located just South of Coeur d'Alene, this casino-style property offers guests a variety of entertainment options. Choose between newer "spa" rooms or more traditional lodge-style units. 300 units. 3-4 stories, interior corridors. **Parking:** on-site and valet. **Terms:** check-in 4 pm. **Amenities:** *Some:* safes. **Dining:** 5 restaurants, also, Chinook Steak & Pasta, High Mountain Buffet, see separate listings. **Pool:** heated indoor. **Activities:** hot tub, regulation golf, exercise room, spa. **Guest Services:** area transportation.

WHERE TO EAT

CHINOOK STEAK & PASTA

208/769-2600

Regional Steak Seafood. Fine Dining. **Address:** 37914 S Nukwalqw Rd 83876

HIGH MOUNTAIN BUFFET

208/686-0248

American. Casual Dining. **Address:** 37914 S Nukwalqw Rd 83876

YELLOWSTONE NATIONAL PARK—See Wyoming p. 214

Glacier National Park

Montana

Under a giant sky varying between shades of azure, turquoise and peacock blue, Montana's landscape—encompassing golden wheat fields, timber-covered mountains, flowing trout streams, rocky bluffs and canyon-carved lakes—is a love affair for the eyes.

The state enjoys the best of both worlds. The Continental Divide in western Montana gave rise to the name *montaña,* Spanish for "mountainous." And although the craggy peaks of the northern Rocky Mountains dominate the west, wide-open space is the name of the game in the east: Expansive, dizzying prairie grasslands in this region coined the state's nickname, Big Sky Country.

While there are differences between Montana's agriculture- and ranching-based Great Plains and its lumber-dominated west, residents have one thing in common: appreciation for the beauty of their surroundings. Still,

Little Bighorn Battlefield National Monument

with a harsh climate and sparse population, no one will argue that living in Montana is a piece of cake. But the view from a ranch window seems to make it worthwhile.

The Treasure State

Vast fortunes were made in Montana, but many would assert they came at the expense of people and land, a notion that doesn't sit well with residents. Many Montanans believe that state resources historically have been exploited in the interests of outsiders.

At Little Bighorn Battlefield National Monument, crooked headstones on a grassy hill attest to the passion that thousands of Lakota, Cheyenne and Arapaho warriors exhibited in an attempt to save their homeland.

And the unearthing of copper ores in Butte began a bitter battle between the "copper kings"—entrepreneurs William A. Clark and Marcus Daly. Today, mining relics are displayed downtown in old mine shafts, cabins and such stately homes as Clark's lavish Copper King Mansion.

Colorful Virginia City sports reminders of its gold mining past with restored buildings. And Helena is home to baroque, Gothic and Italianate mansions recalling the city's golden days.

More recently, locals have exhibited an overwhelming drive to preserve Montana's natural blessings. In the early 1970s, residents amended the state constitution to include strict environmental protection laws, setting a national example.

Spectacular Settings

Take in the snowy peaks, ice-sculpted valleys, and twinkling lakes and waterfalls of Glacier National Park, a majestic region so awe-inspiring the Blackfeet Indians deemed it sacred ground. If the area's resident grizzlies, mountain lions and wolves could talk, they would probably agree.

Your heart will skip a beat on Going-to-the-Sun Road, a mind-boggling scenic byway that snakes around cliffs and climbs 6,646 feet to the summit of Logan Pass.

But save some time for the nation's *first* national park, Yellowstone, which Congress established in 1872. You'll also want to visit the National Bison Range in Moiese, where some 400 buffalo roam the plains.

And, along what is now the Upper Missouri National Wild and Scenic River, you can follow the path of the Lewis and Clark expedition. Journal notes suggest that these explorers were enamored with Montana's scenery as well.

Recreation

What's in the perfect Montana recreation kit? Bear bells. Quick-dry nylon shorts. Ski poles. Maybe some chest waders. Definitely some dry socks. And, of course, a size-2 Sofa Pillow.

The quick-dry shorts will come in handy if you immerse yourself in one of this state's top recreation draws—river rafting. At Glacier National Park you can drift down placid portions of the wild and scenic Flathead River, savoring arching canyon walls and wildflower-filled meadows. Or, you might tackle the bucking, boulder-studded rapids of the Flathead's Middle Fork. And Bear Creek is one of the few runs where mountain goats are regularly sighted, thanks to Goat Lick, a cliff on the waterway's north side that excretes mineral salts irresistible to the horned animals.

As any good fly fisher knows, Montana is trout territory, and that's where the chest waders come in. The best catch must be coaxed out with a deft flick of the wrist and an enticing fly on the end of the line. Such flies can have kind of funny names—hence the Sofa Pillow. For top casting sites, head to Bozeman's outskirts and take your pick of such trout-filled rivers as the Madison, Yellowstone and Gallatin. You'll find plenty of rental boats here, too, complete with guides who will do the rowing for you.

Fly fishing may be out if you hit Bozeman mid-winter, but that doesn't mean you're too late to have fun. Excellent downhill skiing is just around the corner at Big Sky Resort, which averages 400 inches of powder annually. And locals rave about the bowl and chute skiing available at 1,200-acre Bridger Bowl Ski Area. Six cross-country skiing trails rim the region as well, notably the 10-mile Bozeman Creek to Mystic Lake trail and the 4-mile Hyalite Reservoir Ski Loop.

In addition you'll find superb ski venues close to many other Montana towns, including Whitefish Mountain Resort near Whitefish, Red Lodge Mountain near Red Lodge and Snowbowl near Missoula. All make great places to put those ski poles you packed to good use.

Plus, ski poles can often be helpful when hiking Montana's rugged terrain. Such "walking sticks" are especially useful when the only way to follow your trail is to ford a frigid, knee-high creek. The dry socks are for when you get to the other side.

Montana has several great hiking trails, but try not to miss Cinnamon Mountain Lookout Trail in the Gallatin National Forest, or Stoney Indian Pass in Glacier National Park's Belly River Country. Both reward hikers with sudden, stunning vistas of Montana's treasured mountains. One caveat—while such spectacular scenery can be a pleasant surprise, startling an 800-pound grizzly is just plain hazardous. And *that's* why bear bells are number one on any Montana recreational equipment list.

Fly fishing near Bozeman

Historic Timeline

1805	Meriwether Lewis and William Clark arrive in what is now the state of Montana.
1862	Miners strike gold at Grasshopper Creek and later at Diamond City and Virginia City.
1876	Lt. Col. George Armstrong Custer and troops are defeated at the Battle of the Little Bighorn.
1880	Irish immigrant Marcus Daly purchases the Anaconda, a mine with a rich copper reserve that will make him wealthy.
1916	Montana Republican Jeannette Rankin becomes the first U.S. congresswoman; she later voted against both world wars.
1955	The Anaconda Aluminum Co. opens a $65 million plant in northwestern Montana.
1972	Montana's electorate approves a new state constitution.
1984	Launched in 1967, the Libby Dam hydroelectric project is finally completed.
1988	Forest fires sweep through Montana for nearly 3 months, wiping out trees and wildlife in Yellowstone National Park.
1998	Montana Freemen leaders involved in a 1996 armed standoff with FBI agents are convicted of various charges.
2000	Judy Martz is elected governor and becomes the state's first female chief executive.

What To Pack

Temperature Averages Maximum/Minimum	JANUARY	FEBRUARY	MARCH	APRIL	MAY	JUNE	JULY	AUGUST	SEPTEMBER	OCTOBER	NOVEMBER	DECEMBER
Billings	33/13	36/15	43/23	57/34	68/43	76/51	89/58	86/55	75/46	63/37	46/26	39/19
Great Falls	32/14	34/15	41/21	55/33	66/42	72/49	84/56	81/54	70/46	59/38	44/26	37/20
Havre	26/6	29/8	40/18	57/32	69/43	75/51	86/57	83/54	72/44	60/35	42/21	33/12
Kalispell	26/9	32/12	40/19	55/30	65/39	72/46	83/49	80/46	69/39	55/31	37/21	29/16
Medicine Lake	18/-2	27/7	40/18	56/30	68/42	77/51	83/54	82/53	70/42	58/31	36/16	23/3
Miles City	27/6	32/9	42/19	59/33	71/44	79/53	90/60	88/58	75/47	62/36	44/22	34/12

From the records of The Weather Channel Interactive, Inc.

Good Facts To Know

ABOUT THE STATE

POPULATION: 989,415.

AREA: 147,040 square miles; ranks 4th.

CAPITAL: Helena.

HIGHEST POINT: 12,799 ft., Granite Peak.

LOWEST POINT: 1,862 ft., Kootenai River.

TIME ZONE(S): Mountain. DST.

REGULATIONS

TEEN DRIVING LAWS: No more than one unrelated passenger under 18 for the first 6 months and no more than three unrelated passengers under 18 for the second 6 months. Driving is not permitted 11 p.m.-5 a.m. The minimum age for an unrestricted driver's license is 16. Phone (406) 444-3933 for more information about Montana driver's license regulations.

SEAT BELT/CHILD RESTRAINT LAWS: Seat belts are required for driver and all passengers ages 6 and over and at least 60 pounds. Children under age 6 and less than 60 pounds are required to be in a child restraint. AAA recommends the use of seat belts and appropriate child restraints for the driver and all passengers.

HELMETS FOR MOTORCYCLISTS: Required for riders under 18.

RADAR DETECTORS: Permitted. Prohibited for use by commercial vehicles.

MOVE OVER LAW: Driver is required to slow down and vacate the lane nearest stopped police, fire and rescue vehicles using audible or flashing signals. The law also includes tow trucks. If on a highway with a speed limit of 50 mph or greater, the driver must slow down by at least 20 mph below the posted speed limit.

FIREARMS LAWS: Vary by state and/or county. Contact the Montana Department of Justice, Help Desk, 3013 N. Roberts, Room 470, Helena, MT 59601; phone (406) 444-2800.

HOLIDAYS

HOLIDAYS: Jan. 1 ▪ Martin Luther King Jr. Day, Jan. (3rd Mon.) ▪ Lincoln's and Washington's Birthday/Presidents Day, Feb. (3rd Mon.) ▪ Memorial Day, May (last Mon.) ▪ July 4 ▪ Labor Day, Sept. (1st Mon.) ▪ Columbus Day, Oct. (2nd Mon.) ▪ Election Day, Nov. (1st Tues. following 1st Mon.) ▪ Veterans Day, Nov. 11 ▪ Thanksgiving, Nov. (4th Thurs.) ▪ Christmas, Dec. 25.

MONEY

TAXES: Montana does not have a statewide sales tax. Designated resort communities may enact a resort tax of up to 3 percent for goods and services. There is a 7 percent statewide lodging tax.

VISITOR INFORMATION

INFORMATION CENTERS: State welcome centers are on US 2 just 1 mile east of Culbertson ▪ at jct. Main St. and US 2 in Shelby ▪ off I-94 in Wibaux ▪ on I-90 southbound a half-mile east of Hardin ▪ at jct. US 191 and US 20N in West Yellowstone ▪ and off I-15 southbound in Dillon.

ROAD CONDITIONS: The Montana Department of Transportation provides information about highway conditions and construction; phone (406) 444-6201 or (800) 226-7623.

FURTHER INFORMATION FOR VISITORS:

Montana Office of Tourism
301 S. Park Ave.
Helena, MT 59601
(406) 841-2870
(800) 847-4868

NATIONAL FOREST INFORMATION:

U.S. Forest Service
Lolo National Forest
24 Fort Missoula Rd.
Missoula, MT 59804
(406) 329-3750 Supervisor's office
(406) 329-3814 Ranger station

FISHING AND HUNTING REGULATIONS:

Montana Department of Fish, Wildlife & Parks
1420 E. 6th Ave.
P.O. Box 200701
Helena, MT 59620
(406) 444-2535

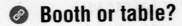

🔗 Booth or table?

AAA.com/travelguides/restaurants

Montana Annual Events

Please call ahead to confirm event details.

 Visit AAA.com/travelguides/events to find AAA-listed events for every day of the year

WINTER

Dec. - First Night Missoula / Missoula
406-541-0860
- Montana Ballet Company's
Nutcracker / Bozeman
406-582-8702

Jan. - Montana PRCA Rodeo Circuit Finals
Great Falls / 406-727-1481
- Seeley Lake Area Winterfest / Seeley
Lake / 406-677-2880

Feb. - Cowtown Beef Breeders Show, Craft
Expo and Ag Trade Show / Miles
City / 406-234-2890
- Whitefish Winter Carnival / Whitefish
406-862-3501

SPRING

Mar. - West Yellowstone Snowmobile EXPO
West Yellowstone / 406-647-7701
- St. Patrick's Day Events / Butte
406-723-3177

Apr. - Ice Breaker Road Race / Great
Falls / 406-771-1265
- International Wildlife Film Festival
Missoula / 406-728-9380

May - MSU-Billings Wine and Food Festival
Billings / 888-430-6782
- Bigfork Whitewater Festival / Bigfork
406-270-1551
- International Migratory Bird Day
Moiese / 406-644-2211, ext. 207

SUMMER

June - Lewis and Clark Festival / Great
Falls / 406-791-7732
- Montana Mule Days / Hamilton
406-777-2331

July - Montana State Fair / Great
Falls / 406-727-8900
- Montana Folk Festival / Butte
406-497-6464

Aug. - MontanaFair / Billings / 406-256-2400
- Sweet Pea Festival / Bozeman
406-586-4003

FALL

Sept. - Havre Festival Days / Havre
406-265-4383

Oct. - Northern International Livestock
Exposition Stock Show, Pro Rodeo
and Western Expo / Billings
406-256-2495
- McIntosh Apple Day / Hamilton
406-363-3338
- Montana Book Festival / Missoula
800-526-3465

Nov. - Parade of Lights / Forsyth
406-347-5656
- Holiday Parade / Billings
406-259-5454
- Seasonal Bazaar & Parade of Lights
Cut Bank / 406-873-4041

Lolo National Forest

Mountain goats

State Capitol, Helena

Glacier National Park

Virginia City

Index: Great Experience for Members

AAA editor's picks of exceptional note

Museum of the
Rockies

Cathedral of St.
Helena

Yellowstone National
Park

C.M. Russell Museum

See Orientation map on p. 90 for corresponding grid coordinates, if applicable.
*Indicates the GEM is temporarily closed.

STAY CONNECTED

TO ALL THE THINGS
MEMBERSHIP CAN DO FOR YOU

- member discounts around you
- cheapest gas nearby
- Diamond Rated hotels and restaurants
- travel information and reservations
- roadside assistance

Download today. Connect every day.
AAA.com/mobile | CAA.ca/mobile

Montana
Atlas Section

ROADS/HIGHWAYS

	INTERSTATE
	CONTROLLED ACCESS
	CONTROLLED ACCESS TOLL
	TOLL ROAD
	PRIMARY DIVIDED
	PRIMARY UNDIVIDED
	SECONDARY DIVIDED
	SECONDARY UNDIVIDED
	LOCAL DIVIDED
	LOCAL UNDIVIDED
	UNPAVED ROAD
	UNDER CONSTRUCTION
	TUNNEL
	PEDESTRIAN ONLY
	AUTO FERRY
	PASSENGER FERRY
	SCENIC BYWAY
10	DISTANCE BETWEEN MARKERS
	EXIT NUMBER-FREE/TOLL
	INTERCHANGE FULL/PARTIAL
	WELCOME/INFORMATION CENTER
	REST AREA/ SERVICE CENTER

BOUNDARIES

	INTERNATIONAL
	STATE
	COUNTY
	TIME ZONE
	CONTINENTAL DIVIDE

ROAD SHIELDS

05 05	INTERSTATE/BUSINESS
22 22 22	U.S./STATE/COUNTY
27 27	FOREST/INDIAN
	TRANS- CANADA
1	PROVINCIAL AUTOROUTE/ KING'S HIGHWAY
1	MEXICO
66	HISTORIC ROUTE 66
VT 41	REFERENCE PAGE INDICATOR

AREAS OF INTEREST

	INDIAN
	MILITARY
	PARK
	FOREST
	GRASSLANDS
	HISTORIC
✈	INT'L/REGIONAL AIRPORT
	INCORPORATED CITY

POINTS OF INTEREST

○	TOWN
⊛	NATIONAL CAPITAL
✸	STATE/PROVINCIAL CAPITAL
■	AAA/CAA CLUB LOCATION
■	FEATURE OF INTEREST
▲	COLLEGE/UNIVERSITY
⊙	CUSTOMS STATION
	HISTORIC
	LIGHTHOUSE
	MONUMENT/MEMORIAL
♣	STATE/PROVINCIAL PARK
♣	NATIONAL WILDLIFE REFUGE
	SKI AREA
○	SPORTS COMPLEX
	DAM

CITIES/TOWNS are color-coded by size, showing where to find AAA Inspected and Approved lodgings or restaurants listed in the AAA TourBook guides and on AAA.com:

- ● Red - major destinations and capitals; many listings
- ● Black - destinations; some listings
- ● Grey - no listings

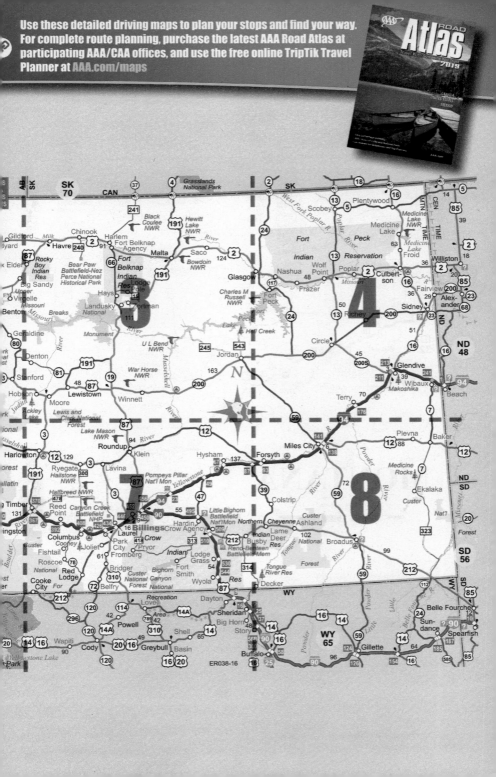

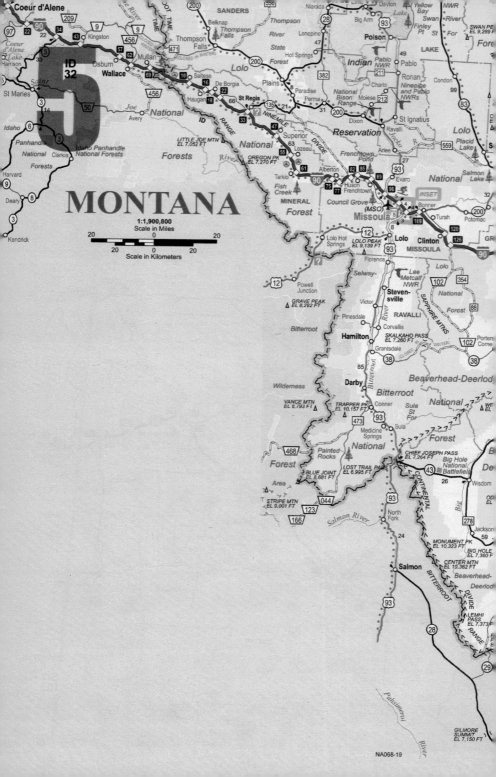

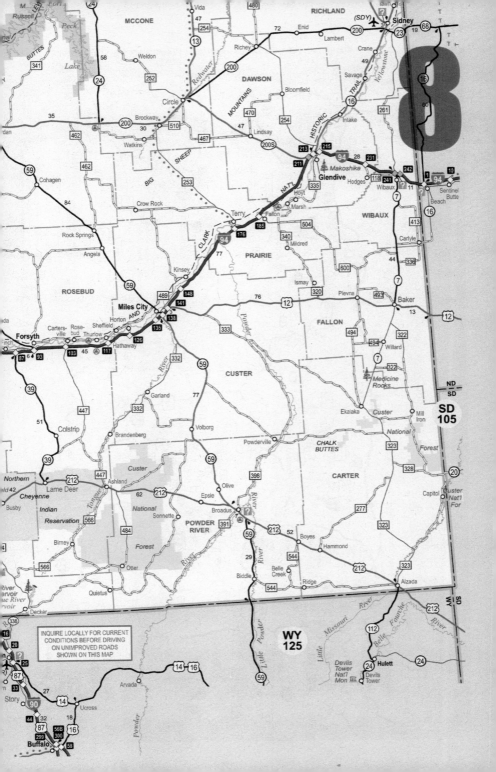

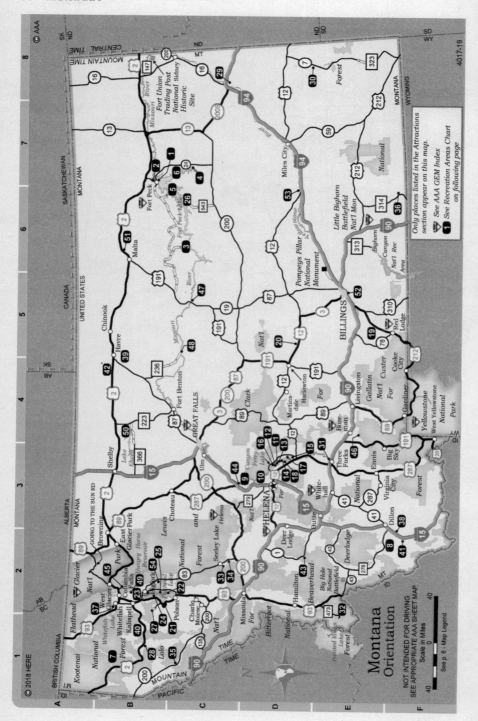

Montana
Orientation

NOT INTENDED FOR DRIVING
SEE APPROPRIATE AAA SHEET MAP.

Scale in Miles

See p. 6 - Map Legend

Only places listed in the Attractions
section appear on this map.

⬥ See AAA GEM Index

🔟 See Recreation Areas Chart
    on following page

Recreation Areas Chart

The map location numerals in column 2 show an area's location on the preceding map.

🔗 **Find thousands of places to camp at AAA.com/campgrounds**

	MAP LOCATION	CAMPING	PICNICKING	HIKING TRAILS	BOATING	BOAT RAMP	BOAT RENTAL	FISHING	SWIMMING	PET FRIENDLY	BICYCLE TRAILS	WINTER SPORTS	VISITOR CENTER	LODGE/CABINS	FOOD SERVICE
NATIONAL PARKS (See place listings.)															
Glacier (A-2) 1,000,000 acres. Horse rental.		•	•	•	•	•	•	•	•	•			•	•	•
NATIONAL FORESTS (See place listings.)															
Beaverhead-Deerlodge (E-2) 3,392,930 acres. Southwestern Montana. Horse rental.		•	•	•	•	•		•	•	•	•	•		•	
Bitterroot (D-1) 1,577,883 acres. Western Montana.		•	•	•	•	•		•	•	•		•		•	
Custer (E-4) 1.3 million acres. Southeastern Montana and north-western South Dakota.		•	•	•				•	•	•		•			
Flathead (A-1) 2,330,029 acres. Northwestern Montana. Horse rental.		•	•	•	•			•	•	•		•		•	
Gallatin (E-4) 1,735,239 acres. South-central Montana. Horse rental.		•	•	•	•	•	•	•	•	•		•		•	
Helena (C-3) 976,000 acres. West-central Montana.		•	•	•	•			•	•	•		•			
Kootenai (A-1) 2.2 million acres. Northwestern Montana. Horse rental.		•	•	•	•	•		•	•	•		•		•	
Lewis and Clark (B-3) 1,843,397 acres. West-central Montana.		•	•	•	•			•	•			•		•	
Lolo (B-1) 2,100,000 acres. Western Montana. Horse rental.		•	•	•	•	•		•	•			•			
NATIONAL RECREATION AREAS (See place listings.)															
Bighorn Canyon (E-6) 120,000 acres in southern Montana and northern Wyoming.		•	•	•	•	•		•	•	•			•		•
ARMY CORPS OF ENGINEERS															
Fort Peck Lake (B-6) off SR 24 in Fort Peck. Bird-watching, canoeing.		•	•	•	•	•		•	•				•		•
Downstream (B-7) 347 acres 1 mi. e. of Fort Peck off SR 117. Bird-watching; museum, playground.	❶	•	•	•	•	•		•		•					
Dredge Cuts (B-7) 650 acres 3 mi. n. of Fort Peck off SR 117.	❷	•	•			•	•	•	•						
Fourchette Bay (C-6) 80 acres 60 mi. s.e. of Malta off SR 191. Bird-watching, canoeing, kayaking.	❸	•	•		•	•		•	•	•	•				
Nelson Creek (C-7) 468 acres 45 mi. s. of Fort Peck off SR 24. Bird-watching, canoeing, kayaking.	❹	•	•		•	•		•	•	•					
The Pines (B-6) 927 acres 4.5 mi. n.w. of Fort Peck on SR 24, 14 mi. s.w. via a gravel road, then 12 mi. s.e. via a gravel road. Bird-watching, canoeing, kayaking; playground.	❺	•	•		•	•		•	•	•	•	•			
Rock Creek (C-7) 345 acres 32 mi. s.e. of Fort Peck off SR 24. Bird-watching; beach.	❻	•	•		•	•		•	•	•					•
Libby Dam (Lake Koocanusa) (B-1) 46,000 acres 13.5 mi. e. of Libby on SR 37, then 3.5 mi. n. on FR 228, following signs. Disc golf; playground.	❼	•	•	•	•	•		•	•	•	•		•		
STATE															
Bannack (F-2) 1,529 acres 17 mi. w. of Dillon on SR 278, then 4 mi. s. on Bannack Rd., following signs. Historic.	❽	•	•	•				•		•			•		
Beartooth Wildlife Management Area (D-3) 27,000 acres 10 mi. s.e. of Wolf Creek via a gravel road.	❾	•	•		•	•		•	•	•					
Black Sandy (D-3) 55 acres 14 mi. n.e. of Helena via I-15 and CR 415.	❿	•	•	•	•	•		•	•	•				•	
Canyon Ferry Lake (D-3) 5,000 acres 20 mi. e. of Helena off US 287. Hunting.			•	•		•	•	•	•	•	•		•	•		•
Cave Bay (D-4) 19 mi. e. of Helena via US 287 and CR 284.	⓫		•		•	•	•	•	•	•					•
Chinaman (D-4) 19 mi. e. of Helena via US 287 and CR 284.	⓬	•	•		•	•		•	•	•					
Court Sheriff (D-4) 18 mi. e. of Helena via US 287 and CR 284.	⓭	•	•		•			•	•	•					
Hellgate (D-3) 27 mi. e. of Helena via US 287 and CR 284.	⓮	•	•		•	•		•	•	•					
Indian Road (D-3) 1 mi. n. of Townsend on US 287.	⓯	•	•		•	•		•		•					
Riverside (D-4) 18 mi. e. of Helena via US 287 and CR 284.	⓰	•	•		•			•		•					

Recreation Areas Chart

The map location numerals in column 2 show an area's location on the preceding map.

Find thousands of places to camp at AAA.com/campgrounds

	MAP LOCATION	CAMPING	PICNICKING	HIKING TRAILS	BOATING	BOAT RAMP	BOAT RENTAL	FISHING	SWIMMING	PET FRIENDLY	BICYCLE TRAILS	WINTER SPORTS	VISITOR CENTER	LODGE/CABINS	FOOD SERVICE
Silos (D-3) 8 mi. n.w. of Townsend off US 287.	17	•	•		•	•		•		•					•
White Earth (D-3) 5 mi. e. of Winston.	18	•	•		•	•		•		•					
Cooney Reservoir (E-5) 304 acres 5 mi. w. of Boyd via a gravel road.	19	•	•	•	•	•		•	•	•					•
Deadman's Basin (D-5) 500 acres 29 mi. e. of Harlowton off US 12.	20	•	•		•	•		•	•	•					
Flathead Lake (C-2) n. of Polson on US 93.															
Big Arm (C-1) 55 acres 15 mi. n. of Polson on US 93.	21	•	•		•	•		•	•	•					
Finley Point (C-2) 24 acres about 12 mi. n.e. of Polson off SR 35.	22	•	•		•	•		•	•	•	•				
Wayfarers (B-2) 68 acres 1 mi. s. of Bigfork off SR 35.	23	•	•		•	•		•	•	•					
West Shore (B-1) 146 acres about 20 mi. s. of Kalispell on US 93.	24	•	•	•	•	•		•	•	•					
Yellow Bay (B-2) 10 acres 20 mi. n.e. of Polson off SR 35.	25	•	•		•	•		•	•	•					
Hell Creek (C-6) 172 acres 26 mi. n. of Jordan via a gravel road on Fort Peck Reservoir.	26	•	•	•	•	•	•	•	•	•				•	•
Lake Mary Ronan (B-1) 76 acres 7 mi. n.w. of Dayton off US 93.	27	•	•		•	•		•	•	•					
Logan (B-1) 18 acres 45 mi. w. of Kalispell off US 2.	28	•	•	•	•	•		•							
Makoshika (C-8) 11,531 acres 1 mi. s. of Glendive at 1301 Snyder Ave.	29	•	•	•						•	•	•	•	•	
Medicine Rocks (D-8) 320 acres 24 mi. s. of Baker on SR 7. Historic.	30	•	•							•	•				
Missouri Headwaters (E-4) 527 acres 3 mi. e. of Three Forks, then 3 mi. n. of US 10 at 1585 Trident Jct.	31	•	•	•	•	•		•		•			•		
Painted Rocks (E-2) 263 acres 20 mi. s.w. of Conner off SR 473.	32	•	•		•	•		•	•	•					
Placid Lake (C-2) 32 acres 6 mi. s.w. of Seeley Lake via CR 83.	33	•	•		•	•		•	•	•	•				
Salmon Lake (C-2) 42 acres 5 mi. s. of Seeley Lake on SR 83.	34	•	•	•	•	•		•	•	•					
Thompson Falls (C-1) 36 acres 3 mi. w. of Thompson Falls off SR 200.	35	•	•		•	•		•		•	•				
Tongue River Reservoir (F-6) 640 acres 6 mi. n. of Decker on CR 314, then 1 mi. e.	36	•	•		•	•		•	•	•					•
Whitefish Lake (A-2) 10 acres 5 mi. w. of Whitefish on US 93.	37	•	•		•	•	•	•	•					•	•
OTHER															
Barretts Park (F-3) 38 acres 8 mi. s.w. of Dillon off I-15.	38	•	•		•			•	•	•					
Beaver Creek (B-5) 10,000 acres 11 mi. s. of Havre on CR 234. Bird-watching.	39	•	•	•	•			•	•	•		•			
Bitterroot Lake (B-1) 36 acres 5 mi. n. of US 2 at Marion.	40	•	•		•	•		•	•					•	
Clark Canyon Reservoir (F-2) 4,131 acres 20 mi. s.w. of Dillon on I-15. Hunting.	41	•	•		•	•	•	•	•	•					
Fresno Reservoir (B-4) 25,668 acres n.w. of Havre. Hunting, water skiing.	42	•	•		•	•		•	•	•					
Georgetown Lake (D-2) 2,850 acres 15 mi. w. of Anaconda on SR 1. Water skiing; playground.	43	•	•	•	•	•		•	•	•		•		•	•
Holter Lake (C-3) 22 acres 2 mi. e. of Wolf Creek on Missouri River Rd., then 3 mi. s. via a gravel road.	44	•	•		•	•		•	•	•				•	•
Hungry Horse Reservoir (B-2) 6,836 acres 10 mi. e. of Columbia Falls on SR 40, then s. 5 mi. via a gravel road. Hunting.	45	•	•	•	•	•		•	•		•	•	•		
Hyalite Canyon (E-3) 35,000 acres 14 mi. s. of Bozeman on SR 85.	46	•	•	•	•	•		•	•	•	•	•			
James Kipp (C-5) 465 acres 65 mi. n.e. of Lewistown off US 191.	47	•	•		•	•		•							
Judith Landing (C-5) 44 mi. s.e. of Big Sandy on CR 236.	48	•			•	•		•							
Lake Blaine (B-2) 13 acres 7 mi. e. of Kalispell.	49	•		•	•	•		•	•	•				•	•
Lake Elwell (B-4) 6,197 acres 18 mi. s.w. of Chester.	50	•	•		•	•		•	•	•					•

Recreation Areas Chart

The map location numerals in column 2 show an area's location on the preceding map.

 Find thousands of places to camp at AAA.com/campgrounds

	MAP LOCATION	CAMPING	PICNICKING	HIKING TRAILS	BOATING	BOAT RAMP	BOAT RENTAL	FISHING	SWIMMING	PET FRIENDLY	BICYCLE TRAILS	WINTER SPORTS	VISITOR CENTER	LODGE/CABINS	FOOD SERVICE
Nelson Reservoir (B-6) 7,702 acres 18 mi. n.e. of Malta off US 2.	51	●	●		●	●		●	●	●					
Riverfront Park (E-5) 1 mi. s. of Billings on CR 416.	52		●	●	●			●			●	●			
Rosebud East (D-6) 32 acres e. of Forsyth off I-94. Bird-watching.	53	●	●	●	●	●		●		●					
Swan Lake (B-2) 10 acres 14 mi. s.e. of Bigfork on SR 83. Water skiing.	54	●	●		●	●		●	●	●					

LET'S GET SOCIAL

Connect with AAA and CAA for the latest updates.

 AAA.com/Facebook

 AAA.com/Twitter

 Instagram.com/aaa_national

 AAA.com/Googleplus

 YouTube.com/AAA

CAA Social Media: CAA.ca/social

BEAVERHEAD-DEERLODGE NATIONAL FOREST (E-2)

Elevations in the forest range from 4,075 ft. in the valleys to 11,361 ft. on Hilgard Peak. Refer to AAA maps for additional elevation information.

Beaverhead-Deerlodge National Forest is part of the huge complex of national forests occupying most of southwestern Montana. In 1996, Deerlodge National Forest's 1,194,124 acres (nearly 100 square miles) were combined with Beaverhead National Forest to form an outdoor recreation area encompassing more than 3.3 million acres.

Glaciated peaks rise from broad valleys in the area to form some of Montana's most majestic ranges—the Anaconda, Bitterroot, Beaverhead, Flint Creek, Gravelly, Highland, Madison, Tobacco Root and Sapphire. Mountains in these ranges are among the loftiest in the state; more than 40 surpass 10,000 feet. Mount Evans rises to 10,604 feet, and several more, including Hilgard Peak, exceed 11,000 feet.

From the snowpack of these ranges spring the Big Hole, Beaverhead and Ruby rivers, which form three major tributaries of the Jefferson River. The high country also supplies some of the tributaries of the Madison River. The Clark Fork River flows from its headwaters west of the Continental Divide to Idaho's Lake Pend Oreille.

Through this maze of mountains and river valleys Sacagawea led Meriwether Lewis and William Clark in their search for a passage to the Pacific. This was the land of Sacagawea's people, the Shoshones, who re-provisioned and led the expedition over Lemhi Pass in 1805 and north to a final passage to the West. Despite the inroads of progress—lumbering, mining and ranching—much of the forest's lands have changed little since Lewis and Clark's visit.

Within the forest are portions of the Anaconda-Pintler and Lee Metcalf wilderness areas and a large number of roadless tracts. Typical features of roadless areas are glacial lakes, trout streams and rugged mountain vistas.

The Anaconda-Pintler Wilderness straddles 30 miles of the Anaconda Range and the Continental Divide. The land gradually rises from dense stands of lodgepole pine to open parks dotted with lakes, culminating in jagged peaks in the heart of the range. Anglers prize the clear mountain streams and alpine lakes for their abundance and variety of trout.

Another major area is the Taylor-Hilgard portion of the Lee Metcalf Wilderness. This unit is one of the four portions of wilderness along the spine of the Madison Range, which lies just northwest of Yellowstone National Park. Soaring peaks, knife-edged ridges and alpine lakes are characteristics of this popular area. Bird-watchers will find more than 260 species frequenting a variety of habitats in the forest. The region provides winter range for bighorn sheep and mountain goats and a home to grizzly and black bears, mule deer, mountain lions, elk and moose.

The bald eagle nests in the southeastern Gravelly Range and winters along the Red Rock, Ruby, Jefferson, Madison, Big Hole and Beaverhead rivers. Most migration and wintering activities occur in the large river valleys adjoining the forest. The gray wolf is an occasional visitor to parts of the Continental Divide southwest of Dillon. Grizzly bears occupy portions of the Madison Range within the Lee Metcalf Wilderness and are occasional visitors to the Tobacco Root Mountains and the Gravelly Range.

The forest offers fishing streams, hiking trails, groomed snowmobile trails, developed campgrounds and sites for motorized boating. Visitors can explore many old mines near Deer Lodge, plus the ghost town of Elkhorn, near Boulder, an 1880s mining town with a few corporeal residents. Fifteen miles west of Anaconda on SR 1 is Georgetown Lake *(see Recreation Areas Chart)*, one of the area's busiest recreation sites, partly due to its excellent fishing. Snowmobiling and cross-country and downhill skiing are available at Discovery Ski Area, north of Georgetown Lake, and at Maverick Mountain near Dillon.

Detailed information about campgrounds and recreational opportunities is available at the district ranger stations in Butte, Deer Lodge, Dillon, Ennis, Philipsburg, Sheridan, Whitehall, Wisdom and Wise River. For further information contact the Beaverhead-Deerlodge National Forest Supervisor's Office, 420 Barrett St., Dillon, MT 59725; phone (406) 683-3900. *See Recreation Areas Chart.*

BELGRADE   pop. 7,389

HOLIDAY INN EXPRESS & SUITES BELGRADE
406/388-7100

Hotel
Rates not provided

Address: 309 W Madison Ave 59714 **Location:** I-90 exit 298, just n on SR 85. **Facility:** 97 units. 3 stories, interior corridors. **Parking:** winter plug-ins. **Amenities:** safes. **Pool:** heated indoor. **Activities:** hot tub, exercise room. **Guest Services:** valet and coin laundry, area transportation. **Featured Amenity:** full hot breakfast.

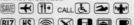

LA QUINTA INN & SUITES BELGRADE/BOZEMAN
(406)388-2222

Hotel. **Address:** 6445 Jackrabbit Ln 59714

QUALITY INN
(406)388-0800

Hotel
$69-$159

Address: 6261 Jackrabbit Ln 59714 **Location:** I-90 exit 298, just s on SR 85. **Facility:** 67 units. 3 stories, interior corridors. **Parking:** winter plug-ins. **Activities:** exercise room. **Guest Services:** coin laundry. **Featured Amenity:** breakfast buffet.

SUPER 8-BELGRADE/BOZEMAN AIRPORT   (406)388-1493
♥♥ Hotel. **Address:** 6450 Jackrabbit Ln 59714

WHERE TO EAT

FIESTA MEXICANA   406/388-8887
♥♥ Mexican. Casual Dining. **Address:** 6220 Jackrabbit Ln 59714

GALLATIN RIVER GRILL   406/388-0148
♥♥♥ Regional American. Casual Dining. **Address:** 9105 Thorpe Rd 59718

MACKENZIE RIVER PIZZA   406/388-0016
♥♥ Pizza. Casual Dining. **Address:** 409 W Main St 59714

THE WOK   406/388-2838
♥♥ Chinese. Casual Dining. **Address:** 312 W Main St, Suite B-10 59714

BIGFORK (B-2) pop. 4,270, elev. 2,968'

On the bay formed by the Swan River on the northeastern shore of Flathead Lake, Bigfork once was a small fishing village and trade center for nearby orchards and farms. Its reputation as an artists' and writers' colony now makes it a popular cultural retreat. Among recreational pursuits are snowmobiling and skiing in winter and a host of water sports in summer.

Glacially formed Flathead Lake (see place listing p. 107) is the largest natural body of fresh water west of the Mississippi River; at points along its 38-mile length the lake stretches 15 miles wide. Jewel Basin, one of the country's most popular hiking areas with 35 miles of trails, is 11 miles north. A Flathead National Forest (see place listing p. 107) ranger station provides information about recreational opportunities in the nearby mountains.

Cultural highlights in Bigfork include the Riverbend Concert Series, which stages Sunday performances throughout the summer. From mid-May through Labor Day, Bigfork Summer Playhouse presents a regular repertory of Broadway musicals; phone (406) 837-4886 for ticket information.

Bigfork Area Chamber of Commerce: 8155 Hwy. 35, P.O. Box 237, Bigfork, MT 59911. **Phone:** (406) 837-5888.

BRIDGE STREET COTTAGES   406/837-2785
♥♥♥ Cottage. **Address:** 309 Bridge St 59911

MOUNTAIN LAKE LODGE   406/837-3800
♥♥♥ Hotel. **Address:** 14735 Sylvan Dr 59911

TIMBERS MOTEL   406/837-6200
♥♥ Motel. **Address:** 8540 Hwy 35 59911

WHERE TO EAT

ECHO LAKE CAFE   406/837-4252
♥♥ Breakfast. Casual Dining. **Address:** 1195 Swan Hwy (SR 83) 59911

EL TOPO CANTINA   406/837-2114
♥♥ Mexican. Casual Dining. **Address:** 7987 SR 35 59911

SHOWTHYME!   406/837-0707
♥♥♥ American. Fine Dining. **Address:** 548 Electric Ave 59911

WHEN IN ROME   406/837-7663
♥♥ Mediterranean Pizza. Casual Dining. **Address:** 8270 Hwy 35 59911

BIG HOLE NATIONAL BATTLEFIELD (E-2)

Big Hole National Battlefield is 10 miles west of Wisdom on SR 43. Covering 655 acres of Nez Perce National Historical Park (see place listing in Idaho p. 56), the site commemorates the battle fought Aug. 9-10, 1877, when U.S. troops aided by civilian volunteers staged a surprise attack against several bands of Nez Perce Indians. The Nez Perce were attempting to escape confinement to a reservation by fleeing to Idaho Territory.

Although victorious at Big Hole, the Nez Perce sustained severe losses—approximately 90 men, women and children were killed. These losses forced their surrender 2 months later on Oct. 5, 1877, in the Bear Paw Mountains. Some 250 Nez Perce escaped to Canada.

The battlefield became a military reserve in 1883, a national monument in 1910 and a national battlefield in 1963. The visitor center displays Native American and military items and presents an audio-visual program about the battle. An observation deck features scopes for wildlife viewing. Interpretive trails traverse the battlefield to the areas where the soldiers retreated and the Nez Perce camped.

Allow 30 minutes minimum for the visitor center and 1 hour, 30 minutes for the battlefield. Battlefield open daily dawn-dusk. Visitor center open daily 9-5, late Apr.-Sept. 30; 10-5, rest of year. Phone for information about tipi-raising sessions. Guided tours are offered daily, July-Aug. Visitor center closed Jan. 1, Martin Luther King Jr. Day, Presidents Day, Columbus Day, Veterans Day, Thanksgiving and Christmas. Battlefield Road is closed to automobile traffic in winter; skiing and snowshoeing are permitted. Free. Phone (406) 689-3155.

BIGHORN CANYON NATIONAL RECREATION AREA (E-6)

In Montana and northern Wyoming, Bighorn Canyon National Recreation Area centers on a 71-mile-long lake bounded by steep canyon walls. Covering about 120,000 acres, the area features facilities for boat launching, picnicking and camping at Ok-A-Beh Marina, 42 miles southwest of Hardin via SR 313.

Horseshoe Bend in Wyoming, 14 miles north of Lovell, Wyo., via SR 37, and Barry's Landing in Montana, 32 miles south of Yellowtail Dam by boat or north of Lovell via SR 37, have areas for swimming, camping, picnicking and boat launching (personal watercraft are permitted). Hunting and fishing also are available.

Admission to the recreation area is $5 for a daily pass. Yellowtail Dam Visitor Center in Fort Smith offers an orientation film about the area as well as exhibits about wildlife, Native American culture and the construction of Yellowtail Dam, said to be the highest dam in the Missouri River Basin. The center is open daily 8:30-5, Memorial Day to Labor Day. Phone (406) 666-9961.

The Bighorn Canyon Visitor Center, at the junction of US 310 and US 14A in Lovell is open daily 8-6, Memorial Day-Labor Day; 8:30-4:30, rest of year. Closed Jan. 1, Thanksgiving and Christmas. Phone (307) 548-5406.

For further information, contact Bighorn Canyon National Recreation Area, P.O. Box 7458, Fort Smith, MT 59035 or 20 US 14A E., Lovell, WY 82431; to verify schedule phone (406) 666-2412 or (307) 548-5406. *See Recreation Areas Chart.*

BIG SKY (E-3) pop. 2,308, elev. 7,218'
• **Hotels & Restaurants map & index p. 220**
• **Part of Yellowstone National Park area — see map p. 214**

Surrounded by the mountain meadows and forested slopes of Gallatin National Forest *(see place listing p. 109)* and the Spanish Peaks Wilderness, Big Sky is an all-year resort community. Lone Mountain serves as the centerpiece for this village conceived and developed by newsman Chet Huntley.

Skiing and snowmobiling are popular in winter, while summer activity revolves around hiking, horseback riding, white-water rafting and mountain biking.

THE LODGE AT BIG SKY   406/995-7858 **23**
▼▼▼ Hotel. **Address:** 75 Sitting Bull Rd 59716

RAINBOW RANCH LODGE   406/995-4132 **24**
▼▼▼ Resort Hotel. **Address:** 42950 Gallatin Rd 59730

WHERE TO EAT

BUCK'S T-4   406/993-5222 **15**
▼▼▼ Regional American. Fine Dining. **Address:** 46625 Gallatin Rd 59716

THE CABIN BAR & GRILL   406/995-4244 **13**
▼▼ Regional American. Casual Dining. **Address:** Big Sky's Mountain Village 59716

THE CORRAL STEAKHOUSE   406/995-4249 **16**

▼▼ ▼
Steak
Casual Dining
$9-$35

AAA Inspector Notes: Comfort food is served in a Western setting at this local favorite that features a large dining/lounge area. A varied menu offers finger foods to full meals including sandwiches, beef or buffalo burgers, fried chicken, rainbow trout, walleye pike and cod, pork chops, pasta and a selection of steaks. **Features:** full bar. **Address:** 42895 Gallatin Rd 59730 **Location:** 5 mi s on US 191. **B** **L** **D**

LOTUS PAD   406/995-2728 **14**
▼▼ Thai. Casual Dining. **Address:** 47 Town Center Ave, Suite D-1 59716

RAINBOW RANCH LODGE   406/995-4132 **17**
▼▼▼ Regional American. Fine Dining. **Address:** 42950 Gallatin Rd 59736

BILLINGS (E-5) pop. 104,170, elev. 3,124'
• **Restaurants p. 98**

In 1823 at Alkali Creek, the site of present-day Billings, 400 Blackfeet attacked American Fur Co. trappers. Some pelts taken by the Blackfeet were traded to Hudson's Bay Co. and later appeared on the London market. An American recognized the stolen pelts, touching off an international incident.

The Northern Pacific Railroad arrived in 1882, literally putting Billings on the map. Refusing to pay the exorbitant prices the landowners in Coulson were demanding, Northern Pacific Railroad laid out a new city 2 miles upriver and named it in honor of its president, Frederick Billings. In 5 months the town grew from a single building to 250 buildings and 2,000 citizens.

The Rimrocks, Billings' most striking natural feature, rise 500 feet above the Yellowstone Valley, running the length of the city and beyond. Legend has it that Crow warriors once rode over Sacrifice Cliff to appease their gods and to halt the spread of smallpox among their people. At the bottom of Chief Black Otter Trail is Boothill Cemetery. The only vestige of the town of Coulson, the cemetery is the final resting place of two dozen individuals, including peace officers, massacre victims and Muggins Taylor, the scout who brought the world the news of Lt. Col. George Armstrong Custer's last stand.

Pictograph Cave State Park, 7 miles southeast at the I-90 Lockwood exit, features caverns that have sheltered people of many Native American cultures. Pictorial records adorn the walls of one cave.

▼ MontanaFair is a 9-day agricultural celebration beginning the second week in August. Exhibits, music, food, entertainment, a carnival and petting zoo add to the experience. One of the region's largest events, the fair is held annually in MetraPark.

Billings Chamber of Commerce/Visit Billings: 815 S. 27th St., P.O. Box 31177, Billings, MT 59107-1177. **Phone:** (406) 245-4111.

Self-guiding tours: A map of historic sites can be obtained at the chamber of commerce.

Shopping: Rimrock Mall, at the junction of Central Avenue and 24th Street West, includes Dillard's and JCPenney among its 95 stores.

MOSS MANSION is at 914 Division St. An Old World-style house designed by architect H.J. Hardenbergh, this massive red sandstone mansion completed in 1903 features an eclectic décor with original carpet and drapes, ornate ceilings and handmade light fixtures. The Moss family occupied the house until 1984 and left the interior intact. The three-story mansion is an unusually complete example of early 20th-century decorative arts.

Hours: Tues.-Sat. 10-4, Sun. 1-3, June 1-Aug. 31. Guided 1-hour tours Fri.-Sat. at 1. Closed Jan. 1, Jan. 10-31, Easter, July 4, Nov. 1-15, Thanksgiving and Christmas. **Cost:** $12; $15 (with guided tour). **Phone:** (406) 256-5100 to confirm schedule. **GT**

YELLOWSTONE ART MUSEUM is at 401 N. 27th St. Housed in the original Yellowstone County jail, the museum offers changing exhibitions of historic and contemporary art. Boundless Visions tells the story of art in Montana with interactive exhibits and works from the museum's 7,500-piece permanent collection. **Time:** Allow 30 minutes minimum. **Hours:** Tues.-Sun. 10-5 (also Thurs.-Fri. 5-8). **Cost:** $15; $12 (ages 65+); $6 (ages 6-18 and college students with ID). Reservations are required for guided tours. **Phone:** (406) 256-6804. GT

BEST WESTERN PLUS CLOCKTOWER INN
(406)259-5511

Hotel
$75-$200

AAA Benefit: Members save up to 15% and earn bonus points!

Address: 2511 1st Ave N 59101 **Location:** On I-90 business loop; downtown. **Facility:** 126 units, some kitchens. 1-3 stories, interior/exterior corridors. **Parking:** winter plug-ins. **Terms:** cancellation fee imposed. **Pool:** heated outdoor. **Activities:** sauna, exercise room. **Guest Services:** valet and coin laundry. **Featured Amenity: full hot breakfast.**

BEST WESTERN PLUS KELLY INN & SUITES
(406)256-9400

Hotel
$140-$180

AAA Benefit: Members save up to 15% and earn bonus points!

Address: 4915 Southgate Dr 59101 **Location:** I-90 exit 447, just w. Across from family fun park. **Facility:** 89 units. 3 stories, interior/exterior corridors. **Parking:** winter plug-ins. **Terms:** check-in 4 pm, cancellation fee imposed, resort fee. **Pool:** heated indoor. **Activities:** hot tub, exercise room. **Guest Services:** valet and coin laundry. **Featured Amenity: continental breakfast.**

BIG HORN RESORT, AN ASCEND HOTEL COLLECTION MEMBER (406)839-9300
Hotel. **Address:** 1801 Majestic Ln 59102

BILLINGS SUPER 8 (406)248-8842
Hotel. **Address:** 5400 Southgate Dr 59101

BOOTHILL INN & SUITES
406/245-2000

Hotel
Rates not provided

Address: 242 E Airport Rd 59105 **Location:** I-90 exit 452, 1.8 mi n on US 87. **Facility:** 69 units. 4 stories, interior corridors. **Parking:** winter plug-ins. **Amenities:** *Some:* safes. **Pool:** heated indoor. **Activities:** hot tub, exercise room. **Guest Services:** coin laundry, area transportation. **Featured Amenity: breakfast buffet.**

C'MON INN 406/655-1100
Hotel. **Address:** 2020 Overland Ave 59102

COUNTRY INN & SUITES BY RADISSON, BILLINGS AT METRA PARK 406/245-9995
Hotel. **Address:** 231 Main St 59105

DAYS INN (406)252-4007
Hotel. **Address:** 843 Parkway Ln 59101

DOUBLETREE BY HILTON
(406)252-7400

Hotel
$99-$289

AAA Benefit: Members save 5% or more!

Address: 27 N 27th St 59101 **Location:** I-90 business loop and SR 3. **Facility:** 289 units. 23 stories, interior corridors. **Terms:** 1-7 night minimum stay, 3 day cancellation notice-fee imposed. **Amenities:** safes. **Activities:** exercise room. **Guest Services:** valet and coin laundry, luggage security pick-up.

EXTENDED STAY AMERICA-BILLINGS-WEST END 406/245-3980
Extended Stay Hotel. **Address:** 4950 Southgate Dr 59101

FAIRFIELD INN & SUITES BY MARRIOTT-BILLINGS (406)652-5330
Hotel. **Address:** 2026 Overland Ave 59102
AAA Benefit: Members save 5% or more!

HAMPTON INN & SUITES BY HILTON 406/656-7511
Hotel. **Address:** 3550 Ember Ln 59102
AAA Benefit: Members save 5% or more!

HAMPTON INN BY HILTON 406/248-4949
Hotel. **Address:** 5110 Southgate Dr 59101
AAA Benefit: Members save 5% or more!

HILLTOP INN BY RIVERSAGE 406/245-5000
Hotel. **Address:** 1116 N 28th St 59101

HILTON GARDEN INN BILLINGS
(406)655-8800

Hotel
$119-$209

AAA Benefit: Members save 5% or more!

Address: 2465 Grant Rd 59102 **Location:** I-90 exit 446, 1.5 mi w, just s on S 24th St W, then just w. **Facility:** 128 units. 5 stories, interior corridors. **Parking:** winter plug-ins. **Terms:** 1-7 night minimum stay, 3 day cancellation notice-fee imposed. **Pool:** heated indoor. **Activities:** hot tub, exercise room. **Guest Services:** valet and coin laundry.

HOLIDAY INN EXPRESS & SUITES 406/652-0111
Hotel. **Address:** 3431 Ember Ln 59102

HOLIDAY INN EXPRESS BILLINGS
406/259-8600
◆◆◆ Hotel. **Address:** 430 Cole St 59101

HOME2 SUITES BY HILTON
406/252-2255
◆◆◆ Extended Stay Hotel. **Address:** 2611 7th Ave 59101

AAA Benefit:
Members save 5%
or more!

HOMEWOOD SUITES BY HILTON
406/656-0525
◆◆◆ Extended Stay Hotel. **Address:** 3420 Ember Ln 59102

AAA Benefit:
Members save 5%
or more!

KELLY INN
406/248-9800
◆◆ Hotel. **Address:** 5610 S Frontage Rd 59101

LA QUINTA INN & SUITES
(406)252-1188
◆◆◆ Hotel. **Address:** 5720 S Frontage Rd 59101

MY PLACE HOTEL
406/259-9970
◆◆ Extended Stay Hotel. **Address:** 4770 King Ave E 59101

QUALITY INN HOMESTEAD
(406)652-1320
◆◆ Hotel. **Address:** 2036 Overland Ave 59102

RESIDENCE INN BY MARRIOTT
(406)656-3900
◆◆◆ Extended Stay Hotel. **Address:** 956 S 25th St W 59102

AAA Benefit:
Members save 5%
or more!

RIVERSAGE BILLINGS INN
406/252-6800
◆◆ Hotel. **Address:** 880 N 29th St 59101

SURESTAY PLUS HOTEL BY BEST WESTERN BILLINGS
406/294-9090
◆◆◆ Hotel. **Address:** 3040 King Ave W 59102

TOWNEPLACE SUITES BY MARRIOTT BILLINGS
(406)652-7106

Extended Stay Hotel
$100-$197

TOWNEPLACE
—SUITES—
MARRIOTT

AAA Benefit: Members save 5% or more!

Address: 2480 Grant Rd 59102 **Location:** Jct King Ave and S 24th St W, 0.4 mi s, then just w. **Facility:** 91 units, some two bedrooms, efficiencies and kitchens. 4 stories, interior corridors. **Terms:** cancellation fee imposed. **Pool:** heated indoor. **Activities:** exercise room. **Guest Services:** valet and coin laundry. **Featured Amenity:** continental breakfast.

WESTERN EXECUTIVE INN
(406)294-8888

◆◆◆
Hotel
$100-$240

Address: 3121 King Ave W 59102 **Location:** I-90 exit 446, 2.5 mi w. **Facility:** 40 units, some kitchens. 2 stories (no elevator), interior corridors. **Parking:** winter plug-ins. **Terms:** cancellation fee imposed. **Guest Services:** valet laundry. **Featured Amenity:** full hot breakfast.

THE ATHENIAN RESTAURANT
406/248-5681
◆◆ Greek. Casual Dining. **Address:** 18 N 29th St 59101

BISTRO ENZO
406/651-0999
◆◆ Mediterranean. Casual Dining. **Address:** 1502 Rehberg Ln 59102

BRUNO'S A TASTE OF ITALY
406/652-4416
◆◆ Italian. Casual Dining. **Address:** 1911 King Ave W 59101

THE BURGER DIVE
406/281-8292
◆ Burgers. Quick Serve. **Address:** 114 N 27th St 59101

CHAM THAI CUISINE
406/256-1812
◆◆ Thai. Casual Dining. **Address:** 2916 1st Ave N 59101

CIAO MAMBO
406/325-5100
◆◆ Italian. Casual Dining. **Address:** 2301 Montana Ave 59101

C J'S BAR & GRILL
406/656-1400
◆◆ American. Casual Dining. **Address:** 2455 Central Ave 59102

DOS MACHOS RESTAURANT
406/652-2020
◆◆ Mexican. Casual Dining. **Address:** 980 S 24th St W 59102

THE FIELDHOUSE
406/534-2556
◆◆◆ American. Fine Dining. **Address:** 2601 Minnesota Ave 59101

GOLDEN PHOENIX RESTAURANT
406/256-0319
◆◆ Chinese. Casual Dining. **Address:** 279 Swords Ln 59105

INDIA GRILL
406/652-9700
◆◆ Indian. Casual Dining. **Address:** 503 N 24th St W 59102

JAKE'S BAR & GRILL
406/252-9375
◆◆ American. Casual Dining. **Address:** 2425 Gabel Rd 59102

JAKES OF BILLINGS
406/259-9375
◆◆ American. Casual Dining. **Address:** 2701 1st Ave N 59101

LILAC
406/969-4959
◆◆◆ American. Fine Dining. **Address:** 2515 Montana Ave 59102

MACKENZIE RIVER PIZZA
◆◆ Pizza. Casual Dining.
LOCATIONS:
Address: 3025 E Grand Ave 59102 **Phone:** 406/651-0068
Address: 405 W Main St 59105 **Phone:** 406/254-0066

MCCORMICK CAFE
406/255-9555
◆ American. Casual Dining. **Address:** 2419 Montana Ave 59101

MONTANA'S RIB & CHOP HOUSE
406/839-9200
◆◆ American. Casual Dining. **Address:** 1849 Majestic Ln 59102

NA RA RESTAURANT SUSHI BAR
406/245-8866
◆◆ Asian. Casual Dining. **Address:** 3 Custer Ave 59101

SIAM THAI
406/652-4315
◆◆ Thai. Casual Dining. **Address:** 3210 Henesta Dr, Suite G 59102

STELLA'S KITCHEN AND BAKERY
406/248-3060
◆◆ Breakfast Breads/Pastries. Casual Dining. **Address:** 2525 1st Ave N 59101

TAO NEW ASIAN
406/655-9898
◆◆ Asian. Casual Dining. **Address:** 900 S 24th St W 59102

UBERBREW 406/534-6960
♥♥ American. Gastropub. **Address:** 2305 Montana Ave 59101

WALKER'S GRILL 406/245-9291
♥♥♥ Regional American. Fine Dining. **Address:** 2700 1st Ave N 59101

THE WINDMILL 406/252-8100
♥♥ American. Casual Dining. **Address:** 3429 Trans Tech Way 59102

BITTERROOT NATIONAL FOREST (D-1)

Elevations in the forest range from 3,500 ft. at the Kootenai Creek Trail to 10,175 ft. on Trapper Peak. Refer to AAA maps for additional elevation information.

Bitterroot National Forest is in Montana and Idaho. The Montana section curves around the headwaters of the Bitterroot River, reaching into the Sapphire and Bitterroot ranges. This is a region of strong contrasts, with rolling subalpine woodland, open parks and lakes, and jagged, glaciated peaks and canyons.

The national forest takes its name from the bitterroot plant, whose pink flowers carpet the valleys and foothills from late April to July. Meriwether Lewis, on his journey through the region, added the bitterroot flower to his botanical collection and sampled the meal that the Native Americans ground from its root. A British botanist later honored Lewis' contribution by using his name as the basis of the flower's Latin name, *Lewisia rediviva*.

As one of the first forest reserves, Bitterroot National Forest also is the site of the nation's oldest surviving ranger station, built in Alta in 1899. The forest's Idaho portion encompasses the headwaters of the Selway River and a stretch of the Salmon River. Both rivers are components of the National Wild and Scenic River system. Portions of the Frank Church-River of No Return Wilderness, the Selway-Bitterroot Wilderness and the Anaconda-Pintler Wilderness occupy about half of the forest's 1.6 million acres. For further information contact Bitterroot National Forest, 1801 N. First St., Hamilton, MT 59840; phone (406) 363-7100. *See Recreation Areas Chart.*

BOZEMAN (E-4) pop. 37,280, elev. 4,755'
• Restaurants p. 100

Bozeman was named for John Bozeman, who brought the first wagon train of pioneers to settle the Gallatin Valley. The trail he blazed became not only a highway for settlers and miners but also a flash point between the Native Americans and the settlers. Three years after bringing settlers to the valley, Bozeman was killed by the Sioux, and his trail remained unused for 9 years because of repeated attacks upon wayfarers.

The valley that Bozeman helped settle once was a neutral and sacred hunting ground known to Native Americans as the "Valley of the Flowers." The area has blossomed into one of the state's more agriculturally productive regions.

Bozeman Area Chamber of Commerce: 2000 Commerce Way, Bozeman, MT 59715.

MUSEUM OF THE ROCKIES is on the Montana State University campus at 600 W. Kagy Blvd. Home to one of the largest dinosaur fossil collections in the United States, the museum's Siebel Dinosaur Complex features a fully mounted Tyrannosaurus rex skeleton as well as other dinosaur specimens, dinosaur eggs, nests and sculptures. Other exhibits include the Paugh History Hall, which offers an array of regional artifacts; Welcome to Yellowstone Country showcases the history of tourism in the national park and examines the life and culture of Native Americans from the Northern Plains and Rockies; the Living History Farm (open in the summer only), a historically accurate, late-1800s Montana homestead; and the Martin Children's Discovery Center.

The museum also features the Taylor Planetarium, which presents a breathtaking journey through the cosmos. **Hours:** Daily 8-6, Memorial Day weekend-Labor Day; Daily 9-5, rest of year. Planetarium shows are given daily. Closed Jan. 1, Thanksgiving and Christmas. **Cost:** Museum (includes planetarium) $14.50; $13.50 (ages 65+); $9.50 (ages 5-17). **Phone:** (406) 994-2251.

BEST WESTERN PLUS GRANTREE INN (406)587-5261

♥♥♥ Hotel $99-$399

Best Western PLUS. **AAA Benefit:** Members save up to 15% and earn bonus points!

Address: 1325 N 7th Ave 59715 **Location:** I-90 exit 306, just s. **Facility:** 120 units. 2 stories, interior corridors. **Parking:** winter plug-ins. **Terms:** cancellation fee imposed. **Amenities:** safes. **Pool:** heated indoor. **Activities:** hot tub, exercise room. **Guest Services:** valet and coin laundry, area transportation.

/ SOME UNITS 🦌

BOZEMAN DAYS INN & SUITES (406)587-5251
♥♥ Hotel. **Address:** 1321 N 7th Ave 59715

C'MON INN 406/587-3555
♥♥♥ Hotel. **Address:** 6139 E Valley Center Rd 59718

COMFORT INN OF BOZEMAN (406)587-2322
♥♥♥ Hotel. **Address:** 1370 N 7th Ave 59715

COMFORT SUITES BOZEMAN (406)587-0800
♥♥♥ Hotel. **Address:** 2515 Catamount St 59718

COUNTRY INN & SUITES BY RADISSON - BOZEMAN
406/586-2230

Hotel
Rates not provided

Address: 5997 E Valley Center Rd 59715 **Location:** I-90 exit 305, 0.3 mi s on 19th Ave. **Facility:** 79 units. 4 stories, interior corridors. **Parking:** winter plug-ins. **Pool:** heated indoor. **Activities:** hot tub, exercise room. **Guest Services:** coin laundry. **Featured Amenity:** breakfast buffet.

ELEMENT BOZEMAN
(406)582-4972

Hotel
$90-$307

AAA Benefit: Members save 5% or more!

Address: 25 E Mendenhall St 59715 **Location:** Jct US 191 and SR 86, just w. **Facility:** 104 units, some efficiencies. 5 stories, interior corridors. **Parking:** winter plug-ins. **Terms:** cancellation fee imposed. **Amenities:** safes. **Pool:** heated indoor. **Activities:** exercise room. **Guest Services:** valet and coin laundry, area transportation.

HAMPTON INN BY HILTON
(406)522-8000

Hotel
$102-$272

AAA Benefit: Members save 5% or more!

Address: 75 Baxter Ln 59715 **Location:** I-90 exit 306, just s, then just n. **Facility:** 70 units. 2 stories, interior corridors. **Parking:** winter plug-ins. **Terms:** 1-7 night minimum stay, 3 day cancellation notice-fee imposed. **Pool:** heated indoor. **Activities:** hot tub, exercise room. **Guest Services:** valet and coin laundry. **Featured Amenity:** continental breakfast.

HILTON GARDEN INN
406/582-9900

Hotel. **Address:** 2023 Commerce Way 59715

AAA Benefit: Members save 5% or more!

HOLIDAY INN EXPRESS & SUITES
406/582-4995

Hotel. **Address:** 2305 Catron St 59718

HOMEWOOD SUITES BY HILTON BOZEMAN
406/587-8180

Extended Stay Hotel. **Address:** 1023 Baxter Ln 59715

AAA Benefit: Members save 5% or more!

HOWLERS INN BED & BREAKFAST
(406)587-5229

Bed & Breakfast. **Address:** 3185 Jackson Creek Rd 59715

LA QUINTA INN & SUITES
(406)585-9300

Hotel. **Address:** 620 Nikles Dr 59715

THE LARK
406/624-3064

Boutique Contemporary Hotel. **Address:** 122 W Main St 59715

MOTEL 6 BOZEMAN #4818
406/585-7888

Hotel. **Address:** 817 Wheat Dr 59718

MOUNTAINVIEW LODGE & SUITES
406/522-8686

Hotel. **Address:** 1121 Reeves Rd W 59718

MY PLACE HOTEL
406/586-8228

Extended Stay Hotel. **Address:** 5889 E Valley Center Rd 59718

RAMADA
(406)585-2626

Hotel
$60-$140

Address: 2020 Wheat Dr 59715 **Location:** I-90 exit 306, just n, then just w. **Facility:** 50 units. 2 stories (no elevator), interior/exterior corridors. **Parking:** winter plug-ins. **Terms:** 3 day cancellation notice-fee imposed. **Pool:** heated indoor. **Activities:** hot tub, exercise room. **Guest Services:** valet and coin laundry.

SPRINGHILL SUITES BOZEMAN
(406)586-5200

Hotel. **Address:** 1601 Baxter Ln 59715

AAA Benefit: Members save 5% or more!

SUPER 8
(406)586-1521

Hotel. **Address:** 800 Wheat Dr 59715

WESTERN HERITAGE INN-TRAVELODGE BY WYNDHAM
(406)586-8534

Hotel
$79-$199

Address: 1200 E Main St 59715 **Location:** I-90 exit 309 (Main St), 0.5 mi w. **Facility:** 38 units, some efficiencies and kitchens. 3 stories (no elevator), interior corridors. **Parking:** winter plug-ins. **Terms:** resort fee. **Amenities:** safes. **Activities:** hot tub, steamroom. **Guest Services:** coin laundry. **Featured Amenity:** continental breakfast.

WHERE TO EAT

14 NORTH
406/404-1800

American. Gastropub. **Address:** 14 N Church Ave 59715

BIANKINI'S THE SANDWICH AND SALAD MARKET
406/587-2405

Sandwiches. Quick Serve. **Address:** 2051 Oak St 59718

CHINATOWN RESTAURANT
406/587-5168

Chinese. Casual Dining. **Address:** 1228 W Main St 59715

CO-OP DOWNTOWN
406/922-2667

Sandwiches. Quick Serve. **Address:** 44 E Main St 59715

COPPER WHISKEY BAR & GRILL
406/404-1700

American. Gastropub. **Address:** 101 E Main St 59715

THE GARAGE
406/585-8558

American. Casual Dining. **Address:** 451 E Main St 59715

LA PARILLA   406/582-9511
▼ Fusion. Quick Serve. **Address:** 1624 W Babcock St 59771

MACKENZIE RIVER PIZZA   406/587-0055
▼▼ Pizza. Casual Dining. **Address:** 232 E Main St 59715

MAIN STREET OVEREASY   406/587-3205
▼ American. Casual Dining. **Address:** 9 E Main St 59715

MONTANA ALE WORKS   406/587-7700
▼▼ American. Casual Dining. **Address:** 611 E Main St 59715

THE NAKED NOODLE   406/585-4501

Noodles Specialty Quick Serve $7-$14

AAA Inspector Notes: This restaurant features an eclectic décor and a great dining concept. Diners choose from seven varieties of pasta, including gluten-free, to add to your favorite sauce, meats, vegetables, seafood and other toppings to create a delicious meal. Can't decide? Choose one of the many tried-and-true combinations or salads posted on the board. **Address:** 27 S Willson Ave 59715 **Location:** Just s; center. **Parking:** on-site and street. [L] [D]

THE NOVA CAFE   406/587-3973
▼▼ American. Casual Dining. **Address:** 312 E Main St 59715

RICE   406/404-1196
▼▼ Thai. Casual Dining. **Address:** 140 E Main St 59715

ROOST FRIED CHICKEN   406/404-1475
▼ Chicken. Quick Serve. **Address:** 1520 W Main St 59715

SAFFRON TABLE   406/586-0800
▼▼▼ Indian. Casual Dining. **Address:** 1511 W Babcock St 59715

SIDEWINDERS AMERICAN GRILL   406/587-8387
▼▼ American. Casual Dining. **Address:** 780 Boardwalk Ave 59715

SOLA CAFE   406/922-7652
▼ Deli Breads/Pastries. Quick Serve. **Address:** 290 W Kagy Blvd 59715

SOUTH 9TH BISTRO   406/404-1244
▼▼▼ American. Casual Dining. **Address:** 721 S 9th Ave 59715

SWEET CHILI - ASIAN BISTRO   406/582-1188
▼▼ Asian. Casual Dining. **Address:** 101 E Main St, Unit 1 59715

BROWNING (B-2) pop. 1,016, elev. 4,366'
• Part of Glacier National Park area — see map
p. 111

Founded in 1895, Browning is the hub of the Blackfeet Nation and a center for reservation activities. It also is the site of the Blackfeet Tribal Headquarters, which includes a nine-member business council, the governing board of the Blackfeet Tribe. Fifteen miles east on the reservation, a monument marks the northernmost point reached by the Lewis and Clark expedition on July 23, 1806. About 7,000 Native Americans live on the Blackfeet Indian Reservation, which covers 1.5 million acres.

BUTTE (E-3) elev. 5,716'
• Hotels p. 102 • Restaurants p. 103

Silver Bow Creek's gold and silver first brought the mineral wealth of remote Butte to the attention of the world. But it was copper that made Butte's reputation as "the richest hill on Earth," producing more

than 20 billion pounds of the metal. "Copper kings" fought for control of Butte's wealth; Marcus Daly's Anaconda Copper Mining Co. eventually gained ownership of every mine in Butte and became the dominant power in Montana.

By 1955, the high-grade copper ore was almost played out and excavation began on Berkeley Open Pit Mine to extract low-grade ore. The mine was one of the larger truck-operated pit mines in the world. The Berkeley Pit Viewing Stand, open daily dawn to dusk from March to mid-November, is $2 for adults and $1 for children and provides an excellent view of the old open mine. As a transportation hub, the city has become one of the nation's larger inland ports, with containerized cargo from the Orient being cleared and routed to points throughout the Midwest.

The Anselmo Mine Yard, uptown at Caledonia and Excelsior streets, is a fine example of surface support facilities that once served the miners. An interpretive center and tours are offered during the summer. The Granite Mountain Mine Memorial, 1308 N. Main St., is dedicated to the 168 men who died in a 1917 mine disaster.

Butte's historic district contains a large concentration of late 19th- and early 20th-century residential and commercial buildings as well as mining relics such as the steel headframes used to lower miners to a network of more than 2,000 miles of tunnels under "the hill."

Butte is surrounded by Beaverhead-Deerlodge National Forest *(see place listing p. 94)*, which offers varied recreational opportunities. Visitors can experience the beauty of the nearby rugged mountains, verdant forests and meadows by driving either north to Helena or south to Monida on I-15.

Butte-Silver Bow Chamber of Commerce and Visitor Center: 1000 George St., Butte, MT 59701. **Phone:** (406) 723-3177 or (800) 735-6814.

Self-guiding tours: Brochures detailing two walking tours of the historic district are available at the chamber of commerce and visitor center.

BUTTE TROLLEY TOUR departs from the Butte-Silver Bow Chamber of Commerce and Visitor Center; take I-90 exit 126 to 1000 George St. These narrated tours relate the city's history. Sites include the Berkeley Pit Viewing Stand and Butte's historic district.

Time: Allow 1 hour, 30 minutes minimum. **Hours:** Tours are given Mon.-Sat. at 10, 12:30 and 3, Sun. at 10 and 12:30, June 1-Labor Day; daily at 12:30, day after Labor Day-Sept. 30. Phone ahead to confirm schedule. **Cost:** $17; $15 (ages 65+); $12 (ages 12-17); $8 (ages 4-11). Fares may vary; phone ahead. **Phone:** (406) 723-3177 or (800) 735-6814.

SAVE **CHARLES W. CLARK CHATEAU** is at 321 W. Broadway. Built in 1898, the residence of Charles W. Clark, eldest son of "copper king" William A. Clark, was modeled after a French château.

Today the building displays exhibits about Butte history and hosts Montana artists in its galleries. Exhibits change periodically. Evening events such as lectures, theater, readings by local authors, live music and dance classes also are offered. **Time:** Allow 1 hour minimum. **Hours:** Thurs.-Sun. noon-4, June-Sept; phone for schedule, rest of year. **Cost:** General admission $7; $5 (ages 65+, and students and military with ID); $25 family (up to five people). Admission with tour $10; $7 (ages 65+, and students and military with ID); $35 family (up to five people). **Phone:** (406) 565-5600.

COPPER KING MANSION is at 219 W. Granite St. The 34-room Victorian house was the residence of William A. Clark, a U.S. senator and "copper king." Now a national historic landmark and bed and breakfast, the restored 1884-88 mansion is furnished in period and serves as a showcase for numerous collections. **Time:** Allow 1 hour minimum. **Hours:** Guided tours are given daily 10-4, May-Sept. **Cost:** $10; $5 (ages 6-14). **Phone:** (406) 782-7580. GT

OUR LADY OF THE ROCKIES is atop the Continental Divide; tours to the site depart from the Plaza Mall, 3100 Harrison Ave. The 90-foot-high statue of the Virgin Mary—a nondenominational tribute to motherhood—took 6 years to build and was airlifted into place in 1985. Visitors may step inside the metal structure. The road to the statue is not open to public traffic. A chapel observatory is available.

Hours: Bus tours lasting 2.5 hours depart daily at 10 and 2, June-Oct. (weather permitting). Reservations are required. **Cost:** $16; $14 (ages 55+); $12 (ages 13-17); $8 (ages 5-12); $2 (ages 0-4). **Phone:** (406) 782-1221 or (800) 800-5239.

SAVE **WORLD MUSEUM OF MINING,** 155 Museum Way, is on the grounds of the Orphan Girl Mine, which operated 1875-1956. The 50-plus structures on the 44-acre site range from a 100-foot-high headframe to the many buildings of Hell Roarin' Gulch, an 1890s mining town. Visitors learn about the evolution of mining technology and about the mining town's culture and ethnic history. A 90-minute underground mine tour is offered.

Time: Allow 2 hours minimum. **Hours:** Complex open Mon.-Fri. 9-6, Sun. 10-6, Apr.-Oct. Last admission at 5. Phone ahead for tour times. **Cost:** Museum only $8.50; $7.50 (ages 65+); $5 (ages 5-17). Museum and underground mine tour $21 (to 100-foot level); $19 (to 65-foot level). Space is limited on the mine tour, so reservations are recommended. **Phone:** (406) 723-7211. GT ⊞

AMERICAS BEST VALUE INN   406/723-5464
🛢🛢 Motel. **Address:** 122001 W Brown's Gulch Rd 59701

BEST WESTERN PLUS BUTTE PLAZA INN
(406)494-3500

🛢🛢🛢
Hotel
$112-$155

AAA Benefit: Members save up to 15% and earn bonus points!

Address: 2900 Harrison Ave 59701 **Location:** I-90/15 exit 127 (Harrison Ave), just s. **Facility:** 133 units. 2 stories, interior corridors. **Parking:** winter plug-ins. **Terms:** cancellation fee imposed. **Pool:** heated indoor. **Activities:** sauna, hot tub, exercise room. **Guest Services:** coin laundry, area transportation.

/SOME UNITS 🐾 HS

CLARION INN COPPER KING CONVENTION CENTER
(406)565-5001
🛢🛢🛢 Hotel. **Address:** 4655 Harrison Ave 59701

COMFORT INN OF BUTTE   (406)494-8850

🛢🛢
Hotel
$99-$150

Address: 2777 Harrison Ave 59701 **Location:** I-90/15 exit 127 (Harrison Ave), just s. **Facility:** 144 units, some efficiencies. 3 stories, interior corridors. **Parking:** winter plug-ins. **Pool:** heated indoor. **Activities:** sauna, hot tub, exercise room. **Guest Services:** coin laundry, area transportation. **Featured Amenity:** full hot breakfast.

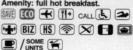

/SOME UNITS 🐾

FAIRFIELD INN & SUITES BY MARRIOTT - BUTTE
(406)494-3000
🛢🛢🛢 Hotel. **Address:** 2340 Cornell Ave 59701   **AAA Benefit:** Members save 5% or more!

FINLEN HOTEL   406/723-5461
🛢🛢 Hotel. **Address:** 100 E Broadway 59701

HAMPTON INN BY HILTON   (406)494-2250

🛢🛢
Hotel
$109-$193

AAA Benefit: Members save 5% or more!

Address: 3499 Harrison Ave 59701 **Location:** I-90/15 exit 127 (Harrison Ave), 0.6 mi s. **Facility:** 91 units. 3 stories, interior corridors. **Parking:** winter plug-ins. **Terms:** 1-7 night minimum stay, 3 day cancellation notice-fee imposed. **Pool:** heated indoor. **Activities:** hot tub, exercise room. **Guest Services:** valet and coin laundry, area transportation. **Featured Amenity:** breakfast buffet.

HOLIDAY INN EXPRESS HOTEL & SUITES BUTTE
406/782-2000
🛢🛢🛢 Hotel. **Address:** 2609 Harrison Ave 59701

LA QUINTA INN & SUITES   (406)494-6999
🛢🛢🛢 Hotel. **Address:** 1 Holiday Park Dr 59701

SUPER 8 OF BUTTE   (406)494-6000
WW Hotel. **Address:** 2929 Harrison Ave 59701

WHERE TO EAT

BROADWAY CAFE   406/723-8711
WW Pizza Natural/Organic. Casual Dining. **Address:** 302 E Broadway 59701

CASAGRANDA'S STEAKHOUSE   406/723-4141
WW American. Casual Dining. **Address:** 800 S Utah Ave 59701

CHRISTINA'S COCINA CAFE   406/723-8444
WW Tex-Mex. Casual Dining. **Address:** 2201 Silver Bow Blvd 59701

FRED'S MESQUITE GRILL   406/723-4440
WW American. Casual Dining. **Address:** 205 S Arizona St 59701

MATT'S PLACE DRIVE IN   406/782-8049
W American. Casual Dining. **Address:** 2339 Placer St 59701

METALS SPORTS BAR & GRILL   406/782-5534
WW American. Casual Dining. **Address:** 8 W Park St 59701

THE MONTANA CLUB   406/494-1400
WW Regional American. Casual Dining. **Address:** 3540 Harrison Ave 59701

MONTANA'S RIB & CHOP HOUSE   406/494-9200
WW American. Casual Dining. **Address:** 4655 Harrison Ave 59701

SOHO ASIAN CUISINE   406/221-7288
WW Chinese. Casual Dining. **Address:** 60 1/2 E Broadway 59701

UPTOWN CAFE   406/723-4735
WW Continental. Casual Dining. **Address:** 47 E Broadway St 59701

CHARLO (C-2) pop. 379, elev. 2,936'

NINEPIPES MUSEUM OF EARLY MONTANA is at 40962 US 93. The extensive and in-depth collections include examples of antique and contemporary beadwork and quillwork, photographs dating from the late 1800s, Western artwork by such notables as Charles M. Russell and E.S. Paxson, and period Western and Native American clothing. A large diorama includes mounted specimens. **Time:** Allow 1 hour minimum. **Hours:** Mon.-Sat. 9-5, Apr. 1-late Nov. Phone ahead to confirm schedule. **Cost:** $5; $4.50 (senior citizens); $4 (students with ID); $2.50 (ages 4-12). **Phone:** (406) 644-3435.

CHINOOK (B-5) pop. 1,203, elev. 2,405'

Chinook was named after the Native American word for the winds that often whip through this area during January and February, causing the temperature to rise as much as 70 degrees in a few hours. Melting the snow and exposing the grass, chinooks have saved many cattle herds from disaster. Charles M. Russell captured the significance of these winds to the range cattleman in his picture of a starving cow titled "Waiting for a Chinook."

BEAR PAW BATTLEFIELD-NEZ PERCE NATIONAL HISTORICAL PARK is off US 2, 16 mi. s. on CR 240, following signs. Chief Joseph, leader of

the Nez Perce Indians, surrendered to Col. Nelson A. Miles on this site Oct. 5, 1877. A 1.5-mile walking trail is available. Blaine County Museum serves as the park's visitor center. **Hours:** Daily dawn-dusk. **Cost:** Free. **Phone:** (406) 357-3130, or (406) 357-2590 for the Blaine County Museum. GT AT

CHOTEAU (C-3) pop. 1,684, elev. 4,000'

Choteau (SHO-toe) was named after French fur trader Pierre Chouteau; the name is spelled with one "u" to distinguish it from the adjoining county, also named after the Frenchman.

Choteau Chamber of Commerce: 815 Main Ave. N., P.O. Box 897, Choteau, MT 59422. **Phone:** (406) 466-5316 or (800) 823-3866.

CHOTEAU STAGE STOP INN   (406)466-5900

WW
Hotel
$109-$150

Address: 1005 N Main Ave 59422 **Location:** On US 89, north of town center. **Facility:** 77 units. 2-3 stories, interior corridors. **Parking:** winter plug-ins. **Pool:** heated indoor. **Activities:** hot tub, exercise room. **Guest Services:** coin laundry. **Featured Amenity: full hot breakfast.**

SAVE [Y] CALL [&] [↝] [♨] BIZ
[🛜] [✕] [📞] [🍴] [💻]

WHERE TO EAT

JOHN HENRY'S   406/466-5642
W American. Casual Dining. **Address:** 215 N Main St 59422

COLUMBIA FALLS (B-2) pop. 4,688, elev. 3,098'

• Hotels p. 104 • Restaurants p. 104
• Hotels & Restaurants map & index p. 116
• Part of Glacier National Park area — see map p. 111

The union of the North and Middle forks of the Flathead River has carved out Bad Rock Canyon, at the entrance of which lies Columbia Falls. The abundance of water and timber in the area supports Weyerhaeuser Company (formerly Plum Creek Timber Co).

Numerous recreational opportunities are available along scenic CR 486, which follows the North Fork of the Flathead River 20 miles north to the Camas Creek entrance to Glacier National Park. Hungry Horse Dam *(see Glacier National Park p. 114)* and the Great Bear and Bob Marshall wilderness areas also are nearby.

SAVE **BIG SKY WATERPARK** is 2 blks. w. of jct. US 2 and SR 206 at 7211 US 2 E. Among the park's amusements are several waterslides, including a family-friendly tube slide; a miniature golf course; bumper cars; an antique carousel; a rock-climbing wall; a "water wars" balloon game; and a video arcade. **Time:** Allow 2 hours minimum. **Hours:** Daily 11-7, July 1 to mid-Aug.; 11-6, mid-June through June 30 and mid-Aug. through Labor

(See map & index p. 116.)

Day. Phone ahead to confirm schedule. **Cost:** Waterpark $27.99; $22.99 (ages 60+ and under 48 inches tall). Waterpark after 3 p.m. $22.99; $17.99 (ages 60+ and under 48 inches tall). Miniature golf $9. **Phone:** (406) 892-5026. 🍽️ 🏕️

BAD ROCK BED & BREAKFAST   (406)892-2829   **9**
💎💎💎 Bed & Breakfast. **Address:** 480 Bad Rock Dr 59912

CEDAR CREEK LODGE & CONFERENCE CENTER
406/897-7070   **7**
💎💎💎 Hotel. **Address:** 930 2nd Ave W 59912

GLACIER TRAVEL INN   406/892-0888   **8**
💎💎 Hotel. **Address:** 7336 US 2 E 59912

MEADOW LAKE RESORT   406/892-8700   **5**
💎💎💎 Vacation Rental Condominium. **Address:** 100 St Andrews Dr 59912

MEADOW LAKE VIEW BED & BREAKFAST
406/892-0900   **4**
💎💎 Bed & Breakfast. **Address:** 180 Meadow Lake Dr 59912

NORTH FORTY RESORT ·   (406)862-7740   **6**
💎💎 Cabin. **Address:** 3765 Hwy 40 W 59912

WHERE TO EAT

THE BACK ROOM/NITE OWL RESTAURANTS
406/892-2191   **4**

💎💎
American Casual Dining
$8-$26

AAA Inspector Notes: Here you're treated to two eateries in one building. The casual Back Room opens at 4 p.m. and features excellent barbecue, steaks and seafood with few frills. Dedicated carnivores can sample any of three styles of ribs served with fry bread. The Nite Owl, open early morning through evening, serves hearty breakfasts all day and comfort foods such as meatloaf and fried chicken. **Features:** full bar, patio dining. **Address:** 522 9th St W 59912 **Location:** Just w of downtown. B L D

LAURIE'S DELI   406/892-2711   **5**
💎 American. Quick Serve. **Address:** 330 9th St W 59912

COOKE CITY (F-4) pop. 75, elev. 7,675'
• Hotels & Restaurants map & index p. 220
• Part of Yellowstone National Park area — see map p. 214

Gold miners settled Cooke City in the early 1870s, and by 1880 the town numbered 7,000 fortune-seeking souls. Gold mining continued until the late 1950s, when commercial mining finally ceased. Gold panning in area streams remains popular.

Cooke City is 4 miles from Yellowstone National Park's northeast gate. Beartooth Scenic Highway (see Red Lodge p. 134), the town's eastern access, usually is open Memorial Day through mid-Oct. Cooke City can be reached all year via the road from Gardiner through Yellowstone.

Colter Pass, Cooke City & Silver Gate Chamber of Commerce: 206 W. Main St., P.O. Box 1071, Cooke City, MT 59020. **Phone:** (406) 838-2495.

ELK HORN LODGE   (406)838-2332   **42**
💎 Motel. **Address:** 103 Main St 59020

CUSTER NATIONAL FOREST (E-4)

Elevations in the forest range from 1,035 ft. in the grasslands of South Dakota to 12,799 ft. at Granite Peak in Montana. Refer to AAA maps for additional elevation information.

Scattered across counties in Montana and South Dakota, Custer National Forest encompasses nearly 1.3 million acres in three unique districts. The mountainous section, or Beartooth District, includes a portion of the Absaroka-Beartooth Wilderness and Granite Peak, the highest point in Montana. The eastern portions range from the pine-clad hills and rough break country of southeastern Montana to the rolling grassland of northwestern South Dakota and the badlands of western North Dakota.

Beartooth Scenic Highway, usually open Memorial Day through mid-October, traverses the mountain country. Other good routes provide access to campgrounds and trailheads. Guide and pack services are available in nearby towns.

Trail information, which can be obtained from Forest Service offices, should be checked and updated at Beartooth Ranger Station before a trip into Absaroka-Beartooth Wilderness is attempted. The ranger station, south of Red Lodge, Mont., on US 212, is open daily 8-4:30, Memorial Day-Labor Day; Mon.-Fri. 8-4:30, rest of year.

For further information contact the Forest Supervisor, P.O. Box 130, 10 E. Backcock Ave., Bozeman, MT 59771; phone (406) 587-6701 or Beartooth Ranger Station, (406) 446-2103. See Recreation Areas Chart.

CUT BANK pop. 2,869

CUT BANK SUPER 8   (406)873-5662

💎💎
Motel
$75-$95

Address: 609 W Main St 59427 **Location:** On US 2, 0.3 mi w. **Facility:** 61 units. 3 stories (no elevator), interior corridors. **Parking:** winter plug-ins. **Pool:** heated indoor. **Activities:** limited exercise equipment. **Guest Services:** coin laundry. **Featured Amenity:** continental breakfast.

SAVE 🍽️ 🏊 📶 ✕ 📺 / SOME UNITS 🛗 🖨️

DEER LODGE (D-3) pop. 3,111, elev. 4,519'
• Restaurants p. 106

The second oldest city in Montana, Deer Lodge is on the Clark Fork River midway between Yellowstone and Glacier national parks. The city was established in 1862 as the result of a nearby gold discovery. With fresh food and a blacksmith as drawing cards, Deer Lodge was a welcome stop for the many settlers and miners who passed through the area.

Southwest Montana: 1105 Main St., Deer Lodge, MT 59722. **Phone:** (800) 879-1159.

Self-guiding tours: Driving tour maps for the surrounding area are available from the Powell County Chamber of Commerce at 1109 Main St.; phone (406) 846-2094.

GRANT-KOHRS RANCH NATIONAL HISTORIC SITE is off I-90 exit 184 or 187. Established in the early 1860s, the ranch had grown to 27,000 acres by the early 1900s, and the owners controlled more than a million acres of public range in four states and Canada. Though much reduced, the 1,500-acre ranch still has livestock and more than 80 buildings, from bunkhouse row to the 23-room ranch house.

Hours: Daily 9-5:30, Memorial Day-Labor Day; 9-4:30, rest of year. Guided historic house tours are given on the hour in the morning and on the half-hour in the afternoon. Closed Jan. 1, Thanksgiving and Christmas. Phone ahead to confirm schedule. **Cost:** Free. **Phone:** (406) 846-2070. *(See ad this page.)* GT

OLD MONTANA PRISON is off I-90 exit 184 or 187 at 1106 Main St. Self-guiding tours of the cell house, maximum-security areas, hole, tunnel and walled prison grounds together with an exhibit of photographs provide insight into early prison life and area history. The facility served as a prison 1871-1979.

Time: Allow 30 minutes minimum. **Hours:** Daily 8-6, mid-May to mid-Sept.; daily 10-4, rest of year. Last admission 50 minutes before closing. Closed for 2 weeks at Christmas. Phone ahead to confirm schedule. **Cost:** (includes Frontier Montana Museum, Montana Auto Museum and Yesterday's Playthings Doll & Toy Museum) $10; $9 (ages 62+ and military with ID); $6 (ages 10-15). **Phone:** (406) 846-3111.

Frontier Montana Museum is at 1106 Main St., at the Old Prison Museum complex. An extensive private collection of Western memorabilia from the 1800s is a highlight of this museum. Also featured are Civil War items, a gun collection comprising 250 weapons, Native American artifacts, a railroad saloon diorama, railroad artifacts and a display of "gambler's essentials." **Hours:** Daily 10-5, mid-May to mid-Sept.; otherwise varies rest of year. Closed

for 2 weeks at Christmas. **Cost:** Entrance included with Old Montana Prison admission of $10; $9 (ages 62+ and military with ID); $6 (ages 10-15). **Phone:** (406) 846-3111.

Montana Auto Museum is at 1106 Main St., at the Old Prison Museum complex. The museum houses a representative collection of vintage automobiles from the 1800s through the 1970s. Included are a 1903 Model A Ford, a 1914 Detroit Electric Car, 1950s Chevrolets and muscle cars from the late 1960s and early '70s. Interpretive displays and photographs enhance the collection.

Hours: Daily 8-6, mid-May to mid-Sept.; daily 10-4, rest of year. Last admission 30 minutes before closing. Closed for 2 weeks at Christmas. Phone ahead to confirm schedule. **Cost:** Entrance included with Old Montana Prison admission of $10; $9 (ages 62+ and military with ID); $6 (ages 10-15). **Phone:** (406) 846-3111.

Powell County Museum is at 1193 Main St., at the Old Prison Museum complex. Permanent and changing exhibits depict the history of Powell County and Deer Lodge Valley. Displays include a woodcarving collection, mining and ranching equipment and household and school items. **Hours:** Daily noon-5, in summer. Phone ahead to confirm schedule. **Cost:** Free. **Phone:** (406) 846-3111.

Yesterday's Playthings Doll & Toy Museum is at 1097 Main St., at the Old Prison Museum complex. The history of children's toys from the 19th century to the present is the focus of this museum. The collection includes an extensive Raggedy Ann and Andy display, dolls from different cultures and dolls made from materials ranging from papier-mâché to china. A model railroad collection also is displayed. **Time:** Allow 30 minutes minimum. **Hours:** Daily 9-6, May-Oct.; 10-4, Nov.-Apr. **Cost:** Entrance included with Old Montana Prison admission of $15; $12 (ages 62+ and military with ID); $8 (ages 10-15). **Phone:** (406) 846-3111.

WESTERN BIG SKY INN   406/846-2590
Motel. **Address:** 210 N Main St 59722

▼ *See AAA listing this page* ▼

WHERE TO EAT

BROKEN ARROW STEAKHOUSE   406/846-3400
♦♦ American. Casual Dining. **Address:** 317 N Main St 59722

DILLON (E-3) pop. 4,134, elev. 5,102'

Dillon was established in 1880 by a group of businessmen who bought out a rancher who refused to give up his land to the railroad. Named for the president of Union Pacific Railroad, Dillon is today a focal point for five rich stock-raising valleys, including Big Hole, Grasshopper and Beaverhead. Beaverhead County is among the top cattle- and hay-producing regions in the state.

West of Dillon is Bannack State Park, on the site of a former mining town. In 1863 Sidney Edgerton, a lawyer from Ohio, arrived in the vicinity and stayed throughout the winter season. When he visited Washington, D.C., in the spring, he advocated the creation of a new territory; President Abraham Lincoln named Edgerton governor and Bannack the temporary capital. The following year the territory's seat was moved to the boomtown of Virginia City.

Fishing is a popular recreational pursuit in the area. Some of Montana's higher mountains can be seen from scenic I-15, which follows the Beaverhead and Red Rock rivers to the Idaho border.

Beaverhead Chamber of Commerce: 10 W. Reeder St., P.O. Box 425, Dillon, MT 59725. **Phone:** (406) 683-5511.

Self-guiding tours: A brochure outlining a walking tour of historic Dillon is available from the chamber of commerce and the Beaverhead County Museum.

BEST WESTERN PARADISE INN   (406)683-4214

♦♦ ♦♦
Hotel
$95-$159

BW **Best Western.** **AAA Benefit:** Members save up to 15% and earn bonus points!

Address: 650 N Montana St 59725 **Location:** I-15 exit 63, 0.3 mi s on SR 41. **Facility:** 63 units, some two bedrooms. 2 stories (no elevator), exterior corridors. **Terms:** cancellation fee imposed. **Pool:** heated indoor. **Activities:** hot tub, exercise room. **Guest Services:** coin laundry.

COMFORT INN OF DILLON   (406)683-6831

♦♦ ♦♦
Hotel
$94-$154

Address: 450 N Interchange 59725 **Location:** I-15 exit 63, just e. **Facility:** 48 units. 2 stories (no elevator), interior corridors. **Parking:** winter plug-ins. **Pool:** heated indoor. **Guest Services:** coin laundry. **Featured Amenity:** full hot breakfast.

FAIRBRIDGE INN EXPRESS   406/683-3636
♦♦ Hotel. **Address:** 580 Sinclair St 59725

SUPER 8 DILLON   406/988-0908
♦♦ Hotel. **Address:** 550 N Montana St 59725

WHERE TO EAT

LION'S DEN   406/683-2051
♦♦ American. Casual Dining. **Address:** 725 N Montana St 59725

PAPA T'S   406/683-6432
♦ American. Casual Dining. **Address:** 10 N Montana St 59725

SPARKY'S GARAGE   406/683-2828
♦♦ American. Casual Dining. **Address:** 420 E Poindexter St 59725

EAST GLACIER PARK (B-2) elev. 4,795'
- **Hotels & Restaurants map & index p. 116**
- **Part of Glacier National Park area — see map p. 111**

In the Two Medicine Valley, East Glacier Park is the recreational center and eastern gateway to Glacier National Park *(see place listing p. 111)*. The community maintains an Old West appearance.

JACOBSON'S SCENIC VIEW COTTAGES   406/226-4422 **12**
♦ Cottage. **Address:** 1204 Hwy 49 59434

MOUNTAIN PINE MOTEL   (406)226-4403 **13**
♦ Motel. **Address:** SR 49 N 59434

WHERE TO EAT

SERRANO'S   406/226-9392 **8**
♦♦ Mexican. Casual Dining. **Address:** 29 Dawson Ave 59434

EMIGRANT pop. 488
- **Part of Yellowstone National Park area — see map p. 214**

PARADISE GATEWAY BED & BREAKFAST & VACATION HOMES   (406)333-4063
♦♦♦ Bed & Breakfast. **Address:** 2644 Hwy 89 S 59027

ENNIS (E-3) pop. 838, elev. 4,939'

Ennis is in the broad, rolling Madison Valley, flanked on both sides by mountain ranges. Built along the Madison River, the town is convenient to the historic gold-mining towns of Virginia City and Nevada City as well as to the trout-filled lakes and streams of the Beaverhead-Deerlodge and Gallatin national forests *(see place listings p. 94 and p. 109)*.

Ennis Chamber of Commerce: 201 E. Main St., P.O. Box 291, Ennis, MT 59729. **Phone:** (406) 682-4388.

FAN MOUNTAIN INN (406)682-5200

◆◆◆ ◆◆◆
Motel
$75-$95

Address: 204 N Main St 59729 **Location:** US 287, just nw of City Center. **Facility:** 27 units. 2 stories (no elevator), exterior corridors. **Parking:** winter plug-ins. **Terms:** 10 day cancellation notice-fee imposed.

SAVE ⎅➔ 🛜 ✕ 🗄 🖵 / SOME UNITS 🐾

WHERE TO EAT

YESTERDAY'S SODA FOUNTAIN 406/682-4246
◆ American. Casual Dining. **Address:** 124 Main St 59729

ESSEX
• Hotels & Restaurants map & index p. 116
• Part of Glacier National Park area — see map p. 111

GLACIER HAVEN INN 406/888-5720 **30**
◆ Motel. **Address:** 14305 US Hwy 2 E 59916

WHERE TO EAT

THE DINING CAR 406/888-5700 **24**
◆◆ American. Casual Dining. **Address:** 290 Izaak Walton Inn Rd 59916

HEALTHY HAVEN CAFE 406/888-5720 **23**
◆ American. Casual Dining. **Address:** 14305 US 2 E 59916

FLATHEAD LAKE (B-2)

A recreational mecca, Flathead Lake appeals to those who enjoy a wide array of activities ranging from water skiing and fishing to sailing and sightseeing. The 28-mile-long, 15-mile-wide lake boasts several islands; sheep, deer, bears, eagles and ospreys inhabit Wild Horse. Nearby communities include Bigfork, Kalispell, Lakeside and Polson *(see individual place listings)*.

FLATHEAD NATIONAL FOREST (A-1)

Elevations in the forest range from 3,500 ft. at the valley floor to 9,289 ft. on Swan Peak in the Swan Valley. Refer to AAA maps for additional elevation information.

Flathead National Forest stretches along the spine of the Rocky Mountains south from the Canadian border for more than 120 miles. With parts of its eastern and northern boundaries bordering Glacier National Park *(see place listing p. 111)*, the forest shares much of the park's spectacular scenery of high ridges and mountains. Its principal rivers are the Swan, Stillwater and the three forks of the Flathead—the North Fork, Middle Fork and South Fork, all in the National Wild and Scenic River system. This is augmented by 3,400 miles of streams and many small lakes.

Almost half the national forest's approximately 2.3 million acres lies within the Bob Marshall Wilderness complex, which includes the Bob Marshall, Great Bear and Scapegoat wilderness areas. The combined 1.5 million acres attracts those who seek out a challenging recreation experience in a natural setting where mechanized travel and equipment are prohibited.

Popularly known as the "Bob," the Bob Marshall Wilderness straddles the Continental Divide. There are many rugged peaks, alpine lakes, mountain valleys, meandering streams, wildflower-strewn meadows and waterfalls. Sunsets often are highlighted by long streamers of wave-shaped clouds, a phenomenon created partly by strong winds blowing perpendicular to a mountain range.

For those seeking utter solitude, winter use of the "Bob" is almost nil. This vast reserve, appropriately named for the man who helped preserve millions of acres of the wilderness system, shelters one of the country's largest wildlife populations, including elk, bighorn sheep, black bears and several hundred grizzly bears. About 50 outfitting and guiding businesses serve the area.

Other areas of interest in the forest are Mission Mountain Wilderness and Hungry Horse Reservoir *(see Recreation Areas Chart and Hungry Horse Dam in Glacier National Park p. 114)*, along the shores of which are almost half of the forest's camping and picnic areas. The 15,000-acre Jewel Basin Hiking Area, reached by forest roads from SRs 83 or 35, is a scenic area of rushing waterways, open meadows and subalpine forests; mechanized vehicles and pack animals are not permitted. Hiking, fishing and floating the three forks of the Flathead River are popular activities.

Information about the forest's 31 campgrounds and recreational opportunities is available at the forest headquarters in Kalispell and at district ranger stations. For further information contact the Supervisor's Office, Flathead National Forest, 650 Wolfpack Way, Kalispell, MT 59901; phone (406) 758-5204. *See Recreation Areas Chart.*

FORSYTH pop. 1,777

RAILS INN MOTEL 406/346-2242
◆ Hotel. **Address:** 290 Front St 59327

SUNDOWNER INN (406)346-2115

◆◆ ◆◆
Motel
$100-$140

Address: 1018 Front St 59327 **Location:** I-94 exit 95, 0.5 mi nw. **Facility:** 40 units. 2 stories (no elevator), exterior corridors. **Parking:** winter plug-ins. **Terms:** resort fee. **Guest Services:** coin laundry. **Featured Amenity:** continental breakfast.

SAVE ⎅➔ BIZ HS 🛜 ✕ 🗄 🖵 🖵 / SOME UNITS 🐾

WESTWIND MOTOR INN 406/346-2038
◆ Motel. **Address:** 225 Westwind Ln 59327

FORT BENTON (C-4) pop. 1,464, elev. 2,632'

At the head of navigation on the Missouri River, Fort Benton is one of Montana's oldest communities and was the link between east and west. Thousands of immigrants and miners marked this landing as the beginning of the way west along Mullan Road or north along WhoopUp Trail. Fort Benton also was their chief means of supply, as all goods were brought by steamboat from St. Louis. In 1868, 39 steamboats unloaded 8,000 tons of freight and 10,000 passengers; one steamboat returned to St. Louis with $1.5 million in gold.

The Lewis and Clark Memorial overlooks the Missouri River from the levee not far from the old fort; the memorial stands as a reminder of the explorers' stay in the area and the role they and Fort Benton played in opening the West. A statue of Lt. John Mullan, the first white man to pave the way west from Fort Benton to Walla Walla, Wash., and for whom the Mullan Trail is named, also stands on the levee.

Fort Benton is on the western fringe of the Upper Missouri River Breaks National Monument, and its corridor traces the Upper Missouri River 149 miles east into the Charles M. Russell National Wildlife Refuge. Recreation information can be obtained from the Upper Missouri River Breaks National Monument Interpretive Center.

Fort Benton Chamber of Commerce: 1421 Front St., P.O. Box 12, Fort Benton, MT 59442. **Phone:** (406) 622-3864.

Self-guiding tours: A brochure outlining a walking and driving tour of Fort Benton is available from the Museum of the Upper Missouri and from the visitor information center on Front Street.

GRAND UNION HOTEL   406/622-1882
▼▼▼ Historic Hotel. **Address:** 1 Grand Union 59442

WHERE TO EAT

UNION GRILLE RESTAURANT   406/622-1882
▼▼▼ Regional American. Fine Dining. **Address:** 1 Grand Union 59442

FORT PECK (B-7) pop. 233, elev. 2,100'

The federal government developed Fort Peck in the early 1930s as a support community for the construction of Fort Peck Dam. Built by the U.S. Army Corps of Engineers, the dam harnesses the Missouri River, providing electric power, irrigation and recreation.

Fort Peck Summer Theatre, 201 Missouri Ave., presents contemporary productions from mid-June to early September; phone the box office at (406) 526-9943.

▼GEM **FORT PECK DAM & LAKE** is on SR 24. The construction of the largest hydraulic earth-filled dam in the world created Fort Peck Lake

(see Recreation Areas Chart), which offers excellent fishing, camping, boating, hiking, bird-watching and other recreation along its 130-mile length.

A testament to the human spirit, the dam was originally authorized in 1933 by President Franklin D. Roosevelt, who believed it would provide jobs for thousands of Depression-era people and serve as flood protection-a concern since the 1860s. Today, a hard-surfaced highway follows the crest of the dam 250 feet above the tunnel outlets. **Phone:** (406) 526-3411. GT 🅰 🅧 🈁

Fort Peck Dam Interpretive Center & Museum, on SR 24, adjacent to the powerhouses, offers exhibits depicting the fauna of the Charles M. Russell National Wildlife Refuge, along with information about the history of the Fort Peck Dam & Lake. A cast of Peck's Rex, a Tyrannosaurus rex specimen found in the area, is on display. A cretaceous sea exhibit features several ocean species hanging from the ceiling; other exhibits spotlight a struthiomimus and an edmontosaur. Two large aquariums housing native and game fish of Fort Peck Lake and the Missouri River can be seen.

A children's discovery area offers hands-on displays for kids. Interpretive programs and theater presentations are available in summer. **Time:** Allow 2 hours minimum. **Hours:** Daily 9-5, May-Sept. Hours vary rest of year; phone for schedule. Closed major holidays, except Memorial Day, July 4 and Labor Day. **Cost:** Free. **Phone:** (406) 526-3493.

Powerhouse Tour departs from the Fort Peck Dam Interpretive Center & Museum adjacent to the dam powerhouses. The tour describes how the power plants at Fort Peck Dam transform flowing water into electricity. Generators, surge tanks and turbines are displayed.

Note: Adult visitors must present a valid, government-issued photo ID. **Time:** Allow 1 hour minimum. **Hours:** Tours depart Mon.-Fri. at 9:30, 11:30, 1:30 and 3:30, Sat.-Sun. and holidays on the hour 9-4, Memorial Day-Labor Day; by appointment, rest of year. Visitors must sign up at least 15 minutes prior to the tour. **Cost:** Free. **Phone:** (406) 526-3493. GT

FORT UNION TRADING POST NATIONAL HISTORIC SITE (B-8)

Fort Union Trading Post National Historic Site, reached via US 2 and SR 1804, is 25 miles southwest of Williston, N.D., and 24 miles northeast of Sidney, Mont. Founded by John Jacob Astor for his American Fur Co. in 1828, the trading post became the center for the fur trade on the Upper Missouri River. The fort was 1,800 miles by river from St. Louis, the nearest supply point.

Excavators unearthed the foundations of the Bourgeois House, palisades, bastions, a Native American trade house, an icehouse and other structures. The trade house has been rebuilt and furnished as it might have appeared in the early 1850s.

The fort's walls and bastions also have been reconstructed. A visitor center in the reconstructed Bourgeois House features exhibits about the fort and the fur trade.

Allow 1 hour minimum. Daily 8-6:30 CST, Memorial Day weekend-Labor Day; 9-5 CST, rest of year. Closed Jan. 1, Thanksgiving and Christmas. Trade house open 10-5 CST, Memorial Day weekend-Labor Day. Free. Phone (701) 572-9083.

GALLATIN NATIONAL FOREST (E-4)

Elevations in the forest range from 4,300 ft. at Derby Gulch to 12,799 ft. on Granite Peak. Refer to AAA maps for additional elevation information.

Gallatin National Forest is in south-central Montana. Some of the most rugged mountains in the state can be found in the 1,735,239-acre forest. On the western side are the Madison and Gallatin ranges; to the east, the Absaroka and Beartooth; and to the north, the Bridger Mountains and the isolated block encompassing the Crazy Mountains.

To some, such as the Crow Indians who sought their visions in the Crazies, these mountains inspire a mystical reverence; to others, such as the mountain men who thought the Beartooth Range resembled the teeth of a familiar predator, they inspire a sense of awe. Much of this region remains unchanged, protected in the forest's two wilderness units, the Lee Metcalf and the Absaroka-Beartooth.

Absaroka-Beartooth Wilderness is named for its two very different mountain ranges. Rugged mountains, broad forested valleys and a variety of plant life characterize the Absaroka Range, which receives precipitation that is unusually abundant for this region. In contrast, the Beartooths present a jagged silhouette of monumental walls and spires soaring to heights of more than 12,000 feet. Forming the roof of these massive peaks are broad plateaus of alpine tundra carpeted with summer wildflowers and hundreds of lakes. The ranges are an integral part of the Yellowstone ecosystem, offering shelter to grizzlies, moose, deer, eagles and turkeys.

The Yellowstone, Gallatin, Madison and Boulder, which are the principal rivers, are renowned for excellent fishing. Natural Bridge State Monument, 28 miles south of Big Timber via SR 289, features a 100-foot waterfall at the mouth of Boulder River Canyon. Several short trails lead from the parking area to observation sites of the falls.

Hikers favor Lee Metcalf Wilderness *(see Beaverhead-Deerlodge National Forest p. 94)* and the Hyalite area of the Gallatin Range. Also scenic are the trails in the Bridger Mountains near Bozeman. To experience the region's beauty by car travel Beartooth Scenic Highway *(see Red Lodge p. 134)* or US 191 from West Yellowstone to Gallatin Gateway; or take a self-guiding tour of the Madison River Canyon Earthquake Area.

Information about the forest's numerous campgrounds and picnic areas is available at district ranger stations. For further information, contact the Bozeman Ranger District, 3710 Fallon St., Ste. C, Bozeman, MT 59718; phone (406) 522-2520. *See Recreation Areas Chart.*

GARDINER (F-4) pop. 875, elev. 5,267'
- Restaurants p. 110
- Hotels & Restaurants map & index p. 220
- Part of Yellowstone National Park area — see map p. 214

The northern entrance to Yellowstone National Park *(see place listing p. 214)*, Gardiner is the only approach open all year. The Devil's Slide, an unusual rock formation 5 miles northwest on US 89, is visible from the highway. A mile north of town by gravel road is a travertine rock quarry. Theodore Roosevelt dedicated Roosevelt Arch in 1903.

Gardiner Chamber of Commerce: 216 Park St., P.O. Box 81, Gardiner, MT 59030. **Phone:** (406) 848-7971.

WILD WEST RAFTING departs from 906 W. Scott St. in the Yellowstone Outpost Mall. Passengers may view and photograph Montana wildlife on a leisurely 5-mile float trip on the Yellowstone River. A guide rows the vessel through Paradise Valley. Other activities as well as white-water rafting excursions also are available.

Time: Allow 2 hours minimum. **Hours:** Scenic float trips depart daily at 9:30, 1 and 4, May 1-Sept. 7. Half-day white-water rafting trips depart daily at 9, 10, 12:30, 3:30 and 5:30, May 1-Sept. 7. **Cost:** Scenic float trip or half-day white-water rafting trip $41; $31 (ages 3-12). **Phone:** (406) 848-2252 or (800) 862-0557.

RECREATIONAL ACTIVITIES
White-water Rafting
- **Montana Whitewater Rafting and ZipLine Co.** is at 603 Scott St. Rafting, ziplining and horseback riding are offered. **Hours:** Trips are offered daily, May-Sept. Departure times vary; phone ahead. **Phone:** (406) 848-7398 or (800) 799-4465.

BEST WESTERN BY MAMMOTH HOT SPRINGS
(406)848-7311 **31**

▼▼▼
Motel
$139-$269

 Best Western. **AAA Benefit:** Members save up to 15% and earn bonus points!

Address: 905 Scott St W 59030 **Location:** 0.5 mi n. **Facility:** 86 units, some two bedrooms and kitchens. 2 stories (no elevator), interior/exterior corridors. **Parking:** winter plug-ins. **Terms:** check-in 4 pm, cancellation fee imposed, resort fee. **Dining:** Yellowstone Mine Restaurant, see separate listing. **Pool:** heated indoor. **Activities:** sauna, hot tub. **Guest Services:** coin laundry.

(See map & index p. 220.)

COMFORT INN YELLOWSTONE NORTH   (406)848-7536   **30**
Hotel. **Address:** 107 Hellroaring St 59030

TRAVELODGE GARDINER AT YELLOWSTONE PARK NORTH ENTRANCE   406/848-7520   **29**
Motel. **Address:** 109 Hellroaring St 59030

YELLOWSTONE BASIN INN   (406)848-7080   **27**
Motel. **Address:** 4 Maiden Basin Dr 59030

YELLOWSTONE RIVER MOTEL   (406)848-7303   **33**
Motel
$78-$199
Address: 14 E Park St 59030 **Location:** Just e of US 89. **Facility:** 38 units, some two bedrooms and kitchens. 1-2 stories (no elevator), exterior corridors. **Terms:** closed 10/24-4/12, cancellation fee imposed, resort fee.

YELLOWSTONE SUPER 8-GARDINER   (406)848-7401   **32**
Hotel. **Address:** 702 Scott St W 59030

YELLOWSTONE VILLAGE INN   406/848-7417   **28**
Hotel. **Address:** Yellowstone Park North Entrance 59030

WHERE TO EAT

THE ANTLER PUB & GRILL   406/848-7536   **20**
American. Casual Dining. **Address:** 107 Hellroaring St 59030

THE RAVEN GRILL   406/848-7600   **23**
American. Casual Dining. **Address:** 220 W Park St 59030

ROSIE'S BISTRO   406/580-0966   **22**
American. Casual Dining. **Address:** 202 Park St 59030

YELLOWSTONE MINE RESTAURANT
406/848-7336   **21**
American
Casual Dining
$9-$22
AAA Inspector Notes: Entering this eatery is like walking into an Old West mine, chock-full of period artifacts on the walls. Chicken, steak and seafood are all good menu choices. During the summer months arrive early to avoid a wait. **Features:** full bar, happy hour. **Address:** 905 Scott St W 59030 **Location:** 0.5 mi n; in Best Western By Mammoth Hot Springs. B D

GLACIER NATIONAL PARK (A-2)

• Hotels p. 119 • Restaurants p. 119
• Attractions map p. 113
• Hotels & Restaurants map & index p. 116

Elevations in the park range from a low of 3,100 ft. in the West Glacier Area to 10,466 ft. on Mt. Cleveland. Refer to AAA maps for additional elevation information.

Glacier National Park is in northwestern Montana. Geologic processes formed and sculpted the peaks, leaving about 25 glaciers and 750 lakes. The mountains are a result of an overthrust of the Earth's crust. Rock layers about a billion years old lie above layers millions of years younger. Some of the finest mountain scenery in America is within this million-acre national park.

The U-shaped valleys, as well as most of the lakes, are the legacy of the last ice age. Most glaciers are accessible only by trail; a few can be viewed from the road. Glacier National Park and Waterton Lakes National Park, in Alberta, together form Waterton-Glacier International Peace Park, although each is administered separately. Scenic Going-to-the-Sun Road *(see attraction listing p. 114)* connects the east and west sections of Glacier National Park.

Though Glacier is a refuge for many large mammals, most of the animals seek the undisturbed areas, and few are seen along the roads during the travel season. The park also is a haven for more than 260 species of birds.

The brilliance and diversity of its floral life is one of Glacier's outstanding features; July marks the height of bloom for many of the alpine species of vascular plants. In the valleys on the east side are dense stands of Engelmann spruce, subalpine fir and lodgepole pine. The western valleys present a different picture with their many dense stands of western red cedars, hemlocks and other conifers.

General Information and Activities

The park's peak travel season is roughly from mid-June to mid-September; however, the park is

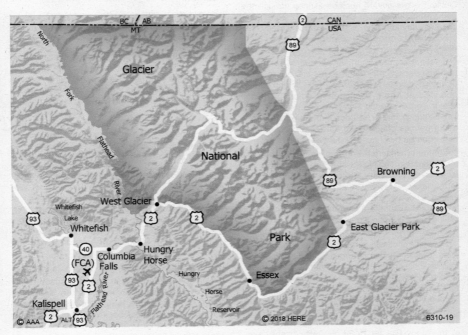

This map shows cities in Glacier National Park where you will find attractions, hotels and restaurants. Cities are listed alphabetically in this book on the following pages.

(See map & index p. 116.)

open year-round. Visitors can use the park's shuttle system for unlimited one-way or round-trip travel to various park locations from 7:30-7, early July through Labor Day. The last shuttle buses leave Logan Pass at 7 p.m. for both Apgar Transit Center and St. Mary Visitor Center. Check the shuttle schedule upon arrival. The shuttle is free with park admission. Canoe and motor boat rentals are available at the Apgar dock; phone (406) 257-2426. Additional docks and rentals are at Lake McDonald Lodge, Two Medicine and Rising Sun.

Note: Vehicles and vehicle combinations longer than 21 feet or wider than 8 feet (including mirrors) are prohibited from traveling the section of the Going-to-the-Sun Road between the Avalanche Creek picnic area and Sun Point parking areas, where they may park.

More than 700 miles of trails penetrate the park, and many points of interest are within easy walking distance of the hotels and chalets. Swan Mountain Outfitter offers guided horseback rides through the park. Tours depart from Lake McDonald Corral near Lake McDonald Lodge, Apgar Corral and Many Glacier Corral; phone (406) 387-4405 or (877) 888-5557.

There are more than 60 campsites for backpackers; backcountry camping permits are required ($5 per person per night, May 1-Nov. 1) and can be obtained at Apgar backcountry office, St. Mary Visitor Center and the Two Medicine, Many Glacier or Polebridge ranger stations. For more information about permits phone (406) 888-7857. Topographic maps can be purchased at the park visitor centers.

Mountain whitefish and cutthroat trout are the most common fish. Lake trout are taken from the larger lakes, principally McDonald, St. Mary and Waterton lakes. Grayling thrive in Elizabeth Lake. A fishing license is not required inside the park; regulations are available at the visitor centers. When fishing or participating in any activity in or near park water, watch for slippery rocks at the water's edge.

Several concessionaires within the park provide tours. Glacier Guides arranges guided backpacking trips for those in search of adventurous things to do. Glacier Park Boat Co. *(see attraction listing this page)* operates guided lake cruises on McDonald, St. Mary, Two Medicine, Swiftcurrent and Josephine lakes. Boats and canoes can be rented at Two Medicine, Swiftcurrent and McDonald lakes and at the Many Glacier Hotel on Swiftcurrent Lake. Shuttle services are available at Upper Waterton Lake.

CCInc. Auto Tape Tours of the park are available at Glacier Gift Shop in West Glacier or St. Mary's Lodge in St. Mary; phone (201) 236-1666.

Trail rides ranging from a 1-hour trip to an all-day journey depart from Lake McDonald Lodge and Many Glacier Hotel. Daily schedules of ranger-led hikes, junior ranger activities, boat trips and campfire programs are printed as a supplement to the *Waterton-Glacier Guide,* the park's newspaper,

which is handed out at the visitor centers. *See Recreation Areas Chart.*

Note: Although the animals in the park might appear tame, they are wild and potentially dangerous. Do not approach, feed, molest or tease them in any manner. Bears and mountain lions especially should be avoided; if one approaches, stay in your closed vehicle. Sightings should be reported to park rangers.

ADMISSION May-Oct. is $35 (per private vehicle); $30 (per motorcyclist); $20 (per person arriving on foot or by bicycle). Admission rest of year is $25 (per private vehicle); $20 (per motorcyclist); $15 (per person arriving on foot or by bicycle). The above fees permit entrance to the park for 7 calendar days from date of purchase.

PETS are permitted in the park only if they are leashed, crated or otherwise physically restrained at all times. They are not allowed on park trails or in the water.

ADDRESS inquiries to the Superintendent, Glacier National Park, P.O. Box 128, West Glacier, MT 59936; phone (406) 888-7800.

AVALANCHE CREEK is on Going-to-the-Sun Rd. A deep, narrow gorge cut through brilliant red mudstone is filled with potholes scoured out by stones swirled in the foaming torrent. From the gorge a 2-mile trail travels to Avalanche Basin and Lake, a semicircular amphitheater with walls more than 2,000 feet high, over which plunge a half-dozen waterfalls. A nature trail with a boardwalk for physically impaired visitors leads to the gorge. **Time:** Allow 30 minutes minimum. **Phone:** (406) 888-7800.

BELLY RIVER COUNTRY is accessible by trail from Many Glacier through Ptarmigan Tunnel, from Waterton Lake over Stoney Indian Pass, or from Chief Mountain customs station on Chief Mountain International Rd. Spurs are available to Helen, Cosley, Glenns, Mokowanis and Elizabeth lakes and Gros Ventre and Dawn Mist falls. The region is wild and heavily forested in some places.

A 33-mile drive through the Chief Mountain area to Waterton Lakes National Park of Canada offers scenic views. Waterton Inter-Nation Shoreline Cruise Co. operates a launch on Waterton Lake early May to mid-October (weather permitting). **Time:** Allow 2 hours minimum. **Cost:** Round-trip launch fare (in Canadian dollars) $46; $23 (ages 13-17); $15 (ages 4-12).

CUT BANK, at the s.e. portion of Glacier National Park off US 89, is a primitive, densely wooded valley. At the head of the valley is 8,020-foot Triple Divide Peak.

GLACIER PARK BOAT CO. departs from Lake McDonald, Many Glacier, Rising Sun and Two Medicine. The company offers scenic cruises aboard classic wooden boats that have plied the lakes here since the park's early days. Narrated trips offer

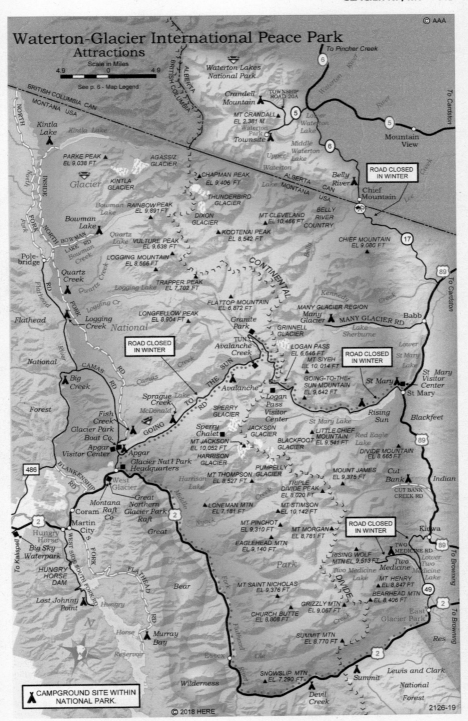

© AAA

Waterton-Glacier International Peace Park
Attractions

Scale in Miles
4.9   0   4.9

See p. 6 - Map Legend

CAMPGROUND SITE WITHIN
NATIONAL PARK.

© 2018 HERE

2126-19

(See map & index p. 116.)

views of wilderness areas, glacial formations, waterfalls and rugged cliffs. Tours last between 45 minutes and 1.5 hours. Guided hikes also are available. Canoes, rowboats, kayaks, paddleboards and motorboats can be rented at Apgar late May through Aug. 31. Rowboats and motorboats can be rented at Lake MacDonald Lodge late May through late September. Rowboats, kayaks and canoes can be rented at Two Medicine early June through Labor Day and at Many Glacier early June through late September.

Hours: Tours depart from Lake McDonald Lodge daily at 11, 1:30, 3, 5:30 and 7, late May-Labor Day; at 1:30, 3 and 5:30, day after Labor Day-late Sept. Tours depart from Many Glacier daily at 8:30, 9, 11, 2 and 4:30, mid-June to mid-Sept. (also at 1 and 3, July 1-Labor Day). Tours depart from Rising Sun daily at 10, noon, 2, 4 and 6:30, mid-June to early Sept. Tours depart from Two Medicine daily at 10:30, 1, 3 and 5, early June-early Sept. (also at 9 a.m., July 1-Labor Day). Phone ahead to confirm schedule. **Cost:** Fares $12.50-$25.45; $6.25-$12.50 (ages 4-12). Rates may vary. Reservations are recommended. **Phone:** (406) 257-2426.

GOING-TO-THE-SUN ROAD joins US 89 at St. Mary and US 2 at West Glacier. Acclaimed as one of the outstanding scenic roadways of the world, the 50-mile route traverses the width of the park, crossing the Continental Divide through Logan Pass at an elevation of 6,646 feet while affording magnificent views of some of the park's loveliest scenery. Several miles of the two-lane highway had to be cut out of steep mountainsides and consequently it took more than a decade to complete.

At its official dedication on July 15, 1933, the road was given its current whimsical name, which comes from a mountain looming over the route east of Logan Pass. The source of the mountain's name is open to debate. It may have originated in a Blackfeet Indian legend or simply been made up by a white explorer with an active imagination.

You could drive Going-to-the-Sun Road from one end to the other in around 2 hours without stopping, but take your time because pulling over at one or more of the road's many scenic overlooks is an essential Glacier National Park experience. Some of the classic photo ops you should look for, from east to west: tiny Wild Goose Island in the midst of St. Mary Lake; Jackson Glacier, one of the few glaciers visible from the road; Bird Woman Falls, a silver ribbon of water falling hundreds of feet down the face of Mount Oberlin; the Weeping Wall, a waterfall that actually splashes onto the roadway; and McDonald Creek, a picturesque boulder-strewn stream.

Several trailheads are just off Going-to-the-Sun Road. Some paths go for miles into the backcountry while others offer short hikes to beauty spots. At Avalanche Creek *(see attraction listing p. 112)*, the Trail of the Cedars offers a pleasant .7-mile boardwalk loop among moisture-loving cedars and hemlocks. At Logan Pass, the Hidden Lake Overlook Trail is a 3-mile roundtrip journey through alpine meadows filled with wildlife and ending with a spectacular view high above a mountain lake.

Note: Logan Pass closes for the season no later than November 1 and reopens in mid-June (weather permitting). *For vehicle restrictions, see General Information and Activities p. 111.* The park's optional, free Going-to-the-Sun Road shuttle stops at various points along the road July through Labor Day. **Road Closures:** Due to an ongoing, multiyear maintenance project, construction delays along sections of Going-to-the-Sun Road are likely. Portions may be entirely closed before and after the main season (roughly mid-June to mid-September, weather permitting) to accelerate the project. **Phone:** (406) 888-7800 for road closure information.

GRANITE PARK is reached from Waterton by the northern portion of the Highline Trail, from Logan Pass along the Highline Trail and from Many Glacier over Swiftcurrent Pass Trail. Exposed is a great mass of lava that once spread over the region. Trails radiate into the surrounding mountains. Granite Park Chalet, operated by a concessioner, is open July 1 through mid-Sept.; reservations are required. **Phone:** (888) 345-2649 for chalet information.

HUNGRY HORSE DAM is 15 mi. s.e. of Glacier National Park. One of the world's largest concrete dams, Hungry Horse's 2,115-foot crest is crossed by a 39-foot-wide roadway. A visitor center 4 miles east of US 2 has interactive displays and a video. *See Recreation Areas Chart.* **Hours:** Visitor center daily 8:30-5. Phone ahead to confirm schedule. **Cost:** Free. **Phone:** (406) 387-5241, ext. 361.

LAKE MCDONALD is reached via Going-to-the-Sun Road, which runs along the eastern shore. Ten miles long and 1 mile wide, the lake is the largest in the park. Its shores are heavily forested, and impressive rocky summits rise 6,000 feet above. Lake McDonald Lodge, near the upper end of the lake, is the focal point for trails to Sperry Chalet, Gunsight Pass, Sperry Glacier, Upper McDonald Valley and the summit of Mount Brown. A cruise boat operates from the lodge Memorial Day weekend through Labor Day. Boat rentals and naturalist programs are available at the lodge and at Apgar.

LOGAN PASS lies between the headwaters of Logan and Reynolds creeks. At an elevation of 6,646 feet, it straddles the Continental Divide and carries Going-to-the-Sun Road from St. Mary to West Glacier. Though there are no overnight stopping places, other than campgrounds along the road, easy access by automobile makes it a favorite starting point for several walks, including the trail to Hidden Lake Overlook. Naturalist-led day trips and orientation talks are offered. **Note:** Parking is limited during peak visiting hours, generally mid-morning to late afternoon.

MANY GLACIER REGION is in the n.e. sector of the park. The area encompasses Swiftcurrent Lake,

(See map & index p. 116.)

from which branch many deep, glaciated valleys. It can be reached by road 13 miles from US 89 at Babb or by trail from Siyeh Bend, Granite Park, Belly River and Waterton Lake. Launch trips on Swiftcurrent and Josephine lakes depart daily, late July-late Sept.

RED EAGLE LAKE is in Red Eagle Valley. Access to the valley is by trail from the St. Mary park entrance, from Sun Point via Red Eagle Trail and from Cut Bank over Triple Divide Pass.

ST. MARY LAKE lies at the foot of the Lewis Range. Peaks of the front barrier of the Rockies soar a mile above lake waters. A trail radiating from Sun Point is the shortest and best trail to Baring Falls. Red Eagle Trail along the south shore leads to Red Eagle Lake. Programs are presented nightly in summer at the visitor center and at Rising Sun campground. Launch trips and boat tours are available at the boat landing at Rising Sun from mid-June to late August.

SPERRY CHALET can be reached only by foot or on horseback from Lake McDonald and by foot from the St. Mary Valley via Gunsight and Lincoln passes.

In a high, steep hollow at the upper end of a mountain valley, the chalet is hemmed in on three sides by precipitous peaks. Hiking and exploring the Sperry Glacier and fishing in nearby Lake Ellen Wilson are the chief diversions. Mountain goats frequently are seen on the cirque walls, usually during the late afternoon. **Hours:** Open mid-July to mid-Sept. **Phone:** (888) 345-2649.

TWO MEDICINE VALLEY is 11 mi. from East Glacier and 7 mi. off SR 49. Features include a lake surrounded by majestic peaks separated by deep, glaciated valleys. Trails for hikers and saddle horse parties radiate to adjacent points of interest; one short trail leads through dense evergreen forest to the foot of Twin Falls. Launch trips across Two Medicine Lake depart daily, early July to early September.

A readily accessible .3-mile scenic trail is at Running Eagle Falls, 2 miles below the lake near the road bridge across Two Medicine Creek. A portion of the falls' waters flows from a cave beneath the brink of the main falls. Early in the year it appears to be an ordinary waterfall, but late in the season water issues from the cave alone, and the waterfall above it is dry.

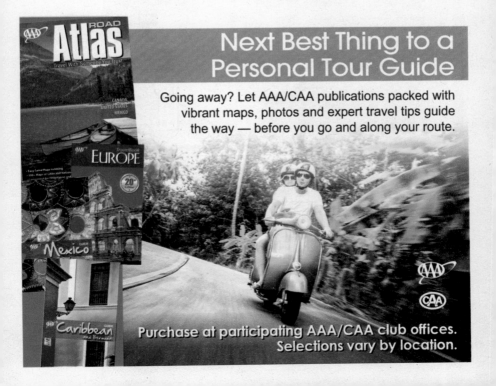

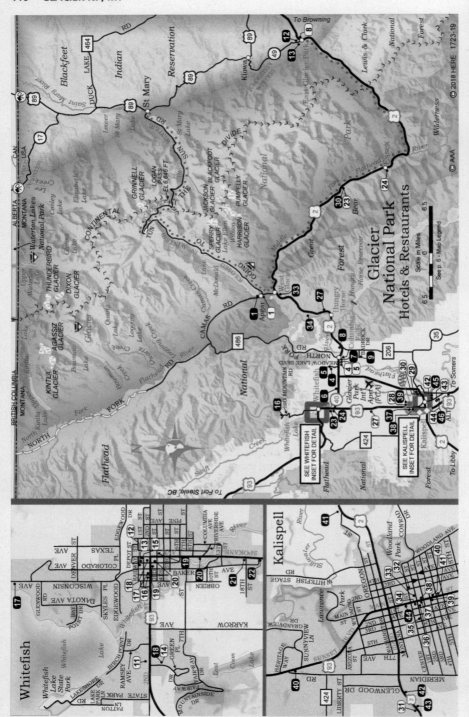

Glacier National Park
Hotels & Restaurants

See p. 6 - Map Legend

Scale in Miles

Whitefish

Kalispell

© 2018 HERE 1723-19

Glacier National Park

This index helps you "spot" where approved hotels and restaurants are located on the corresponding detailed maps. Hotel daily rate range is for comparison only. Restaurant price range is a combination of lunch and/or dinner. Turn to the listing page for more information and consult display ads for special promotions.

 For more details, rates and reservations: AAA.com/travelguides/hotels

GLACIER NATIONAL PARK

Map Page	Hotel	Diamond Rated	Rate Range	Page
1 p. 116	Apgar Village Lodge	◈	Rates not provided	119

Map Page	Restaurant	Diamond Rated	Cuisine	Price Range	Page
① p. 116	Eddie's Restaurant	◈	American	$9-$16	119

COLUMBIA FALLS

Map Page	Hotels	Diamond Rated	Rate Range	Page
4 p. 116	Meadow Lake View Bed & Breakfast	◈◈	Rates not provided	104
5 p. 116	Meadow Lake Resort	◈◈◈	Rates not provided	104
6 p. 116	North Forty Resort	◈◈	$119-$289	104
7 p. 116	Cedar Creek Lodge & Conference Center	◈◈◈	Rates not provided	104
8 p. 116	Glacier Travel Inn	◈◈	Rates not provided	104
9 p. 116	Bad Rock Bed & Breakfast	◈◈◈	$169-$249	104

Map Page	Restaurants	Diamond Rated	Cuisine	Price Range	Page
④ p. 116	**The Back Room/Nite Owl Restaurants**	◈◈	American	$8-$26	104
⑤ p. 116	Laurie's Deli	◈	American	$4-$8	104

EAST GLACIER PARK

Map Page	Hotels	Diamond Rated	Rate Range	Page
12 p. 116	Jacobson's Scenic View Cottages	◈	Rates not provided	106
13 p. 116	Mountain Pine Motel	◈	$79-$123	106

Map Page	Restaurant	Diamond Rated	Cuisine	Price Range	Page
⑧ p. 116	Serrano's	◈◈	Mexican	$9-$18	106

WHITEFISH

Map Page	Hotels	Diamond Rated	Rate Range	Page
16 p. 116	Whitefish Mountain Resort	◈◈	Rates not provided	142
17 p. 116	**The Lodge at Whitefish Lake**	◈◈◈◈	$109-$369 (SAVE)	142
18 p. 116	Grouse Mountain Lodge	◈◈◈	Rates not provided	141
19 p. 116	The Firebrand Hotel	◈◈◈	Rates not provided	141
20 p. 116	**Pine Lodge** *(See ad p. 141.)*	◈◈	Rates not provided (SAVE)	142
21 p. 116	**Best Western Rocky Mountain Lodge** *(See ad p. 141.)*	◈◈◈	$109-$320 (SAVE)	141
22 p. 116	**Chalet Motel**	◈◈	$79-$179 (SAVE)	141
23 p. 116	TownePlace Suites by Marriott	◈◈◈	$70-$329	142
24 p. 116	Hampton Inn & Suites by Hilton - Whitefish	◈◈◈	Rates not provided	141

Map Page	Restaurants	Diamond Rated	Cuisine	Price Range	Page
⑪ p. 116	**Whitefish Lake Restaurant**	◈◈◈	American	$12-$46	142
⑫ p. 116	Craggy Range Bar & Grill	◈◈	American	$9-$26	142

Map Page	Restaurants (cont'd)	Diamond Rated	Cuisine	Price Range	Page
13 p. 116	**Tupelo Grille and Wine Bar**	◆◆◆	Continental	$16-$42	142
14 p. 116	Logan's Grill	◆◆◆	American	$9-$38	142
15 p. 116	Jersey Boys Pizzeria	◆	Pizza	$9-$26	142
16 p. 116	Ciao Mambo	◆◆◆	Italian	$10-$25	142
17 p. 116	Loula's	◆◆	American	$9-$24	142
18 p. 116	Latitude 48	◆◆◆	American	$11-$34	142
19 p. 116	**Wasabi Sushi Bar & The Ginger Grill**	◆◆◆	Asian	$8-$45	142
20 p. 116	Buffalo Cafe	◆◆	American	$8-$25	142

HUNGRY HORSE

Map Page	Hotel	Diamond Rated	Rate Range	Page
27 p. 116	**Historic Tamarack Lodge & Cabins**	◆◆	Rates not provided [SAVE]	125

ESSEX

Map Page	Hotel	Diamond Rated	Rate Range	Page
30 p. 116	Glacier Haven Inn	◆	Rates not provided	107

Map Page	Restaurants	Diamond Rated	Cuisine	Price Range	Page
23 p. 116	Healthy Haven Cafe	◆	American	$10-$26	107
24 p. 116	The Dining Car	◆◆	American	$10-$33	107

WEST GLACIER

Map Page	Hotels	Diamond Rated	Rate Range	Page
33 p. 116	**Glacier Raft Company Cabins at Glacier Outdoor Center**	◆◆	Rates not provided [SAVE]	137
34 p. 116	**Silverwolf Log Chalets**	◆◆	Rates not provided [SAVE]	137

KALISPELL

Map Page	Hotels	Diamond Rated	Rate Range	Page
37 p. 116	Holiday Inn Express & Suites	◆◆◆	Rates not provided	126
38 p. 116	**SpringHill Suites by Marriott Kalispell**	◆◆◆	$63-$318 [SAVE]	126
39 p. 116	Homewood Suites by Hilton	◆◆◆	Rates not provided	126
40 p. 116	Americas Best Value Inn	◆◆	Rates not provided	126
41 p. 116	La Quinta Inn & Suites Kalispell	◆◆◆	$84-$179	126
42 p. 116	**Hampton Inn by Hilton Kalispell**	◆◆◆	$92-$390 [SAVE]	126
43 p. 116	Quality Inn	◆◆	$69-$226	126
44 p. 116	Red Lion Hotel Kalispell	◆◆◆	Rates not provided	126
45 p. 116	Super 8-Kalispell/Glacier National Park	◆◆	$53-$123	126
46 p. 116	**Hilton Garden Inn Kalispell**	◆◆◆	$79-$309 [SAVE]	126

Map Page	Restaurants	Diamond Rated	Cuisine	Price Range	Page
27 p. 116	Spencer & Co	◆◆	Steak	$14-$30	127
28 p. 116	Bullman's Wood Fired Pizza	◆◆	Pizza	$8-$19	127
29 p. 116	Cislo's	◆◆	American	$8-$16	127
30 p. 116	Nickel Charlie's Casino & Eatery	◆◆	American	$8-$24	127
31 p. 116	Bojangles' Diner	◆◆	American	$4-$13	126
32 p. 116	Julie's Center Street Cafe	◆◆	American	$6-$10	127

Map Page	Restaurants (cont'd)	Diamond Rated	Cuisine	Price Range	Page
㉝ p. 116	Bonelli's Bistro	◆◆	Mediterranean	$6-$12	126
㉞ p. 116	Norm's News	◆	Burgers	$4-$10	127
㉟ p. 116	The Desoto Grill	◆◆	American	$10-$22	127
㊱ p. 116	The Alley Connection	◆◆	Chinese	$6-$18	126
㊲ p. 116	ScottiBelli's Ristorante Italiano	◆◆	Italian	$15-$32	127
㊳ p. 116	Hops Downtown Grill	◆◆	Western Burgers	$10-$25	127
㊴ p. 116	Genki	◆◆	Asian Sushi	$8-$19	127
㊵ p. 116	Thai Palace Restaurant	◆◆	Thai	$12-$22	127
㊶ p. 116	Wheat Montana Bakery & Deli	◆	Breads/Pastries Deli	$5-$10	127
㊷ p. 116	The Montana Club	◆◆	Western Steak Seafood	$8-$24	127
㊸ p. 116	Casa Mexico	◆◆	Mexican	$8-$18	127
㊹ p. 116	Blue Canyon Kitchen & Tavern	◆◆	American	$12-$34	126

APGAR VILLAGE LODGE   406/888-5484   **1**
◆ Cabin. **Address:** 200 Going to the Sun Rd 59936

WHERE TO EAT

EDDIE'S RESTAURANT   406/888-5361   ①
◆ American. Casual Dining. **Address:** 1 Fish Creek Rd 59936

GREAT FALLS (C-4) pop. 58,505, elev. 3,312'
• Hotels p. 121 • Restaurants p. 121

Meriwether Lewis and William Clark visited the Great Falls of the Missouri River in 1805. Clark mapped the area while the other expedition members portaged around a series of five falls. The party returned to this site on its trip from the Pacific coast a year later. In 1882 Paris Gibson visited the site; he returned in the spring of 1883 with a surveyor and an attorney, and a townsite soon was plotted and named Great Falls. Important contributors to the economy are Malmstrom Air Force Base, agriculture and tourism.

Symbolizing the importance of the railroad in the city's development are two former railroad stations, both of which are located downtown near the east bank of the Missouri River. Built in 1909, the Great Northern Depot, now an office building, is just south of First Avenue. North of First Avenue, the impressive Milwaukee Road Depot was erected in 1915 and sports a handsome "flash" brick facade. Its 135-foot tower is emblazoned with the railroad's name, which is spelled out in red, yellow and white tiles.

River's Edge Trail, which begins north of US 89 on River Drive and stretches along the Missouri River, is popular with pedestrians and bicyclists. The trail's 40-plus miles include both paved and graveled sections.

A large American flag marks the visitor center on the Broadwater Overlook; follow directional signs on the approach and throughout the city. The center can provide information about guided tours; phone (406) 771-0885. An audio tour tracing 34 miles of the Lewis and Clark National Historic Trail is available from The History Museum, 422 Second St. S.; phone (406) 452-3462.

The ➳ Lewis and Clark Festival features historic re-enactments, foods that were typically eaten on the expedition, tours, exhibits and demonstrations. Other events also include outdoor art, a dinner gala, and live and silent auctions. The 3-day celebration in late June takes place at various locations, including the Lewis and Clark National Historic Trail Interpretive Center (see attraction listing p. 120) and Giant Springs State Park.

Great Falls Area Convention and Visitors Bureau: 1106 9th St. S., Great Falls, MT 59405. **Phone:** (406) 770-3078 or (800) 735-8535.

Shopping: Holiday Village Mall, 2.5 miles east of US 15 at 1200 10th Ave. S., houses 95 stores including Herberger's, JCPenney and SCHEELS.

⬥ (SAVE) **C.M. RUSSELL MUSEUM,** 400 13th
GEM St. N., pays homage to the cowboy artist Charles Marion Russell. The complex contains a museum, Russell's home and log studio, and a sculpture garden. Russell's observation of life, personal philosophy and love of Montana greatly influenced his paintings and sculpture. Though Russell was an established artist at the time of his death in 1926, creating art was not always his ambition. Rather, he was attracted to the exciting life of a cowboy.

Just days after celebrating his 16th birthday, Russell moved from St. Louis to Judith Basin in Montana where he tended sheep for a brief stint. He spent 2 years learning from a hunter and trapper. His experience led him to become a night wrangler and he seized the time and opportunity to closely observe and sketch all the daily and nightly activities of the camp. After 11 years of being a ranch hand, he retired to pursue his life as a full-time artist.

Russell's great admiration of Native Americans, especially those of the Northern Plains, is quite evident in his detailed works on the subject. The cowboy's life is romanticized in many works. In addition, images of bison, wolves, elk and other wild animals also feature in his paintings and reflect his life in Montana.

A visit to the museum reveals several galleries of Russell's watercolors, sculptures, oil paintings and illustrated cards and letters. Also featured are historical photographs of the Old West; a collection of Browning firearms; and the permanent exhibition, The Bison: American Icon, Heart of Plains Indian Culture. Changing temporary exhibitions showcase contemporary Western artists and historic artists, including O.C. Seltzer, Winold Reiss, Henry Farny and J.H. Sharp.

Time: Allow 2 hours minimum. **Hours:** Tues.-Sun. 10-5, May-Oct.; Wed.-Sun. 10-5, rest of year. Closed Jan. 1, Easter, Thanksgiving and Christmas. Phone ahead to confirm schedule. **Cost:** (includes C.M. Russell Home and Log Studio of C.M. Russell) $9; $7 (ages 60+ and retired military with ID); $4 (students with ID); free (ages 0-5 and active military with ID and their family members). Additional fees may be charged for special exhibitions. Reservations are required for guided tours. **Phone:** (406) 727-8787. GT

C.M. Russell Home is at the C.M. Russell Museum complex, 400 13th St. N. Russell's permanent residence was built in 1900 and presents a personal look into the lives of both Charlie and Nancy Russell. . **Hours:** Tues.-Sun. 11-4, May-Oct. Phone ahead to confirm schedule. **Cost:** Included in C.M. Russell Museum admission of $9; $7 (ages 60+ and retired military with ID); $4 (students with ID); free

(ages 0-5 and active military with ID and their family members). **Phone:** (406) 727-8787.

Log Studio of C.M. Russell is at the C.M. Russell Museum complex, 400 13th St. N. Built in 1903, the studio contains Russell's pallet and brushes, cowboy memorabilia and Native American artifacts he used as models. **Hours:** Tues.-Sun. 10-4:45, May-Oct.; Wed.-Sun. 10-4:45, rest of year. Phone ahead to confirm schedule. **Cost:** Included in C.M. Russell Museum admission of $9; $7 (ages 60+ and retired military with ID); $4 (students with ID); free (ages 0-5 and active military with ID and their family members). **Phone:** (406) 727-8787.

LEWIS AND CLARK NATIONAL HISTORIC TRAIL INTERPRETIVE CENTER is at 4201 Giant Springs Rd. Exhibits detail the 1804-06 Lewis and Clark expedition, particularly the portion that took place in what is now Montana. Highlighted are the Indian tribes of the Plains and Pacific Northwest who aided the explorers. Rangers demonstrate skills used on the journey. A 30-minute introductory film by Ken Burns sets the stage for the visitor's own discovery journey. A second 20-minute movie depicts the arduous journey around the Great Falls of the Missouri River.

The interpretive center, managed by the USDA Forest Service, overlooks the Missouri River. Onsite features include walking trails, scenic overlooks and grounds landscaped with plants described in the explorers' journals. Outdoor living-history programs are presented in the summer. Audio tours are available in several languages.

Time: Allow 2 hours minimum. **Hours:** Daily 9-6, Memorial Day weekend-Sept. 30; Tues.-Sat. 9-5, Sun. noon-5, rest of year. Closed Jan. 1, Thanksgiving and Christmas. **Cost:** $8; free (ages 0-15). **Phone:** (406) 727-8733.

▼ See AAA listing p. 121 ▼

COMFORT INN & SUITES (406)455-1000
Hotel. **Address:** 1801 Market Place Dr 59404

COMFORT INN BY CHOICE HOTELS (406)454-2727

Hotel
$82-$160

Address: 1120 9th St S 59405 **Location:** I-15 exit 278, 3 mi e on 10th Ave S, US 87/89 and SR 3/200, then just s. Next to a mall. **Facility:** 64 units. 3 stories, interior corridors. **Parking:** winter plug-ins. **Amenities:** safes. **Pool:** heated indoor. **Guest Services:** valet and coin laundry. **Featured Amenity:** full hot breakfast.

CRYSTAL INN HOTEL & SUITES GREAT FALLS 406/727-7788
Hotel. **Address:** 3701 31st St SW 59404 *(See ad p. 120.)*

DAYS INN OF GREAT FALLS (406)727-6565
Hotel. **Address:** 101 14th Ave NW 59404

EXTENDED STAY AMERICA-GREAT FALLS-MISSOURI RIVER 406/761-7524
Extended Stay Hotel. **Address:** 800 River Dr S 59405

THE GREAT FALLS INN BY RIVERSAGE 406/453-6000
Hotel. **Address:** 1400 28th St S 59405

HAMPTON INN BY HILTON 406/453-2675
Hotel. **Address:** 2301 14th St SW 59404

AAA Benefit: Members save 5% or more!

HERITAGE INN 406/761-1900

Hotel
Rates not provided

Address: 1700 Fox Farm Rd 59404 **Location:** I-15 exit 278, 0.8 mi e on 10th Ave S, US 87/89 and SR 3/200. **Facility:** 230 units, some kitchens. 2 stories, interior corridors. **Parking:** winter plug-ins. **Pool:** heated indoor. **Activities:** sauna, hot tub, exercise room. **Guest Services:** valet and coin laundry.

HILTON GARDEN INN 406/452-1000
Hotel. **Address:** 2520 14th St SW 59404

AAA Benefit: Members save 5% or more!

HOLIDAY INN EXPRESS & SUITES 406/453-4000
Hotel. **Address:** 1625 Market Place Dr 59404

LA QUINTA INN & SUITES RIVERSIDE (406)761-2600
Hotel. **Address:** 600 River Dr S 59405

MOTEL 6 #4238 406/453-1602
Motel. **Address:** 2 Treasure State Dr 59404

O'HAIRE MOTOR INN 406/454-2141
Motel. **Address:** 17 7th St S 59401

STAYBRIDGE SUITES 406/761-4903
Extended Stay Hotel. **Address:** 201 3rd St NW (US 87) 59404

WINGATE BY WYNDHAM GREAT FALLS 406/454-3000
Hotel. **Address:** 1000 9th Ave S 59405

WHERE TO EAT

BERT & ERNIE'S 406/453-0601
American. Casual Dining. **Address:** 300 1st Ave S 59401

THE CATTLEMEN'S CUT SUPPER CLUB BAR & CASINO 406/452-0702
Steak Seafood. Casual Dining. **Address:** 369 Vaughn Frontage Rd 59404

THE CELTIC COWBOY 406/952-0393
Irish. Gastropub. **Address:** 116 1st Ave S 59401

DANTE'S CREATIVE CUISINE 406/453-9599
Italian. Casual Dining. **Address:** 1325 8th Ave N 59401

JAKER'S BAR AND GRILL 406/727-1033
American. Casual Dining. **Address:** 1500 10th Ave S 59405

KOBE SEAFOOD & STEAK 406/315-3775
Japanese. Casual Dining. **Address:** 115 3rd St NW 59404

MACKENZIE RIVER PIZZA 406/761-0085
Pizza. Casual Dining. **Address:** 500 River Dr S 59405

RIKKI'S PIZZA & PASTA 406/761-8052
American. Casual Dining. **Address:** 1220 9th St S 59405

SUKI CAFE 406/770-3038
Thai Sushi. Casual Dining. **Address:** 1229 10th Ave S 59405

WHEAT MONTANA BAKERY AND DELI 406/771-7456
Breads/Pastries Deli. Casual Dining. **Address:** 1116 9th St S 59405

HAMILTON (D-2) pop. 4,348, elev. 3,572'

The seat of Ravalli County and headquarters of Bitterroot National Forest, Hamilton was founded by 19th-century copper magnate Marcus Daly.

Bitterroot Valley Chamber of Commerce: 105 E. Main St., Hamilton, MT 59840. **Phone:** (406) 363-2400.

BITTERROOT RIVER INN & CONFERENCE CENTER 406/375-2525
Hotel. **Address:** 139 Bitterroot Plaza Dr 59840

QUALITY INN (406)363-6600

Hotel
$73-$164

Address: 1113 N 1st St 59840 **Location:** On US 93, n of City Center. **Facility:** 62 units. 2 stories (no elevator), interior corridors. **Parking:** winter plug-ins. **Activities:** sauna, exercise room. **Guest Services:** coin laundry. **Featured Amenity:** full hot breakfast.

WHERE TO EAT

SPICE OF LIFE   406/363-4433
▼▼ American. Casual Dining. **Address:** 163 S 2nd St 59840

HARLOWTON (D-4) pop. 997, elev. 4,206'

UPPER MUSSELSHELL MUSEUM is at 36 S. Central Ave. Life in the early 1900s is depicted through replicas of a general store, schoolroom, kitchen and living room. Supplementing these exhibits are displays of period clothing, farm tools and other artifacts. Also displayed is a replica of an avaceratops lammersi dinosaur whose remains were found north of town on Careless Creek. The museum is one of several stops along the Montana Dinosaur Trail. **Time:** Allow 30 minutes minimum. **Hours:** Mon.-Sat. 10-5, Memorial Day-Labor Day; by appointment rest of year. **Cost:** $5; $2.50 (ages 55+); free (ages 0-16). **Phone:** (406) 632-5519.

HAVRE (B-5) pop. 9,310, elev. 2,493'

Havre's beginnings as a transportation hub were forged by the railroad, which brought supplies to trappers, miners and the military at nearby Fort Assinniboine. The town was named by railroad officials after the French city Le Havre, but its citizens gave it a different pronunciation: HAV-er.

Guided tours of Fort Assinniboine, 8 miles southwest off US 87, are offered for a fee daily (weather permitting), June 1-Labor Day. High Line Heritage Resources Walking Tours offers 1-hour tours of the downtown area departing from 124 Third St. A separate hour-long walking tour leaving from the corner of Third Avenue and Main Street explores a 36-block residential historic district. High Line's tours are available by appointment Memorial Day weekend through the last weekend in December (weather permitting); phone (406) 399-5225.

Area geography can best be described as dichotomous. Here, rolling plains meet the Bear Paw Mountains, providing unlimited summer and winter recreation opportunities. Beaver Creek Park, a 17-mile-long, 1-mile-wide strip park 11 miles south on CR 234, encases Beaver Creek and two lakes and offers a variety of activities including camping, fishing, hiking, cross-country skiing and snowshoeing (see Recreation Areas Chart).

Havre Chamber of Commerce: 130 Fifth Ave., P.O. Box 308, Havre, MT 59501. **Phone:** (406) 265-4383.

Self-guiding tours: Brochures for self-guiding walking tours of the 36-block historic district are available from the chamber of commerce.

HAVRE BENEATH THE STREETS is at 120 Third Ave. This guided walking tour takes visitors through the city's historical underground. Many of the original buildings built in 1904 are now beneath the city streets. Included are a Chinese laundry, post office, bordello, meat market, bakery, opium den, barbershop and saloon. **Time:** Allow 1 hour minimum. **Hours:** Tours depart daily 9:30-3:30, Memorial Day to mid-Sept.; Mon.-Sat. 10:30-2:30, rest of year. Closed major holidays. **Cost:** $15; $13 (ages 65+); $12 (ages 13-17); $9 (ages 6-12). Prices may vary; phone ahead. Reservations are recommended. **Phone:** (406) 265-8888.

AMERICINN LODGE & SUITES OF HAVRE   (406)395-5000
▼▼ Hotel. **Address:** 2520 Hwy 2 W 59501

BEST WESTERN PLUS GREAT NORTHERN INN
               (406)265-4200

Hotel
$110-$159

Best Western PLUS   **AAA Benefit:** Members save up to 15% and earn bonus points!

Address: 1345 1st St 59501 **Location:** On US 2, 0.7 mi e of town center. **Facility:** 74 units. 3 stories, interior corridors. **Parking:** winter plug-ins. **Terms:** cancellation fee imposed. **Pool:** heated indoor. **Activities:** hot tub, steamroom, exercise room. **Guest Services:** valet laundry.

/ SOME UNITS [HS]

BEST WESTERN PLUS HAVRE INN & SUITES
               (406)265-2888

Hotel
$100-$160

Best Western PLUS   **AAA Benefit:** Members save up to 15% and earn bonus points!

Address: 1425 2 Hwy NW 59501 **Location:** On US 2, 1 mi w of town. **Facility:** 68 units. 3 stories, interior corridors. **Pool:** heated indoor. **Activities:** hot tub, exercise room. **Guest Services:** valet and coin laundry, area transportation.

 CALL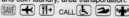
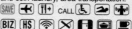

WHERE TO EAT

WOLFER'S DINER   406/265-2111
▼ American. Casual Dining. **Address:** 126 3rd Ave 59501

HELENA (D-3) pop. 28,190, elev. 4,047'
• Restaurants p. 124

Helena succeeded the other gold camps of Bannack and Virginia City as the territorial capital in 1875. It became the state capital in 1889 after a hotly contested fight between "copper kings" William A. Clark and Marcus Daly. The city owes its existence to "The Georgians," four weary and discouraged Southern prospectors, who in 1864 stumbled down a gulch and grimly dubbed it "Last Chance Gulch," only to find gold where the city's main street now runs.

Later a more suitable name, Helena (He-LAY-na), was put to a vote. But the miners and the bull-whackers did not like the name's feminine ring. Consequently, the emphasis was shifted to the first syllable, with the second "e" almost silent, and HEL-e-na became the accepted pronunciation. The gold rush faded quickly, and Helena settled down to become a trade center for the surrounding goldfields.

Reminders of the early days can be found in the architecture of the buildings that line Reeder's Alley off the 200 block of South Park Avenue in southwest Helena. Said to be the oldest structure in Helena, the 1864 Pioneer Cabin, 210 Park Ave., is furnished with pioneer artifacts.

Helena Tourism Alliance: 105 Reeder's Alley, Helena, MT 59601. **Phone:** (406) 449-1270.

Self-guiding tours: The Helena Montana Geocaching Tour, available through the tourism alliance, highlights 38 historic, scenic and cultural sites located in the city and in the surrounding area. The GPS-directed treasure hunt includes the Mansion District, landmark structures such as the Capitol building and the "Guardian of the Gulch" Fire Tower, and Centennial Park.

Shopping: Once the quarters of miners, muleskinners and Chinese laborers during the gold rush, the buildings along Reeder's Alley, 100 S. Park Ave., now contain specialty shops as well as an 1864 cabin furnished with pioneer artifacts.

CATHEDRAL OF ST. HELENA is at 530 N. Ewing St. This handsome Victorian Gothic structure was modeled after the Votive Church of the Sacred Heart in Vienna, Austria, and completed in 1914. Interior finishings are of Carrara marble, and the stained-glass windows were made in Munich, Germany, by F.X. Zettler Co. An open-air sculpture gallery contains 29 statues of historical persons from the arts, sciences and religion.

Time: Allow 30 minutes minimum. **Hours:** Mon.-Fri. 6:30-4, Sat. 8-5, Sun. 6:30-11. Guided tours are given Tues.-Thurs. 1-3, late May-Labor Day; by reservation rest of year. **Cost:** Donations. **Phone:** (406) 442-5825. GT

LAST CHANCE TOUR TRAIN departs from the Montana Historical Society Museum, Library and Archives at 225 N. Roberts St. This 1-hour jaunt makes a circuit through Helena's present and past on an automotive tour train. Passengers view such whimsical downtown architectural features as giant lizards, thumbprints and gargoyles; the Cathedral of St. Helena's splendid 230-foot-tall spires; Reeder's Alley; and the city's mansion district.

Hours: Tours depart Mon.-Sat. at 11, 1, 3 and 5:30, July-Aug.; at 11, 1 and 3, June 15-30; at 11 and 3, June 1-14 and Sept. 1-15. **Cost:** $9; $8 (ages 60+); $7 (ages 4-12). **Phone:** (406) 442-1023.

MONTANA HISTORICAL SOCIETY MUSEUM, LIBRARY AND ARCHIVES is across from the state Capitol at 225 N. Roberts St. The history of Montana and the West is recounted through an extensive collection of Charles M. Russell's paintings and sculpture in addition to frequently changing exhibits. The Montana Homeland exhibition uses more than 2,000 artifacts, photographs and documents to trace Montana history from the end of the most recent ice age through World War II. A highlight is the display of "Big Medicine," a rare white bison with blue eyes and tan hooves born in 1933.

Hours: Mon.-Sat. 9-5. Closed major holidays. **Cost:** $5; $1 (ages 5-18); $12 (family, two adults and children ages 0-18). **Phone:** (406) 444-2694.

STATE CAPITOL is at 1301 Sixth St. Faced with sandstone and Montana granite, the capitol is topped by a dome of Montana copper. The cornerstone was laid July 4, 1899, and the building was dedicated July 4, 1902. Historical paintings and statues decorate the interior; prominent among these is Charles M. Russell's largest painting, the 12-by-25-foot "Lewis and Clark Meeting Indians at Ross' Hole," in the House of Representatives.

Time: Allow 45 minutes minimum. **Hours:** Mon.-Fri. 8-5, Sat.-Sun. and holidays 9-3. Guided tours are given on the hour Mon.-Sat. 10-2, May-Sept.; Sat. 10-2, Oct.-Dec. The Jan.-Apr. tour schedule in even-numbered years is Sat. 10-2; Mon.-Sat. 10-2 in odd-numbered years. Closed Jan. 1, Thanksgiving and Christmas. Phone ahead to confirm schedule. **Cost:** Free. **Phone:** (406) 444-4789. GT

BARRISTER BED & BREAKFAST   406/443-7330
♥♥♥ Historic Bed & Breakfast. **Address:** 416 N Ewing St 59601

BEST WESTERN PREMIER HELENA GREAT NORTHERN HOTEL   (406)457-5500

♥♥♥♦ **Hotel** $180-$300

BWP PREMIER BEST WESTERN.

AAA Benefit: Members save up to 15% and earn bonus points!

Address: 835 Great Northern Blvd 59601 **Location:** I-15 exit 193 (Cedar St), 2 mi w, just w on Lyndale Ave, then just s on Getchell St; downtown. **Facility:** 100 units. 4 stories, interior corridors. **Parking:** winter plug-ins. **Terms:** cancellation fee imposed. **Amenities:** safes. **Dining:** Silver Star Steak Company, see separate listing. **Pool:** heated indoor. **Activities:** hot tub, exercise room. **Guest Services:** valet and coin laundry.

SAVE ✈ 🍽 🛎 CALL 🛗 ➤ 🛗 BIZ HS 📶 ✉ 📱 🖥 🖨 /SOME UNITS 🐾

COMFORT SUITES

(406)495-0505

Hotel
$100-$172

Address: 3180 N Washington St 59602 **Location:** I-15 exit 194 (Custer Ave), just e. **Facility:** 90 units, some efficiencies. 3 stories, interior corridors. **Parking:** winter plug-ins. **Amenities:** safes. **Pool:** heated indoor. **Activities:** hot tub, exercise room. **Guest Services:** valet and coin laundry, area transportation. **Featured Amenity: full hot breakfast.**

SAVE ✈ ❤️ CALL 🅰 🛳 🚲
BIZ HS 📶 ✕ 🖥 💺 💻
/ SOME UNITS 🖥

DAYS INN HELENA

(406)442-3280

Hotel. **Address:** 2001 Prospect Ave 59601

DELTA HOTELS BY MARRIOTT HELENA COLONIAL

(406)443-2100

Hotel. **Address:** 2301 Colonial Dr 59601

AAA Benefit: Members save 5% or more!

FAIRFIELD INN & SUITES BY MARRIOTT

(406)449-9944

Hotel
$75-$204

Fairfield

AAA Benefit: Members save 5% or more!

Address: 2150 11th Ave 59601 **Location:** I-15 exit 192 (Prospect Ave), just sw. **Facility:** 58 units. 3 stories, interior corridors. **Parking:** winter plug-ins. **Terms:** check-in 4 pm, cancellation fee imposed. **Pool:** heated indoor. **Activities:** hot tub, exercise room. **Guest Services:** valet and coin laundry. **Featured Amenity: breakfast buffet.**

SAVE ✈ ❤️ CALL 🅰 🛳 🚲

BIZ HS 📶 ✕ 🖥 💺 💻

HAMPTON INN BY HILTON-HELENA

(406)443-5800

Hotel
$128-$179

Hampton by Hilton

AAA Benefit: Members save 5% or more!

Address: 725 Carter Dr 59601 **Location:** I-15 exit 192 (Prospect Ave), just e. **Facility:** 81 units. 3 stories, interior corridors. **Parking:** winter plug-ins. **Terms:** 1-7 night minimum stay, 3 day cancellation notice-fee imposed. **Pool:** heated indoor. **Activities:** hot tub, exercise room. **Guest Services:** valet and coin laundry, area transportation. **Featured Amenity: full hot breakfast.**

SAVE ✈ ❤️ CALL 🅰 🛳 🚲 BIZ 📶 ✕ 🖥
💺 💻

HOLIDAY INN EXPRESS HOTEL & SUITES

406/442-7500

Hotel. **Address:** 3170 N Sanders St 59602

HOME2 SUITES BY HILTON

406/502-2222

Extended Stay Contemporary Hotel. **Address:** 3325 N Sanders St 59602

AAA Benefit: Members save 5% or more!

LA QUINTA INN & SUITES HELENA

(406)449-4000

Hotel. **Address:** 701 Washington St 59601

RESIDENCE INN BY MARRIOTT

(406)443-8010

Extended Stay Hotel. **Address:** 2500 E Custer Ave 59602

AAA Benefit: Members save 5% or more!

THE SANDERS-HELENA'S BED & BREAKFAST

(406)442-3309

Historic Bed & Breakfast. **Address:** 328 N Ewing St 59601

WINGATE BY WYNDHAM

(406)449-3000

Hotel. **Address:** 2007 N Oakes St 59601

WHERE TO EAT

BENNY'S BISTRO

406/443-0105

American
Casual Dining
$9-$27

AAA Inspector Notes: Whether you choose to dine here at lunch or at dinner, you'll always be served fresh, delicious, innovative cuisine. The focaccia bread is wonderful for any sandwich creation or as an accompaniment to an entrée. Tapas are served daily. Be sure to ask about the soup du jour and the chef's choice for cheesecake. **Features:** beer & wine. **Address:** 108 E 6th Ave 59601 **Location:** Center; in historic downtown; across from Chamber of Commerce. **Parking:** street only. L D

BREWHOUSE PUB & GRILLE

406/457-9390

American. Brewpub. **Address:** 939 Getchell St 59601

JADE GARDEN

406/443-8899

Chinese. Casual Dining. **Address:** 3128 N Montana Ave 59602

LUCCA'S

406/457-8311

Italian. Casual Dining. **Address:** 56 N Last Chance Gulch 59601

MACKENZIE RIVER PIZZA

406/443-0033

Pizza. Casual Dining. **Address:** 1110 Road Runner Dr 59602

MEDITERRANEAN GRILL

406/495-1212

Mediterranean. Casual Dining. **Address:** 42 S Park Ave 59601

NAGOYA JAPANESE STEAKHOUSE & SUSHI

406/449-2742

Japanese Sushi. Casual Dining. **Address:** 2790 Washington St 59602

ON BROADWAY

406/443-1929

Italian. Casual Dining. **Address:** 106 Broadway St 59601

SILVER STAR STEAK COMPANY

406/495-0677

Steak. Casual Dining. **Address:** 833 Great Northern Blvd 59601

STEVE'S CAFE

406/449-6666

American. Casual Dining. **Address:** 630 N Montana Ave 59601

STEVE'S CAFE

406/444-5010

Breakfast. Casual Dining. **Address:** 1225 E Custer Ave 59601

TOI'S THAI CUISINE

406/443-6656

Thai. Casual Dining. **Address:** 423 N Last Chance Gulch St 59601

WINDBAG SALOON

406/443-9669

American. Casual Dining. **Address:** 19 S Last Chance Gulch 59601

HELENA NATIONAL FOREST (C-3)

Elevations in the forest range from 3,600 ft. at the gates of the Missouri River to 9,411 ft. on Red Mountain in the Lincoln district. Refer to AAA maps for additional elevation information.

In west-central Montana, Helena National Forest encompasses 976,000 acres. The forest straddles the Continental Divide and embraces the Big Belt and the Elkhorn mountains. The Missouri River passes through the Helena Valley near the center of the forest. Vegetation ranges from sagebrush and bunchgrass to Douglas fir, lodgepole pine and spruce.

There are more than 1,000 miles of trails and 1,600 miles of forest roads. Continental Divide National Scenic Trail passes through the forest. Ten campgrounds, picnic grounds, good hunting and fishing, historic sites, wilderness areas and several ghost towns are among the forest's attractions. For further information contact the Forest Supervisor, Helena National Forest, 2880 Skyway Dr., Helena, MT 59602; phone (406) 449-5201. *See Recreation Areas Chart.*

THE GATES OF THE MOUNTAINS RECREATION AREA is 20 mi. n. of Helena via I-15 exit 209 to Gates of the Mountains Landing and is reached by boat or trails. In 1805, the members of the Lewis and Clark expedition were fortunate to gaze upon the majestic natural wonder that lay before them. Limestone walls towering 1,200 feet stood like rock sentries within the canyon where the Missouri River pushes through the Big Belt Range. Named by Meriwether Lewis as "gates of the mountains," the name stuck and today visitors continue to marvel at the splendor of the rock formations.

Wildlife that call the canyon home include bighorn sheep, mountain goats, deer, mountain lions, black bears, ospreys and falcons. The recreation area provides swimming, hiking, fishing and narrated boat trip opportunities. A dinner cruise also is available.

Hours: Narrated 2-hour boat trips depart Mon.-Fri. at 9, 11, 1 and 3, Sat.-Sun. and holidays on the hour 10-4, in July; Mon.-Fri. at 11, 1 and 3, Sat.-Sun. on the hour 10-4, Aug. 1-Labor Day; Mon.-Fri. at 11 and 2, Sat.-Sun. and holidays at 10, noon, 2 and 4 in June; Wed.-Fri. at 11 and 2, Sat.-Sun. and holidays at 11, 1 and 3, day after Labor Day-Sept. 30. Dinner cruises Fri. at 6, mid-July to mid-Aug. **Cost:** Narrated boat trip $16; $14 (ages 60+ and military with ID); $10 (ages 4-17). Dinner cruise $44. Reservations are required. **Phone:** (406) 458-5241.

**🔗 For more details,
rates and reservations:
AAA.com/travelguides/hotels**

HUNGRY HORSE pop. 826

- Hotels & Restaurants map & index p. 116
- Part of Glacier National Park area — see map p. 111

HISTORIC TAMARACK LODGE & CABINS

406/387-4420

Cabin
Rates not provided

Address: 9549 US 2 E 59919 **Location:** 1.6 mi n. **Facility:** 30 units, some cabins. 1 story, interior/exterior corridors. **Activities:** fishing, cross country skiing, lawn sports, picnic facilities, trails.

KALISPELL (B-2) pop. 19,927, elev. 2,956'

- Hotels p. 126 • Restaurants p. 126
- Hotels & Restaurants map & index p. 116
- Part of Glacier National Park area — see map p. 111

Kalispell (KAL-is-pell) is in the Flathead Valley between Glacier National Park *(see place listing p. 111)* and Flathead Lake, a region noted for the production of sweet cherries. The area was known only to the Salish, who called it "the land between the mountains," until 1891 when the Great Northern Railroad laid track to this point. The nearby settlements of Demersville and Ashley were moved to create Kalispell.

Kalispell is circled by dense forests, lakes, rivers and mountains. To the east is the Swan Range of the Rocky Mountains, and to the west, the Kootenai Range. Flathead National Forest *(see place listing p. 107)* has its headquarters in the city.

Local parks include Woodland Park, with lagoons, formal gardens and picnicking. Three forks of the Flathead River drain into Flathead Lake, making the area an ideal place for fly fishing, white-water rafting, kayaking and sailing.

Kalispell Chamber of Commerce/Convention & Visitor Bureau: 15 Depot Park, Kalispell, MT 59901-4008. **Phone:** (406) 758-2200 or (888) 888-2308.

Self-guiding tours: Information about walking tours of the historic district is available from the Kalispell Chamber of Commerce; phone (406) 758-2811. For information about the greater northwestern Montana area contact Glacier Country at (800) 338-5072.

Shopping: The Kalispell Farmers Market, in the Flathead Valley Community College parking lot, offers more than 100 vendors selling homemade and homegrown products Saturdays 9-12:30 from spring through fall.

CONRAD MANSION MUSEUM is 6 blks. e. of Main St. at 330 Woodland Ave. Built in 1895 for Kalispell's founder, Charles E. Conrad, who traded and freighted on the Missouri River, the 26-room mansion has been restored to its Victorian

(See map & index p. 116.)

splendor and contains original furnishings. Visitors can take guided tours of the mansion and self-guiding tours of the 3-acre site's gardens.

Time: Allow 1 hour minimum. **Hours:** Guided tours are given Tues.-Sun. on the hour 10-4, mid-June to mid-Oct.; Wed.-Sun. 10-4, mid-May to mid-June. Holiday tours are offered Thanksgiving weekend-late Dec. Phone ahead to confirm schedule. **Cost:** $12; $11 (ages 65+); $8 (ages 12-17); $6 (ages 0-11). **Phone:** (406) 755-2166. [GT]

HOCKADAY MUSEUM OF ART is at 302 Second Ave. E. Permanent and rotating exhibits showcase the art and culture of Montana, with special focus on Glacier National Park and the Northern Plains and Blackfeet Indians. **Time:** Allow 1 hour minimum. **Hours:** Tues.-Fri. 10-5, Sat. 10-4. **Cost:** $5; $4 (ages 60+); $2 (college students with ID); free (ages 0-18). **Phone:** (406) 755-5268.

AMERICAS BEST VALUE INN   406/756-3222 [40]
Hotel. **Address:** 1550 Hwy 93 N 59901

BEST WESTERN PLUS FLATHEAD LAKE INN & SUITES
(406)857-2400

Hotel
$89-$329

Best Western PLUS
AAA Benefit: Members save up to 15% and earn bonus points!

Address: 4824 Hwy 93 S 59901 **Location:** 7 mi s; jct SR 82. **Facility:** 59 units. 3 stories, interior corridors. **Parking:** winter plug-ins. **Terms:** cancellation fee imposed. **Pool:** heated indoor. **Activities:** hot tub, exercise room. **Guest Services:** coin laundry. **Featured Amenity: full hot breakfast.**

/ SOME UNITS

HAMPTON INN BY HILTON KALISPELL
(406)755-7900 [42]

Hotel
$92-$390

Hampton by Hilton
AAA Benefit: Members save 5% or more!

Address: 1140 US 2 W 59901 **Location:** 0.9 mi w on US 2 from jct US 93. **Facility:** 120 units. 3 stories, interior corridors. **Parking:** winter plug-ins. **Terms:** 1-7 night minimum stay, 3 day cancellation notice-fee imposed. **Pool:** heated indoor. **Activities:** hot tub, exercise room. **Guest Services:** valet and coin laundry, area transportation. **Featured Amenity: full hot breakfast.**

AAA.com/discounts—Your first stop for travel and shopping savings

HILTON GARDEN INN KALISPELL   (406)756-4500 [46]

Hotel
$79-$309

Hilton Garden Inn
AAA Benefit: Members save 5% or more!

Address: 1840 US 93 S 59901 **Location:** 1.4 mi s on US 93 from jct US 2. **Facility:** 144 units. 4 stories, interior corridors. **Parking:** winter plug-ins. **Terms:** 1-7 night minimum stay, 3 day cancellation notice-fee imposed. **Dining:** Blue Canyon Kitchen & Tavern, see separate listing. **Pool:** heated indoor. **Activities:** hot tub, exercise room. **Guest Services:** valet and coin laundry, area transportation.

HOLIDAY INN EXPRESS & SUITES   406/755-7405 [37]
Hotel. **Address:** 275 Treeline Rd 59901

HOMEWOOD SUITES BY HILTON   406/755-8080 [39]
Extended Stay Hotel. **Address:** 195 Hutton Ranch Rd 59901

AAA Benefit: Members save 5% or more!

LA QUINTA INN & SUITES KALISPELL   (406)257-5255 [41]
Hotel. **Address:** 255 Montclair Dr 59901

QUALITY INN   (406)755-6700 [43]
Hotel. **Address:** 1330 Hwy 2 W 59901

RED LION HOTEL KALISPELL   406/751-5050 [44]
Hotel. **Address:** 20 N Main St 59901

SPRINGHILL SUITES BY MARRIOTT KALISPELL
(406)314-6600 [38]

Hotel
$63-$318

SPRINGHILL SUITES MARRIOTT
AAA Benefit: Members save 5% or more!

Address: 250 Old Reserve Dr 59901 **Location:** Jct US 93 and Reserve Loop, just w. **Facility:** 101 units. 4 stories, interior corridors. **Terms:** cancellation fee imposed. **Pool:** heated indoor. **Activities:** exercise room. **Guest Services:** valet and coin laundry. **Featured Amenity: breakfast buffet.**

SUPER 8-KALISPELL/GLACIER NATIONAL PARK
(406)755-1888 [45]
Hotel. **Address:** 1341 1st Ave E 59901

WHERE TO EAT

THE ALLEY CONNECTION   406/752-7077 [36]
Chinese. Casual Dining. **Address:** 22 1st St W 59901

BLUE CANYON KITCHEN & TAVERN   406/758-2583 [44]
American. Casual Dining. **Address:** 1840 US 93 59901

BOJANGLES' DINER   406/755-3222 [31]
American. Casual Dining. **Address:** 1319 US 2 59901

BONELLI'S BISTRO   406/257-8669 [33]
Mediterranean. Casual Dining. **Address:** 38 1st Ave E 59901

(See map & index p. 116.)

BULLMAN'S WOOD FIRED PIZZA   406/257-3473   (28)
💎💎 Pizza. Casual Dining. **Address:** 175 Hutton Ranch Rd 59901

CASA MEXICO   406/752-6800   (43)
💎💎 Mexican. Casual Dining. **Address:** 1600 93 Hwy S 59901

CISLO'S   406/756-7330   (29)
💎💎 American. Casual Dining. **Address:** 2046 US 2 E 59901

THE DESOTO GRILL   406/314-6095   (35)
💎💎 American. Casual Dining. **Address:** 227 1st St W 59901

GENKI   406/257-8889   (39)
💎💎 Asian Sushi. Casual Dining. **Address:** 302 Main St 59901

HOPS DOWNTOWN GRILL   406/755-7687   (38)
💎💎 Western Burgers. Gastropub. **Address:** 121 Main St 59903

JULIE'S CENTER STREET CAFE   406/755-7171   (32)
💎💎 American. Casual Dining. **Address:** 200 E Center St 59901

MACKENZIE RIVER PIZZA   406/756-3030
💎💎 Pizza. Casual Dining. **Address:** 45 Treeline Rd 59901

THE MONTANA CLUB   406/260-4401   (42)
💎💎 Western Steak Seafood. Casual Dining. **Address:** 1301 S Main St 59901

NICKEL CHARLIE'S CASINO & EATERY   406/257-7756   (30)
💎💎 American. Casual Dining. **Address:** 1275 US 2 E 59901

NORM'S NEWS   406/756-5466   (34)
💎 Burgers. Casual Dining. **Address:** 34 Main St 59901

SCOTTIBELLI'S RISTORANTE ITALIANO   406/890-7800   (37)
💎💎 Italian. Casual Dining. **Address:** 110 Main St 59901

SPENCER & CO   406/756-8941   (27)
💎💎 Steak. Casual Dining. **Address:** 4010 US 93 N 59901

THAI PALACE RESTAURANT   406/756-7956   (40)
💎💎 Thai. Casual Dining. **Address:** 319 Main St 59901

WHEAT MONTANA BAKERY & DELI   406/257-6530   (41)
💎 Breads/Pastries Deli. Casual Dining. **Address:** 405 Main St 59901

KOOTENAI NATIONAL FOREST (A-1)

Elevations in the forest range from 1,862 ft. where the Kootenai River crosses into Idaho to 8,736 ft. on Snowshoe Peak. Refer to AAA maps for additional elevation information.

Kootenai National Forest is in the northwest corner of Montana, with a small section extending into Idaho. High, craggy peaks characterize the 2.2 million-acre region; portions of the Cabinet, Whitefish and Purcell mountains are the main ranges, attaining elevations as high as 8,700 feet. The area's climate is modified Pacific Maritime, and as a result Kootenai has an abundance of plant species more common to the Pacific Coast than to other parts of Montana.

There are diverse wildlife species, including bear, elk, deer, mountain goats, bighorn sheep and wolves. The forest also is home to many non-game species. Throughout the year bald eagles can be seen along the Kootenai River north of Libby; 205 species of birds have been recorded in the forest. Cabinet Mountains Wilderness has 85 small lakes; many are scenic, stocked with fish and reached by trail. Ski facilities are available northwest of Libby. The area has more than 50 campgrounds and 1,500 miles of hiking trails.

Ross Creek Cedars Scenic Area, off SR 56 southwest of Libby, and Ten Lakes Scenic Area, on the Canadian border northeast of Eureka, are reached by local and forest roads. Lake Koocanusa also is a popular recreational spot.

For further information, contact the Forest Supervisor, Kootenai National Forest, 31374 US 2, Libby, MT 59923; phone (406) 293-6211. *See Recreation Areas Chart.*

LAUREL pop. 6,718

BEST WESTERN YELLOWSTONE CROSSING
(406)628-6888

💎💎
Hotel
$79-$159

Best Western. **AAA Benefit:** Members save up to 15% and earn bonus points!

Address: 205 SE 4th St 59044 **Location:** I-90 exit 434, just n, then just e. **Facility:** 60 units. 3 stories, interior corridors. **Parking:** winter plug-ins. **Terms:** cancellation fee imposed. **Amenities:** safes. **Pool:** heated indoor. **Activities:** hot tub. **Guest Services:** coin laundry.

LEWIS AND CLARK NATIONAL FOREST (B-3)

Elevations in the forest range from 4,000 ft. in the valley bottoms to 9,204 ft. on Scapegoat Mountain. Refer to AAA maps for additional elevation information.

Lewis and Clark National Forest is in west-central Montana. Consisting of 1,843,397 acres, the forest has two units. The Rocky Mountain Unit, which embraces about half of the acreage, lies along the eastern slope of the Continental Divide south of Glacier National Park. It includes portions of the Bob Marshall *(see Flathead National Forest p. 107)* and Scapegoat wildernesses.

The Rocky Mountain Unit rises sharply from grasslands to peaks between 7,000 and 8,000 feet in elevation. Access to the area is by a number of gravel roads off US 89 that connect with forest roads and trailheads and serve several campgrounds.

Southeast of Great Falls is the Jefferson Unit, scattered inland mountain ranges dotting the prairie, including the Little Belt, Castle, Highwoods, Big Snowy and Little Snowy mountain ranges and the north end of the Crazy Mountains. The Jefferson Division has short, dome-like mountains rather than jagged peaks.

The mountains are forest-covered and have moderate slopes that present less demanding hiking and riding trails than those found in the Rocky Mountain Unit. There are many streams but no large rivers or lakes.

Winter sports are available near Kings Hill Summit, some 40 miles north of White Sulphur Springs, Monarch and Neihart. For further information contact the Forest Supervisor, Lewis and Clark National Forest, 1220 38 St. N., Great Falls, MT 59405; phone (406) 791-7700. *See Recreation Areas Chart.*

LITTLE BIGHORN BATTLEFIELD NATIONAL MONUMENT (E-6)

The main entrance to Little Bighorn Battlefield National Monument is 15 miles southeast of Hardin via exit 510 off I-90, then a half-mile east via US 212. In the Valley of the Little Bighorn River in June 1876, Lt. Col. George Armstrong Custer and the 210 men of the 7th Cavalry Regiment under his command made their last stand against several thousand Lakota, Arapaho and Northern Cheyenne, many of whom were fleeing the restrictions of the reservation. Covering 1.2 square miles, the monument commemorates the dramatic climax of the Indian Wars by preserving the site of this Native American victory.

The monument embraces a national cemetery established in 1879, various monuments and memorials, and a historical museum with maps, photographs and dioramas depicting the battle. Just inside the entrance is a visitor center where park rangers provide tour information and self-guiding tour brochures.

Auto tours with maps are available at the center and from Big Horn County Historical Museum and State Visitor Center and other local outlets; phone (406) 665-1671.

Monument 8-8, Memorial Day-Labor Day; 8-6, Apr. 1-day before Memorial Day and day after Labor Day-Sept. 30; 8-4:30, rest of year. Closed Jan. 1, Thanksgiving and Christmas. Admission $25 (per private vehicle); $20 (per motorcycle); $15 (per person arriving by other means). Cemetery free. Phone (406) 638-2621.

APSAALOOKE TOURS departs from the Little Bighorn Battlefield National Monument Visitor Center. Narrated van tours of the site of the Battle of the Little Bighorn are given by Native American guides. **Time:** Allow 1 hour minimum. **Hours:** Tours are given daily at 10, 11, noon and 3, Memorial Day-Labor Day; other times by appointment. **Cost:** $10; $8 (ages 65+); $5 (ages 4-12). **Phone:** (406) 638-2621. GT

LIVINGSTON (E-4) pop. 7,044, elev. 4,501'
• Part of Yellowstone National Park area — see map p. 214

The lush grasses of Paradise Valley were ideal for raising cattle, and the valley's warm Chinook winds protected the area from bitter Montana winters. When the Northern Pacific Railroad laid tracks in 1882, both the cattle industry and Livingston flourished. Among the town's more memorable residents was Calamity Jane.

Livingston is at the head of Paradise Valley, through which flows the Yellowstone River and around which rise the Crazy Mountains and the Absaroka and Gallatin ranges of the Rockies. The area offers opportunities for wildlife viewing, hunting, fishing, rafting, backpacking, camping, skiing and snowmobiling.

A scenic drive, US 89, connects Livingston to Gardiner and the northern entrance to Yellowstone National Park *(see place listing p. 214).* Livingston was the original entrance to Yellowstone.

Livingston Area Chamber of Commerce: 303 E. Park St., Livingston, MT 59047. **Phone:** (406) 222-0850.

Self-guiding tours: A brochure outlining a walking tour of the historic business district is available at Yellowstone Gateway Museum *(see attraction listing this page)* and the chamber of commerce.

SAVE **YELLOWSTONE GATEWAY MUSEUM** is off I-90 exit 333 at 118 W. Chinook St. Housed in a three-story, 1907 schoolhouse, the museum features a variety of local history exhibits, including Yellowstone National Park memorabilia and stagecoaches once used within the park. Historic vehicles include a turn-of-the-20th-century Northern Pacific Railway caboose.

A map traces William Clark's route through the area. Rounding out the museum's offerings are exhibits about military, fire and transportation history; American Indian artifacts; local Yellowstone art; and household items from area pioneers. **Time:** Allow 30 minutes minimum. **Hours:** Daily 10-5, Memorial Day-Sept. 30; Thurs.-Sat. 10-5, rest of year. **Cost:** $5; $4 (ages 55+); free (ages 0-18). **Phone:** (406) 222-4184.

LIVINGSTON COMFORT INN   (406)222-4400
♦♦ Hotel. **Address:** 114 Loves Ln 59047

SUPER 8 LIVINGSTON   (406)224-4099

♦♦
Motel
$70-$140

Address: 105 Centennial Dr 59047 **Location:** I-90 exit 333, just s on US 89. **Facility:** 37 units, some kitchens. 2 stories (no elevator), interior corridors. **Parking:** winter plug-ins. **Amenities:** safes. **Guest Services:** coin laundry. **Featured Amenity:** continental breakfast.

TRAVELODGE LIVINGSTON   (406)222-6320

♦♦
Motel
$60-$180

Address: 102 Rogers Ln 59047 **Location:** I-90 exit 333, just n on US 89, then just w. **Facility:** 44 units. 1 story, interior/exterior corridors. **Parking:** winter plug-ins. **Amenities:** safes. **Pool:** heated indoor. **Guest Services:** coin laundry.

YELLOWSTONE PIONEER LODGE   406/222-6110
▼▼ **Hotel. Address:** 1515 W Park St 59047

**YELLOWSTONE VALLEY LODGE, AN ASCEND HOTEL
COLLECTION MEMBER**   406/333-4787

**Resort Cabin
Rates not provided**

Address: 3840 US Hwy 89 S 59047 **Location:** I-90 exit 333, 15 mi s on US 89 S; between MM 38 and 39. **Facility:** There are two outside fire pits for fun evening gatherings. Each unit offers a deck overlooking the river. Choose a cabin with basic accommodations or a newer upscale room. 23 cabins, some two bedrooms and kitchens. 1 story, exterior corridors. **Activities:** fishing. **Featured Amenity: full hot breakfast.**

WHERE TO EAT

2ND STREET BISTRO   406/222-9463
▼▼ Regional American. Casual Dining. **Address:** 123 N 2nd St 59047

GIL'S GOODS   406/222-9463
▼▼ Pizza Breads/Pastries. Casual Dining. **Address:** 207 W Park St 59047

MONTANA'S RIB & CHOP HOUSE   406/222-9200
▼▼ American. Casual Dining. **Address:** 305 E Park Rd 59047

LOLO NATIONAL FOREST (B-1)

Lolo National Forest is in western Montana. With boundaries stretching from the Swan Range in the northeast to the Idaho border, an area 120 miles long and 40 to 80 miles wide, the forest embraces about 2,100,000 acres. Although the Lolo is an important timber producer, many of its south-facing slopes are open and grassy. It also is one of the principal elk areas in western Montana.

Wilderness areas within the forest include the 33,000-acre Rattlesnake National Recreation Area and Wilderness as well as Welcome Creek and portions of Scapegoat.

Recreational opportunities abound on 3,500 miles of streams, including Rock Creek, a haven for trout-fishing enthusiasts. Approximately 485 species of fish and wildlife inhabit the forest, which has numerous camping and/or picnic sites and 1,780 miles of hiking trails; winter activities include downhill and cross-country skiing, snowmobiling along 360 miles of designated trails and ice fishing. Some recreation facilities are designed for physically impaired access; inquire at a ranger station.

The forest has five offices: the Ninemile Ranger Station in Huson; the Missoula Ranger Station at Fort Missoula; and stations in the outlying districts of Seeley Lake, Superior and Plains/Thompson Falls.

· For further information, contact Lolo National Forest, 24 Fort Missoula Rd., Missoula, MT 59804; phone (406) 329-3750. *See Recreation Areas Chart.*

MALTA (B-6) pop. 1,997, elev. 2,248'
• Restaurants p. 129

Named for the island in the Mediterranean, Malta was the center of a cattle empire that reached from Glasgow to Havre and from the Missouri River to Canada during the late 19th century. Wheat and alfalfa have joined cattle as the area's leading products.

A large boulder at the intersection of US 2 and Sleeping Buffalo Resort looks like a sleeping buffalo. The Assiniboine Indians revered it, and the markings on it had a part in their tribal rituals.

The Little Rocky Mountains, called "island mountains" by early Native Americans, are 40 miles southwest on US 191. Gold was discovered in the mountains in 1884, and the historic remains set the scene for the mountain communities of Zortman and Landusky.

Notable Wild Bunch outlaws Butch Cassidy and Landusky resident Harvey "Kid Curry" Logan hid out in the area in 1901 after robbing a Great Northern passenger train, making off with around $60,000.

The Charles M. Russell National Wildlife Refuge, 60 miles south of Malta via US 191, sprawls across 1,100,000 acres around Fort Peck Reservoir. Drivers can access a scenic, 19-mile, self-guiding automobile tour route from two points along US 191. Signs along the way describe the area's history, geology and wildlife. Phone (406) 538-8706.

Malta Area Chamber of Commerce: 10½ S. 4th St. E., P.O. Box 1420, Malta, MT 59538. **Phone:** (406) 654-1776.

PHILLIPS COUNTY MUSEUM is at 431 E. US 2. Visitors are greeted by Elvis, a 33-foot brachylophosaurus, and meet the Outlaw Kid Curry, ranchers and homesteaders inside the museum. A collection of Native American beadwork and numerous fossils are on display. The refurbished, historic H.G. Robinson House and Gardens are next door. **Time:** Allow 1 hour minimum. **Hours:** Mon.-Sat. 10-5, Apr.-Dec. **Cost:** $5; $3 (ages 5-18); $12 (family). **Phone:** (406) 654-1037.

EDGEWATER INN & RV PARK   406/654-1302
▼ Motel. **Address:** 101 Hwy 2 W 59538

MALTANA MOTEL   406/654-2610

▼
**Motel
Rates not provided**

Address: 138 S 1st Ave W 59538 **Location:** Just s of US 2 via US 191, just w; downtown. **Facility:** 19 units. 1 story, exterior corridors. **Parking:** winter plug-ins. **Guest Services:** area transportation.

WHERE TO EAT

GREAT NORTHERN STEAKHOUSE   406/654-2100
▼▼ American. Casual Dining. **Address:** 2 S 1st Ave E 59538

MARTINSDALE (D-4) pop. 64, elev. 4,819'

BAIR FAMILY MUSEUM is at 2751 SR 294. Charles M. Bair moved to Montana in 1883. He went into ranching and made his fortune in the Alaskan Gold Rush. The circa 1890s Bair ranch comprises antiques and paintings. Highlights include a collection of Paul Storr silver and an 18th-century British sideboard. **Time:** Allow 1 hour minimum. **Hours:** Daily 10-5, Memorial Day-Labor Day.; Wed.-Sun. 10-5, day after Labor Day-Oct. 31. Last tour begins 1 hour before closing. **Cost:** $5; $3 (ages 62+); $2 (ages 6-16). **Phone:** (406) 572-3314. 🏧

MILES CITY (D-7) pop. 8,410, elev. 2,364'

Miles City developed on the bottomland at the confluence of the Tongue and Yellowstone rivers. Gen. Nelson A. Miles arrived at the mouth of the Tongue River in August 1876 to force the Cheyenne and Sioux to return to the reservations. Miles built Fort Keogh at the site in 1877 and used it as a base for controlling the local tribes.

Main Street in times past was a block of saloons, gambling dens and brothels on the south, and banks, businesses and pawn shops on the north. Miles City has become a growing retail and service hub for eastern Montana and a center for cattle, sheep and crop farms.

Miles City Area Chamber of Commerce: 511 Pleasant St., Miles City, MT 59301. **Phone:** (406) 234-2890.

BEST WESTERN WAR BONNET INN   (406)234-4560

Motel
$105-$135

Best Western. **AAA Benefit:** Members save up to 15% and earn bonus points!

Address: 1015 S Haynes Ave 59301 **Location:** I-94 exit 138 (Broadus), 0.3 mi n. **Facility:** 53 units. 2 stories (no elevator), exterior corridors. **Parking:** winter plug-ins. **Terms:** cancellation fee imposed. **Pool:** heated indoor. **Activities:** sauna, hot tub.

[SAVE] [▥] [▨] [BIZ] [▨] [✕] [▤] [▨] [▨] [/SOME UNITS] [▨] [HS]

SLEEP INN & SUITES MILES CITY   (406)232-3000

Hotel
$99-$208

Address: 1006 S Haynes Ave 59301 **Location:** I-94 exit 138 (S Haynes Ave), 0.3 mi n. **Facility:** 90 units, some efficiencies. 3 stories, interior corridors. **Parking:** winter plug-ins. **Amenities:** safes. **Pool:** heated indoor. **Activities:** exercise room. **Guest Services:** coin laundry. **Featured Amenity:** full hot breakfast.

[SAVE] [▥] [CALL] [▨] [▨] [▨] [BIZ] [HS] [▨] [✕] [▤] [▨] [▨] [/SOME UNITS] [▨]

WHERE TO EAT

BLACK IRON GRILL & ROTISSERIE   406/234-4766
American. Casual Dining. **Address:** 2901 Boutelle St 59301

CITYBREW   406/234-6106
Coffee/Tea. Casual Dining. **Address:** 719 S Haynes Ave 59301

MISSOULA (D-2) pop. 66,788, elev. 3,223'
• Restaurants p. 132

Missoula lies astride the Clark Fork River, a tributary of the Columbia River named for William Clark. The town also occupies a valley that was once part of Glacial Lake Missoula, a prehistoric lake.

At the mouth of Hell Gate Canyon, Missoula straddles the route the Salish Indians traveled to reach the Great Plains hunting buffalo. Meriwether Lewis and William Clark later followed the same route through the canyon and camped approximately 9 miles southwest at Travellers Rest, near present-day Lolo. Many Native Americans died in the canyon, as the Blackfoot regularly ambushed the Salish, which prompted French-Canadian trappers to christen the site Porte de L'Enfer, "Gate of Hell."

One of the first lumber mills in the region began in Missoula. Lumber remains not only a major industry but also a major concern. The U.S. Forest Service maintains in Missoula its Region No. 1 headquarters, a research station devoted to forest fire research and the 'smokejumpers' training center. The University of Montana supports these studies with a 22,000-acre experimental forest in addition to conservation and wildlife research stations.

A short drive in any direction will lead into a national forest or a wilderness area. The Rattlesnake National Recreation Area and Wilderness, 6 miles north of downtown, has many small lakes, streams and trails.

A Carousel for Missoula near Caras Park is a hand-carved 1918 merry-go-round created by volunteers. Rides are offered year-round; phone (406) 549-8382.

The International Wildlife Film Festival provides an opportunity for wildlife and conservation filmmakers, broadcasters, scientists, educators and students to network and share ideas relating to projects. The 8-day event takes place in spring.

The 5-day Montana Book Festival takes place in September. It is a literary celebration that features some 50 events showcasing more than 70 writers in a variety of demonstrations, exhibits, readings, receptions, signings and workshops.

Missoula Convention & Visitors Bureau: 101 E. Main St., Missoula, MT 59802. **Phone:** (406) 532-3250 or (800) 526-3465.

Self-guiding tours: Brochures outlining walking tours of public art and historical buildings in the downtown district are available from the convention and visitors bureau.

Shopping: Southgate Mall, US 93 and South Avenue, counts Dillard's, Herberger's and JCPenney among its 105 stores. The restored historic downtown, with a lighted riverfront nearby, also offers distinctive shopping opportunities. Montana Antique Mall, 331 W. Railroad St., has four floors of dealers in the red-bricked Hotel Montana building, which was built in 1890.

GARNET GHOST TOWN, I-90 e. to exit 109 (Bonner), then 23 mi. e. on SR 200, after mile marker 22 turn s. on Garnet Range Rd. and proceed 11 mi. on gravel road to parking lot. Lost in time, this intact mining town still reflects life as the community knew it at the end of the 19th century. Different from typical mining towns of the era, gold miners were encouraged to bring their families. After the 1930s, the town fell into disrepair and the last resident died in 1947. The remaining buildings, including the Wells Hotel, Davey Store and Kelly Saloon, have been preserved.

Time: Allow 2 hours minimum. **Hours:** Daily 9:30-4:30, Memorial Day-Sept. 30. Phone for schedule rest of year. Although the site is open year-round the roads are generally closed due to snow mid-Dec. to early May. **Cost:** $3; free (ages 0-15). **Phone:** (406) 329-3914.

Turn dreams into plans using AAA travel planning tools: AAA.com/maps

MISSOULA ART MUSEUM, 335 N. Pattee St., is housed in the old public library and hosts more than 25 rotating exhibitions from local and international artists each year. Artworks reflect the culture of the American West with a focus on contemporary Montana artists. **Time:** Allow 1 hour minimum. **Hours:** Tues.-Sat. 10-5. Closed major holidays. **Phone:** (406) 728-0447.

BEST WESTERN PLUS GRANT CREEK INN
(406)543-0700

Hotel
$99-$209

Best Western PLUS. **AAA Benefit:** Members save up to 15% and earn bonus points!

Address: 5280 Grant Creek Rd 59808 **Location:** I-90 exit 101 (Reserve St), just n. **Facility:** 126 units. 4 stories, interior corridors. **Parking:** winter plug-ins. **Terms:** cancellation fee imposed. **Pool:** heated indoor. **Activities:** sauna, hot tub, steamroom, exercise room. **Guest Services:** valet and coin laundry.

CAMPUS INN   406/549-5134
Motel. **Address:** 744 E Broadway 59802

C'MON INN   406/543-4600
Hotel. **Address:** 2775 Expo Pkwy 59808

COMFORT INN - UNIVERSITY   (406)549-7600
Hotel. **Address:** 1021 E Broadway 59802

DAYS INN/MISSOULA AIRPORT   (406)721-9776
Hotel. **Address:** 8600 Truck Stop Rd 59808

▼ See AAA listing p. 132 ▼

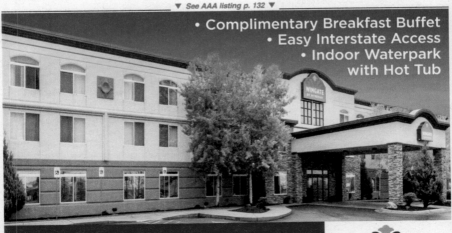

• Complimentary Breakfast Buffet
• Easy Interstate Access
• Indoor Waterpark with Hot Tub

406-541-8000 | mslawingate.com
5252 Airway Blvd. Missoula, MT 59808

WINGATE BY WYNDHAM

DOUBLETREE BY HILTON HOTEL MISSOULA - EDGEWATER
(406)728-3100

Hotel
$119-$309

AAA Benefit: Members save 5% or more!

Address: 100 Madison St 59802 **Location:** I-90 exit 105 (Van Buren St), just s, then just w on Front St. **Facility:** 172 units. 2-3 stories, interior corridors. **Parking:** winter plug-ins. **Terms:** 1-7 night minimum stay, 3 day cancellation notice-fee imposed. **Dining:** Finn & Porter, see separate listing. **Pool:** heated outdoor. **Activities:** hot tub, exercise room. **Guest Services:** valet laundry.

ECONO LODGE   (406)542-7550
Hotel. **Address:** 4953 N Reserve St 59808

HAMPTON INN BY HILTON
(406)549-1800

Hotel
$99-$189

AAA Benefit: Members save 5% or more!

Address: 4805 N Reserve St 59808 **Location:** I-90 exit 101 (Reserve St), just s. **Facility:** 61 units. 4 stories, interior corridors. **Parking:** winter plug-ins. **Terms:** 1-7 night minimum stay, 3 day cancellation notice-fee imposed. **Pool:** heated indoor. **Activities:** hot tub, exercise room. **Guest Services:** valet and coin laundry. **Featured Amenity: breakfast buffet.**

HILTON GARDEN INN MISSOULA AND MISSOULA CONFERENCE CENTER
406/532-5300
Hotel. **Address:** 3720 N Reserve St 59808

AAA Benefit: Members save 5% or more!

HOLIDAY INN EXPRESS & SUITES   406/830-3100
Hotel. **Address:** 150 Expressway Blvd 59808

HOLIDAY INN MISSOULA-DOWNTOWN   406/721-8550
Hotel. **Address:** 200 S Pattee St 59802

LA QUINTA INN MISSOULA   (406)549-9000
Hotel. **Address:** 5059 N Reserve St 59808

MY PLACE HOTEL   406/926-1001
Extended Stay Hotel. **Address:** 2951 Expo Pkwy 59808

QUALITY INN & SUITES-MISSOULA   (406)542-0888
Hotel. **Address:** 4545 N Reserve St 59808

RUBY'S INN & CONVENTION CENTER
406/721-0990

Hotel
Rates not provided

Address: 4825 N Reserve St 59808 **Location:** I-90 exit 101 (Reserve St), just s. **Facility:** 124 units, some kitchens. 2 stories, interior/exterior corridors. **Parking:** winter plug-ins. **Pool:** heated outdoor. **Activities:** sauna, hot tub, exercise room. **Guest Services:** valet and coin laundry. **Featured Amenity: full hot breakfast.**

SLEEP INN BY CHOICE HOTELS   (406)543-5883
Hotel. **Address:** 3425 Dore Ln 59801

STAYBRIDGE SUITES   406/830-3900
Extended Stay Hotel. **Address:** 120 Expressway Blvd 59808

STONECREEK LODGE   406/541-3600
Extended Stay Hotel. **Address:** 5145 Airway Blvd 59808

SUPER 8-BROOKS ST   (406)251-2255
Hotel. **Address:** 3901 Brooks St 59804

SUPER 8-RESERVE ST   (406)549-1199
Hotel. **Address:** 4703 N Reserve St 59808

TOWNEPLACE SUITES BY MARRIOTT MISSOULA
(406)721-6000
Extended Stay Hotel. **Address:** 3055 Stockyard Rd 59808

AAA Benefit: Members save 5% or more!

WINGATE BY WYNDHAM
(406)541-8000

Hotel
$89-$199

Address: 5252 Airway Blvd 59808 **Location:** I-90 exit 99 (Airway Blvd), just s to E Harrier Dr. **Facility:** 100 units. 3 stories, interior corridors. **Parking:** winter plug-ins. **Terms:** check-in 4 pm. **Amenities:** safes. **Pool:** heated indoor. **Activities:** hot tub, exercise room. **Guest Services:** valet and coin laundry, area transportation. *(See ad p. 131.)*

WHERE TO EAT

BAGELS ON BROADWAY   406/728-8900
Deli. Quick Serve. **Address:** 223 W Broadway 59802

BIGA PIZZA   406/728-2579
Pizza Natural/Organic. Casual Dining. **Address:** 241 W Main St 59802

BLUE CANYON KITCHEN & TAVERN   406/541-2583
American. Casual Dining. **Address:** 32720 N Reserve St 59808

CATALYST   406/542-1337
American. Casual Dining. **Address:** 111 N Higgins Ave 59802

CHINA GARDEN   406/721-1785
Chinese. Casual Dining. **Address:** 2100 Stephens Ave 59801

CIAO MAMBO   406/543-0377
Italian. Casual Dining. **Address:** 541 S Higgins Ave 59801

THE DEPOT   406/728-7007
▼▼ American. Casual Dining. **Address:** 201 W Railroad St 59802

EL CAZADOR   406/728-3657
▼▼ Mexican. Casual Dining. **Address:** 101 S Higgins Ave 59801

FINN & PORTER   406/542-4660
▼▼▼ American. Fine Dining. **Address:** 100 Madison St 59802

IRON HORSE BAR & GRILL   406/728-8866
▼▼ American. Casual Dining. **Address:** 501 N Higgins Ave 59802

IZA ASIAN RESTAURANT   406/830-3237
▼▼ Asian. Casual Dining. **Address:** 529 S Higgins Ave 59801

JAKER'S BAR & GRILL   406/721-1312
▼▼ American. Casual Dining. **Address:** 3515 Brooks St 59801

THE KEEP   406/728-5132
▼▼▼ American. Fine Dining. **Address:** 102 Ben Hogan Dr 59803

KOBE SEAFOOD AND STEAK HOUSE   406/540-4480
▼▼ Asian Sushi. Casual Dining. **Address:** 3331 N Reserve St 59808

MACKENZIE RIVER PIZZA   406/251-3424
▼▼ Pizza. Casual Dining. **Address:** 3820 S Reserve St 59801

THE MONTANA CLUB   406/543-3200
▼▼ Regional American. Casual Dining. **Address:** 2620 Brooks St 59801

THE MONTANA CLUB   406/541-8141
▼▼ Regional American. Casual Dining. **Address:** 4561 N Reserve St 59808

THE MUSTARD SEED ASIAN CAFE   406/542-7333
▼▼ Asian. Casual Dining. **Address:** 2901 Brooks St 59801

PARADISE FALLS RESTAURANT, LOUNGE & CASINO
    406/728-3228
▼▼ American. Casual Dining. **Address:** 3621 Brooks St 59801

THE PEARL CAFE   406/541-0231
▼▼▼ Regional American. Fine Dining. **Address:** 231 E Front St 59802

RED BIRD   406/549-2906
▼▼▼ American. Fine Dining. **Address:** 111 N Higgins Ave, Suite 100 59802

RUMOUR   406/549-7575
▼▼▼ American. Casual Dining. **Address:** 1855 Stephens Ave 59801

SA-WAD-DEE   406/543-9966
▼ Thai. Casual Dining. **Address:** 221 W Broadway St 59802

SCOTTY'S TABLE   406/549-2790
▼▼▼ International. Fine Dining. **Address:** 131 S Higgins Ave, Unit P3 59802

SEAN KELLY'S, THE STONE OF ACCORD   406/830-3210
▼▼ Irish. Gastropub. **Address:** 4951 N Reserve St 59801

THE SHACK CAFÉ   406/549-9903
▼▼ American. Casual Dining. **Address:** 222 W Main St 59802

SUSHI HANA   406/549-7979
▼ Japanese. Casual Dining. **Address:** 403 N Higgins Ave 59802

TIA'S BIG SKY   406/317-1817
▼ Mexican. Quick Serve. **Address:** 1016 W Broadway St 59802

VIETNAM GRILL   406/721-3410
▼▼ Vietnamese. Casual Dining. **Address:** 420 N Higgins Ave 59802

VIETNAM NOODLE RESTAURANT   406/542-8299
▼▼ Vietnamese. Casual Dining. **Address:** 2100 Stephens Ave, Suite 103 59801

WHEAT MONTANA BAKERY & DELI   406/327-0900
▼ Breads/Pastries Deli. Casual Dining. **Address:** 2520 S 3rd St W 59804

WHEAT MONTANA FARMS & BAKERY   406/728-8182
▼ Breads/Pastries Deli. Quick Serve. **Address:** 8800 Truck Stop Rd 59808

MOIESE (C-2) elev. 2,600'

NATIONAL BISON RANGE is s.w. via SR 212. Up to 400 bison as well as herds of elk, pronghorn antelope, deer and bighorn sheep live on the 18,700-acre range. Visitors can also see more than 210 species of birds. From mid-May to mid-October the refuge can be explored via a 19-mile self-guiding driving tour on a one-way gravel road. The tour takes about 2 hours. Only portions of the site are open the rest of the year.

Note: Two-wheeled vehicles are not allowed off the paved roads. Trailers and larger motor homes are restricted to the West Loop Drive; check at the visitor center. The gravel and dirt roads present some long climbs and steep downgrades. Visitors must keep their vehicles on the tour road and must remain in or near them. **Hours:** Range open daily dawn-dusk. Visitor center open daily 9-5, mid-May through Sept.; Thurs.-Mon. 9-5, rest of year. Closed holidays Oct.-May. **Cost:** $5 (per private vehicle). **Phone:** (406) 644-2211.

POLSON (C-2) pop. 4,488, elev. 2,931'
• Hotels p. 134 • Restaurants p. 134

Polson is in a natural amphitheater at the foot of Flathead Lake. During May and June water pours through the 200- to 500-foot perpendicular walls of the Flathead River Gorge at the rate of 500,000 gallons per second. Legend has it that Paul Bunyan dug the channel connecting the river and the lake.

Polson Chamber of Commerce: 402 1st St. E., Suite 102, Polson, MT 59860. **Phone:** (406) 883-5969.

AMERICAS BEST VALUE PORT POLSON INN   (406)883-5385
♦♦ Motel. **Address:** 49825 US Hwy 93 E 59860

KWATAQNUK RESORT AND CASINO   (406)883-3636

♦♦♦
Hotel
$95-$240

Address: 49708 US Hwy 93 E 59860 **Location:** Waterfront. Just s of downtown. **Facility:** 106 units. 2-3 stories, interior corridors. **Terms:** check-in 4 pm, 3 day cancellation notice-fee imposed, resort fee. **Pool:** heated indoor. **Activities:** sauna, hot tub, marina, exercise room. **Guest Services:** valet laundry.

WHERE TO EAT

CHERRIES BBQ PIT   406/571-2227
♦ Barbecue. Quick Serve. **Address:** 105 2nd St E 59860

HOT SPOT THAI CAFE   406/883-4444
♦ Thai. Casual Dining. **Address:** 50440 US Hwy 93 E 59860

POMPEYS PILLAR NATIONAL MONUMENT (D-6)

Pompeys Pillar National Monument is 1 mi. n. of Pompeys Pillar off I-94 exit 23. William Clark carved his name on this huge sandstone formation in 1806; it is the only physical evidence of the Lewis and Clark expedition through the area. Clark named the rock after guides Charbonneau and Sacagawea's son, Baptiste, whom he nicknamed Pomp. The pillar also bears Native American pictographs and the names of early trappers, soldiers and settlers. Interpretive tours are available upon request at the visitor center.

Daily 8:30-6, early May-Sept. 30. The site is accessible the rest of the year only by a half-mile walk from a parking area. Admission $7 (per private vehicle). Phone (406) 875-2400 for the visitor center, or (406) 896-5013 for the Bureau of Land Management.

RED LODGE (F-5) pop. 2,125, elev. 5,548'
• **Hotels & Restaurants map & index p. 220**
• **Part of Yellowstone National Park area — see map p. 214**

At the base of the Beartooth Mountains, Red Lodge is an all-year resort town. Winter sports include downhill and cross-country skiing, while summer pursuits range from trout fishing and boating to water skiing on Cooney Reservoir *(see Recreation Areas Chart)*.

Local legend attributes the town's name to a tribe of Crow Indians called the Red Lodge Clan, who covered their tepees with the local red clay. Coal-mining operations later drew many Europeans to the area.

The Carbon County Arts Guild & Depot Gallery, 11 W. Eighth St., displays the works of local and regional artists in the 1889 Northern Pacific Depot building; phone (406) 446-1370. A red Northern Pacific caboose sits on a section of restored track adjacent to the depot.

Red Lodge Area Chamber of Commerce and Visitors Center: 701 Broadway Ave. N., P.O. Box 988, Red Lodge, MT 59068. **Phone:** (406) 446-1718.

Self-guiding tours: A guide distributed by the chamber of commerce features a walking tour of the historic district and includes buildings that once served as schools, jails, courthouses, banks and hospitals.

BEARTOOTH SCENIC HIGHWAY is US 212 from Red Lodge to the northeastern entrance of Yellowstone National Park via Cooke City. The Native Americans called the original Beartooth Pass the "trail above the eagles." This 64-mile road begins at 5,650 feet and rises to the Beartooth Plateau via a series of switchbacks.

After cresting the plateau at an elevation of almost 11,000 feet, where an unobstructed view of more than 75 miles is possible, the road winds past snowfields, small lakes and fields of flowers. Finally it descends into a dense pine forest, passing tumbling waterfalls and streams interspersed with occasional jagged peaks.

Many scenic overlooks have been constructed. Even in mid-summer, cool temperatures can be expected at higher elevations; a jacket or sweater is recommended. **Time:** Allow 3 hours minimum. **Hours:** The two-lane highway is usually open Memorial Day to mid-Oct. Phone ahead to confirm schedule. **Phone:** (406) 446-1718.

COMFORT INN BY CHOICE HOTELS OF RED LODGE
(406)446-4469 **36**
♦♦ Hotel. **Address:** 612 N Broadway 59068

THE POLLARD   406/446-0001 **37**
♦♦ Historic Hotel. **Address:** 2 N Broadway Ave 59068

ROCK CREEK RESORT   406/446-1111 **39**
♦♦ Resort Hotel. **Address:** 6380 US Hwy 212 S 59068

YODELER MOTEL   406/446-1435 **38**
♦♦ Historic Motel. **Address:** 601 S Broadway Ave 59068

WHERE TO EAT

BOGART'S   406/446-1784 **28**
♦♦ American. Casual Dining. **Address:** 11 S Broadway Ave 59068

CARBON COUNTY STEAKHOUSE   406/446-4025 **30**
♦♦♦ Steak. Casual Dining. **Address:** 121 S Broadway Ave 59068

(See map & index p. 220.)

CHINA GARDEN   406/446-9909   31
◆◆ Chinese. Casual Dining. **Address:** 202 S Broadway Ave 59068

THE DINING ROOM AT THE POLLARD   406/446-0001   27
◆◆◆ Regional American. Casual Dining. **Address:** 2 N Broadway Ave 59068

OLD PINEY DELL   406/446-1196   32
◆◆◆ American. Casual Dining. **Address:** 6380 US Hwy 212 S 59068

THE PUB AT THE POLLARD   406/446-0001   26
◆◆◆ American. Gastropub. **Address:** 2 N Broadway Ave 59068

RED LODGE PIZZA CO.   406/446-3333   29
◆◆ Pizza. Casual Dining. **Address:** 115 S Broadway Ave 59068

ST. REGIS pop. 319

LITTLE RIVER MOTEL   (406)649-2713

Motel
$60-$100

Address: 424 Little River Ln 59866 **Location:** I-90 exit 33, just n to flashing light, just w, then just sw. **Facility:** 11 units, some cottages. 1 story, exterior corridors. **Parking:** winter plug-ins. **Featured Amenity: continental breakfast.**

SUPER 8 - ST. REGIS   (406)649-2422

◆◆◆
Hotel
$65-$149

Address: 9 Old Hwy 10 E 59866 **Location:** I-90 exit 33, just n. **Facility:** 53 units, some kitchens. 2 stories (no elevator), interior/exterior corridors. **Parking:** winter plug-ins. **Activities:** hot tub. **Guest Services:** coin laundry. **Featured Amenity: continental breakfast.**

SEELEY LAKE (C-2) pop. 1,659, elev. 4,028'

Seeley Lake is a year-round recreation area tucked between the Mission Mountains and Swan Range on scenic SR 83. In summer visitors can indulge in camping, hiking, golf, fishing, swimming, boating, backpacking and horseback riding. Fewer than 10 miles from town are Placid Lake and Salmon Lake state parks (see Recreation Areas Chart); Seeley Lake itself has three Forest Service campgrounds, and at the north end of the lake is the 3.5-mile-long Clearwater Canoe Trail. Northeast of Seeley Lake is the 2.5-mile-long Morrell Falls National Recreation Trail, rated as "easy." Just east of the Morrell Falls trailhead access road is the Pyramid Pass Trail into Bob Marshall Wilderness. Head north to enjoy the 1.6-mile-long Holland Falls National Recreation Trail.

In the winter the average snow on the ground is about 3 feet. With a Nordic ski trail system for cross-country skiing and more than 300 miles of groomed snowmobile trails, the Seeley-Swan area provides good opportunities for winter recreation. Contact the Seeley Lake Ranger District office, 3 miles north of town on SR 83, for maps and brochures about access to trails and wildlife in the area; phone (406) 677-2233. Other local wintertime diversions include cultural presentations, ice fishing and dog sledding.

Seeley Lake Area Chamber of Commerce: 2920 SR 83 N., P.O. Box 516, Seeley Lake, MT 59868. **Phone:** (406) 677-2880.

SHELBY (B-3) pop. 3,376, elev. 3,276'
• Restaurants p. 136

Shelby was one of the towns that the Great Northern Railroad left in its path as it pushed across the prairie. In its heyday, the town was paradise to cowboys after months on the range. A Saturday night might include carousing, horse racing, or—as once happened—holding up a passing opera troupe and making the train conductor do a clog dance to the rhythm of bullets.

Ranching, farming and the railroad supported the town until the 1922 discovery of oil in the Kevin-Sunburst fields. The area retains a few working oil pumps. Shelby's location on major transportation corridors established its right as an inland port for truck and rail shipping via the Northwest Express Transportation Authority.

Shelby Area Chamber of Commerce Office and Visitor Information Center: 100 Montana Ave., P.O. Box 865, Shelby, MT 59474. **Phone:** (406) 434-7184.

BEST WESTERN SHELBY INN & SUITES (406)424-4560

Hotel
$89-$189

Best Western.

AAA Benefit: Members save up to 15% and earn bonus points!

Address: 1948 Roosevelt Hwy 59474 **Location:** I-15 exit 363, just w. **Facility:** 74 units. 3 stories, interior corridors. **Terms:** cancellation fee imposed. **Pool:** heated indoor. **Activities:** hot tub, exercise room. **Guest Services:** coin laundry, area transportation. **Featured Amenity: breakfast buffet.**

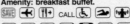

COMFORT INN OF SHELBY   (406)434-2212

◆◆◆
Hotel
$99-$159

Address: 455 McKinley Ave 59474 **Location:** I-15 exit 363, just e, then just s. **Facility:** 128 units, some efficiencies. 3 stories, interior corridors. **Parking:** winter plug-ins. **Amenities:** Some: safes. **Pool:** heated indoor. **Activities:** sauna, hot tub, exercise room. **Guest Services:** coin laundry, area transportation. **Featured Amenity: full hot breakfast.**

KOW LOON RESTAURANT   406/434-2030
🍴🍴 Chinese. Casual Dining. **Address:** 220 Main St 59474

SIDNEY (B-8) pop. 5,191, elev. 1,950'

Sidney is a marketing center for sugar beets and wheat and serves an active oil drilling and coal mining region. One of the larger auction houses in Montana, the Sidney Livestock Market Center on E. Main Street conducts cattle auctions on Wednesdays.

Sidney Area Chamber of Commerce and Agriculture: 909 S. Central Ave., Sidney, MT 59270. **Phone:** (406) 433-1916.

BEST WESTERN GOLDEN PRAIRIE INN & SUITES
(406)433-4560

Hotel
$70-$120

AAA Benefit: Members save up to 15% and earn bonus points!

Address: 820 S Central Ave 59270 **Location:** 1.8 mi n of jct SR 16 and 200. **Facility:** 72 units. 4 stories, interior corridors. **Pool:** heated indoor. **Activities:** hot tub, exercise room. **Guest Services:** coin laundry, area transportation.

CANDLEWOOD SUITES SIDNEY   406/482-9692
🍴🍴🍴 Extended Stay Hotel. **Address:** 201 6th St NW 59270

HOLIDAY INN EXPRESS & SUITES   406/433-3200
🍴🍴🍴 Hotel. **Address:** 251 W Holly St 59270

MICROTEL INN & SUITES BY WYNDHAM SIDNEY
(406)482-9011
🍴🍴 Hotel. **Address:** 1500 S Central Ave 59270

RICHLAND INN & SUITES   406/433-6400
🍴🍴 Motel. **Address:** 1200 S Central Ave 59270

WINGATE BY WYNDHAM-SIDNEY   (406)433-3100
🍴🍴🍴 Hotel. **Address:** 1490 S Central Ave 59270

RODIRON GRILL   406/433-3300
🍴🍴 American. Casual Dining. **Address:** 520 N Central Ave 59270

THREE FORKS pop. 1,869, elev. 4,061'

Three Forks was a favorite Native American hunting ground near the headwaters of the Missouri River. In 1805 Meriwether Lewis and William Clark documented their exploration of the beginning of the world's longest river system. Sacajawea (Sacagawea), the wife of one of their guides, was kidnapped and raised by the Minnetaree. A plaque in Sacajawea Park downtown commemorates her contribution to the success of the Lewis and Clark expedition. A statue, commissioned by the Three Forks Area Historical Society in 2005, depicts Sacajawea with her baby.

A trading post was established by fur trappers in 1810. The first permanent non-native settlement was established nearby in 1862. As railroads and highways provided access to the area, settlers arrived, and Three Forks was founded in 1908. Excellent hunting and fishing opportunities continue to attract visitors today.

Three Forks Chamber of Commerce: 110 N. Main St., P.O. Box 1103, Three Forks, MT 59752. **Phone:** (406) 285-4753 or (406) 595-4755.

 LEWIS AND CLARK CAVERNS STATE PARK—see Whitehall p. 142.

BROKEN SPUR MOTEL   406/285-3237
🍴 Motel. **Address:** 124 W Elm (Hwy 2) 59752

TRAVELODGE THREE FORKS   (406)285-3233
🍴 Motel. **Address:** 10776 Hwy 287 59752

POMPEY'S GRILL   406/285-6515
🍴🍴🍴 Western American. Casual Dining. **Address:** 5 N Main St 59752

WHEAT MONTANA FARMS BAKERY & DELI   406/285-3614
🍴 Breads/Pastries Deli. Quick Serve. **Address:** 10778 Hwy 287 59752

ULM (C-3) pop. 738, elev. 3,346'

FIRST PEOPLES BUFFALO JUMP STATE PARK is off I-15 exit 270, then 3.5 mi. w. on Ulm-Vaughn Rd. The park preserves one of the largest known buffalo jump sites and interprets the buffalo culture. Exhibits depict how Native Americans hunted bison by stampeding them over the cliffs. Featured are several mounted buffalo, implements fashioned from buffalo remains and a furnished tepee made of buffalo hides. Interpretive trails to the cliffs and grasslands are available.

Time: Allow 1 hour minimum. **Hours:** Daily 8-6, Apr.-Sept.; Wed.-Sat. 10-4, Sun. noon-4, rest of year. **Cost:** $6 (nonresidents per private vehicle); $4 (nonresidents arriving by other means); free (Montana residents with ID). **Phone:** (406) 866-2217.

VIRGINIA CITY (E-3) pop. 190, elev. 5,822'

After fruitless panning along the Yellowstone River, six prospectors stumbled onto Alder Creek in May 1863, and their discovery of gold led to the establishment of a town. The settlement attracted thousands of miners and a band of renegades said to have committed more than 190 murders in 6 months. The miners formed a secret group called The Vigilantes, who captured and hanged 21 of the criminals, including the outlaws' leader, the sheriff.

One of the older cities in the state, Virginia City served as territorial capital 1865-75. More than 130 early buildings have been preserved; others have been reconstructed and can be visited. Among these are the state's first newspaper office, an equipped pharmacy of the period, the Wells Fargo Express Office, the Bale of Hay Saloon and general stores carrying 1860-80 merchandise. Boot Hill Cemetery contains the graves of road agents hanged by vigilantes in 1864.

Gold panning, hunting and fishing opportunities are available. A 1935 gold dredge can be seen at the River of Gold Mining Museum. All facilities are open Memorial Day through Labor Day.

Virginia City Visitor Information Center: 300 W. Wallace St., P.O. Box 338, Virginia City, MT 59755. **Phone:** (406) 843-5247 or (800) 829-2969.

WEST GLACIER (B-2) pop. 227, elev. 3,215'
• Hotels & Restaurants map & index p. 116
• Part of Glacier National Park area — see map p. 111

West Glacier is the western rail and highway entrance to Glacier National Park *(see place listing p. 111)*. White-water rafting, skiing, hiking and year-round camping are the area's most popular recreational activities. Fishing and golf also draw visitors in pursuit of outdoor fun. One golf course cites this rule on the scorecards: "players may move balls without penalty to avoid elk tracks."

GLACIER RAFT COMPANY CABINS AT GLACIER OUTDOOR CENTER   406/888-5454

Cabin
Rates not provided

Address: 12400 US Hwy 2 E 59936 **Location:** On US 2, 0.5 mi w. **Facility:** 26 cabins, some two bedrooms. 1-2 stories (no elevator), exterior corridors. **Terms:** check-in 4 pm. **Activities:** fishing, lawn sports, picnic facilities.

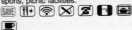

SILVERWOLF LOG CHALETS   406/387-4448

Cabin
Rates not provided

Address: 160 Gladys Glen Rd 59936 **Location:** 6 mi sw on US 2; close to Coram, outside of park. Located in a quiet rural area. **Facility:** 10 cabins, some two bedrooms and kitchens. 1 story, exterior corridors. **Bath:** shower only. **Featured Amenity: continental breakfast.**

WEST YELLOWSTONE (F-4) pop. 1,271, elev. 6,667'
- Restaurants p. 140
- Hotels & Restaurants map & index p. 220
- Part of Yellowstone National Park area — see map p. 214

As its name suggests, West Yellowstone is at the west entrance to Yellowstone National Park *(see place listing p. 214)*. Due to this strategic location, the town's major industry is tourism. Numerous outfitters and rental operations supply visitors with various sports equipment, particularly snowmobiles and cross-country skis, for use in the park and in bordering national forest areas. Fly fishing, hiking and horseback riding can be enjoyed during summer.

Two miles north of West Yellowstone on US 287, the Interagency Aerial Fire Control Center provides tours explaining firefighting techniques in summer, when staff is available; phone (406) 646-7691.

For evening entertainment The Playmill Theatre at 29 Madison Ave. presents 2-hour musical comedy performances Monday through Saturday nights, mid-May through early September. Saturday matinées also are offered. Reservations are recommended. For more information and schedules contact the theater; phone (406) 646-7757.

West Yellowstone Chamber of Commerce: 30 Yellowstone Ave., P.O. Box 458, W. Yellowstone, MT 59758. **Phone:** (406) 646-7701.

GRIZZLY & WOLF DISCOVERY CENTER is 1 blk. s. of the Yellowstone National Park west entrance at 201 S. Canyon St. in Grizzly Park. Live grizzly bears and wolves can be viewed in naturalistic habitats as well as river otters. Also offered are educational presentations, Yellowstone ranger talks, live birds of prey exhibits, safety in bear country and wolf enrichment programs, films, an interactive bear museum, and wolf enrichment. **Time:** Allow 1 hour minimum. **Hours:** Daily 8:30-dusk. **Cost:** (valid for 2 consecutive days) $13; $12.25 (ages 62+); $8 (ages 5-12). **Phone:** (406) 646-7001 or (800) 257-2570.

ALPINE MOTEL   (406)646-7544   56
Motel
$109-$199

Address: 120 Madison Ave 59758 **Location:** Just w of US 191 (Canyon St) and Madison Ave; 0.3 mi nw of park entrance. **Facility:** 15 units, some kitchens. 1-2 stories (no elevator), exterior corridors. **Terms:** 7 day cancellation notice-fee imposed. **Activities:** picnic facilities.

BEST WESTERN DESERT INN   (406)646-7376   52
Hotel
$105-$320

BW Best Western. AAA Benefit: Members save up to 15% and earn bonus points!

Address: 133 N Canyon St 59758 **Location:** Jct US 191 (N Canyon St) and Firehole Ave; 0.3 mi n of park entrance. **Facility:** 76 units. 3 stories, interior corridors. **Parking:** winter plug-ins. **Terms:** cancellation fee imposed, resort fee. **Pool:** heated indoor. **Activities:** hot tub. **Guest Services:** coin laundry.

BEST WESTERN WESTON INN   (406)646-7373   46
Motel
$139-$329

BW Best Western. AAA Benefit: Members save up to 15% and earn bonus points!

Address: 103 Gibbon Ave 59758 **Location:** Jct US 191 (N Canyon St) and Gibbon Ave; 0.5 mi n of park entrance. Across from West Yellowstone Town Park. **Facility:** 66 units. 2-3 stories (no elevator), interior/exterior corridors. **Terms:** closed 10/16-4/30, cancellation fee imposed. **Pool:** heated outdoor. **Activities:** hot tub.

BRANDIN' IRON INN   (406)646-9411   51
Motel
$79-$239

Address: 201 N Canyon St 59758 **Location:** Jct US 20 (Firehole Ave) and 191 (Canyon St); 0.3 mi s of park entrance. **Facility:** 80 units, some kitchens. 2 stories (no elevator), exterior corridors. **Parking:** winter plug-ins. **Terms:** 3 day cancellation notice-fee imposed. **Activities:** hot tub, snowmobiling, trails. **Guest Services:** coin laundry. **Featured Amenity:** continental breakfast.

Free Expanded Continental Breakfast & High-Speed Internet

CLUBHOUSE INN   (406)646-4892   59
Hotel. **Address:** 105 S Electric St 59758

CROSSWINDS INN   406/646-9557   50
Motel
Rates not provided

Address: 201 Firehole Ave 59758 **Location:** At US 20 (Firehole Ave) and Dunraven St; 0.5 mi n of park entrance. Across from West Yellowstone Town Park. **Facility:** 70 units. 2 stories (no elevator), exterior corridors. **Terms:** check-in 4 pm. **Pool:** heated indoor. **Activities:** hot tub. **Guest Services:** coin laundry. **Featured Amenity:** breakfast buffet.

(See map & index p. 220.)

DAYS INN WEST YELLOWSTONE (406)646-7656 **54**

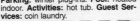

Hotel
$100-$278

Address: 301 Madison Ave 59758 **Location:** At Madison Ave and Electric St; 0.5 mi nw of park entrance. **Facility:** 133 units. 3 stories, interior corridors. **Parking:** winter plug-ins. **Pool:** heated indoor. **Activities:** hot tub. **Guest Services:** coin laundry.

EVERGREEN MOTEL 406/646-7655 **48**

Motel. **Address:** 229 Firehole Ave 59758

EXPLORER CABINS AT YELLOWSTONE 406/646-7075 **60**

Cabin
Rates not provided

Address: 201 Grizzly Ave 59758 **Location:** 0.5 mi sw of park entrance. **Facility:** A front porch, fire pit, luxurious bedding, two flat-panel TVs, walk-in shower, plush robes, enhanced personal care products and dishwasher are just some of the highlights of these upscale cabins. 50 efficiency cabin units, some two bedrooms. 1 story, exterior corridors. *Bath:* shower only. **Terms:** off-site registration. **Amenities:** safes. **Activities:** cross country skiing, snowmobiling, trails. **Guest Services:** complimentary laundry. *(See ad this page.)*

GRAY WOLF INN & SUITES (406)646-0000 **63**

Hotel
$89-$329

Address: 250 S Canyon St 59758 **Location:** Just w of park entrance, then just s. Across from Grizzly & Wolf Discovery Center. **Facility:** 103 units, some two bedrooms and kitchens. 3 stories, interior corridors. **Terms:** check-in 4 pm, 3 day cancellation notice-fee imposed, resort fee. **Pool:** heated indoor. **Activities:** sauna, hot tub. **Guest Services:** coin laundry. **Featured Amenity:** continental breakfast. *(See ad this page.)*

HOLIDAY INN WEST YELLOWSTONE CONFERENCE HOTEL 406/646-7365 **57**

Hotel
Rates not provided

Address: 315 Yellowstone Ave 59758 **Location:** 0.4 mi w of park entrance. **Facility:** 123 units. 3 stories, interior corridors. **Parking:** winter plug-ins. **Amenities:** video games. **Pool:** heated indoor. **Activities:** sauna, hot tub, game room, exercise room. **Guest Services:** complimentary laundry, area transportation. *(See ad this page.)*

(See map & index p. 220.)

LAZY G MOTEL   (406)646-7586   49

Motel
$119

Address: 123 Hayden St 59758 **Location:** Just s of Firehole Ave and Hayden St; 0.9 mi w of park entrance. **Facility:** 15 units, some two bedrooms and efficiencies. 1-2 stories (no elevator), exterior corridors. **Parking:** winter plug-ins. **Terms:** closed 4/1-5/1 & 10/18-11/20, 2 night minimum stay - seasonal and/or weekends, 5 day cancellation notice-fee imposed. **Activities:** picnic facilities.

[SAVE] [🍴+] [📶] [✕] [♨] [📶]
[/SOME/UNITS] [📠] [📺]

ONE HORSE MOTEL   (406)646-7677   47

Motel
$122-$148

Address: 216 Dunraven St 59758 **Location:** Just n of Firehole Ave and Dunraven St; 0.6 mi nw of park entrance. Across from West Yellowstone Town Park. **Facility:** 19 units. 1 story, exterior corridors. **Terms:** closed 10/6-5/16, 7 day cancellation notice-fee imposed. **Activities:** playground, picnic facilities. **Guest Services:** coin laundry. **Featured Amenity: continental breakfast.**

[SAVE] [✈] [🍴+] [📶] [✕] [⏲] [📶]
[📺]

SUPER 8 WEST YELLOWSTONE   (406)646-9584   45

Hotel
$113-$325

Address: 1545 Targhee Pass Hwy (US 20) 59758 **Location:** 7 mi w of downtown. Adjacent to Gallatin National Forest. **Facility:** 44 units. 2 stories (no elevator), interior corridors. **Terms:** closed 10/16-5/14. **Activities:** fishing, playground, lawn sports, trails. **Guest Services:** coin laundry. **Featured Amenity: continental breakfast.**

[SAVE] [🍴] [CALL] [♿] [📶] [✕] [📶]
[📺]

THREE BEAR LODGE   406/646-7353   58
Hotel. **Address:** 217 Yellowstone Ave 59758

WEST YELLOWSTONE CITY CENTER MOTEL
          406/646-7337   55
Motel. **Address:** 214 Madison Ave 59758

YELLOWSTONE LODGE   406/646-0020   62
Hotel. **Address:** 251 S Electric St 59758

YELLOWSTONE PARK HOTEL   (406)646-0255   61

Hotel
$89-$329

Address: 201 Grizzly Ave 59758 **Location:** 0.5 mi sw of park entrance. **Facility:** 66 units. 3 stories, interior corridors. **Terms:** closed 10/21-4/20, check-in 4 pm, 3 day cancellation notice-fee imposed, resort fee. **Pool:** heated indoor. **Activities:** hot tub, bicycles, trails, exercise room. **Guest Services:** complimentary laundry. **Featured Amenity: continental breakfast.** *(See ad p. 139.)*

[SAVE] [✈] [🍴] [Y] [CALL] [♿] [🚲]
[📶] [BIZ] [📶] [✕] [📶] [📠] [📺]

YELLOWSTONE WEST GATE HOTEL   406/646-4212   53
Hotel. **Address:** 638 Madison Ave 59758

WHERE TO EAT

ARROWLEAF ICE CREAM PARLOR & GRILL
          406/646-9776   46
Burgers. Quick Serve. **Address:** 27 N Canyon St 59758

BULLWINKLE'S SALOON & EATERY   406-646-7974   40
American. Casual Dining. **Address:** 115 N Canyon St 59758

CAFE MADRIZ   406/646-9245   35
Spanish Small Plates. Casual Dining. **Address:** 311 N Canyon St 59758

CANYON STREET GRILL   406/646-7548   47
Burgers Sandwiches. Casual Dining. **Address:** 22 Canyon St 59758

ERNIE'S BAKERY, SANDWICH SHOP & DELI
          406/646-9467   36
Breakfast Sandwiches. Quick Serve. **Address:** 406 Hwy 20 59758

EURO CAFE   406/646-1170   37
Breakfast Sandwiches. Casual Dining. **Address:** 237 Firehole Ave W 59758

GUSHER PIZZA AND SANDWICH SHOPPE
          406/646-9050   42
American. Casual Dining. **Address:** 40 Dunraven St 59758

MADISON CROSSING LOUNGE   406/646-7621   43
American. Casual Dining. **Address:** 121 Madison Ave 59758

PETE'S ROCKY MOUNTAIN PIZZA & PASTA
          406/646-7820   41
Pizza Sandwiches. Casual Dining. **Address:** 112 Canyon St 59758

RED LOTUS   406/646-7002   44
Chinese. Casual Dining. **Address:** 19 Madison Ave 59758

RUNNING BEAR PANCAKE HOUSE   406/646-7703   39
Breakfast Sandwiches. Casual Dining. **Address:** 538 Madison Ave 59758

SERENITY BISTRO   406/646-7660   48
New French. Casual Dining. **Address:** 38 N Canyon St 59758

SLIPPERY OTTER PUB & EATERY   406/646-7050   38
American. Casual Dining. **Address:** 139 Canyon St 59758

THREE BEAR RESTAURANT   406/646-7811   49

American Casual Dining
$8-$25

AAA Inspector Notes: Varied dishes ranging from selections of beef and fish to sandwiches, soups and salads are likely to please just about anyone at this family restaurant. Home-baked pastries are mouth-watering treats. The décor is certainly Northwestern with a feel reminiscent of what it was like in Yellowstone's early days. The staff here makes you feel like a welcome guest. **Features:** full bar. **Address:** 205 Yellowstone Ave 59758 **Location:** At Yellowstone Ave and Dunraven St, just w of park entrance; next to Three Bear Lodge. **Parking:** street only. [B] [D]

TIMBERLINE CAFE   406/646-9349   50
American. Casual Dining. **Address:** 135 Yellowstone Ave 59758

WILD WEST PIZZERIA & SALOON   406/646-4400   45
Pizza Sandwiches. Casual Dining. **Address:** 14 Madison Ave 59758

WHITEFISH (B-2) pop. 6,357, elev. 3,033'

Whitefish Lake borders Whitefish and extends 7 miles north. The area offers scenic vistas, fishing, swimming, boating and beach activities.

Restored to its 1927 chalet-like appearance, the Great Northern Railway Depot houses railroad artifacts and area memorabilia. On the grounds is the Great Northern Locomotive #181, one of only seven ever built.

Offering spectacular views of the Flathead Valley and Glacier National Park, the Whitefish Mountain Resort Scenic Lift carries passengers to the 7,000-foot summit; phone (406) 862-2900.

BEST WESTERN ROCKY MOUNTAIN LODGE
(406)862-2569 **21**

**Hotel
$109-$320**

AAA Benefit: Members save up to 15% and earn bonus points!

Address: 6510 Hwy 93 S 59937 **Location:** 1.3 mi s on US 93 from jct SR 487. **Facility:** 67 units. 2-3 stories, interior/exterior corridors. **Parking:** winter plug-ins. **Terms:** cancellation fee imposed. **Pool:** heated outdoor. **Activities:** hot tub, exercise room. **Guest Services:** complimentary laundry, area transportation. *(See ad this page.)*

CHALET MOTEL
(406)862-5581 **22**

**Motel
$79-$179**

Address: 6430 US 93 S 59937 **Location:** 1 mi n on US 93 from jct SR 40. **Facility:** 34 units. 2 stories (no elevator), exterior corridors. **Parking:** winter plug-ins. **Terms:** 2 night minimum stay - seasonal, cancellation fee imposed, resort fee. **Pool:** heated indoor. **Guest Services:** coin laundry. **Featured Amenity:** continental breakfast.

THE FIREBRAND HOTEL
406/863-1900 **19**
Hotel. **Address:** 650 E 3rd St 59937

GROUSE MOUNTAIN LODGE
406/862-3000 **18**
Hotel. **Address:** 2 Fairway Dr 59937

HAMPTON INN & SUITES BY HILTON - WHITEFISH
406/730-8901 **24**
Hotel. **Address:** 6340 Hwy 93 S 59937

AAA Benefit: Members save 5% or more!

(See map & index p. 116.)

THE LODGE AT WHITEFISH LAKE (406)863-4000 [17]

Hotel
$109-$369

Address: 1380 Wisconsin Ave 59937 **Location:** Waterfront. Jct US 93 and SR 487, 1.5 mi n on SR 487. **Facility:** Surrounded by mountains and a wildlife preserve, this lodge offers amenities for all seasons. All rooms are luxurious with western décor and feature both a shower and a tub. 117 units, some kitchens. 3 stories, interior/exterior corridors. **Parking:** on-site and valet, winter plug-ins. **Terms:** check-in 4 pm, 1-5 night minimum stay - seasonal and/or weekends, 14 day cancellation notice. **Amenities:** safes. Some: video games. **Dining:** 2 restaurants. **Pool:** heated outdoor, heated indoor. **Activities:** sauna, hot tub, steamroom, limited beach access, motor boats, self-propelled boats, marina, bicycles, exercise room, spa. **Guest Services:** valet and coin laundry, area transportation.

[icons: SAVE, etc.]

PINE LODGE 406/862-7600 [20]

Hotel
Rates not provided

Address: 920 Spokane Ave 59937 **Location:** 1 mi s on US 93 from jct SR 487. **Facility:** 76 units, some kitchens. 3 stories, interior corridors. **Parking:** winter plug-ins. **Terms:** check-in 4 pm. **Pool:** heated outdoor. **Activities:** hot tub, exercise room. **Guest Services:** valet and coin laundry, area transportation. **Featured Amenity:** continental breakfast. *(See ad p. 141.)*

[icons: SAVE, BIZ, etc.]

TOWNEPLACE SUITES BY MARRIOTT (406)890-2053 [23]
Extended Stay Hotel. **Address:** 300 Akers Ln 59937

AAA Benefit:
Members save 5%
or more!

WHITEFISH MOUNTAIN RESORT 406/862-1960 [16]
Vacation Rental Condominium. **Address:** 3889 Big Mountain Rd 59937

WHERE TO EAT

BUFFALO CAFE 406/862-2833 [20]
American. Casual Dining. **Address:** 514 3rd St E 59937

CIAO MAMBO 406/863-9600 [16]
Italian. Casual Dining. **Address:** 234 E 2nd St E 59937

CRAGGY RANGE BAR & GRILL 406/862-7550 [12]
American. Quick Serve. **Address:** 10 Central Ave 59937

JERSEY BOYS PIZZERIA 406/862-2212 [15]
Pizza. Quick Serve. **Address:** 550 E 1st St 59937

LATITUDE 48 406/863-2323 [18]
American. Fine Dining. **Address:** 147 Central Ave 59937

LOGAN'S GRILL 406/862-3000 [14]
American. Fine Dining. **Address:** 2 Fairway Dr 59937

LOULA'S 406/862-5614 [17]
American. Casual Dining. **Address:** 300 2nd St E 59937

TUPELO GRILLE AND WINE BAR 406/862-6136 [13]

Continental
Casual Dining
$16-$42

AAA Inspector Notes: In keeping with the experience of the owners, who hail from the South, the menu's Continental dishes show hints of Southern Creole and Cajun influences. Chicken and dumplings, Cajun penne pasta, ahi poke and Southern bayou catfish are some of the offerings found here. **Features:** beer & wine. **Reservations:** suggested. **Address:** 17 Central Ave 59937 **Location:** Downtown. **Parking:** street only. [D]

WASABI SUSHI BAR & THE GINGER GRILL 406/863-9283 [19]

Asian
Casual Dining
$8-$45

AAA Inspector Notes: The menu centers on sushi and Asia-influenced dishes grilled with a contemporary flair. The lively, colorful dining room displays original artwork in oils, acrylics and fiber. **Features:** beer & wine. **Reservations:** suggested. **Address:** 419 E 2nd St 59937 **Location:** Downtown. **Parking:** street only. [D]

WHITEFISH LAKE RESTAURANT 406/862-5285 [11]

American
Casual Dining
$12-$46

AAA Inspector Notes: On one of the area's finest golf courses, the restaurant is housed in a structure made of logs from the surrounding forests. Guests dine on steak and seafood as well as inventive specials created nightly. **Features:** full bar, patio dining. **Reservations:** suggested. **Address:** 1200 US Hwy 93 N 59937 **Location:** 1 mi w on US 93 from jct SR 487. [L] [D]

WHITEHALL (E-3) pop. 1,038, elev. 4,351'

LEWIS AND CLARK CAVERNS STATE PARK is 7.3 mi. e. on SR 2 to 25 Lewis and Clark Rd. Dedicated in 1941, Montana's first state park includes a limestone cavern of vaulted chambers, intricate passageways and delicate, varicolored formations that make this one of the most beautiful caverns in the country. On the surface, 10 miles of hiking trails showcase the rugged site's 3,000 acres.

Note: The 2-hour guided cavern tours involve walking a total of 2 miles and require visitors to negotiate 600 (mostly descending) steps; full mobility is required and rubber-soled shoes are advised. Because the cavern temperature remains around 50 F, a jacket is recommended. Pets are not permitted in the cavern.

Hours: Park open daily 9-9, mid-June. to mid-Aug.; 9-5, rest of year. Cavern tours are given daily 9-6:30, mid-June to mid-Aug.; 9-4:30, May 1 to mid-June and mid-Aug. through Sept. 30. Candlelight cave tours are offered are offered in late December; reservations are required. **Cost:** Park admission $6 (nonresidents per private vehicle); $4 (nonresidents arriving by other means); free (Montana residents with ID). Two-hour, 2-mile guided cavern tour $12; $5 (ages 6-11). **Phone:** (406) 287-3541.

[icons: GT, etc.]

YELLOWSTONE NATIONAL PARK—See Wyoming p. 214

Experience the
DIAMOND Difference

With so many hotel and restaurant rating systems, it's hard to know who to trust. That's why AAA uses professional inspectors to conduct in-person evaluations using guidelines based on member priorities.

5 FIVE REASONS TO TRUST AAA

1 - Inspection visits are unscheduled
2 - Our guidelines are an open book
3 - We're in it for members
4 - We know travel inside out
5 - We're picky

Every AAA Inspected & Approved establishment is good for the kind of experience it offers. So the only question is, how many Diamonds are right for your needs?

Inspected & Approved

Visit AAA.com/Diamonds

Grand Teton National Park

Wyoming

You could say that Wyoming is *Mecheweami-ing* to the max. The Delaware Native American word meaning "at the great plains" or "on the great plain"—helpfully simplified to the present state name—is certainly geographically apt. But Wyoming's mountains, grasslands, canyons, deserts and other natural attributes also are worthy of greatness.

The Continental Divide cuts a diagonal swath across this almost precisely rectangular state, bisecting it into the Missouri and Columbia and Colorado river basins. The divide winds northwest to southeast along the curved, jagged spine of the Rocky Mountains, and some of Wyoming's most scenic jewels can be found in this formidably mountainous territory.

Grand Teton National Park fully deserves gushing adjectives like "breathtaking" and "magnificent"; it was first photographed way back in 1872, and ever since shutterbugs

Bighorn Canyon National Recreation Area

have commemorated for posterity the region's sparkling blue lakes, impressive glaciers, mammoth snowfields and lush green stands of fir, pine and spruce. This awesome natural setting begat Jackson Hole, an outdoor recreation paradise offering thrill seekers a range of temptations from mountain climbing and windsurfing to skiing and whitewater rafting.

Yellowstone is the nation's first national park, and one of its most beloved. It's also a hot spot for geyser activity, the result of a volcanic eruption some 600,000 years ago. The thermal theatrics of Old Faithful receive top billing; this cone geyser shoots up to 8,000 gallons of boiling water some 150 feet in the air every 90 or so minutes, providing a spectacular show. But Yellowstone offers everything from the terrace-like formations of Mammoth Hot Springs and colorful hot clay bubbling from vivid paint pots to photographic encounters with the likes of grizzlies, black bears, elk, bison and bighorn sheep.

In Bighorn Canyon National Recreation Area, shared with neighboring Montana, canyon walls of sculpted rock rise up and encircle a 55-mile stretch of serene Bighorn Lake. Imposing Shell and Crazy Woman canyons punctuate the terrain of Bighorn National Forest. The Green River carved the backdrop of appropriately named Flaming Gorge National Recreation Area; as Creedence Clearwater Revival once observed in a song, you can kick your feet way down in shallow water and skip a flat rock across Green River.

Like a bad haircut, sagebrush crowns the massive monolith that is the centerpiece of Devils Tower National Monument. The remarkably well-preserved remains of fish, insects, reptiles, plants and birds at Fossil Butte National Monument provide compelling evidence that the region basked in a subtropical environment some 50 million years ago.

Rolling Westward

Wyoming's topographic highlights must have been eye-popping to the 19th-century pioneers who rumbled along the Oregon Trail in a series of wagon train processions, heading to a new life in California and the Pacific Northwest. Western lore is well documented at places like Fort Laramie National Historic Site, a fur-trading post established in 1834 that witnessed the unfolding drama of westward expansion as well as its varied cast: trappers, traders, missionaries, treasure seekers, homesteaders, cowboys and the Native American tribes that fiercely resisted the encroachments on their land.

Museums like The Nelson Museum of the West in Cheyenne, the Buffalo Bill Center of the West in Cody, the Wyoming Pioneer Memorial Museum in Douglas and the Wyoming Territorial Prison State Historic Site in Laramie all are repositories for this rich heritage. Cody not only pays tribute to its founder, Col. William "Buffalo Bill" F. Cody, but to Harry Longabaugh—or the Sundance Kid—who adopted his better-known moniker from the Wyoming town in which he once served time. And as fans of Paul Newman and Robert Redford know, that particular Wyoming legend was made into a pretty darn good movie.

Recreation

Wyoming lets you experience Wild West life without having to put up with Wild West hardships. Mount a trusty horse at the crack of dawn and head into the mountains, experience breathtakingly unspoiled wilderness and end the day relaxing around an open campfire. Outfitters offer everything from cattle herding adventures to overnight chuck wagon trips.

Yellowstone has more than 1,000 miles of hiking trails ranging from easy loops to strenuous treks; many visitors opt for a trail that ventures past at least one of the park's bubbling geysers. Yellowstone Lake is tops for boating; Shoshone Lake is a favorite for canoeing. If you're in the mood for a less demanding activity, the Togwotee Trail (US 26/287 through Fremont and Teton counties) offers scenery that is magnificent viewed from the passenger seat of a car.

A short skip south is Wyoming's *other* national park, Grand Teton. Extreme adventure enthusiasts will relish the challenge of climbing one of the park's four principal mountains—Grand Teton, Middle Teton, Buck Mountain and Mount Moran. Allow 2 days for a summertime ascent of Grand Teton; the Owen-Spaulding route, a 7-mile trek, is the most popular scramble to the top of this 13,770-foot peak.

There's another natural landmark in the state's opposite (northeastern) corner. Devils Tower, the nation's first national monument, soars 1,267 feet above the Belle Fourche River. Climbing the formation's fluted, nearly perpendicular heights is permitted, but most folks are content to hike the popular 1.3-mile Tower Trail that circles it.

White-water rafting in the vicinity of Jackson Hole has the bonus of spectacular mountain backdrops. The upper Snake River's relatively gentle water is well-suited for novices, but the lower Snake's white water will take you for a wild ride. And winter in Wyoming brings lots of snow and plenty of terrain for cross-country and downhill skiing; the packed powder typical of Snow King Mountain in Jackson Hole makes it a good spot for beginners.

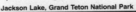
Jackson Lake, Grand Teton National Park

Historic Timeline

1807	John Colter, a member of the Lewis and Clark Expedition, spends months alone in a wilderness of mountains and geysers.
1834	Fur traders William Sublette and Robert Campbell establish a trading post at Fort Laramie.
1849	The United States buys Fort Laramie to use as a base to protect and supply travelers along the Oregon Trail.
1863	The Wyoming Territory's first newspaper, *The Daily Telegraph*, begins printing in Fort Bridger.
1869	Wyoming women become the first in the nation to obtain the right to vote.
1890	Wyoming becomes the 44th state.
1872	The wilderness area John Colter described as "Colter's Hell" is designated Yellowstone, the country's first national park.
1925	Nellie Tayloe Ross is sworn in as Wyoming's—and the nation's—first woman governor.
1958	The 4320th Strategic Missile Wing is established at F.E. Warren Air Force Base in Cheyenne.
1988	Wildfires in Yellowstone National Park scorch more than 1 million acres.
2016	Yellowstone receives more than 4 million visitors for the second year, setting the record for highest annual visitation rate.

What To Pack

Temperature Averages Maximum/Minimum	JANUARY	FEBRUARY	MARCH	APRIL	MAY	JUNE	JULY	AUGUST	SEPTEMBER	OCTOBER	NOVEMBER	DECEMBER
Casper	33/14	37/16	43/21	56/31	66/40	77/49	87/56	85/55	74/45	61/36	44/23	37/18
Cheyenne	38/14	40/15	44/20	55/29	64/39	76/48	84/54	82/53	73/43	62/33	47/22	42/18
Evanston	29/10	34/12	42/19	52/26	61/33	72/40	79/46	78/45	68/37	57/28	40/18	32/10
Lander	31/8	36/12	45/20	56/31	66/40	76/48	86/55	84/54	73/45	60/34	43/19	35/12
Sheridan	34/9	36/11	43/19	56/31	67/40	75/48	87/56	86/53	74/43	62/33	46/21	39/14
Yellowstone NP	26/10	30/11	37/17	48/26	57/33	67/41	76/47	74/45	64/37	52/29	38/20	28/12

From the records of The Weather Channel Interactive, Inc.

Good Facts To Know

ABOUT THE STATE

POPULATION: 563,626.

AREA: 97,813 square miles; ranks 10th.

CAPITAL: Cheyenne.

HIGHEST POINT: 13,804 ft., Gannett Peak.

LOWEST POINT: 3,099 ft., Belle Fourche River Valley.

TIME ZONE(S): Mountain. DST.

GAMBLING

MINIMUM AGE FOR GAMBLING: 18.

REGULATIONS

TEEN DRIVING LAWS: No more than one passenger under the age of 18 is permitted (family members are exempt). Driving is not permitted 11 p.m.-5 a.m. The minimum age for an unrestricted driver's license is 16 and 6 months with driver's education course and 17 without driver's education course. Phone (307) 777-4800 for more information about Wyoming driver's license regulations.

SEAT BELT/CHILD RESTRAINT LAWS: Seat belts are required for driver and all passengers ages 9 and over. Children under age 9 are required to be in a child restraint in the rear seat, if possible. AAA recommends the use of seat belts and appropriate child restraints for the driver and all passengers.

CELLPHONE RESTRICTIONS: All drivers are banned from text messaging.

HELMETS FOR MOTORCYCLISTS: Required for riders under 18.

RADAR DETECTORS: Permitted. Prohibited for use by commercial vehicles.

MOVE OVER LAW: Driver is required to slow down to 20 mph under the posted speed limit and vacate the lane nearest stopped police, fire, rescue, including tow trucks, and municipal, utility and road maintenance vehicles using audible or flashing signals.

FIREARMS LAWS: Vary by state and/or county. Contact the Wyoming Highway Patrol, 5300 Bishop Blvd., Cheyenne, WY 82009; phone (307) 777-4301.

HOLIDAYS

HOLIDAYS: Jan. 1 ▪ Martin Luther King Jr. Day, Jan. (3rd Mon.) ▪ Washington's Birthday/Presidents Day, Feb. (3rd Mon.) ▪ Memorial Day, May (last Mon.) ▪ July 4 ▪ Labor Day, Sept. (1st Mon.) ▪ Veterans Day, Nov. 11 ▪ Thanksgiving, Nov. (4th Thurs.) ▪ Christmas, Dec. 25.

MONEY

TAXES: Wyoming's statewide sales tax is 4 percent, with local options for an additional increment up to 2 percent. Localities may also impose a lodging tax of up to 4 percent.

VISITOR INFORMATION

INFORMATION CENTERS: State welcome centers are on I-90 exit 23 east of Sheridan ▪ on I-90 exit 199 at Sundance ▪ on US 26/89/187 on north edge of Jackson ▪ 1 mile south of Cheyenne at I-25 exit 4 on High Plains Road ▪ on I-80 on east edge of Evanston ▪ on I-80 exit 401 south of Pine Bluffs ▪ and on I-80, 10 miles east of Laramie at Sherman Hill exit. The centers are open daily 8-6, Memorial Day-Labor Day, and daily 8-5, rest of year.

FURTHER INFORMATION FOR VISITORS:
Wyoming Office of Tourism
5611 High Plains Rd.
Cheyenne, WY 82007
(307) 777-7777
(307) 777-2877
(800) 225-5996

NATIONAL FOREST INFORMATION:
USDA Forest Service, Ogden Ranger District
U.S. Forest Service, Rocky Mountain Region
740 Simms St.
Golden, CO 80401
(303) 275-5350

FISHING AND HUNTING REGULATIONS:
Wyoming Game and Fish Department
5400 Bishop Blvd.
Cheyenne, WY 82006
(307) 777-4600

RECREATION INFORMATION:
Wyoming State Parks and Cultural Resources
Barrett Building
2301 Central Ave.
Cheyenne, WY 82002
(307) 777-6303

STATE PARK INFORMATION:
Division of State Parks and Historic Sites
Barrett Building
2301 Central Ave., 4th Floor
Cheyenne, WY 82002
(307) 777-6323

Wyoming Annual Events

Please call ahead to confirm event details.

 Visit **AAA.com/travelguides/events** to find
AAA-listed events for every day of the year

WINTER

Dec. - Lighted Christmas Parade / Buffalo
307-684-5544
- Mountain Man Christmas / Pinedale
307-367-2242
- Powell Country Christmas / Powell
307-754-3494

Jan. - Wild West Winter Carnival / Riverton
307-856-4801

Feb. - Buffalo Bill Birthday Ball / Cody
307-527-5626
- Sulphur Creek Ice Fishing Derby
Evanston / 307-679-7377

SPRING

Mar. - World Championship Snowmobile Hill
Climb / Jackson / 307-734-9653
- Ceili at the Roundhouse Celtic
Festival / Evanston / 307-679-2348
- Jackson Hole Rendezvous / Teton
Village / 307-733-2292

Apr. - Spring Home and Garden Show
Rock Springs / 307-752-5359
- Society of Petroleum Engineers
Crawfish Boil / Gillette
307-680-6789
- Western Spirit Art Show and Sale
Cheyenne / 307-778-7290

May - ElkFest and Antler Auction / Jackson
307-733-3316
- Cody's Wild West Days / Cody
307-587-4221
- Old West Days / Jackson
307-733-3316

SUMMER

June - Flaming Gorge Days / Green
River / 307-778-3133
- Cody Nite Rodeo / Cody
800-207-0744

July - Green River Rendezvous / Pinedale
307-367-4101
- Cheyenne Frontier Days / Cheyenne
307-778-7222
- Sheridan-Wyo-Rodeo / Sheridan
307-751-1832

Aug. - Wyoming State Fair & Rodeo
Douglas / 307-358-2398
- Gift of the Waters Pageant & Parade
Thermopolis / 370-258-9861

FALL

Sept. - Rendezvous Royale / Cody
307-587-5002
- Jackson Hole Fall Arts Festival
Jackson / 307-733-3316

Oct. - Trick or Treat on Town Square
Jackson / 307-733-3316
- Chili Cook-Off / Gillette
307-687-5213
- Moonlight Madness / Thermopolis
877-864-3192

Nov. - Cheyenne Christmas Parade,
Concert and Craft Show / Cheyenne
307-637-3376
- Christmas Stroll / Sheridan
307-672-2485
- Cody Christmas Celebration / Cody
307-587-2777

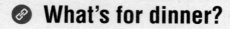 **What's for dinner?**

AAA.com/travelguides/restaurants

Bald eagle at Jenny Lake,
Grand Teton National Park

Autumn at Jackson Hole

Cheyenne Frontier Days

Midway Geyser Basin, Yellowstone National Park

Herd of bison

Index: Great Experience for Members

AAA editor's picks of exceptional note

Cheyenne Frontier
Days Old West
Museum

Devils Tower National
Monument

Wyoming Territorial
Prison State Historic
Site

Yellowstone National
Park

See Orientation map on p. 160 for corresponding grid coordinates, if applicable.
*Indicates the GEM is temporarily closed.

Big Horn (B-4)
The Brinton Museum *(See p. 163.)*

Casper (D-4)
National Historic Trails Interpretive Center
(See p. 167.)

Cheyenne (E-6)
Cheyenne Frontier Days Old West Museum
(See p. 169.)
The Nelson Museum of the West *(See p. 169.)*
Wyoming State Museum *(See p. 170.)*

Cody (B-2)
Buffalo Bill Center of the West *(See p. 172.)*
Old Trail Town *(See p. 174.)*

Devils Tower National Monument
(B-6)
Devils Tower National Monument *(See p. 175.)*

Douglas (D-5)
Wyoming Pioneer Memorial Museum
(See p. 176.)

Fort Laramie National Historic Site
(D-6)
Fort Laramie National Historic Site
(See p. 178.)

Grand Teton National Park (B-1)
Grand Teton National Park *(See p. 180.)*

Laramie (E-5)
Wyoming Territorial Prison State Historic Site
(See p. 200.)

Powell (B-3)
Heart Mountain Interpretive Center
(See p. 203.)

Yellowstone National Park (B-2)
Yellowstone National Park *(See p. 214.)*

STAY CONNECTED

TO ALL THE THINGS MEMBERSHIP CAN DO FOR YOU

- member discounts around you
- cheapest gas nearby
- Diamond Rated hotels and restaurants
- travel information and reservations
- roadside assistance

Download today. Connect every day.
AAA.com/mobile | CAA.ca/mobile

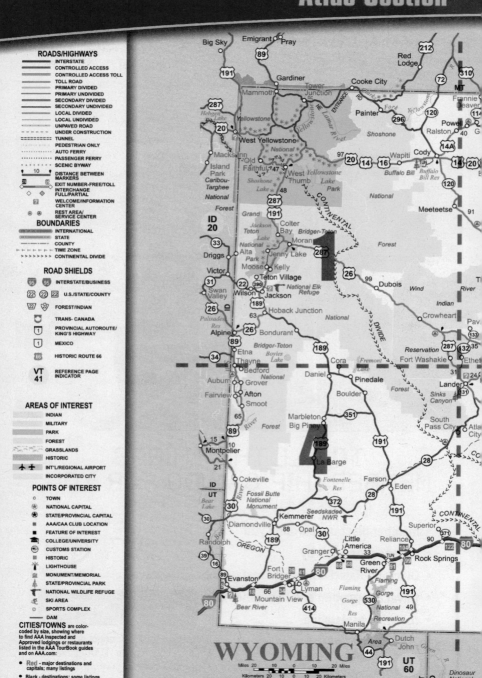

Wyoming
Atlas Section

ROADS/HIGHWAYS
- INTERSTATE
- CONTROLLED ACCESS
- CONTROLLED ACCESS TOLL
- TOLL ROAD
- PRIMARY DIVIDED
- PRIMARY UNDIVIDED
- SECONDARY DIVIDED
- SECONDARY UNDIVIDED
- LOCAL DIVIDED
- LOCAL UNDIVIDED
- UNPAVED ROAD
- UNDER CONSTRUCTION
- TUNNEL
- PEDESTRIAN ONLY
- AUTO FERRY
- PASSENGER FERRY
- SCENIC BYWAY
- DISTANCE BETWEEN MARKERS
- EXIT NUMBER-FREE/TOLL
- INTERCHANGE FULL/PARTIAL
- WELCOME/INFORMATION CENTER
- REST AREA/ SERVICE CENTER

BOUNDARIES
- INTERNATIONAL
- STATE
- COUNTY
- TIME ZONE
- CONTINENTAL DIVIDE

ROAD SHIELDS
- INTERSTATE/BUSINESS
- U.S./STATE/COUNTY
- FOREST/INDIAN
- TRANS- CANADA
- PROVINCIAL AUTOROUTE/ KING'S HIGHWAY
- MEXICO
- HISTORIC ROUTE 66
- VT 41 REFERENCE PAGE INDICATOR

AREAS OF INTEREST
- INDIAN
- MILITARY
- PARK
- FOREST
- GRASSLANDS
- HISTORIC
- INT'L/REGIONAL AIRPORT
- INCORPORATED CITY

POINTS OF INTEREST
- TOWN
- NATIONAL CAPITAL
- STATE/PROVINCIAL CAPITAL
- AAA/CAA CLUB LOCATION
- FEATURE OF INTEREST
- COLLEGE/UNIVERSITY
- CUSTOMS STATION
- HISTORIC
- LIGHTHOUSE
- MONUMENT/MEMORIAL
- STATE/PROVINCIAL PARK
- NATIONAL WILDLIFE REFUGE
- SKI AREA
- SPORTS COMPLEX
- DAM

CITIES/TOWNS are color-coded by size, showing where to find AAA Inspected and Approved lodgings or restaurants listed in the AAA TourBook guides and on AAA.com:
- Red - major destinations and capitals; many listings
- Black - destinations; some listings
- Grey - no listings

Miles 20   10   0   10   20 Miles
Kilometers 20 10 0 10 20 Kilometers
ONE INCH EQUALS APPROXIMATELY 33 MILES OR 53.11 KILOMETERS   1:2,090,880

MT 38

Lodge Grass 530
90 549
Bighom Parkman 87
Ranchester 23
Dayton 25
14 Sheridan
Big Horn 49
79 14 National
Shell Story
Clearmont 14 Arvada 16
90 Ucross 14
87 16
300/566 58
Buffalo 299
Manderson 31 Hyattville 16
16 89
Ten Sleep 25
Forest
Ten Sleep

2

N

Kaycee 254
Powder
387

oshoni 26 97
20
South 189

Thermopolis
ne Springs

59 River
River 212
112
59 85
Thunder Hulett 24 34
Basin Devils Belle Fourche
National Tower Black Sundance Spearfish
Grassland Nat'l Mon 61 14 Keyhole 20 14A
Devils Tower Keyhole 185 187
Gillette 14 64 90 585 43
124 Rozet 154 National
129 Moorcroft Thunder
99 Upton Osage 85
59 16 54 Newcastle 16
3 450 Basin 85 28
Wright National 18
Grassland 46 18
59 SD
SD
NE

Evansville SD/NE
Bar Edness Rolling Hills Manville Lusk
Nunn Kimball Glenrock Douglas 18 20 20
189 Wilkins 165 63 25 140 26 41 47
Casper 58B OREGON 126 85 NE
Medicine Glendo Res 39
220 Alcova Glendo NE
80 Alcova Bow Glendo
effrey Res Guernsey Fort 38 Laramie
City Pathfinder National Ft Laramie NHS
72 Res 291 Forest Guern- Lingle
Barroil 487 sey Torrington 26
42 78 73 Yoder TRAIL
287 Seminoe Wheatland 85
Seminoe 65 Slater Hawk
Res Medicine 54 Springs
Hanna Bow Chugwater LaGrange
Rawlins Sinclair 287 Wheatland Res 2 34
187 80 30 Rock River 84
3 29 211 215 219 260 13 30
Wam- 235 Arlington 287 25 87
sutter Elk Mountain 272 311 Laramie FE
789 Saratoga 130 Medicine 80 143 Medicine Bow Warren Pine Bluffs
53 Bow Nat'l AFB **Cheyenne** 401
Medicine Riverside 130 Centennial 210 For 30 80
Encampment 313 323 Curt 42
70 National 230 Gowdy 0/395 362 85
Baggs Forest Foxpark 362
13 230 127 287 85
DIVIDE 125 25
CO Walden 14 Laporte 14
CO 12 14 14 Ft Collins 269 ER065-16

5

6

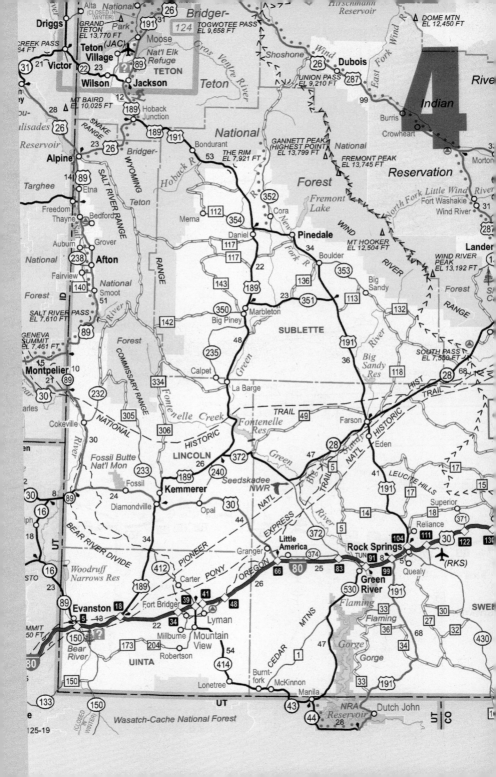

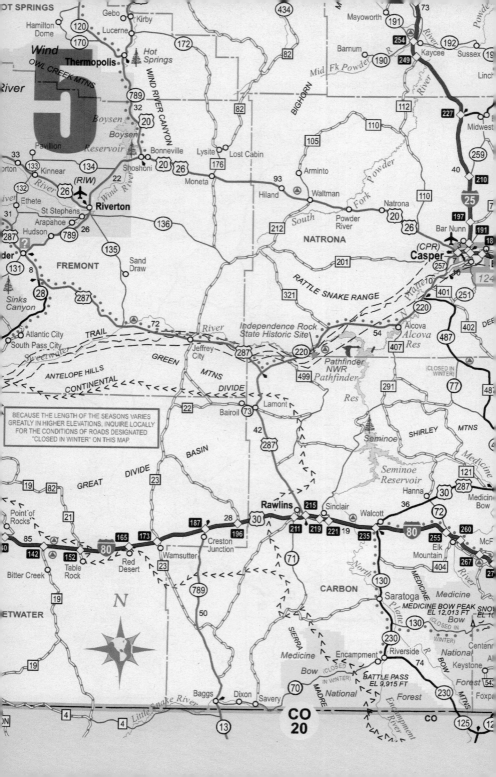

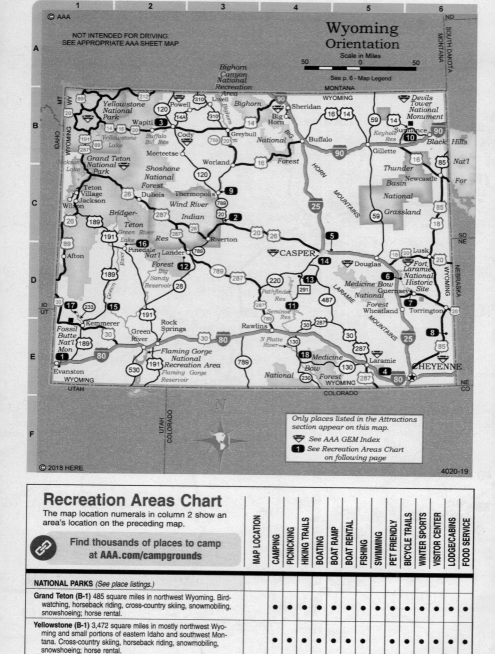

© AAA

NOT INTENDED FOR DRIVING.
SEE APPROPRIATE AAA SHEET MAP.

Wyoming
Orientation

Scale in Miles

50 ___ 0 ___ 50

See p. 6 - Map Legend

Only places listed in the Attractions section appear on this map.

⬡ *See AAA GEM Index*

1 *See Recreation Areas Chart on following page*

© 2018 HERE

4020-19

Recreation Areas Chart

The map location numerals in column 2 show an area's location on the preceding map.

🔗 **Find thousands of places to camp at AAA.com/campgrounds**

	MAP LOCATION	CAMPING	PICNICKING	HIKING TRAILS	BOATING	BOAT RAMP	BOAT RENTAL	FISHING	SWIMMING	PET FRIENDLY	BICYCLE TRAILS	WINTER SPORTS	VISITOR CENTER	LODGE/CABINS	FOOD SERVICE
NATIONAL PARKS *(See place listings.)*															
Grand Teton (B-1) 485 square miles in northwest Wyoming. Bird-watching, horseback riding, cross-country skiing, snowmobiling, snowshoeing; horse rental.		●	●	●	●	●	●	●	●	●	●	●	●	●	●
Yellowstone (B-1) 3,472 square miles in mostly northwest Wyoming and small portions of eastern Idaho and southwest Montana. Cross-country skiing, horseback riding, snowmobiling, snowshoeing; horse rental.		●	●	●	●	●	●	●	●	●	●	●	●	●	●

Recreation Areas Chart

The map location numerals in column 2 show an area's location on the preceding map.

Find thousands of places to camp at AAA.com/campgrounds

	MAP LOCATION	CAMPING	PICNICKING	HIKING TRAILS	BOATING	BOAT RAMP	BOAT RENTAL	FISHING	SWIMMING	PET FRIENDLY	BICYCLE TRAILS	WINTER SPORTS	VISITOR CENTER	LODGE/CABINS	FOOD SERVICE
NATIONAL FORESTS (See place listings.)															
Bighorn (B-3) 1,115,073 acres in north-central Wyoming. Cross-country and downhill skiing, horseback riding, snowmobiling, snowshoeing; horse rental.		•	•	•	•	•		•		•		•	•	•	•
Black Hills (B-6) 1,246,660 acres. Southwestern South Dakota and northeastern Wyoming.		•	•	•	•	•	•	•	•			•	•		•
Bridger-Teton (C-2) 3,439,809 acres in western Wyoming. Cross-country and downhill skiing, horseback riding, snowmobiling, snowshoeing; horse rental.		•	•	•	•	•		•		•		•	•	•	•
Medicine Bow (D-5) 1,093,618 acres in eastern Wyoming. Cross-country and downhill skiing, horseback riding, rock climbing, snowmobiling, snowshoeing; horse rental.		•	•	•	•	•		•		•		•	•	•	•
Shoshone (C-2) 2,466,586 acres in northwestern Wyoming. Geocaching.		•	•	•	•	•		•		•	•	•	•	•	•
NATIONAL MONUMENTS (See place listings.)															
Devils Tower (B-6) 1,347 acres in northeast Wyoming.		•	•	•				•		•	•		•	•	
NATIONAL RECREATION AREAS (See place listings.)															
Bighorn Canyon (A-3) 120,000 acres in southern Montana and northern Wyoming.		•	•	•	•	•	•	•	•	•			•		•
Flaming Gorge (E-2) 207,363 acres in northeast Utah and southwest Wyoming. Cross-country skiing, horseback riding, hunting, ice fishing, parasailing, rafting, snowmobiling, water skiing.		•	•	•	•	•	•	•	•	•	•	•	•	•	•
STATE															
Bear River (E-1) 320 acres on I-80 near Evanston. Skiing; captive bison herd, playground.	**1**		•	•				•	•	•	•	•	•		
Boysen (C-3) 39,545 acres 14 mi. n.w. of Shoshoni off US 20. Beach, playground.	**2**	•	•		•	•		•	•	•		•	•		•
Buffalo Bill (B-2) 12,000 acres 9 mi. w. of Cody on US 14/16/20. Beach, playground	**3**	•	•	•	•	•		•		•		•	•		
Curt Gowdy (E-5) 1,960 acres 26 mi. w. of Cheyenne off SR 210. Bird-watching, horseback riding; amphitheater, archery range, playground.	**4**	•	•	•	•	•		•		•	•		•	•	
Edness Kimball Wilkins (C-5) 315 acres 6 mi. e. of Casper off I-25. Bird-watching; beach, playground.	**5**		•	•				•	•	•	•		•		
Glendo (D-5) 22,430 acres 4 mi. e. of Glendo off US 87. Beach, marina, playground.	**6**	•	•	•	•	•	•	•	•	•	•		•		•
Guernsey (D-6) 8,638 acres 3 mi. w. of Guernsey off US 26. Bird-watching; beach, playground.	**7**	•	•	•	•	•		•	•	•			•	•	
Hawk Springs (E-6) 2,000 acres 39 mi. s. of Torrington off US 85. Bird-watching; beach, playground.	**8**	•	•		•	•		•	•	•					
Hot Springs (C-3) 1,034 acres in n.e. Thermopolis on SR 789 and US 20. Playground, pool.	**9**		•	•				•	•	•			•		•
Keyhole (B-6) 15,674 acres 7 mi. n. of I-90 between Moorcroft and Sundance. Beach, cabins, marina, playground.	**10**	•	•	•	•	•	•	•	•	•			•	•	•
Seminoe (D-4) 10,381 acres 35 mi. n. of Sinclair off I-80. Beach, playground.	**11**	•	•		•	•		•	•	•			•	•	
Sinks Canyon (D-2) 600 acres 7.5 mi. s.w. of Lander on SR 131. Playground.	**12**	•	•	•				•		•			•		
OTHER															
Alcova Reservoir (D-4) 2,470 acres 4 mi. s. of Alcova off SR 220. Beach, playground.	**13**	•	•	•	•	•	•	•	•	•					•
Casper Mountain Park (D-4) 3,315 acres 7 mi. s. of Casper on SR 251. Cross-country and downhill skiing, horseback riding, snowmobiling; archery range, braille nature trail.	**14**	•	•	•							•	•	•		•
Fontenelle Reservoir (D-2) 8,000 acres 35 mi. n. of Kemmerer via US 189.	**15**	•	•	•	•	•	•		•	•					

Recreation Areas Chart

The map location numerals in column 2 show an area's location on the preceding map.

 Find thousands of places to camp at AAA.com/campgrounds

	MAP LOCATION	CAMPING	PICNICKING	HIKING TRAILS	BOATING	BOAT RAMP	BOAT RENTAL	FISHING	SWIMMING	PET FRIENDLY	BICYCLE TRAILS	WINTER SPORTS	VISITOR CENTER	LODGE/CABINS	FOOD SERVICE
Fremont Lake (D-2) 5,000-acre lake 3.5 mi. n.e. of Pinedale off Fremont Lake Rd. Ice fishing, cross-country skiing, skating, snowmobiling.	16	•	•	•	•	•	•	•	•	•	•	•	•	•	•
Lake Viva Naughton (D-1) 1,375 acres 12 mi. n. of Kemmerer via SR 233.	17	•			•	•		•							
Saratoga Lake (E-4) 270-acre lake 1.5 mi. n. of Saratoga off SR 130.	18	•	•	•	•	•		•	•	•	•	•			

Make the Connection

AAA guidebooks are just the beginning. Open the door to a whole lot more on **AAA.com**. Get extra travel insight, more information and online booking.

AFTON (D-1) pop. 1,911, elev. 6,267'

Mormon emigrants surveyed the already-settled site of Afton in 1896, using a carpenter's square, a rope and an almanac and taking their bearings from the North Star and the sun. An official survey made years later found the plot only about 5 feet off.

In addition to the arch of 3,011 elk antlers that spans Washington Street at the center of town, Afton is noted for Periodic Spring, a natural cold-water geyser. The spring is 5 miles east in Bridger-Teton National Forest *(see place listing p. 164).*

Afton lies in Star Valley along the scenic portion of US 89, which runs 255 miles between Mammoth Hot Springs in Yellowstone National Park *(see place listing p. 218)* and Geneva on the Idaho border.

Star Valley Chamber of Commerce: 150 S. Washington St., P.O. Box 190, Afton, WY 83110. **Phone:** (307) 855-2759 or (800) 426-8833.

FAIRFIELD INN & SUITES BY MARRIOTT AFTON
(307)885-4040
Contemporary Hotel. **Ad-dress:** 53 E 1st Ave 83110

AAA Benefit: Members save 5% or more!

LAZY B MOTEL   307/885-3187
Motel. **Address:** 219 S Washington St (US 89) 83110

WHERE TO EAT

ROCKY MOUNTAIN SEAFOOD   307/885-2722
Seafood. Quick Serve. **Address:** 492 S Washington St (US 89) 83110

ALPINE pop. 828
• Part of Jackson Hole Including Grand Teton National Park area — see map p. 193
FLYING SADDLE RESORT RESTAURANT   307/654-4422
American. Casual Dining. **Address:** 118878 Jct US 26 & 89 83128

BIG HORN (B-4) pop. 490, elev. 4,081'

THE BRINTON MUSEUM, 239 Brinton Rd., interprets the atmosphere of Western ranch life. The main house was built in 1892; businessman Bradford Brinton bought the property in 1923 and built several additions 1927-28. A large collection of Western art includes paintings, sculpture and etchings by John James Audubon, Edward Borein, Frank Tenney Johnson, Frederic Remington and Charles M. Russell.

Extensive collections of equipment, Plains Native American crafts, rare books and documents (including letters and manuscripts by William Penn, George Washington and Abraham Lincoln), and items pertaining to the history of the ranch are displayed in their original setting in the fully furnished ranch house and outbuildings. The Forrest E. Mars, Jr., Building features four galleries of Western and Native American art and artifacts, including changing exhibits of living artists' works and items on loan from other institutions.

Time: Allow 1 hour minimum. **Hours:** Daily 9:30-5, Memorial Day-Labor Day; Wed.-Sun. 9:30-5, day after Labor Day-Dec. 23 and March 15-day before Memorial Day. **Cost:** $10; $8 (ages 62+ and students with ID); free (ages 0-12). **Phone:** (307) 672-3173.

BIGHORN NATIONAL FOREST (B-3)

Elevations in the forest range from 4,600 ft. in the northern section to 13,165 ft. at Cloud Peak. Refer to AAA maps for additional elevation information.

In the Bighorn Mountains of north-central Wyoming, the Bighorn National Forest encompasses 1,115,073 acres. The forest is traversed by US 14 (Bighorn Scenic Byway), which crosses 8,950-foot Granite Pass and winds through scenic Shell Canyon and Falls; US 14A (Medicine Wheel Passage), which passes by Medicine Mountain near the enigmatic Medicine Wheel; and US 16 (Cloud Peak Skyway), which crosses 9,677-foot Powder River Pass and threads through beautiful Ten Sleep Canyon.

Cloud Peak is the highest peak within the forest. Motorists pulling trailers should use caution on US 14/14A.

Backpacking and saddle and pack trips can be taken into 189,039-acre Cloud Peak Wilderness; horse and foot trails begin at trail heads accessible via gravel roads off US 14 and US 16. This scenic area has miles of streams and more than 200 lakes containing brook, cutthroat, golden and rainbow trout. Hunters come in search of deer and elk.

Throughout the forest are 30 campgrounds, 10 picnic grounds and a good trail network, including the Bucking Mule Falls National Recreation Trail. Downhill skiing is available east of Worland (west of Buffalo); cross-country skiing can be pursued in all sections of the forest. Mountain climbing and snowmobiling also are popular.

Maps of the forest are available at the District Ranger's office in Sheridan at 2013 Eastside Second St., (307) 674-2600; in Greybull at 95 US 16/20, (307) 765-4435; and in Buffalo at 1415 Fort St., (307) 684-7806. Offices are open Mon.-Fri. 8-4:30; closed federal holidays. Offices are open Mon.-Fri. 8-4:30; closed federal holidays.

Shell Falls Wayside Visitor Center is on US 14, 5 miles west of Burgess Junction. The Center offers nature trails, exhibits, maps and other information about the forest, recreational activities and nearby communities; open daily 9:30-5, Memorial Day weekend through Labor Day. For additional information contact the Forest Supervisor's Office, 2013 Eastside Second St., Sheridan, WY 82801; phone (307) 674-2600. See Recreation Areas Chart.

MEDICINE WHEEL is off US 14A on Medicine Mountain, about 27 mi. e. of Lovell. The pre-Columbian structure, a circular arrangement of stones 245 feet in circumference with 28 spokes extending from a central cairn, is believed to have been used for religious ceremonies or celestial observations. **Note:** The road to Medicine Wheel is closed to vehicular traffic. Visitors are required to walk 1.5 miles to the site. Exceptions can be made for elderly or physically impaired visitors.

SHELL CANYON AND FALLS is 22 mi. e. of Greybull on US 14. The site can be seen from the Shell Falls overlook on US 14. An interpretive trail provides views of the imposing limestone cliffs and deep granite gorge cut by Shell Creek. **Hours:** Daily 9:30-5, Memorial Day to mid-Sept. **Cost:** Free. **Phone:** (307) 765-4435.

BLACK HILLS NATIONAL FOREST (B-6)

Elevations in the forest range from 3,300 ft. south of Hot Springs to 7,242 ft. at Black Elk Peak (formerly Harney Peak). Refer to AAA maps for additional elevation information.

In the scenic Black Hills of South Dakota and extending westward into Wyoming, the Black Hills National Forest covers more than 1.2 million acres. It was established in 1897. Stands of ponderosa pine, spruce and aspen are home to mountain lions, white-tailed and mule deer, elk and turkeys. Mountain goats and bighorn sheep are sometimes seen throughout the hills. Visitors should note that while summer days are warm, the nights can be quite cool.

Various routes make for a scenic drive. Peter Norbeck Scenic Byway creates a 70-mile loop via the Needles Highway, Iron Mountain Road—with its views of Mount Rushmore framed by tunnels—and

the pigtail bridges. Norbeck Overlook, on Iron Mountain Road (US 16A south from Keystone, S.D.), offers a view of the Black Elk Wilderness area.

The 20-mile Spearfish Canyon Scenic Byway along US 14A follows the pine- and spruce-covered banks of Spearfish Creek. Hiking trails to the canyon rims offer views of canyon walls and forests. Beautiful fall colors may be seen along this route in late September and early October.

The 111-mile Centennial Trail runs the length of the Black Hills from Bear Butte State Park to Wind Cave National Park. With more than 30 access points, portions of the route are open to motorized vehicles, horseback riders and mountain bicycles.

The forest's visitor center at Pactola Reservoir, on US 385 west of Rapid City, S.D., provides information about the history and management of the forest, including wildlife, scenery and recreation areas. Maps and information also are available at the forest supervisor's office in Custer City, S.D., and at district rangers' offices in Custer City, Rapid City and Spearfish, S.D., and in Sundance and Newcastle, Wyo. Allow 30 minutes minimum. Visitor center open daily 9-5, mid-May through Labor Day. Free.

Most of the forest's developed recreational facilities are in South Dakota, but the Wyoming segment does have four campgrounds with 76 sites. Entrance to the forest is free, but there are fees for day-use areas and camping. For further information contact the Forest Supervisor's Office, 1019 N. 5th St., Custer City, SD 57730; phone (605) 673-9200. See Recreation Areas Chart.

BRIDGER-TETON NATIONAL FOREST (C-2)

Elevations in the forest range from 5,660 ft. near Alpine to 13,804 ft. at Gannett Peak. Refer to AAA maps for additional elevation information.

Bordering Grand Teton (see place listing p. 180) and Yellowstone (see place listing p. 214) national parks, Bridger-Teton National Forest covers 3,439,809 acres in the Gros Ventre, Salt River, Teton, Wind River and Wyoming ranges. Within the forest are several live glaciers, an outstanding example of a geologic landslide and the state's highest mountain, Gannett Peak, shared by Shoshone National Forest (see place listing p. 208). Fishing, hunting, white-water rafting and winter sports attract visitors to the area.

The forest has three wilderness areas, all accessible only on foot or horseback. The Bridger Wilderness, 428,169 acres of scenic mountain country, lies on the west slope of the Continental Divide in the Wind River Range. More than 1,300 lakes, Gannett Peak and many glaciers highlight this rugged landscape, which is traversed by more than 500 miles of hiking and snowmobiling trails.

The Green River, beginning at the base of Gannett Peak, races through the Wind River Mountains before turning southward to join the Colorado River.

The Teton Wilderness preserves 585,468 acres in the northern section of the forest. Snow sometimes stays on the ground until early July in this barren alpine country of broad meadows, lakes, steep canyons, streams and waterfalls.

At Two Ocean Pass, Two Ocean Creek divides and sends one stream to the Pacific Ocean and another to the Atlantic; this geographic phenomenon supposedly exists nowhere else on the continent. The 287,000-acre Gros Ventre Wilderness, immediately east of Jackson, also is rugged, mountainous country ideally suited to backpacking, fishing and hunting.

Gros Ventre Slide is 5 miles east of Kelly on Gros Ventre Road. When the landslide occurred on the morning of June 23, 1925, this large earth movement dammed up the Gros Ventre (Big Belly) River. In a matter of minutes, trees and land fell from an elevation of 9,000 feet. Two years later part of the slide gave way, and the resulting wall of water, mud and rock destroyed the town of Kelly.

Scenic drives include Centennial National Scenic Byway from Dubois to Pinedale, the Green River Road from Pinedale north to the Green River Lakes, and the Skyline Drive from Pinedale northeast to Elkhart Park. Greys River Road leaves US 89 near Alpine and follows the river on its southward run; from its headwaters roads lead to US 89 near Geneva and to US 189 at Big Piney or Fontenelle reservoirs.

Pinedale *(see place listing p. 203)* and the resort town of Jackson *(see place listing p. 186)* are recreational activity centers. Near these two towns are the forest's three ski areas; trails for cross-country skiing also are available. Nearby hot springs include Granite Hot Springs, 35 miles southeast of Jackson on US 189, then 9 miles north. The Jackson Hole & Greater Yellowstone Visitor Center, 532 N. Cache St., Jackson, is open daily 8-7, late May-Sept.; 9-5, rest of year; phone (307) 733-3316

For additional information contact the Forest Supervisor's Office, 340 N. Cache St., P.O. Box 1888, Jackson, WY 83001; phone (307) 739-5500. *See Recreation Areas Chart.*

INSIDER INFO:
High-Altitude Health

Temples throbbing, gasping for breath and nauseated, you barely notice the scudding clouds or the spectacular view.

You might be suffering from Acute Mountain Sickness (AMS). Usually striking at around 8,000 feet (2,450 m) in altitude, AMS is your body's way of coping with the reduced oxygen and humidity of high altitudes. Among the symptoms are headaches, shortness of breath, loss of appetite, insomnia and lethargy. Some people complain of temporary weight gain or swelling in the face, hands and feet.

You can reduce the effect of high altitude by being in top condition. If you smoke or suffer from heart or lung ailments, consult your physician before your trip. Certain drugs will intensify the symptoms. To avoid Acute Mountain Sickness, adjust to elevations slowly; a gradual ascent with a couple days of acclimatization is best if you have time. For example, if you are planning a trip to the Rocky Mountains of Colorado, you might want to spend the first night in a lower altitude city such as Denver as opposed to heading directly to an environment with extreme elevations.

On the way up, eat light, nutritious meals and stay hydrated by drinking a large amount of water, taking care to avoid caffeine, alcohol and salt. In addition, your doctor may be able to prescribe medication that can offset the effects of high-altitude.

If you develop AMS, you should stop ascending; you will recover in a few days. If the AMS is mild, a quick descent will end the suffering immediately.

Other high-altitude health problems include sunburn and hypothermia. Dress in layers to protect yourself from the intense sun and wide fluctuations in temperature.

Finally, after you lounge in the sauna or hot tub at your lodgings, remember to stand up carefully, for the heat has relaxed your blood vessels and lowered your blood pressure.

PERIODIC SPRING is about 5 mi. e. of Afton on FR 10211 (Swift Creek Rd.). In late summer the spring ceases to flow every 18 minutes, then gradually builds to a thundering, ice-cold torrent. This cycle occurs regularly for 9 months and fluctuates during the period of highest snow melt, from about mid-May to mid-August. A narrow dirt road leads to within half a mile of the spring; the last 200 yards of the hike are very steep. The road, not recommended for trailers, is closed during winter. ⛏

BUFFALO (B-4) pop. 4,585, elev. 4,645'
• Hotels p. 166 • Restaurants p. 166

Retaining the atmosphere and hospitality of the Old West, Buffalo is a ranching town on the eastern slope of the Bighorn Mountains. Many Native American battles took place in this area 1866-77, triggered by the presence of the Bozeman Trail and the forts built to protect it.

After the area was opened to settlement, Buffalo was founded in 1879. Buffalo became known as the "Rustlers' Capital," and by 1892 the tensions between the region's big cattlemen and farmers, or "nesters," had erupted into the Johnson County War. It took the U.S. Army to restore order.

The growth of sheep ranching in the late 1890s brought Basque herders, who were drawn to Buffalo because of the Bighorn Mountains' resemblance to their homeland in the Pyrenees. Basque descendants continue to practice their time-honored traditions.

Guided saddle trips and jeep tours of nearby scenic and historical attractions can be arranged through local operators. Sightseeing is most rewarding along the Cloud Peak Scenic Byway portion of US 16 that runs between Buffalo and Ten Sleep.

Hunters can visit the Hunters Information Station in the chamber of commerce building.

Buffalo Chamber of Commerce: 55 N. Main St., Buffalo, WY 82834. **Phone:** (307) 684-5544 or (800) 227-5122.

Self-guiding tours: Information about walking and driving tours is available from the chamber of commerce.

JIM GATCHELL MEMORIAL MUSEUM is at 100 Fort St. The museum, which honors a frontier pharmacist known for his friendship with and knowledge of the Plains Native Americans, houses more than 30,000 artifacts. Included in the displays are a variety of firearms, historical photographs depicting the early days of the West, Native American artifacts and pioneer items. **Hours:** Mon.-Fri. 8-6, Sat. 9-5, Sun. noon-5, Memorial Day weekend-Labor Day; Mon.-Fri. 8-4, rest of the year. Closed Columbus Day, Veterans Day, Thanksgiving and Christmas. Phone ahead to confirm schedule. **Cost:** $7; $5 (ages 12-18 and 65+); $3 (ages 6-11). **Phone:** (307) 684-9331.

MUSEUM OF THE OCCIDENTAL HOTEL is at 10 N. Main St. Founded in a tent in 1879, the Occidental quickly became one of the state's most renowned hotels. Guests included Buffalo Bill Cody, Teddy Roosevelt and Calamity Jane. Reputedly the only fully restored frontier hotel in Wyoming, antique furnishings and Old World ambience reflect its original grandeur. The lobby's embossed ceilings and the 1908 saloon's original back bar are particularly noteworthy. **Hours:** Daily 8-8. **Cost:** Donations. **Phone:** (307) 684-0451. 🍴

BUFFALO INN   307/684-7000
🛡🛡 Hotel. **Address:** 100 Flatiron Dr 82834

HAMPTON INN & SUITES BY HILTON BUFFALO
                                              307/684-8899
🛡🛡🛡 Hotel. **Address:** 85 US Hwy | **AAA Benefit:**
16 E 82834 | Members save 5%
                                          | or more!

HOLIDAY INN EXPRESS HOTEL & SUITES BUFFALO
                                              307/684-9900
🛡🛡🛡 Hotel. **Address:** 106 US Hwy 16 E 82834

THE OCCIDENTAL HOTEL   307/684-0451

Historic Hotel
Rates not provided

Address: 10 N Main St 82834 **Location:** Downtown. **Facility:** This historic property—consisting of a hotel, restaurant and bar—spans one city block. Most rooms are themed after Western characters, and the décor includes antiques and period pieces. 19 units, some two and three bedrooms. 2 stories (no elevator), interior corridors. **Parking:** onsite and street. **Dining:** The Virginian Restaurant, see separate listing.

SAVE 🍴 🍷 📶 ✕ ☎ / SOME UNITS 🧳

SURESTAY PLUS HOTEL BY BEST WESTERN
                                      307/684-9564

Hotel
Rates not provided

Address: 65 US Hwy 16 E 82834 **Location:** I-25 exit 299 (US 16), just e; I-90 exit 58, 1.3 mi w. **Facility:** 63 units. 2 stories, interior/exterior corridors. **Parking:** winter plug-ins. **Pool:** heated indoor. **Activities:** hot tub, exercise room. **Guest Services:** coin laundry. **Featured Amenity:** full hot breakfast.

SAVE 🍴 CALL 🐾 ➔ ✚ BIZ 📶 ✕ 🛏 📷 💻 / SOME UNITS 🔔

WHERE TO EAT

BOZEMAN'S TRAIL STEAKHOUSE   307/684-5555

American
Casual Dining
$9-$28

AAA Inspector Notes: The steakhouse's varied menu lists not only burgers, buffalo steak and the house specialty baby back ribs but also shrimp dinners and a few Mexican items. The décor contributes to a Western and Plains Indian atmosphere. **Features:** full bar. **Address:** 675 E Hart St 82834 **Location:** I-25 exit 299 (US 16), just w. L D

CHINA GARDENS   307/684-9208
🛡🛡 Chinese. Casual Dining. **Address:** 386 N Main St 82834

CLEAR CREEK CANTINA   307/684-5317
🛡🛡 Tex-Mex. Casual Dining. **Address:** 4 S Main St 82834

THE VIRGINIAN RESTAURANT   307/684-5976
🛡🛡 Steak Seafood. Fine Dining. **Address:** 10 N Main St 82834

WINCHESTER STEAK HOUSE   307/684-8636
🛡🛡 Steak. Casual Dining. **Address:** 117 US Hwy 16 E 82834

CARIBOU-TARGHEE NATIONAL FOREST—See Idaho p. 38

CASPER (D-4) pop. 55,316, elev. 5,123'
• Restaurants p. 168

Casper's roots are buried in commerce. The town began as a ferry site on the Oregon Trail in 1847, when a group of Mormon immigrants who were camping realized that there was money to be made by boating travelers across the North Platte River. The idea caught on, and in the early 1850s a toll bridge was built; soon a military post was established to protect the span and its traffic.

The town's real asset, however, was not discovered until 1889, when the first well in the Salt Creek oil field was tapped; by 1915 the town was in an oil boom that matched the frenzy of the California, Colorado and Montana gold rushes.

The boom brought not only prosperity but also a national scandal over the nearby Teapot Dome oil field. In 1927 the U.S. Supreme Court handed down verdicts in the case, which included sentencing Secretary of the Interior Albert Fall to prison for secretly leasing the rich field to Mammoth Crude Oil Co. without taking competitive bids.

Casper is a major service and supply center for mineral, oil, natural gas, uranium and coal industries, as well as a center for many medical and financial services.

Stargazers can view astronomy-related programs throughout the year at Casper Planetarium, a half-mile north of I-25 exit 188B at 904 N. Poplar, phone (307) 577-0310. Along SRs 20/26 and 220, markers identify the California, Mormon, Oregon and Pony Express trails.

Casper Area Convention and Visitors Bureau: 139 W. Second St., Suite 1B, Casper, WY 82601. **Phone:** (307) 234-5362 or (800) 852-1889.

FORT CASPAR MUSEUM AND HISTORIC SITE is .5 mi. n. of SR 220 off Wyoming Blvd. at 4001 Fort Caspar Rd. This site on the Oregon, California, Mormon, and Pony Express trails includes reconstructions of an 1847 Mormon Trail ferry, an 1859 Guinard bridge and an 1865 frontier Army fort. Museum exhibits recount the history of central Wyoming, from prehistory to the present.

Hours: Museum daily 8-5, May-Sept.; Tues.-Sat. 8-5, rest of year. Reconstructed buildings daily 8:30-4:30 May-Sept. **Cost:** May-Sept. $3; $2 (ages 13-18). Rest of year $1.50; $1 (ages 13-18). **Phone:** (307) 235-8462.

HISTORIC TRAILS WEST departs from the National Historic Trails Interpretive Center, 1501 N. Poplar St. The tour features a wagon train that travels along the actual ruts of the Oregon, California, Mormon and Pony Express trails. Visitors also can take an excursion where they ride horses as Pony Express riders did alongside the wagons. Historical accounts are given. Dutch-oven cookouts and overnight, 3- and 5-day expeditions also are available.

Hours: Daily, May-Oct. (weather permitting). **Cost:** Trips lasting 2 hours to overnight $55-$175. Trips lasting 3 to 5 days $895-$1,495. Reservations are recommended. **Phone:** (307) 266-4868. GT

NATIONAL HISTORIC TRAILS INTERPRETIVE CENTER is off I-25 exit 189, then 1 mi. n. to 1501 N. Poplar St. Seven galleries represent Western trail history through interactive and multimedia exhibits and dioramas. Visitors can sit in a covered wagon and experience a simulated crossing of the North Platte River. A five-screen theater features an audiovisual presentation illustrating pioneer and Native American life. During the summer months, encampment reenactments take place and interpreters in period costume perform demonstrations.

Time: Allow 2 hours minimum. **Hours:** Tues.-Sun. 8-5, late May-early Sept.; Tues.-Sat. 9-4:30, rest of year. Closed most federal holidays; phone ahead. **Cost:** Free. **Phone:** (307) 265-8030.

TATE GEOLOGICAL MUSEUM is on the Casper College campus at 125 College Dr.; take Wolcott St./Casper Mountain Rd. s. Almost 3,000 fossil and mineral specimens are on display. You can tour a fossil preparation lab and meet "Dee," said to be one of the world's largest mounted Columbian mammoths. **Time:** Allow 1 hour minimum. **Hours:** Mon.-Fri. 9-5, Sat. and holidays 10-4. **Cost:** Donations. **Phone:** (307) 268-2447.

WERNER WILDLIFE MUSEUM is s. via Wolcott St. to 405 E. 15th St. The museum houses a pronghorn antelope diorama, a collection of Western birds and mounted specimens of wildlife native to Wyoming and other parts of North America. The Werner Trophy Room exhibits specimens from around the world. **Hours:** Mon.-Fri. 9-5. Closed Jan. 1, Thanksgiving and Christmas. Phone ahead to confirm schedule. **Cost:** Free. **Phone:** (307) 235-2108.

BEST WESTERN PLUS CASPER INN & SUITES
(307)472-1120

 Contemporary Hotel $109-$189

 Best Western PLUS **AAA Benefit:** Members save up to 15% and earn bonus points!

Address: 651 Granite Peak Dr 82609 **Location:** I-25 exit 182, just s on Hat Six Rd, just w on E 2nd St, then just n. **Facility:** 97 units. 4 stories, interior corridors. **Parking:** winter plug-ins. **Terms:** cancellation fee imposed. **Pool:** heated indoor. **Activities:** hot tub, exercise room. **Guest Services:** valet and coin laundry.

COURTYARD BY MARRIOTT CASPER (307)473-2600
Hotel. **Address:** 4260 Hospitality Ln 82609
AAA Benefit: Members save 5% or more!

HAMPTON INN & SUITES BY HILTON CASPER 307/235-6668
Hotel. **Address:** 1100 N Poplar St 82601
AAA Benefit: Members save 5% or more!

HILTON GARDEN INN CASPER 307/266-1300
Hotel. **Address:** 1150 N Poplar St 82601
AAA Benefit: Members save 5% or more!

HOLIDAY INN CASPER EAST 307/577-5000
Hotel. **Address:** 721 Granite Peak Dr 82609

MAINSTAY SUITES CASPER (307)472-7829
Extended Stay Hotel. **Address:** 551 Granite Peak Dr 82609

QUALITY INN & SUITES CASPER (307)266-2400
Hotel. **Address:** 821 N Poplar St 82601

RAMKOTA HOTEL & CONFERENCE CENTER
307/266-6000

Hotel
Rates not provided

Address: 800 N Poplar St 82601 **Location:** I-25 exit 188B (N Poplar St), just nw. **Facility:** 230 units. 6 stories, interior corridors. **Parking:** winter plug-ins. **Pool:** heated indoor. **Activities:** hot tub, bicycles, exercise room. **Guest Services:** valet and coin laundry, area transportation. **Featured Amenity:** breakfast buffet.

[SAVE] [icons] CALL [icons] / SOME UNITS [icon]

RESIDENCE INN BY MARRIOTT CASPER   (307)234-9008
Extended Stay Contemporary Hotel. **Address:** 4930 E 2nd St 82609

AAA Benefit: Members save 5% or more!

SUPER 8 CASPER WEST   (307)266-3480
Hotel. **Address:** 3838 CY Ave 82604

WHERE TO EAT

BOSCO'S ITALIAN RESTAURANTE   307/265-9658
Italian. Casual Dining. **Address:** 847 E 'A' St 82601

THE COTTAGE CAFE   307/234-1157
Small Plates Sandwiches. Casual Dining. **Address:** 116 S Lincoln St 82601

DSASUMO ASIAN BISTRO   307/237-7874
Thai Fusion. Casual Dining. **Address:** 320 W 1st St 82601

EGGINGTON'S RESTAURANT   307/265-8700
Breakfast Comfort Food. Casual Dining. **Address:** 229 E 2nd St 82602

FIRE ROCK STEAK HOUSE   307/234-2333
Steak Seafood. Casual Dining. **Address:** 6100 E 2nd St 82609

JOHNNY J'S DINER   307/234-4204
American. Casual Dining. **Address:** 1705 E 2nd St 82601

J'S PUB & GRILL   307/472-3100
American. Casual Dining. **Address:** 3201 SW Wyoming Blvd 82604

LA COCINA   307/266-1414
Mexican. Casual Dining. **Address:** 321 E 'E' St 82601

LIME LEAF ASIAN BISTRO   307/315-6888
Asian. Casual Dining. **Address:** 845 E 2nd St 82601

SANFORD'S GRUB & PUB   307/315-6040
American. Casual Dining. **Address:** 61 SE Wyoming Blvd 82609

SILVER FOX STEAKHOUSE   307/235-3000
Steak. Casual Dining. **Address:** 3422 S Energy Ln 82604

CHEYENNE (E-6) pop. 59,466, elev. 6,060'
• Hotels p. 170 • Restaurants p. 171

Cheyenne was named for the tribe of Plains Native Americans that once roamed southeastern Wyoming. In 1867 Union Pacific Railroad chief engineer Maj. Gen. Grenville M. Dodge built a depot on the site, situated at the junction of several roads leading to military camps.

Before the track even reached town, it was overrun by gamblers, cowboys, speculators, shopkeepers and real estate salesmen, thus earning Cheyenne the nickname "Hell on Wheels." The town's reputation was so widespread that in 1868 a resident received a letter from Pennsylvania addressed simply "Cheyenne."

By 1869 Cheyenne had outgrown some of its cow-town adolescence to assume the more mature stature of territorial capital, an honor it retained when Wyoming became the 44th state in 1890.

Noted town residents include Nellie Tayloe Ross, the first woman governor in the United States; and Esther Morris, a pioneer for women's suffrage in Wyoming and former justice of the peace of South Pass City. A statue honoring Morris is on Capitol Avenue. The Cowgirls of the West Museum, 205 W. 17th St., preserves the role of women in Western culture with exhibits of rodeo and ranching memorabilia including saddles, photographs and clothing; phone (307) 638-4994.

"Big Boy," one of the world's largest steam locomotives, is on permanent display in Holliday Park.

Since it was established in 1867 as a headquarters for the cavalry troops protecting pioneers and railroad construction workers, F.E. Warren Air Force Base has served various branches of the military, including the nation's first intercontinental ballistic missile group.

Happy Jack Road (SR 210) is a 38-mile scenic byway to Laramie that runs from rolling grasslands to the rocky foothills of the Pole Mountain Division of Medicine Bow National Forest. Equally interesting is a trip to Snowy Range, a region of fishing streams and mountain lakes.

In July Cheyenne Frontier Days recaptures the city's Wild West heritage with horse races, parades, nightly entertainment and what is claimed to be the world's largest outdoor rodeo.

Visit Cheyenne: 121 W. 15th St., Suite 202, Cheyenne, WY 82001. **Phone:** (307) 778-3133 or (800) 426-5009. *(See ad on inside front cover.)*

Shopping: Frontier Mall, 1400 Dell Range Blvd., has more than 75 stores including Dillard's and JCPenney.

Self-guiding tours: A pamphlet describing a self-guiding walking tour of Cheyenne's historic downtown area is available at Visit Cheyenne.

CHEYENNE BOTANIC GARDENS, 710 S. Lions Park Dr., has a variety of themed gardens, including annual and perennial displays, xeriscape, rose and herb gardens. A 6,800-square-foot solar-heated greenhouse conservatory houses tropical foliage, cacti, herbs and roses as well as a waterfall and a pond. Visitors can walk through a seven-circuit labyrinth; for blind and physically impaired visitors there are four stone benches inscribed with "finger labyrinths." Wyoming's oldest steam locomotive is on the grounds. The 28,000-square-foot Grand Conservatory contains a Navy submarine periscope along with telescope and microscope stations.

Kids learn about sustainability as they explore Paul Smith Children's Village. This LEED-certified site has a solar-powered discovery lab, a solar-heated and solar-powered greenhouse, a wetlands area, a tepee village, a secret garden and an amphitheater where kids can put on puppet shows. Special activities and events are offered.

Time: Allow 1 hour, 30 minutes minimum. **Hours:** Grounds daily dawn-dusk. Conservatory Wed.-Sun. 10-6. Paul Smith Children's Village Tues.-Sun. 10-5. Closed major holidays. **Cost:** Free. **Phone:** (307) 637-6458. *(See ad on inside front cover.)* 🏦

CHEYENNE DEPOT MUSEUM is housed in the restored Union Pacific Railroad Depot at 121 W. 15th St. Regional railroad history is depicted through photographs, narratives, artifacts and a brief film presentation. Exhibits focus on the impact that Union Pacific Railroad operations had on the town and its residents. The second floor baggage room houses The Union Central and Northern Model Railroad layout created by Harry S. Brunk. He spent more than 30 years handcrafting everything from the scenery to the rolling stock for this HO scale of the narrow gauge Clear Creek Lines, which includes the Colorado and Southern Railway.

Hours: Mon.-Fri. 9-7, Sat. 9-5, Sun. 10:45-4, June-Sept.; Mon.-Fri. 9-5, Sat. 9-3, Sun. 11-3, rest of year. Closed major holidays. **Cost:** $8; $7 (ages 60+ and military with ID); free (ages 0-12). **Phone:** (307) 632-3905. *(See ad on inside front cover.)*

CHEYENNE FRONTIER DAYS OLD WEST MUSEUM is in Frontier Park at 4610 N. Carey Ave. The museum has some 149,000 artifacts, including a collection of more than 150 horse-drawn carriages and wagons, and classic Western and folk art. Also included is authentic clothing dating from the 1850s and an interactive children's gallery.

Hours: Daily 9-5, with extended hours during Cheyenne Frontier Days. Closed Jan. 1, Easter, Thanksgiving and Christmas. **Cost:** $10; $9 (ages

65+ and military with ID); free (ages 0-12 with adult). **Phone:** (307) 778-7290. *(See ad on inside front cover.)*

CHEYENNE STREET RAILWAY TROLLEY departs the Cheyenne Depot Square at 121 W. 15th St. Highlights of the 90-minute sightseeing tour include the Cheyenne Frontier Days Old West Museum, State Capitol and Wyoming State Museum. **Hours:** Tours depart Mon.-Fri. at 10, 11:30, 1, 2:30 and 4, Sat. at 10, noon and 2, Sun. at noon and 2, early May-Sept. **Cost:** $12; $6 (ages 2-12). Trolley Plus Tour (includes 90-minute tour and entrance to Cheyenne Frontier Days Old West Museum, Nelson Museum of the West and Cheyenne Depot) $19. **Phone:** (307) 778-3133 or (800) 426-5009. *(See ad on inside front cover, this page.)* GT

THE NELSON MUSEUM OF THE WEST is at 1714 Carey Ave. The museum celebrates the American West through exhibits of antique weapons, cowboy saddles, spurs, chaps, Native American beadwork, pottery, baskets and weavings. Cowgirl, outlaw and lawmen memorabilia is featured in addition to the "Cavalry in the West" exhibit. Mounted taxidermy from all continents also is highlighted. **Time:** Allow 1 hour minimum. **Hours:** Mon.-Sat. 9-4:30, June-Aug.; Mon.-Fri. 9-4:30, in May and Sept.-Oct. **Cost:** $5; $4 (senior citizens); free (ages 0-12). **Phone:** (307) 635-7670.

STATE CAPITOL is on Capitol Ave. between 24th and 25th sts. This neoclassic sandstone building, with a golden dome 50 feet in diameter, is architecturally uncommon for the region. Within the building are murals, woodwork, marble floors and displays of native wildlife. **Note:** The interior of the capitol is closed. Renovations are scheduled to be complete in mid-2019. **Phone:** (307) 777-7220.

TERRY BISON RANCH is accessed by taking I-80 to I-25S, then taking exit 2 off I-25S, then s. on Terry Ranch Rd. to ranch entrance at 51 I-25 Service Rd. E. The historic working bison ranch has more than 3,000 bison. Fishing (no state license required), horseback rides, ATV tours and train tours are offered. Day-long horseback cattle drives that include breakfast and dinner are offered.

▼ *See AAA listing this page* ▼

Hours: Bison tours daily dawn-dusk (weather permitting). Cattle drives, mid-June to mid-Sept.; phone ahead for schedule. **Cost:** Bison tours $12; $6 (ages 4-12). Horseback rides $45 per hour; $8 pony ride. Ages 0-7 are not permitted on horseback rides, but 15-minute pony rides are available for ages 0-9. ATV tour $55 per hour (driver); $40 per hour (passenger); ages 0-4 are not permitted. Cattle drive $150. **Phone:** (307) 634-4171. *(See ad on inside front cover.)* GT

WYOMING STATE MUSEUM, in the Barrett Building of the Capitol complex at 2301 Central Ave., features a variety of permanent and changing exhibits that allow visitors to delve into Wyoming's history.

The Drawn to This Land gallery catalogs the reasons people and businesses chose Wyoming as a place to flourish, and Swamped with Coal traces the development of the mining industry. Social history is the theme of the Living in Wyoming exhibition.

Visitors encounter a skeletal replica of a camptosaur—one of Wyoming's earliest inhabitants—in the R.I.P.-Rex in Pieces gallery; Wild Bunch focuses on other animals that have called the state home.

An interactive map pinpointing historical sites is the highlight of the Wyoming's Story collection; guns, a cowboy diorama and Native American baskets and jewelry are just some of the items on display in the Barber Gallery. Designed for the little ones, the Hands-on History Room has a kid-size tepee, a chuck wagon and a curiosity cabinet.

The museum is hosting the Wyoming State Capitol exhibit into mid-2019 while the State Capitol is closed for restoration. **Time:** Allow 2 hours minimum. **Hours:** Mon.-Sat. 9-4:30. **Cost:** Free. **Phone:** (307) 777-7022. *(See ad on inside front cover.)*

BEST WESTERN PLUS FRONTIER INN   (307)638-8891

Hotel
$129-$309

AAA Benefit: Members save up to 15% and earn bonus points!

Address: 8101 Hutchins Dr 82007 **Location:** I-80 exit 367, just n. **Facility:** 74 units. 3 stories, interior corridors. **Parking:** winter plug-ins. **Terms:** cancellation fee imposed. **Amenities:** safes. **Pool:** heated indoor. **Activities:** hot tub, exercise room. **Guest Services:** valet and coin laundry. **Featured Amenity: full hot breakfast.**

CANDLEWOOD SUITES CHEYENNE   307-634-6622
Extended Stay Hotel. **Address:** 2335 Tura Pkwy 82001

COMFORT INN & SUITES CHEYENNE   (307)514-6051
Hotel. **Address:** 201 W Fox Farm Rd 82007

DAYS INN CHEYENNE   (307)778-8877
Hotel. **Address:** 2360 W Lincolnway 82001

FAIRFIELD INN & SUITES BY MARRIOTT AIRPORT   (307)637-4070
Hotel. **Address:** 1415 Stillwater Ave 82009

AAA Benefit: Members save 5% or more!

FAIRFIELD INN & SUITES BY MARRIOTT CHEYENNE SOUTHWEST/DOWNTOWN AREA   (307)634-0401

Hotel
$72-$438

Fairfield
AAA Benefit: Members save 5% or more!

Address: 1820 W Lincolnway 82001 **Location:** I-25 exit 9, 0.8 mi ne on US 80. **Facility:** 84 units. 4 stories, interior corridors. **Parking:** winter plug-ins. **Terms:** cancellation fee imposed. **Pool:** heated indoor. **Activities:** hot tub, picnic facilities, exercise room. **Guest Services:** valet and coin laundry, area transportation.

HAMPTON INN CHEYENNE   (307)632-2747

Hotel
$102-$359

Hampton by Hilton
AAA Benefit: Members save 5% or more!

Address: 1781 Fleischli Pkwy 82001 **Location:** I-25 exit 9, just e on I-80 business loop/US 30, then just n. **Facility:** 64 units. 3 stories, interior corridors. **Terms:** 1-7 night minimum stay, 3 day cancellation notice-fee imposed. **Pool:** heated indoor. **Activities:** hot tub, exercise room. **Guest Services:** valet and coin laundry. **Featured Amenity: full hot breakfast.**

HOLIDAY INN EXPRESS HOTEL & SUITES CHEYENNE   307/433-0751
Hotel. **Address:** 1741 Fleischli Pkwy 82001

LITTLE AMERICA HOTEL & RESORT-CHEYENNE   307/775-8400

Hotel
Rates not provided

Address: 2800 W Lincolnway 82009 **Location:** I-25 exit 9, just w on US 30. Located in a quiet secluded area. **Facility:** 188 units. 1-3 stories (no elevator), interior/exterior corridors. **Parking:** winter plug-ins. **Amenities:** safes. **Dining:** Hathaway's Restaurant & Lounge, see separate listing. **Pool:** heated outdoor. **Activities:** regulation golf, par 3 golf, playground, exercise room. **Guest Services:** valet and coin laundry.

MICROTEL INN & SUITES BY WYNDHAM CHEYENNE   (307)634-3200
Hotel. **Address:** 1400 W Lincolnway 82001

MY PLACE HOTEL - CHEYENNE   307/634-1400
Extended Stay Hotel. **Address:** 1920 W Lincolnway 82001

NAGLE WARREN MANSION BED & BREAKFAST
(307)637-3333

♦♦♦
Historic Bed & Breakfast
$158-$192

Address: 222 E 17th St 82001 **Location:** I-80 exit 362, 1.2 mi n on I-25 business loop/US 85/87 business route, then just e; jct House St; downtown. **Facility:** Handmade tiles adorn the fireplaces in most guest rooms at this Romanesque-style 1888 building. Furnishings include a variety of period antiques, and fabulous architectural features throughout. 12 units. 3 stories (no elevator), interior corridors. **Parking:** street only. **Terms:** 3 day cancellation notice-fee imposed. **Activities:** hot tub, exercise room, massage. **Guest Services:** valet laundry. **Featured Amenity:** full hot breakfast. *(See ad this page.)*

SAVE ❙❙➕ 🖥 🛜 ✕ / SOME UNITS 🐾

SPRINGHILL SUITES BY MARRIOTT CHEYENNE
(307)635-0006

♦♦♦ Contemporary Hotel. **Address:** 416 W Fox Farm Rd 82007

AAA Benefit:
Members save 5% or more!

STAYBRIDGE SUITES CHEYENNE
307/634-6370

♦♦♦ Extended Stay Contemporary Hotel. **Address:** 5109 Frontier Mall Dr 82009

SUPER 8 CHEYENNE
(307)635-8741

♦♦ Motel. **Address:** 1900 W Lincolnway 82001

▼ See AAA listing this page ▼

WHERE TO EAT

2 DOORS DOWN
307/634-6008

♦ Burgers. Quick Serve. **Address:** 118 E 17th St 82001

THE ALBANY
307/638-3507

♦♦
American Casual Dining
$8-$24

AAA Inspector Notes: *Classic Historic.* In business since 1942, this restaurant is in a large brick building and features high-back booths, wood floors and casual, friendly service. Serving steaks, seafood and chicken, the eatery is a good value at lunch and a bit more upscale at dinner. **Features:** full bar. **Address:** 1506 Capitol Ave 82001 **Location:** Jct Lincolnway, just s; downtown.

L D

ANONG'S THAI CUISINE
307/638-8597

♦♦ Thai. Casual Dining. **Address:** 620 Central Ave 82007

BELLA FUOCO WOOD-FIRED PIZZA & WINE BAR
307/514-2855

♦♦ Italian. Casual Dining. **Address:** 2115 Warren Ave 82001

BREAD BASKET BAKERY & SANDWICH SHOPPE
307/432-2525

♦ Breads/Pastries Sandwiches. Quick Serve. **Address:** 1819 Maxwell Ave 82001

BUNKHOUSE SALOON & STEAKHOUSE
307/632-6184

♦♦ American. Casual Dining. **Address:** 1064 Happy Jack Rd (SR 210) 82009

GUADALAJARA MEXICAN RESTAURANT
307/432-6803

♦♦ Mexican. Casual Dining. **Address:** 1745 Dell Range Blvd 82009

HATHAWAY'S RESTAURANT & LOUNGE   307/775-8400
▼▼▼▼ American. Casual Dining. **Address:** 2800 W Lincolnway 82009

KOREAN HOUSE RESTAURANT   307/638-7938
▼▼ Korean. Casual Dining. **Address:** 3219 Snyder Ave 82001

L'OSTERIA MONDELLO ITALIAN CUCINA   307/778-6068
▼▼ Italian. Casual Dining. **Address:** 1507 Stillwater Ave 82009

LUXURY DINER   307/638-8971
▼ Breakfast Comfort Food. Casual Dining. **Address:** 1401 W Lincolnway 82001

MORT'S BAGELS   307/637-5400
▼ Breads/Pastries Sandwiches. Quick Serve. **Address:** 1815 Carey Ave 82001

POOR RICHARD'S   307/635-5114
▼▼ American. Casual Dining. **Address:** 2233 E Lincolnway 82001

R & B BREAKFAST CLUB   307/433-0023
▼▼ American. Casual Dining. **Address:** 2102 E Lincolnway 82001

RIB & CHOP HOUSE   307/514-0271
▼▼ American. Casual Dining. **Address:** 400 W Lincolnway 82001

RUBYJUICE   307/634-3022
▼ Deli. Quick Serve. **Address:** 113 E 17th St 82001

SANFORD'S GRUB & PUB   307/634-3381
▼▼ American. Casual Dining. **Address:** 115 E 17th St 82001

SENATOR'S RESTAURANT & BRASS BUFFALO SALOON   307/634-4171

▼▼ ▼▼
Steak
Casual Dining
$8-$39

AAA Inspector Notes: Resembling an old Western barn, this rustic pine dining room at this working guest ranch has dark wood walls and floors and a casual décor. For those that do not opt for the specialty, barbecued and grilled bison, there are other choices and a salad bar. The more basic lunch menu lists just sandwiches. This place is in a rural area along the interstate frontage road and is surrounded by various buildings. The casually dressed staff carries out friendly service. **Features:** full bar, patio dining. **Address:** 51 I-25 Service Rd E 82007 **Location:** I-25 exit 2, just e, then 2.5 mi s; in Terry Bison Ranch. [L] [D] CALL [♿]

TWIN DRAGON   307/637-6622
▼▼ Chinese. Casual Dining. **Address:** 1809 Carey Ave 82001

WASABI JAPANESE GRILL & BAR   307/514-5606
▼▼ Japanese. Casual Dining. **Address:** 4620 Grandview Ave #205 82009

CODY (B-2) pop. 9,520, elev. 5,095'

- Hotels p. 175 • Restaurants p. 175
- Hotels & Restaurants map & index p. 220
- Part of Yellowstone National Park area — see map p. 214

Founded by Col. William "Buffalo Bill" F. Cody in 1896, Cody is near the east and northeast entrances to Yellowstone National Park (see place listing p. 214). Some of the state's most scenic areas, including Shoshone National Forest (see place listing p. 208), Sunlight Basin, the Absaroka and Beartooth mountains and the Bighorn Canyon National Recreation Area (see place listing p. 95), are nearby.

US 14/16/20, alternately known as the Buffalo Bill Cody Scenic Byway, has been called the most scenic 52 miles in America. Along the route are many unusual rock formations as well as the State of Wyoming Veterans Memorial Park (near Yellowstone Regional Airport), which honors those who served in World War II, the Korean and Vietnam wars and the Iraq and Afghanistan wars. The highway runs 182 miles between Ranchester and Yellowstone National Park. Cody also is the northern terminus of the scenic section of SR 120 that travels 83 miles southeast to Thermopolis (see place listing p. 209). Scenic US 14A heads 107 miles northeast to Burgess Junction.

Outfitters offer fishing, hayrides, horseback riding, hunting and pack trips and river float trips. Scenic flights overlooking the Bighorn Mountains and Grand Teton and Yellowstone national parks can be arranged through Choice Aviation, (307) 587-9262.

Of interest downtown are historic buildings dating from the beginning of the 20th century. Irma Hotel, 12th Street and Sheridan Avenue, has been a meeting place for local cattlemen, oilmen and shepherds since the early 1900s. Its $100,000 bar was a gift from Queen Victoria to Buffalo Bill in appreciation of his Wild West Show. Pahaska Tepee, Buffalo Bill's first hunting lodge, is at the east entrance to Yellowstone National Park.

Cody Chamber of Commerce: 836 Sheridan Ave., Cody, WY 82414. **Phone:** (307) 587-2777. **(See ad p. 173, p. 216.)**

▼GEM **BUFFALO BILL CENTER OF THE WEST** is at 720 Sheridan Ave. The five museums that comprise the center are dedicated to the art, artifacts, crafts, cultures, traditions and history of the American West. In addition, the McCracken Research Library contains book and manuscript collections and thousands of historic photographs. Daily raptor shows are offered as well as other daily events June through September.

Time: Allow 4 hours minimum. **Hours:** Daily 8-6, May 1 to mid-Sept.; daily 8-5, mid-Sept. through Oct. 31; daily 10-5, Mar.-Apr. and in Nov.; Thurs.-Sun. 10-5, rest of year. Closed Jan. 1, Thanksgiving and Christmas. **Cost:** (Valid for 2 consecutive days for all five museums) $19.50; $18.50 (ages 65+); $18 (students ages 18+ with ID); $13 (ages 6-17). **Phone:** (307) 587-4771. [🍴]

SAVE **Buffalo Bill Museum** is at 720 Sheridan Ave. at Buffalo Bill Center of the West. The museum displays belongings of the showman and scout, one of the most famous men of his time, along with possessions of Annie Oakley and artifacts of the early West. Exhibits provide insight into the history of the American cowboy, conservation and dude ranching.

Hours: Daily 8-6, May 1 to mid-Sept.; daily 8-5, mid-Sept. through Oct. 31; daily 10-5, Mar.-Apr. and in Nov.; Thurs.-Sun. 10-5, rest of year. Closed Jan. 1, Thanksgiving and Christmas. **Cost:** Included with

WHERE AMERICA'S ALWAYS BEEN GREAT.

Cody YELLOWSTONE

THE GREAT AMERICAN ADVENTURE

(See map & index p. 220.)
Buffalo Bill Center of the West admission of $19.50; $18.50 (ages 65+); $18 (students ages 18+ with ID); $13 (ages 6-17). **Phone:** (307) 587-4771.

Cody Firearms Museum is at 720 Sheridan Ave. at Buffalo Bill Center of the West. The museum is noted for its exhibits of American firearms, including the Winchester collection. The museum, featuring some 30,000 firearms-related artifacts, traces the development of firearms from the early 16th century. Examples range from centuries-old projectile arms to flintlocks and Gatling guns to modern sport rifles.

Hours: Daily 8-6, May 1 to mid-Sept.; daily 8-5, mid-Sept. through Oct. 31; daily 10-5, Mar.-Apr. and in Nov.; Thurs.-Sun. 10-5, rest of year. Closed Jan. 1, Thanksgiving and Christmas. **Cost:** Included with Buffalo Bill Center of the West admission of $19.50; $18.50 (ages 65+); $18 (students ages 18+ with ID); $13 (ages 6-17). **Phone:** (307) 587-4771.

Draper Natural History Museum is at 720 Sheridan Ave. at Buffalo Bill Center of the West. The museum features exhibits about the Yellowstone region's natural history and human influence from early explorers to ranchers. A highlight is a virtual expedition through mountain forests and valleys. A live raptor program allows an up-close visit with such birds of prey as owls, eagles and falcons.

Hours: Daily 8-6, May 1 to mid-Sept.; daily 8-5, mid-Sept. through Oct. 31; daily 10-5, Mar.-Apr. and in Nov.; Thurs.-Sun. 10-5, rest of year. Closed Jan. 1, Thanksgiving and Christmas. **Cost:** Included with Buffalo Bill Center of the West admission of $19.50; $18.50 (ages 65+); $18 (students ages 18+ with ID); $13 (ages 6-17). **Phone:** (307) 587-4771.

The Plains Indian Museum is at 720 Sheridan Ave. at Buffalo Bill Center of the West. The museum has an extensive collection of art, artifacts, ceremonial items and beadwork as well as dress and weaponry of the Arapaho, Blackfeet, Cheyenne, Crow, Shoshone and Sioux tribes. Exhibits depict the everyday existence of these Plains tribes.

Hours: Daily 8-6, May 1 to mid-Sept.; daily 8-5, mid-Sept. through Oct. 31; daily 10-5, Mar.-Apr. and in Nov.; Thurs.-Sun. 10-5, rest of year. Closed Jan. 1, Thanksgiving and Christmas. **Cost:** Included with Buffalo Bill Center of the West admission of $19.50; $18.50 (ages 65+); $18 (students ages 18+ with ID); $13 (ages 6-17). **Phone:** (307) 587-4771.

Whitney Western Art Museum is at 720 Sheridan Ave. at Buffalo Bill Center of the West. The gallery houses a comprehensive collection of paintings, sculpture and prints depicting the West. Artists represented include Albert Bierstadt, George Catlin, Thomas Moran, Frederic Remington, Charles M. Russell and Joseph Henry Sharp. Reconstructed studios enable visitors to view artists' work areas.

Hours: Daily 8-6, May 1 to mid-Sept.; daily 8-5, mid-Sept. through Oct. 31; daily 10-5, Mar.-Apr. and in Nov.; Thurs.-Sun. 10-5, rest of year. Closed Jan.

1, Thanksgiving and Christmas. **Cost:** Included with Buffalo Bill Center of the West admission of $19.50; $18.50 (ages 65+); $18 (students ages 18+ with ID); $13 (ages 6-17). **Phone:** (307) 587-4771.

BUFFALO BILL DAM VISITOR CENTER is 6 mi. w. on US 14/16/20 at 4808 North Fork Hwy. In addition to a dam overlook, the visitor center has views of Shoshone Canyon, area wildlife displays, dinosaur and fossil exhibits and a short movie. Self-guiding historical audio tours are available. **Time:** Allow 30 minutes minimum. **Hours:** Mon.-Fri. 8-7, Sat.-Sun. 9-5, June-Aug.; Mon.-Fri. 8-6, Sat.-Sun. 9-5 in May and Sept. **Cost:** Free. **Phone:** (307) 527-6076.

THE CODY CATTLE COMPANY, 2.9 mi. w. on US 14/16/20, then .4 mi. n.w. to 1910 Demaris St., offers a chuck wagon supper and a live Western musical show. Dinner guests have the option of eating before or during the hour-long performance. Seating is in a large mess hall with a stage in front; special lighting and a backdrop create the illusion of being outdoors.

Time: Allow 1 hour minimum. **Hours:** Supper daily 5:30-7:30, June-Sept. Show daily at 6:30, June-Sept. **Cost:** Show only $16; $8 (ages 3-12). Dinner and show $30; $15 (ages 3-12). A combination ticket for the dinner, the show and admission to Cody Nite Rodeo *(see attraction listing this page)* is available most days June-Aug. and costs $47; $25 (ages 7-12); $15 (ages 3-6). Reservations are recommended. **Phone:** (307) 272-5770. 🍴

CODY NITE RODEO is 2 mi. w. on US 14/16/20 at 519 W. Yellowstone Ave. The 2-hour rodeo fea-

tures events like bronc riding, bull riding, team roping and barrel racing. Little ones can participate in the kids' calf scramble. **Hours:** Daily at 8 p.m., June-Aug (gates open at 7 p.m.). Special performances are held July 1-4 during Stampede Days. **Cost:** $20; $10 (ages 7-12). A combination ticket with the dinner and the show at The Cody Cattle Company *(see attraction listing this page)* is available most days June-Aug. and costs $47; $25 (ages 7-12); $15 (ages 3-6). **Phone:** (307) 587-5155 or (800) 207-0744.

OLD TRAIL TOWN is 3 mi. w. on US 14/16/20 at 1831 DeMaris Dr. Featured is a group of historic buildings with indoor exhibits reassembled on the first site of the frontier town of Old Cody. Highlights include the grave of John "Jeremiah" Johnson and a log cabin used as a hideout by Butch Cassidy, the Sundance Kid and other members of the Wild Bunch.

The Museum of the Old West houses guns, carriages, clothing and many prehistoric and historic Plains Native American relics. **Hours:** Daily 8-7, May 15-Sept. 30. **Cost:** $10; $9 (ages 65+); $5 (ages 6-12); free (ages 0-5 and active military with ID). **Phone:** (307) 587-5302.

(See map & index p. 220.)

RECREATIONAL ACTIVITIES

White-water Rafting

- **Wyoming River Trips** depart from 233 Yellowstone Ave. **Hours:** Trips offered several times daily, May-Sept. **Phone:** (307) 587-6661 or (800) 586-6661. GT

A WESTERN ROSE MOTEL   (307)587-4258   **13**
Motel. **Address:** 1807 Sheridan Ave 82414

BEST WESTERN PREMIER IVY INN & SUITES
(307)587-2572   **15**

Hotel
$125-$315

AAA Benefit: Members save up to 15% and earn bonus points!

Address: 1800 8th St 82414 **Location:** 1 mi w on US 14/16/20. **Facility:** 70 units. 3 stories, interior corridors. **Parking:** winter plug-ins. **Terms:** cancellation fee imposed. **Amenities:** safes. **Dining:** 8th Street at the Ivy, see separate listing. **Pool:** heated indoor. **Activities:** hot tub, exercise room. **Guest Services:** complimentary and valet laundry.

BEST WESTERN SUNSET INN   (307)587-4265   **14**

Motel
$151-$250

AAA Benefit: Members save up to 15% and earn bonus points!

Address: 1601 8th St 82414 **Location:** 0.8 mi w on US 14/16/20. **Facility:** 120 units. 1-2 stories (no elevator), exterior corridors. **Terms:** closed 10/10-5/1, cancellation fee imposed. **Pool:** heated outdoor, heated indoor. **Activities:** hot tub, playground, exercise room. **Guest Services:** coin laundry. **Featured Amenity:** full hot breakfast.

BUFFALO BILL VILLAGE   307/587-5544   **12**
Historic Cabin. **Address:** 1701 Sheridan Ave 82414

THE CODY   307/587-5915   **16**
Hotel. **Address:** 232 W Yellowstone Ave 82414

CODY MOTOR LODGE   307/527-6291   **9**

Motel
Rates not provided

Address: 1455 Sheridan Ave 82414 **Location:** Just w on US 14/16/20 and SR 120. **Facility:** 30 units. 2 stories (no elevator), interior corridors. **Guest Services:** coin laundry. **Featured Amenity:** continental breakfast.

COMFORT INN AT BUFFALO BILL VILLAGE RESORT
(307)587-5556   **10**
Hotel. **Address:** 1601 Sheridan Ave 82414

HOLIDAY INN AT BUFFALO BILL VILLAGE RESORT
307/587-5555   **11**
Hotel. **Address:** 1701 Sheridan Ave 82414

MOOSE CREEK LODGE & SUITES   307/587-2221   **8**
Hotel. **Address:** 1015 Sheridan Ave 82414

RODEWAY INN   (307)587-4201   **17**

Motel
$75-$162

Address: 1919 17th St 82414 **Location:** 0.8 mi e on US 14/16/20 and SR 120. **Facility:** 48 units. 1-2 stories (no elevator), exterior corridors. **Featured Amenity:** continental breakfast.

WHERE TO EAT

8TH STREET AT THE IVY   307/587-2572   **8**
Western American. Casual Dining. **Address:** 1800 8th St 82414

ADRIANO'S ITALIAN RESTAURANT   307/527-7320   **5**
Italian. Casual Dining. **Address:** 1244 Sheridan Ave 82414

THE BREADBOARD   307/527-5788   **10**
Sandwiches. Quick Serve. **Address:** 1725 17th St 82414

BUBBA'S BAR-B-QUE RESTAURANT   307/587-7427   **9**
Barbecue. Casual Dining. **Address:** 512 Yellowstone Ave 82414

HERITAGE BAKERY & BISTRO   307/587-2622   **4**
American. Casual Dining. **Address:** 1532 Wyoming Ave 82414

WYOMING'S RIB & CHOP HOUSE   307/527-7731   **6**
American. Casual Dining. **Address:** 1367 Sheridan Ave 82414

ZAPATA'S   307/527-7181   **7**
Mexican. Casual Dining. **Address:** 1362 Sheridan Ave 82414

DEVILS TOWER NATIONAL MONUMENT (B-6)

Devils Tower National Monument is accessible from SR 24, north off I-90 via US 14 or west from Belle Fourche, S.D.; from Alzada, Mont., SR 112 runs southwest off US 212. Occupying 1,347 acres in the area between Sundance and Hulett, the monument contains Devils Tower, the most conspicuous landmark in northeastern Wyoming.

The tower, a huge monolith resembling a colossal stone tree stump, rises 867 feet from its base and 1,267 feet above the Belle Fourche River. The 1.5-acre top has a growth of sagebrush and grass, and the almost perpendicular sides are fluted columns. The tower was formed when numerous sedimentary layers eroded from around a volcanic intrusion that had cooled in a teardrop formation.

About a half-mile from the entrance is a prairie dog colony. Near the monument's campground is an outdoor amphitheater. Ranger-naturalists conduct summer interpretive walks, talks and campfire programs.

The Tower Trail encircles Devils Tower. Climbing on the tower is permitted, but climbers must sign in before and after expeditions. **Note:** During the month of June, the National Park Service asks climbers to voluntarily refrain from climbing on the tower and hikers to voluntarily refrain from scrambling within the interior of the Tower Trail Loop out of respect for the Native American tribes that consider the tower a sacred site.

A visitor center about 3 miles from the park entrance contains geological specimens, artifacts and exhibits. Dogs, which must be leashed, are not permitted on the trails.

Allow 2 hours, 30 minutes minimum. The monument is open daily 24 hours; closed Jan 1 and Dec. 25. The visitor center is open daily 8-7 (weather permitting). Admission $15 per private vehicle; $7 per person arriving on foot, bicycle or motorcycle; free (ages 0-15 and to all on certain National Park days and federal holidays). Phone (307) 467-5283, ext. 635 Mon.-Fri. 8-4. *See Recreation Areas Chart.*

DOUGLAS (D-5) pop. 6,120, elev. 4,815'

Known as Tent Town at its founding in 1886, Douglas served as a supply post for cattlemen and a distribution point for railroad consignments. The town's history is typical of the colorful, brawling days when cavalrymen, cowboys and railroad crews were opening the West, but in contrast to many other towns, few killings were recorded.

One of the town's rowdiest characters was George Pike, a cowhand whose rustling habits were so well-known that the cattle companies decided to hire him so he would at least benefit his current employer. One company thought so highly of Pike that at his death it erected an expensive tombstone with the following inscription:

Underneath this stone in eternal rest, Sleeps the wildest one of the wayward west. He was a gambler and sport and cowboy, too, And he led the pace in an outlaw crew. He was sure on the trigger and staid to the end, But was never known to quit on a friend. In the relations of death all mankind's alike, But in life there was only one George Pike.

Douglas also is said to be the original home of the "jackalope," a fanciful creation of Wyoming's taxidermists. Doubters are confronted with dozens of convincing mounted specimens of this animal—best described as a jackrabbit sporting antlers—displayed throughout the state. A 10-foot replica of the "hybrid" stands downtown in Centennial Jackalope Square at 3rd and Center streets and at the Douglas Area Chamber of Commerce, which is housed in a historic train depot.

Scenic River Path, running along the bank of the North Platte River in downtown, offers 2.5 miles of trails for walking, bicycling and observing nature. The river also provides opportunities for trout fishing, canoeing and float trips. Washington Park

contains the burial monument of racehorse Sir Barton, the first triple crown winner in the United States.

The Wyoming State Fair, off I-25 adjacent to the town's business district, occurs for 8 days in mid-August. Visitors can enjoy livestock and horticultural exhibits as well as a demolition derby and rodeos; for information phone (307) 358-2398.

Douglas Area Chamber of Commerce: 121 Brownfield Rd., Douglas, WY 82633. **Phone:** (307) 358-2950.

WYOMING PIONEER MEMORIAL MUSEUM is on the state fairgrounds at 400 W. Center St. The museum began as a log structure in 1925 and has since enlarged to accommodate one of the largest displays of historic artifacts in the state. The museum contains an extensive collection of Wyoming pioneer items, military relics, Native American artifacts, maps, charts, newspapers and photographs from the late 1800s.

The Johnson Gallery houses the museum's Native American collection that includes such highlights as an 1864 Sioux-style teepee used in the movie "Dances with Wolves," numerous examples of decorative arts and multiple displays of Native American sculpture. Other museum highlights include clothing worn during Wyoming's territorial period, an art display with changing exhibits, a research library about Wyoming history and two 1885 one-room schoolhouses. **Hours:** Mon.-Fri. 8-5 (also Sat. 1-5, June-Sept.). **Cost:** Free. **Phone:** (307) 358-9288.

HAMPTON INN & SUITES BY HILTON DOUGLAS

307/358-0707

▼▼▼▼ Hotel. **Address:** 1730 Muirfield Ct 82633

AAA Benefit: Members save 5% or more!

HOLIDAY INN EXPRESS & SUITES DOUGLAS   307/358-4500
▼▼▼▼ Hotel. **Address:** 900 W Yellowstone Hwy 82633

SLEEP INN & SUITES DOUGLAS   (307)358-2777
▼▼▼▼ Hotel. **Address:** 508 Cortez Dr 82633

WHERE TO EAT

THE DEPOT RESTAURANT   307/358-9999
▼▼ American. Casual Dining. **Address:** 100 E Walnut St 82633

SAPPORO JAPANESE STEAK HOUSE   307/298-4113
▼▼ Japanese. Casual Dining. **Address:** 206 E Walnut St 82633

DUBOIS (C-2) pop. 971, elev. 6,917'

Dubois grew from a rendezvous point for French, American and Native American trappers at the head of the Wind River Valley into a headquarters for cattle outfits, tie hack crews and river tie drives. From 1914 to 1946, stacked decks of railroad ties were floated down the Wind River from tie camps west of town to the railhead at Riverton. Dubois now is bordered by extensive cattle and dude ranching operations.

Northwest of Dubois is Union Pass, said to be the only place in the United States from which three rivers flow in different directions: Fish Creek is the source of the Columbia River, Jakeys Fork flows to the Mississippi, and Roaring Fork is part of the Colorado River drainage system.

Pack trips leave Dubois for Gannett Peak, Wyoming's highest peak, and the Fitzpatrick Wilderness, where there are 44 active glaciers.

Snowmobiling, dog sledding and cross-country skiing are popular at Union Pass and Togwotee Pass; both cross the Continental Divide west of Dubois.

Dubois Chamber of Commerce: 20 Stalnaker St., P.O. Box 632, Dubois, WY 82513. **Phone:** (307) 455-2556 or (888) 518-0502.

LONGHORN RANCH LODGE AND RV RESORT
(307)455-2337

Motel
$99-$179

Address: 5810 US Hwy 26 82513 **Location:** Jct US 26 and 287, 3 mi e. Next to Wind River. **Facility:** 24 units, some two bedrooms, kitchens and cabins. 1 story, exterior corridors. **Terms:** closed 10/15-5/1, cancellation fee imposed. **Activities:** fishing, playground, picnic facilities, massage. **Guest Services:** coin laundry. **Featured Amenity:** continental breakfast.

STAGECOACH INN & SUITES DUBOIS
(307)455-2303

Motel
$69-$139

Address: 103 Ramshorn St 82513 **Location:** On US 26 and 287; downtown. **Facility:** 46 units, some kitchens. 1-2 stories (no elevator), exterior corridors. **Parking:** winter plug-ins. **Terms:** cancellation fee imposed. **Pool:** heated outdoor. **Activities:** hot tub, fishing, playground, lawn sports. **Guest Services:** coin laundry.

WHERE TO EAT

COWBOY CAFE   307/455-2595
American. Casual Dining. **Address:** 115 E Ramshorn St 82513

NOSTALGIA BISTRO   307/455-3528
American. Casual Dining. **Address:** 202 E Ramshorn St 82513

PERCH COFFEE HOUSE & EATERY   307/455-2764
Coffee/Tea Sandwiches. Quick Serve. **Address:** 132 E Ramshorn St 82513

EVANSTON (E-1) pop. 12,359, elev. 6,743'

Designated the seat of Uinta County in 1870, Evanston lies in the center of the energy-rich Overthrust Belt. It also is a departure point for trips into the Uinta Mountains to the south. Depot Square Park is the center of such summer activities as band concerts and barbecues. Other recreational opportunities include water sports at Woodruff Narrows Reservoir, north via US 89, and cross-country skiing at Bear River State Park (see Recreation Areas Chart).

Bear River State Park and Travel Information Center: 601 Bear River Dr., Evanston, WY 82930. **Phone:** (307) 789-6547.

Evanston Chamber of Commerce: 1020 Front St., Evanston, WY 82930. **Phone:** (307) 783-0370.

BEST WESTERN DUNMAR INN
(307)789-3770

Hotel
$110-$160

Best Western. AAA Benefit: Members save up to 15% and earn bonus points!

Address: 1601 Harrison Dr 82930 **Location:** I-80 exit 3 (Harrison Dr), just n. **Facility:** 165 units. 1 story, exterior corridors. **Parking:** winter plug-ins. **Terms:** cancellation fee imposed. **Dining:** Legal Tender Restaurant & Lounge, see separate listing. **Pool:** heated outdoor. **Activities:** sauna, hot tub, exercise room. **Guest Services:** valet laundry. **Featured Amenity:** full hot breakfast.

HAMPTON INN BY HILTON EVANSTON   307/789-5678
Hotel. **Address:** 101 Wasatch Rd 82930

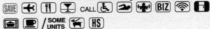
AAA Benefit: Members save 5% or more!

HOLIDAY INN EXPRESS & SUITES EVANSTON
(307)789-7999

Hotel
$99-$169

Address: 1965 Harrison Dr 82930 **Location:** I-80 exit 3 (Harrison Dr), just n. **Facility:** 62 units. 3 stories, interior corridors. **Parking:** winter plug-ins. **Terms:** cancellation fee imposed. **Pool:** heated indoor. **Activities:** hot tub, exercise room. **Guest Services:** valet and coin laundry. **Featured Amenity:** full hot breakfast.

WHERE TO EAT

LEGAL TENDER RESTAURANT & LOUNGE
307/789-3770

American
Casual Dining
$8-$29

AAA Inspector Notes: This restaurant provides friendly service in a relaxed atmosphere. Walls are adorned with memorabilia from the original owner's career as an FBI agent. The steaks and salad bar are a favorite among guests. **Features:** full bar, early bird specials, senior menu. **Address:** 1601 Harrison Dr 82930 **Location:** I-80 exit 3 (Harrison Dr), just n; in Best Western Dunmar Inn.
B L D CALL

SUDS BROTHERS BREWERY   307/444-7837
American. Casual Dining. **Address:** 1012 Main St 82930

FLAMING GORGE NATIONAL RECREATION AREA (E-2)

Reached by SR 530 or US 191 from I-80 in Wyoming or US 191 from Utah, Flaming Gorge National Recreation Area straddles the border between Wyoming and Utah. The area includes a 91-mile-long reservoir and the Flaming Gorge and Red canyons, which were carved through the Uinta Mountains by the Green River.

Lake Flaming Gorge is bounded primarily by Red Canyon to the south and by rolling hills and occasional abrupt cliffs and promontories to the north. Of geologic interest are the exposed strata in Firehole Canyon and the Sheep Creek Geological Loop.

Once belonging to Mexico, Wyoming's portion of the Flaming Gorge region was annexed to the United States after the Mexican War. John Wesley Powell, a one-armed Army major and professor, mapped the area on his way down the Green River in the late 1860s and early 1870s, naming Flaming Gorge and many other prominent landmarks.

I-80 is connected to SR 530 and US 191. In Utah, US 191 joins with SRs 43 and 44, which then link with SR 530 again, to form a complete 160-mile loop around the recreation area. Along the route are the Flaming Gorge Dam and Visitor Center, off US 191 adjacent to the Bureau of Reclamation offices; the Red Canyon Visitor Center and Overlook, which offers a spectacular view from 1,400 feet above Red Canyon and Flaming Gorge Reservoir off SR 44; the Sheep Creek Geological Loop; and Flaming Gorge.

Known for its bountiful fishing waters, Lake Flaming Gorge also is a popular setting for swimming, boating and water skiing. Large boat ramps are found near campgrounds at convenient access points along the western and eastern sides of the lake.

The western shore, accessible from Buckboard, Wyo., and Lucerne Valley, Utah, has campsites and two marinas that provide boat rentals and supplies. Cedar Springs to the southeast is similarly equipped; the latter has a dock and marina. Other campgrounds are scattered throughout the Utah and Wyoming sections.

The reservoir contains a broad sampling of fish, including German brown, lake, rainbow and cutthroat trout; small-mouth bass; and kokanee salmon. Fishing is permitted all year. A license from either Utah or Wyoming is required.

Seasonal hunting is permitted except near public-use facilities. Cross-country skiing, snowmobiling and ice fishing are popular winter activities. For further information, contact the Flaming Gorge Ranger District, Flaming Gorge National Recreation Area, P.O. Box 279, Manila, UT 84046.

The recreation area is open all year, but most developed facilities are closed during the winter. The Red Canyon Visitor Center is open daily 10-5, Memorial Day to Labor Day; phone for schedule, rest of year. The Flaming Gorge Dam Visitor Center is open daily 9-5, mid-Apr. to mid-Oct. Guided tours of the dam depart from the visitor center daily every 20 minutes; phone ahead to confirm schedule.

A use fee pass is required for all facilities. Passes are $5 (1 day), $15 (7 days) and $35 (annual), beginning from the date of purchase. America the Beautiful–National Parks and Federal Recreational Lands Pass holders enter free. Phone (435) 784-3445 for the ranger district, (435) 889-3713 for the Red Canyon Visitor Center, or (435) 885-3135 for the Flaming Gorge Dam and Visitor Center. *See Recreation Areas Chart.*

FLAMING GORGE DAM is off US 191 near Dutch John, Utah. The dam is a concrete arch structure rising 502 feet above bedrock. **Note:** Pets are allowed only in the parking lot, not on the dam. **Hours:** Guided 1-hour tours are offered every 20 minutes daily 9:10-3:50, mid-Mar. to mid-Oct. Hours may vary in spring and fall. Phone ahead to confirm schedule. **Cost:** Free. **Phone:** (435) 885-3135. GT

JOHN JARVIE HISTORIC RANCH is about 8 mi. n.w. of Dutch John, Utah, on US 191, then 22 mi. e. on a gravel road, following signs to Browns Park. A turn-of-the-20th-century hideout for outlaws, Browns Park was also the site of a successful ranching operation started by Scottish immigrant John Jarvie in the 1880s. On the grounds is a replica of a general store built in 1881, a blacksmith shop, a corral and the two-room dugout where Jarvie lived.

A 15-minute orientation video is shown in the on-site museum. **Time:** Allow 1 hour minimum. **Hours:** Daily 10-4:30, Memorial Day-Labor Day; Tues.-Sat. 10-4:30, rest of year (dependent on staff availability). Phone ahead to confirm schedule. **Cost:** Donations. **Phone:** (435) 885-3307 or (435) 781-4400. GT 🅰

RED CANYON VISITOR CENTER is 40 mi. n. of Vernal via US 44. The center contains exhibits about natural and cultural history. An observation deck overlooks the Flaming Gorge National Recreation Area and the Uinta Mountains. **Hours:** Mon.-Fri. 10-5, Sat.-Sun. 9-6, Memorial Day-Labor Day; phone for schedule rest of year. **Cost:** Free. **Phone:** (435) 889-3713.

▽ GEM FORT LARAMIE NATIONAL HISTORIC SITE (D-6)

Fort Laramie National Historic Site is off US 26, 3 miles southwest of the town of Fort Laramie. Near the confluence of the Laramie and North Platte rivers, the site covers 832 acres. From its founding as Fort William in 1834 and until 1849, the fort was an important fur-trading post. Purchased by the U.S. government in 1849 and renamed Fort Laramie, the fort served to aid in the migrations to Oregon and California. By 1890 the fort had outlived its usefulness and was abandoned, its land and buildings sold at public auction.

Eleven structures, including the 1874 cavalry barracks, have been restored and refurnished to recall the flavor of daily life at this post. A visitor center museum displays artifacts relating to civilian, military and Native American history on the northern Plains. From June to mid-August, staff members in period clothing demonstrate aspects of both military and civilian life in the 1870s. A vehicle for the physically impaired is available when the number of staff permits. An 1875 iron Army bridge that spans the North Platte River is 2 miles above the fort.

Grounds open daily dawn-dusk. Visitor center open daily 8-6, Memorial Day weekend-Labor Day; 8-4:30, rest of year. Visitor center closed Jan. 1, Thanksgiving and Christmas. Free. Phone (307) 837-2221 (ext. 3012 on weekends).

FOSSIL BUTTE NATIONAL MONUMENT (E-1)

Fourteen miles west of Kemmerer on US 30, Fossil Butte National Monument rises nearly 1,000 feet above the Twin Creek Valley. The buff-to-white beds of the Green River Formation contain one of the world's largest deposits of the fossils of freshwater fish that lived 50 million years ago. Fossils of mammals, reptiles, fish, insects and plants can be seen at the visitor center; a video presentation also is available.

A self-guiding hiking trail, 2.5 miles long, leads to the site of a historic fossil quarry, and a 1.5-mile trail takes visitors through an aspen tree grove. Interpretive programs are offered June through August.

Allow 2 hours, 30 minutes minimum. Grounds open all year but may be snow-covered Oct.-Apr. Visitor center daily 8-6, Memorial Day-Labor Day; daily 8-4:30, Mar. 1-day before Memorial Day and day after Labor Day-Dec. 1; Mon.-Sat. 8-4:30, rest of year. Closed winter holidays. Free. Phone (307) 877-4455.

GILLETTE (B-5) pop. 29,087, elev. 4,538'
• Restaurants p. 180

Gillette lies on a high plateau between the Black Hills and the Bighorn Mountains. The town's livestock industry dates from the early 1800s. Mule deer, pronghorns and buffalo graze on unspoiled land nearby.

Named for railroad surveyor Edward Gillette, the town was developed as a ranching area and became a hub for transporting livestock to market. Now coal and oil industries fuel Gillette's economy. During summer, coal mine tours can be arranged through the convention and visitors bureau. The bureau also offers an assistance program for hunters interested in the mule deer, pronghorn antelopes and elk populations in the area.

Campbell County Convention and Visitors Bureau: 1810 S. Douglas Hwy., Suite A, Gillette, WY 82718. **Phone:** (307) 686-0040.

ARBUCKLE LODGE   307/685-6363
◆◆◆ Hotel. **Address:** 1400 S Garner Lake Rd 82718

BEST WESTERN TOWER WEST LODGE GILLETTE
(307)686-2210

Hotel
$80-$230

 Best Western. AAA Benefit: Members save up to 15% and earn bonus points!

Address: 109 N US 14-16 82716 **Location:** I-90 exit 124, just n. **Facility:** 190 units. 2 stories (no elevator), interior corridors. **Parking:** winter plug-ins. **Terms:** cancellation fee imposed. **Pool:** heated indoor. **Activities:** hot tub, exercise room. **Guest Services:** valet and coin laundry.

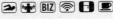
/ SOME UNITS

CANDLEWOOD SUITES GILLETTE   (307)682-6100
◆◆◆ Extended Stay Hotel. **Address:** 904 Country Club Rd 82718

COMFORT INN & SUITES GILLETTE   (307)685-2223

Hotel
$74-$120

Address: 1607 W 2nd St 82716 **Location:** I-90 exit 124, just ne. **Facility:** 60 units. 3 stories, interior corridors. **Parking:** winter plug-ins. **Pool:** heated indoor. **Activities:** hot tub, exercise room. **Guest Services:** valet and coin laundry. **Featured Amenity:** continental breakfast.

/ SOME UNITS

COUNTRY INN & SUITES BY RADISSON   307/682-0505

Hotel
Rates not provided

Address: 2597 S Douglas Hwy (SR 59) 82718 **Location:** I-90 exit 126, 0.5 mi se. **Facility:** 80 units. 3 stories, interior corridors. **Pool:** heated indoor. **Activities:** hot tub, exercise room. **Guest Services:** valet and coin laundry. **Featured Amenity:** full hot breakfast.

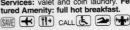

FAIRFIELD INN & SUITES BY MARRIOTT GILLETTE
(307)682-1717
◆◆◆ Hotel. **Address:** 2577 S Douglas Hwy (SR 59) 82718   **AAA Benefit:** Members save 5% or more!

HAMPTON INN BY HILTON GILLETTE   307/686-2000
◆◆◆ Hotel. **Address:** 211 Decker Ct 82716   **AAA Benefit:** Members save 5% or more!

HOLIDAY INN EXPRESS & SUITES GILLETTE   (307)686-9576
◆◆◆ Hotel. **Address:** 1908 Cliff Davis Dr 82718

HOME2 SUITES BY HILTON GILLETTE   307/257-7040
◆◆◆ Extended Stay Hotel. **Address:** 1120 E Boxelder Rd 82718   **AAA Benefit:** Members save 5% or more!

LA QUINTA INN & SUITES GILLETTE (307)686-6000
🔷🔷🔷 Contemporary Hotel. **Address:** 450 E Boxelder Rd 82718

TOWNEPLACE SUITES BY MARRIOTT GILLETTE
(307)682-1464
🔷🔷🔷 Extended Stay Hotel. **Address:** 1715 W 2nd St 82716

AAA Benefit:
Members save 5% or more!

WINGATE BY WYNDHAM GILLETTE (307)685-2700
🔷🔷🔷 Hotel. **Address:** 1801 Cliff Davis Dr 82718

WHERE TO EAT

ARMANDO'S TACO & PASTA SHOP 307/682-2922
🔷🔷 Mexican. Casual Dining. **Address:** 2700 S Douglas Hwy 82718

THE COOP ROTISSERIE HOUSE 307/257-7460
🔷🔷 Latin American. Casual Dining. **Address:** 208 W 2nd St 82716

GILLETTE BREWING COMPANY 307/670-8948
🔷 Pizza. Brewpub. **Address:** 301 S Gillette Ave 82716

LOS COMPADRES 307/682-1101
🔷🔷 Mexican. Casual Dining. **Address:** 1700 W 2nd St 82716

THE MAIN BAGEL COMPANY 307/687-1616
🔷 Deli Coffee/Tea. Quick Serve. **Address:** 2610 S Douglas Hwy 82718

PIZZA CARRELLO 307/363-1743
🔷 Pizza Small Plates. Casual Dining. **Address:** 601 S Douglas Hwy (SR 59) 82716

POKEY'S BARBEQUE AND SMOKEHOUSE 307/687-7653
🔷🔷 Barbecue. Casual Dining. **Address:** 408 S Douglas Hwy (SR 59) 82716

THE PRIME RIB RESTAURANT & WINE CELLAR
307/682-2944

🔷🔷🔷
American Casual Dining $10-$50

AAA Inspector Notes: This bustling upscale restaurant offers patrons many variations of well-prepared steaks, prime rib and seafood. An extensive selection of wine is kept in a state-of-the-art, glass-enclosed wine case. Open for dinner only on Saturday and Sunday. **Features:** full bar, senior menu, happy hour. **Reservations:** suggested. **Address:** 1205 S Douglas Hwy 82717 **Location:** I-90 exit 126, 0.5 mi n. Ⓛ Ⓓ CALL ♿

RAILYARD 307/687-7245
🔷🔷 American. Casual Dining. **Address:** 113 S Gillette Ave 82716

SMILING MOOSE DELI 307/363-4104
🔷 Deli. Quick Serve. **Address:** 2711 Douglas Hwy 82718

GRAND TETON NATIONAL PARK
(B-1)

Elevations in the park range from 6,800 ft. at the valley floor to 13,770 ft. at Grand Teton Peak. Refer to AAA maps for additional elevation information.

Grand Teton National Park's southern entrance is north of Jackson on US 26/89/191; an eastern entrance is at Moran Junction on US 26/287. From this point US 89/191/287 heads north through the park into Yellowstone National Park *(see place listing p. 214).* The park's 485 square miles include the major portion of Wyoming's Teton Range and the valley of Jackson Hole. Together the mountain range and valley frame a majestic landscape of eight large lakes and many smaller ones, glaciers, numerous snowfields and extensive pine, fir and spruce forests.

The Tetons are among the youngest mountains on the continent. The elevations established by the U.S. Geological Survey for the major peaks are Grand Teton, 13,770 feet; Mount Owen, 12,928 feet; Middle Teton, 12,804 feet; Mount Moran, 12,605 feet; South Teton, 12,514 feet; Teewinot Mountain, 12,325 feet; Thor Peak, 12,028 feet; Buck Mountain, 11,938 feet; Nez Perce Peak, 11,901 feet; Mount Wister, 11,490 feet; and Mount St. John, 11,430 feet.

Few mountain ranges have a greater variety of glaciated canyons than the Tetons. The fault-block mountains of this alpine park are rare in this country. Part of the park area lies above the tree line, which is at about 10,000 feet.

The Tetons were first photographed by William H. Jackson, a member of the Hayden Expedition sent by the government to survey the area in 1872.

General Information and Activities

The park is open all year, although most park facilities operate only from mid-May to mid-October. Visitor information is available at Colter Bay and Jenny Lake visitor centers, the Craig Thomas Discovery & Visitor Center in Moose and the Laurance S. Rockefeller Preserve Center on the Moose-Wilson Road. Free ranger-led activities in summer include hikes. Entrance stations and visitor centers distribute a park newspaper listing the schedule of activities.

More than 250 miles of trails afford short walks, strenuous hikes and overnight backcountry trips. Trail booklets can be found at some trail heads and at the visitor centers. Campsites along backcountry trails require a camping permit, available at the visitor centers and the Jenny Lake Ranger Station.

Game fish include brook, brown, cutthroat, Mackinaw, and rainbow trout, as well as whitefish. Fish can be taken with artificial flies and lures during most of the summer and autumn, but the Mackinaw trout in Jackson and Jenny lakes are best caught by trolling with heavy tackle.

A Wyoming fishing license is required; a nonresident 1-day license is available for $14; a full-year permit is $92. Special fishing regulations apply in the park, and changes are made annually regarding limits and waters open to fishing; check the current regulations.

Mountain climbing is a popular summer pastime. Authorized guide services are available, and because of the difficulty of the Teton peaks, climbers are urged to use them. Prospective climbers should

(See map & index p. 195.)

consult rangers for information about routes and appropriate equipment. The Jenny Lake Ranger Station is the park's climbing information center.

Standard alpine equipment is essential: ice axes, ropes and rubber-soled boots or climbing shoes. Two park-approved mountaineering schools offer lessons and guide service.

The climbing season in Grand Teton National Park ordinarily spans mid-June to mid-September, but conditions are best from July to early September. In most cases it is advisable to allow 2 days for an ascent of Grand Teton, Mount Owen or Mount Moran and 1 or 2 days for all the other peaks, depending upon your experience.

Riding on horses trained for mountain trails is another popular way to explore the park. From corrals at Colter Bay Village and Jackson Lake Lodge, the Grand Teton Lodge Company conducts daily guided 1- and 2-hour rides, half-day trail rides and wagon rides; phone (307) 543-2811.

Morning and evening wagon rides with breakfast or dinner also are available for $44-$56. Guide fees vary according to trail, but all rates are regulated by the park and range from $43-$80. Restrictions apply to horseback riding.

If water levels allow, boat and canoe rentals, guided fishing trips and scenic boat trips can be arranged at the Colter Bay Marina at Colter Bay Village, the Bridge Bay Marina on Yellowstone Lake and the booking office at Jackson Lake Lodge. Canoe and kayak rentals are $20-$23 per hour or $75-$88 per day. Two-person kayaks are $25 per hour or $99 per day. Boat rentals are $10 per hour for a rowboat, $44 per hour or $181 per 8-hour day for a motorized boat (including gas and oil); there is a 2-hour minimum boat rental.

Jackson Lake boat cruises lasting 1 hour, 30 minutes leave the Colter Bay Marina several times daily, if water levels allow. Daily trout breakfast cruises to Elk Island as well as Monday, Wednesday, Friday and Saturday evening dinner cruises also are offered. Cruise rates range from $32 to $67; $14 to $38(ages 3-11). Contact the Grand Teton Lodge Co. for schedules and exact fares; phone (307) 543-2811.

Jenny Lake Boating Co. offers scenic cruises on Jenny Lake for $19; $17 (ages 62+); $11 (ages 2-11). The booking office is at the south end of Jenny Lake near the ranger station; phone (307) 734-9227, mid-May to mid-September.

Motorboats can be operated on Jackson and Jenny lakes, but motors more than 10 horsepower cannot be used on Jenny Lake. Hand-propelled craft are permitted on Bearpaw, Bradley, Emma Matilda, Jackson, Jenny, Leigh, Phelps, String, Taggart and Two Ocean lakes and on the Snake River. Water skiing and windsurfing are permitted only on Jackson Lake.

Mandatory boating permits can be purchased at the visitor centers. Permits are $10 for nonmotorized

craft and $40 for motorized craft. In addition, privately owned boats must be inspected prior to launch and display an Aquatic Invasive Species (AIS) decal from the Wyoming Game & Fish Department; phone (307) 777-4600 for information and border inspection locations. AIS fees are $5 for nonmotorized boats and $10 for motorized boats for Wyoming boat owners; $15 for non-motorized boats and $30 for motorized boats that come from outside Wyoming.

Several companies offer scenic float trips on the Snake River from May through September (see attraction listings). Reservations for these relaxing excursions are recommended (and, in some cases, required).

Winter activities include cross-country skiing, snowshoe hikes and ice fishing. Marked trails for cross-country skiing also are provided.

Five campgrounds, Colter Bay, Gros Ventre, Jenny Lake, Lizard Creek and Signal Mountain, are open on a first-come, first-served basis. Opening dates vary from early May to early June; closing dates are from early September to mid-October. Per night rates for campers with vehicles are $25; $13 (Golden Age Passport holders). Per night rates for bicyclists and hikers are $12; $6 (Golden Age Passport holders). Reservations are not accepted. *See Recreation Areas Chart.*

ADMISSION to the park is by private vehicle permit ($35), motorcycle permit ($30) and by single nonmotorized entry ($20), valid in Grand Teton and the John D. Rockefeller, Jr. Memorial Parkway for 7 days. Park Annual Pass ($70) or Interagency Annual Pass ($80 for entrance to most federal sites) also is available. An Interagency Lifetime Senior Pass for U.S. citizens ages 62+ is $80; an Interagency Access Passport for physically impaired U.S. citizens provides free admission.

PETS are permitted in the park only if they are on a leash or otherwise physically restricted at all times. They are not permitted on trails, in the backcountry or in any public building.

ADDRESS inquiries to Grand Teton National Park, P.O. Drawer 170, Moose, WY 83012-0170; phone (307) 739-3300.

AMPHITHEATER LAKE TRAIL extends up the eastern slope of Disappointment Peak to two alpine lakes, Surprise and Amphitheater, both at altitudes of more than 9,000 feet. Amphitheater Lake occupies a protected glacial cirque, or steep hollow. An overlook, reached by several trails climbing 3,000 feet above the valley floor, offers a sweeping panorama of Jackson Hole and a view extending eastward 80 miles to the Wind River Mountains. A branch from the trail leads into Garnet Canyon. Trail conditions are available at the visitor centers. **Time:** Allow 6 hours minimum.

CASCADE CANYON TRAIL, 25 mi. n. of Jackson in the center of the park, explores the deepest recesses of the Tetons, passing through a broad,

© 2018 HERE   © AAA

Grand Teton
National Park
Attractions

Scale in Miles

3.8   0   3.8

See p. 6 - Map Legend

⚑ CAMPGROUND SITE WITHIN
NATIONAL PARK.

2120-19

(See map & index p. 195.)

glacier-carved canyon with walls that rise thousands of feet on either side. Lake Solitude, near the head of the canyon at the tree line, is a pristine example of an alpine lake. **Time:** Allow 7 hours minimum.

CHAPEL OF THE TRANSFIGURATION is off Chapel of the Transfiguration Rd. near Moose. Above the altar of the 1925 log chapel is a large window framing a view of the Teton Range. Episcopal services are held during the summer; schedules are posted on a board outside the chapel and in park newspapers. **Time:** Allow 30 minutes minimum.

COLTER BAY VISITOR CENTER is 25 mi. n. of Moose near Jackson Lake. Videos featuring local wildlife and scenery are shown daily in the amphitheater. **Hours:** Daily 8-7, early June-Labor Day; 8-5, early May-early June and day after Labor Day-early Oct. **Cost:** Free. **Phone:** (307) 739-3594.

CRAIG THOMAS DISCOVERY & VISITOR CENTER is across the street from the park headquarters in Moose. The center orients visitors to the unique natural and cultural history of the area and features stories about conservation and stewardship. Maps and permits are available. **Hours:** Daily 8-7, early June to mid-Sept.; 8-5, May 1-early June and mid-Sept. to late Oct.; daily 9-5, in Apr.; daily 10-4, early Mar.-Mar. 31. **Cost:** Free. **Phone:** (307) 739-3399.

(See map & index p. 195.)

CUNNINGHAM CABIN HISTORIC SITE is 6 mi. s. of Moran Junction on US 26/89/191. The site was the base of pioneer Pierce Cunningham's Bar Flying U Ranch that once comprised some 560 acres. The site now contains the foundations of the house, barn, shed and outbuildings as well as the remains of a cabin. A leaflet outlining a self-guiding trail through the area also describes the life of the homesteader in Jackson Hole. **Time:** Allow 30 minutes minimum.

DEATH CANYON TRAIL, about 3 mi. s. of Moose, traverses the length of a canyon of profound depth and grandeur to broad meadows. No canyon better illustrates the contrasts of the Teton area. **Time:** Allow 6 hours minimum.

FLAGG RANCH INFORMATION STATION is at Flagg Ranch, 16 mi. n. of Colter Bay on US 89/191/287. The station provides information about John D. Rockefeller, Jr. Memorial Parkway and the Yellowstone area. **Hours:** Daily 9-4, early June-Labor Day. The site may be closed during lunch hours; phone ahead to confirm schedule. **Cost:** Free. **Phone:** (307) 543-2372.

HIDDEN FALLS AND INSPIRATION POINT TRAILS lead from the southern shore of Jenny Lake off Teton Park Rd. A boat ride to the trailhead is available in the summer. Ranger-guided tours to Hidden Falls and Inspiration Point depart the trailhead daily at 8:30 in season; departure time may vary. **Time:** Allow 2 hours minimum. GT

JENNY LAKE VISITOR CENTER is 8 mi. n. of Moose Junction on Teton Park Rd. The visitor center has exhibits about geology. **Hours:** Daily 8-7, early June-Labor Day; 8-5, late May to early June and day after Labor Day-late Sept. **Cost:** Free. **Phone:** (307) 739-3392.

MENOR'S FERRY is near the Chapel of the Transfiguration in Moose. The ferry is a reconstruction of the craft that was once the only means of crossing the Snake River in central Jackson Hole country. The original home of Bill Menor, one of the area's first settlers, is in the area; it contains historical objects and exhibits. **Time:** Allow 30 minutes minimum. **Hours:** Daily 10-4, early July-Aug. 31, weather and staff permitting. Phone ahead to confirm schedule.

PAINTBRUSH TRAIL starts near the outlet of Leigh Lake, follows the bottom of Paintbrush Canyon, crosses Paintbrush Divide and joins the Cascade Canyon Trail at Lake Solitude. The many wildflowers along this trail give the canyon its name. Wildlife, especially moose, can be seen near lakes and marshes. This trail affords several good views of Jackson and Leigh lakes. Since dangerous snow and ice remain on the divide until late in the year, check conditions at the visitor centers. Horses cannot be taken over the divide to Lake Solitude until late August.

▼ See AAA listing p. 184 ▼

(See map & index p. 195.)

SIGNAL MOUNTAIN is 3 mi. s. of Jackson Lake Junction on Teton Park Rd. The mountain affords a panorama of the valley, Jackson Lake, a portion of southern Yellowstone and the Teton, Gros Ventre and Hoback mountain ranges. A narrow, paved road that's 5 miles long leads to the summit. Trailers are not allowed on this road.

TETON CREST TRAIL traverses the Tetons from Teton Pass to Cascade Canyon. This high alpine country can be explored on foot or horseback.

VALLEY TRAIL runs parallel to the mountains from the e. shore of Leigh Lake s. to Teton Village. The trail is the point of origin of all trails into the Teton Range. From this point, trails run westward into Cascade, Death, Granite, Open and Paintbrush canyons; others encircle String Lake, Jenny Lake and Hermitage Point on Jackson Lake. A popular hike follows the south shore of Jenny Lake to Hidden Falls.

Float Trips

Float Trips, on the Snake River through Grand Teton National Park, are conducted by experienced guides who thread rubber rafts down the river. These trips, which offer spectacular mountain scenery and opportunities to view native wildlife, are carefully supervised by the National Park Service.

Note: A minimum weight of 35-40 pounds is required for most float trips.

BARKER-EWING SCENIC FLOAT TRIPS depart from the float-trip parking lot at Moose Village; transportation from the parking lot to the launch area is provided. Scenic 10-mile trips are conducted entirely within the park's natural environment and provide opportunities to view wildlife and the Teton peaks. **Hours:** Trips depart several times daily, mid-May to late Sept. **Cost:** $80; $50 (ages 6-15); ages 0-5 not permitted. Reservations are required. **Phone:** (307) 733-1800 or (800) 365-1800. GT

DORNAN'S SNAKE RIVER SCENIC FLOAT TRIPS originate at 185 N. Center St. in Jackson or at 12170 Dornan Rd. in Moose. Lasting 3 to 3.5 hours, the 14-mile scenic float trips provide good opportunities for photography and for observing elk, bear and other wildlife. Visitors should arrive 30 minutes before departure. **Hours:** Trips depart daily at 8, noon and 4, mid-May to mid-Oct. (weather and water conditions permitting). **Cost:** $70; $55 (ages 0-11, with a 40-lb. minimum weight). Reservations are recommended. **Phone:** (307) 733-3699. GT

GRAND TETON LODGE COMPANY WILD AND SCENIC RAFTING TRIPS is 5 mi. n.w. of Moran Junction on US 89/191/287. The company offers 3- to 4-hour float trips as well as luncheon and dinner trips; transportation to and from the river is provided.

Hours: Three- to 4-hour float trips and luncheon trips run daily at 6:45, 8, 9, 1:30 and 6, late May-late Sept. Dinner trips run Tues., Thurs. and Sat., late May-late Sept. Phone ahead to confirm schedule. **Cost:**

Three- to 4-hour float trip $75; $48 (ages 6-11). Luncheon trip $78; $55 (ages 6-11). Dinner trip $88; $60 (ages 6-11). Fares may vary; phone ahead. Ages 0-5 are not permitted. **Phone:** (307) 543-2811. GT

SIGNAL MOUNTAIN LODGE FLOAT TRIPS meets at Signal Mountain Lodge, on Inner Park Rd. in Moran; transportation to and from the Snake River is provided. A 10-mile scenic float ride down the river lasts 3.5 hours and features wildlife viewing opportunities. **Hours:** Morning and evening trips depart daily (times vary), early May-Sept. 30 (weather and water conditions permitting). **Cost:** $79; $59 (ages 6-12). Fares may vary; phone ahead. Ages 0-5 not permitted. **Phone:** (307) 543-2831. GT

SOLITUDE FLOAT TRIPS departs the float-trip parking lot across from the Moose Visitor Center. Ten-mile scenic trips are available. **Hours:** Trips are offered daily at 9:30, 1:30, 4:30, 5 and 5:30 (also 6 a.m., Mon.-Fri.), May-Sept. (weather and water conditions permitting). **Cost:** $75; $55 (ages 5-17). Reservations are recommended. **Phone:** (307) 733-2871 or (888) 704-2800. GT

SAVE **TRIANGLE X RANCH FLOAT TRIPS** meets in the float-trip parking lot across from the Craig Thomas Discovery & Visitor Center. Ten-mile sunrise, mid-day and evening wildlife floats take visitors along the Snake River. Enjoy a hearty meal on the 12-mile scenic dinner float. **Hours:** Trips depart several times daily, May-Sept. **Cost:** Ten-mile float trip $75; $54 (ages 5-18). Twelve-mile dinner float $88; $69 (ages 5-18). Fares may vary; phone ahead. Reservations are required. **Phone:** (307) 733-5500 or (888) 860-0005. *(See ad p. 183, p. 187.)* GT

HEADWATERS LODGE & CABINS AT FLAGG RANCH
307/543-2861
◆◆ Cabin. **Address:** Hwy 89 2 mi s of Yellowstone 83013

JACKSON LAKE LODGE   307/543-2811
◆◆◆ Resort Hotel. **Address:** US Hwy 89 83013

JENNY LAKE LODGE   307/543-3351

◆◆◆◆ **Address:** 1 Jenny Lake Inner Park Rd 83012 **Location:** 3 mi off Inner Park Rd; jct N Jenny Lake. Located in a secluded area. **Facility:** At the foot of the majestic **Resort Cabin** Tetons, log cabins are named after wildflowers and offer hardwood floors, area **Rates not provided** rugs, high-beamed ceilings, pine furnishings, upscale bedding and thoughtful amenities. 37 cabins. 1 story, exterior corridors. **Terms:** check-in 4 pm. **Amenities:** safes. **Dining:** Jenny Lake Lodge Dining Room, see separate listing. **Activities:** recreation programs in summer, bicycles, lawn sports, trails. **Guest Services:** valet laundry, area transportation.

SIGNAL MOUNTAIN LODGE   307/543-2831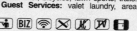
◆◆◆ Resort Hotel. **Address:** 1 Inner Park Rd 83013

TOGWOTEE MOUNTAIN LODGE & CABINS
307/543-2847
◆◆ Hotel. **Address:** 27655 Hwy US 26 & 287 83013

(See map & index p. 195.)

(See map & index p. 195.)

WHERE TO EAT

GRIZZLY GRILL & RED FOX SALOON AT TOGWOTEE
MOUNTAIN LODGE 307/543-2847 ⑤
♦♦ American. Casual Dining. **Address:** 27655 Hwy 26 & 287
83012

JENNY LAKE LODGE DINING ROOM
307/733-4647 ④

Regional American Fine Dining
$10-$85

AAA Inspector Notes: Visit this intimate restaurant for a memorable dining experience. Some tables offer unparalleled views of the Tetons. The five-course menu might feature a wild game crepe, horseradish crusted lamb with garlic fried green tomato, coconut braised ono, grilled red trout with asparagus potato puree or pan seared elk with braised beet greens and port raisin syrup. Vegetarian items are available. For dinner, jackets are suggested, but sweaters and slacks are suitable. **Features:** full bar. **Reservations:** required. Semiformal attire. **Address:** Jenny Lake Inner Park Rd 83013 **Location:** 3 mi off Inner Park Rd; jct N Jenny Lake; in Jenny Lake Lodge.

B L D CALL

LEEK'S MARINA & PIZZERIA 307/543-2494 ①
♦ Pizza Sandwiches. Quick Serve. **Address:** 89 National Park Rd 83013

THE MURAL ROOM 307/543-2811 ②
♦♦♦♦ Regional American. Fine Dining. **Address:** US Hwy 89 83013

PEAKS RESTAURANT AT SIGNAL MOUNTAIN LODGE
307/543-2831 ③
♦♦ American. Casual Dining. **Address:** 1 Inner Park Rd 83013

GREEN RIVER (E-2) pop. 12,515, elev. 6,082'

The northern gateway to the Flaming Gorge National Recreation Area *(see place listing p. 178)*, Green River developed as a stop along the Overland Trail in the mid-1800s. One prominent traveler was Maj. John Wesley Powell, who began his explorations of the Green and Colorado rivers in 1869. The town is a railroad center and the seat of Sweetwater County.

Green River Chamber of Commerce: 1155 W. Flaming Gorge Way, Green River, WY 82935. **Phone:** (307) 875-5711 or (800) 354-6743.

HAMPTON INN & SUITES BY HILTON GREEN RIVER
307/875-5300
♦♦♦♦ Hotel. **Address:** 1055 Wild Horse Canyon Rd 82935

AAA Benefit: Members save 5% or more!

WHERE TO EAT

GET REAL COFFEE & CAFE 307/871-9874
♦ Coffee/Tea. Quick Serve. **Address:** 71 Uinta Dr 82935

HITCHING POST RESTAURANT & SALOON 307/875-2246
♦♦ American. Casual Dining. **Address:** 580 E Flaming Gorge Way 82935

GREYBULL (B-3) pop. 1,847, elev. 3,788'

Greybull derives its name from a local Native American legend that claimed a great albino buffalo once roamed the area. The Native Americans revered the bull, considering it a sign from their Great Spirit. Native American arrowheads, fossils and semiprecious stones can be found around town. The site of widespread oil and mineral activity, Greybull recently has focused its attention on bentonite mining.

Scenic attractions in the vicinity include Shell Canyon and Falls *(see Bighorn National Forest p. 163)*, 24 miles east of US 14, and the drive over the Bighorn Mountains via scenic US 14 to Sheridan. Devil's Kitchen, a few miles northeast, and Sheep Mountain to the north are interesting geological formations.

Greybull Chamber of Commerce: 521 Greybull Ave., Greybull, WY 82426. **Phone:** (307) 765-2100.

WHEELS MOTEL 307/765-2105

Motel
Rates not provided

Address: 1324 N 6th St 82426 **Location:** On US 14/16/20, north end of town. **Facility:** 29 units. 1 story, exterior corridors. **Parking:** winter plug-ins. **Guest Services:** coin laundry.

WHERE TO EAT

BEIJING GARDEN 307/765-9826
♦ Chinese. Casual Dining. **Address:** 510 Greybull Ave 82426

LISA'S 307/765-4765

♦♦ **American Casual Dining** **$9-$40**

AAA Inspector Notes: Relax and unwind amid stucco walls and an adobe fireplace at this spot which serves up a mixture of Western and Southwestern courses as well as a number of microbrewed beers. Locally raised beef is featured on the varied steak menu. Farmer's pasta, fajitas, shrimp and hot sandwiches also are available. The salsa is always fresh. **Features:** full bar. **Reservations:** suggested. **Address:** 200 Greybull Ave 82426 **Location:** On US 14, 0.4 mi e. L D

GUERNSEY (D-6) pop. 1,147, elev. 4,361'

Just below the mouth of Platte River Canyon, Guernsey is in an area known for its limestone beds and a profusion of such artifacts as agricultural and war implements. Native Americans driven from their homes east of the Mississippi River and pioneers headed westward followed the river through this area.

During one of his expeditions in 1842, John C. Fremont camped near what is now the Oregon Trail Ruts State Historic Site. The small prairie next to the river (the present town site) impressed him as a good spot for a military installation because of its cottonwood trees, pines and abundant rock for building.

Prospectors discovered early that the rock formations around Guernsey were good for more than just building. Moss agate stone, unearthed from what is believed to be the first commercially developed deposit of moss agate in the nation, was found in the Guernsey-Hartville region and exported to Germany in the late 1800s. The additional discovery of copper led to the founding of nearby communities Hartville and Sunrise.

Guernsey Visitors Center: 90 S. Wyoming, P.O. Box 667, Guernsey, WY 82214. **Phone:** (307) 836-2715.

REGISTER CLIFF STATE HISTORIC SITE is 3 mi. s. on S. Wyoming Ave. from US 26 exit 92. The site contains a 100-foot cliff with the carved names of thousands of pioneers who journeyed past this point. Many of the inscriptions were made 1840-60. A walkway and an explanatory sign are at the base of the cliff. **Phone:** (307) 836-2900.

HULETT   pop. 383

BEST WESTERN DEVILS TOWER INN   (307)467-5747

Hotel
$90-$170

AAA Benefit: Members save up to 15% and earn bonus points!

Address: 229 Hwy 24 82720 **Location:** North end of downtown. **Facility:** 40 units. 2 stories (no elevator), interior corridors. **Parking:** winter plug-ins. **Terms:** cancellation fee imposed. **Pool:** heated indoor. **Activities:** hot tub. **Guest Services:** coin laundry.

WHERE TO EAT

PONDEROSA CAFE & BAR   307/467-5335
American. Casual Dining. **Address:** 115 Main St 82720

JACKSON   (C-1) pop. 9,577, elev. 6,123'
• Restaurants p. 192
• Hotels & Restaurants map & index p. 195
• Part of Jackson Hole Including Grand Teton National Park area — see map p. 193

The southern entrance to Grand Teton National Park (see place listing p. 180), Jackson is on a scenic portion of US 89 that extends south 255 miles from Mammoth Hot Springs to Geneva, Idaho. It is the supply point and center of activity for ranchers and vacationers in Jackson Hole country. Recreation in the mountain-rimmed valley includes boating, fishing, hiking, horseback riding, mountain climbing, downhill and cross-country skiing, snowmobiling, white-water rafting and windsurfing on Jackson Lake.

Jackson's historic town square is the hub of activity, with plentiful dining and nightlife options. Visitors enjoy strolling amid a setting of Western architecture, with such accents as wooden sidewalks and elk antler arches. Shopping opportunities range from outdoor gear to trendy boutiques.

Live musical comedies are presented in summer at Jackson Hole Playhouse; phone (307) 733-6994. The J.H. Rodeo also operates in the summer; phone (307) 733-7927. Jackson Hole EcoTour Adventures offers wildlife tours of Grand Teton and Yellowstone national parks; for schedules and reservations phone (307) 690-9533.

While Snow King Scenic Chairlift provides uphill transportation for skiers in winter, summer passengers can enjoy scenic panoramas of Jackson Hole and the Tetons; phone (307) 201-5667.

Jackson Hole Chamber of Commerce: 112 Center St., P.O. Box 550, Jackson, WY 83001. **Phone:** (307) 733-3316.

BRUSHBUCK GUIDE SERVICES, 490 US 89S, picks up passengers from the clock tower in Teton Village. With a knowledgeable guide in the driver's seat, visitors ride in a safari-style van through scenic Grand Teton National Park. Among the wildlife that may be seen on this 4-hour tour are bison, grizzly and black bears, eagles, elk, moose, wolves and pronghorn antelope. The tour includes snacks and beverages and the use of binoculars, spotting scopes, blankets and rain gear. Yellowstone National Park tours, multiday tours and private tours also are offered.

Note: The tour may include a walk through sagebrush flats; comfortable, durable clothing is recommended. **Hours:** Grand Teton tour departs daily at dawn (between 6 and 6:30) and dusk (between 4:30 and 5:15). Phone for other tour schedules. **Cost:** Grand Teton tour $125, plus $20 park entrance fee. Yellowstone tour $189-$900, depending on number of people on the tour, plus $20 per person park entrance fee. Phone for other tour prices. Grand Teton tours require a minimum of two people. A 50 percent deposit is required for all tours. Reservations are required. **Phone:** (888) 282-5868 or (307) 699-2999.

NATIONAL MUSEUM OF WILDLIFE ART is on Rungius Rd. across from the National Elk Refuge. The museum is in a stone building wedged into a hillside so that it appears to be more part of its surroundings. The collection includes more than 5,000 paintings, sculptures and photos of wildlife. Artists include Albert Bierstadt, George Catlin, John Clymer, Bob Kuhn, Georgia O'Keeffe, Carl Rungius, C.M. Russell and Conrad Schwiering.

Of note are the JKM Collection of big game animals and the Conservation Gallery. The museum also houses a children's discovery gallery and changing exhibits. **Hours:** Daily 9-5, May-Oct.; Tues.-Sat. 9-5, Sun. 11-5, rest of year. Closed Veterans Day, Thanksgiving and Christmas. **Cost:** $14; $12 (ages 60+); $6 (ages 5-18 with adult). **Phone:** (307) 733-5771.

RECREATIONAL ACTIVITIES
White-water Rafting
• **Barker-Ewing River Trips, Whitewater and Scenic Floats** meets at 945 W. Broadway. Other trips are offered. **Hours:** Trips depart daily, May 1 to mid-Sept. **Phone:** (800) 448-4202.

• **Dave Hansen Whitewater and Scenic River Trips** operate from 225 W. Broadway. **Hours:** Five trips depart daily at various times, mid-May to late Oct. **Phone:** (307) 733-6295 or (800) 732-6295.

• **Jackson Hole Whitewater** is at 650 W. Broadway. Other activities are offered. **Hours:** Trips depart several times daily, May 15-Oct. 15. **Phone:** (307) 733-1007, or (800) 700-7238 out of Wyoming.

• **Mad River Boat Trips** is at 1255 US 89S. Other activities are offered. **Hours:** Trips depart 15 times daily, mid-May to mid-Sept. **Phone:** (307)

(See map & index p. 195.)

733-6203 or (800) 458-7238. *(See ad this page.)* GT

49'ER INN & SUITES   307/733-7550 28
◇◇◇
Hotel
Rates not provided

Address: 330 W Pearl St 83001 **Location:** 0.3 mi e of US 89 and 191 (W Broadway Ave) and Pearl St. **Facility:** 142 units, some kitchens. 3 stories (no elevator), interior/exterior corridors. **Parking:** winter plug-ins. **Amenities:** safes. **Pool:** heated indoor. **Activities:** hot tub, exercise room. **Guest Services:** valet and coin laundry, area transportation. **Featured Amenity:** continental breakfast. *(See ad p. 189, opposite inside front cover.)*

  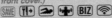

4 WINDS MOTEL   307/733-2474 20
◇ Motel. **Address:** 150 N Millward St 83001

ANTLER INN   (307)733-2535 29
◇◇◇
Motel
$100-$400

Address: 43 W Pearl St 83001 **Location:** Just w of S Cache and W Pearl sts; just s of Town Square. **Facility:** 106 units, some kitchens. 2 stories (no elevator), interior/exterior corridors. **Parking:** winter plug-ins. **Terms:** 4 day cancellation notice-fee imposed, resort fee. **Activities:** sauna, hot tub, exercise room. **Guest Services:** coin laundry. *(See ad p. 189, opposite inside front cover.)*

COWBOY VILLAGE RESORT   (307)733-3121 30
◇◇◇
Cabin
$99-$314

Address: 120 S Flat Creek Dr 83001 **Location:** 0.4 mi w of Town Square to Flat Creek Dr, then just s. **Facility:** 84 efficiency cabin units. 1 story, exterior corridors. **Parking:** winter plug-ins. **Terms:** cancellation fee imposed, resort fee. **Amenities:** safes. **Pool:** heated indoor. **Activities:** hot tub, bicycles, picnic facilities, exercise room. **Guest Services:** coin laundry, area transportation. *(See ad p. 189, opposite inside front cover.)*

▼ See AAA listing p. 186 ▼

▼ See AAA listing p. 184 ▼

(See map & index p. 195.)

ELK COUNTRY INN

307/733-2364 **27**

Hotel
Rates not provided

Address: 480 W Pearl Ave 83001 **Location:** 0.4 mi w of Town Square; just e of jct US 89/191 (W Broadway Ave) and Pearl Ave. **Facility:** 90 units, some efficiencies, kitchens and cabins. 1-2 stories (no elevator), interior/exterior corridors. **Parking:** winter plug-ins. **Amenities:** safes. **Activities:** hot tub, playground, picnic facilities, exercise room. **Guest Services:** valet and coin laundry, area transportation. *(See ad p. 189, opposite inside front cover.)*

[SAVE] [⟷] [⟷] [BIZ] [📶] [✕] [🛗]
[◻] [◻] / SOME UNITS [🐾]

FLAT CREEK INN

307/733-5276 **14**

Motel. **Address:** 1935 N US Hwy 89 83001

GOLDEN EAGLE INN

307/733-2042 **26**

Motel. **Address:** 325 E Broadway 83001

HAMPTON INN BY HILTON JACKSON HOLE

(307)733-0033 **34**

Hotel
$123-$462

AAA Benefit:
Members save 5% or more!

Address: 350 S US Hwy 89 83002 **Location:** Just s of jct US 89 and 191 (W Broadway Ave) and SR 22 (Teton Pass); 1.7 mi sw of Town Square. **Facility:** 88 units. 3 stories, interior corridors. **Parking:** winter plug-ins. **Terms:** check-in 4 pm, 1-7 night minimum stay, 3 day cancellation notice-fee imposed. **Amenities:** safes. **Activities:** hot tub, exercise room. **Guest Services:** valet and coin laundry. **Featured Amenity:** breakfast buffet. *(See ad this page.)*

[SAVE] [⟷] CALL [🛗] [⟷] [BIZ] [📶] [🛗] [✕] [◻]

HOMEWOOD SUITES BY HILTON JACKSON HOLE

307/739-0808 **17**

Extended Stay Hotel. **Address:** 260 N Millward St 83001

AAA Benefit:
Members save 5% or more!

HOTEL JACKSON

307/733-2200 **21**

Boutique Hotel
Rates not provided

Address: 120 N Glenwood St 83001 **Location:** Just n of Broadway Ave (US 89 and 191) and Glenwood St. **Facility:** Guest rooms feature a surround-sound speaker system on the nightstand, fine bedding, leather headboards and luxurious bathrooms; some with a separate shower and/or deep soaking tub. 58 units. 4 stories, interior corridors. **Parking:** valet only. **Amenities:** safes. **Dining:** 2 restaurants, also, Figs Restaurant & Bar, see separate listing. **Activities:** hot tub, exercise room. **Guest Services:** valet laundry, area transportation.

[SAVE] [⟷] [⟷] [Y] CALL [🛗] [⟷] [BIZ] [📶] [✕] [🛗]
[◻]

HOTEL JACKSON

307/733-2200 **21**

Boutique Hotel
Rates not provided

Address: 120 N Glenwood St 83001 **Location:** Just n of Broadway Ave (US 89 and 191) and Glenwood St. **Facility:** Guest rooms feature a surround-sound speaker system on the nightstand, fine bedding, leather headboards and luxurious bathrooms; some with a separate shower and/or deep soaking tub. 58 units. 4 stories, interior corridors. **Parking:** valet only. **Amenities:** safes. **Dining:** 2 restaurants, also, Figs Restaurant & Bar, see separate listing. **Activities:** hot tub, exercise room. **Guest Services:** valet laundry, area transportation.

[SAVE] [⟷] [⟷] [Y] CALL [🛗] [⟷] [BIZ] [📶] [✕] [🛗]
[◻]

(See map & index p. 195.)

JACKSON HOLE LODGE
(307)733-2992

Motel
$89-$459

Address: 420 W Broadway 83001 **Location:** 0.3 mi w of Town Square. **Facility:** 59 units, some two bedrooms, kitchens and condominiums. 2-3 stories (no elevator), interior/exterior corridors. **Parking:** winter plug-ins. **Terms:** check-in 4 pm, 14 day cancellation notice-fee imposed. **Pool:** heated outdoor. **Activities:** hot tub, picnic facilities. *(See ad p. 191.)*

[icons]

PARKWAY INN OF JACKSON HOLE
(307)733-3143 **22**

Hotel
$129-$339

Address: 125 N Jackson St 83001 **Location:** Just n of jct US 89 and 191 (W Broadway Ave) and Jackson St; 0.3 mi w of Town Square. Across from Miller Park. **Facility:** 47 units. 2 stories (no elevator), interior/exterior corridors. **Parking:** winter plug-ins. **Terms:** 14 day cancellation notice-fee imposed. **Pool:** heated indoor. **Activities:** sauna, hot tub, exercise room. **Guest Services:** valet laundry. **Featured Amenity:** continental breakfast.

[icons]

LEXINGTON AT JACKSON HOLE HOTEL & SUITES
(307)733-2648 **18**
Hotel. **Address:** 285 N Cache St 83001

THE LODGE AT JACKSON HOLE HOTEL & CONFERENCE CENTER
307/739-9703 **33**

Hotel
Rates not provided

Address: 80 Scott Ln 83002 **Location:** 1.2 mi sw of Town Square to Scott Ln, then just s; 0.3 mi e of jct US 26/89/191. **Facility:** 154 units. 3 stories, interior corridors. **Parking:** winter plug-ins. **Terms:** check-in 4 pm. **Amenities:** safes. **Pool:** heated outdoor, heated indoor. **Activities:** sauna, hot tub, exercise room, massage. **Guest Services:** valet and coin laundry, area transportation. **Featured Amenity:** breakfast buffet.

[icons]

RUSTIC INN CREEKSIDE RESORT & SPA AT JACKSON HOLE
307/733-2357 **16**

Resort Hotel
Rates not provided

Address: 475 N Cache St 83001 **Location:** Waterfront. 0.5 mi n of Town Square. Across from National Elk Refuge and Visitor Center. **Facility:** On 15 acres, you will enjoy the nature walk that leads to a pond, a bridge to hiking trails, and manicured landscaping on both sides of a creek with red Adirondack chairs and lovely evening lights. 167 units, some two bedrooms, kitchens and cabins. 2 stories (no elevator), interior/exterior corridors. **Parking:** on-site (fee), winter plug-ins. **Terms:** check-in 4 pm. **Amenities:** safes. **Pool:** heated outdoor. **Activities:** sauna, hot tub, fishing, recreation programs in season, trails, exercise room, spa. **Guest Services:** valet and coin laundry, area transportation. **Featured Amenity:** breakfast buffet.

[icons]

MOUNTAIN MODERN MOTEL
(307)733-4340 **25**
Motel. **Address:** 380 W Broadway Ave 83001

▼ See AAA listing p. 192 ▼

For complete hotel, dining and attraction listings: AAA.com/travelguides

(See map & index p. 195.)

RUSTY PARROT LODGE & SPA (307)733-2000 19

Boutique Country Inn
$230-$580

Address: 175 N Jackson St 83001 **Location:** Just n of Town Square to W Gill Ave, then just w to N Jackson St. Across from Miller Park. **Facility:** Tucked away in a quiet corner of downtown, rooms and bathrooms at this beautiful inn feature a large desk, outlets, lavish bedding, robes, makeup mirror, deep soaking tub and heavenly bath products. 32 units. 3 stories (no elevator), interior corridors. **Parking:** winter plug-ins. **Terms:** check-in 4 pm, 3 night minimum stay - seasonal and/or weekends, 14 day cancellation notice-fee imposed, resort fee. **Amenities:** safes. **Dining:** The Wild Sage, see separate listing. **Activities:** hot tub, bicycles, spa. **Guest Services:** valet laundry, area transportation.

[icons: SAVE, restaurant, child, dry cleaning, BIZ, wifi, no smoking / SOME UNITS, refrigerator]

Make the Connection

Find this symbol for places to look, book and save on AAA.com.

SNOW KING RESORT HOTEL (307)733-5200 35

Resort Hotel. Address: 400 E Snow King Ave 83001

SPRING CREEK RANCH 307/733-8833 15

Resort Hotel
Rates not provided

Address: 1800 Spirit Dance Rd 83001 **Location:** 2 mi w on US 26/89/191, 0.5 mi w on SR 22, then 1 mi n on Spring Gulch Rd. **Facility:** This activity-oriented property offers sweeping views of the majestic Tetons. Rustic guest rooms offer a wood burning fireplace, balcony or patio and some have a washer and dryer. 117 units, some kitchens and condominiums. 2 stories (no elevator), exterior corridors. **Terms:** check-in 4 pm. **Dining:** Granary Restaurant at Spring Creek Ranch, see separate listing. **Pool:** heated outdoor. **Activities:** hot tub, tennis, cross country skiing, recreation programs in summer, exercise room, spa. **Guest Services:** valet laundry, area transportation.

[icons: SAVE, sports, restaurant, child, dry cleaning, CALL, accessible, pool, transport, BIZ, wifi, no smoking / SOME UNITS, refrigerator]

SPRINGHILL SUITES BY MARRIOTT JACKSON HOLE (307)201-5320 31

Contemporary Hotel. **Address:** 150 W Simpson Ave 83001

SUPER 8 JACKSON (307)733-6833 36

Hotel. **Address:** 750 S US Hwy 89 83001

▼ See AAA listing p. 190 ▼

(See map & index p. 195.)

THE WORT HOTEL   (307)733-2190   **23**

Historic Boutique Hotel
$229-$479

Address: 50 N Glenwood St 83001 **Location:** Just n of US 89 and 191 (W Broadway Ave) and S Glenwood St; just w of Town Square. **Facility:** Expect an authentic Western lodging experience. Guest room and bathroom highlights include hand-crafted furnishings, a yellow rose, elegant bedding, robes and lavish bath amenities. 55 units. 2 stories, interior corridors. **Parking:** on-site and valet. **Terms:** check-in 4 pm, 14 day cancellation notice-fee imposed, resort fee. **Amenities:** safes. **Dining:** Silver Dollar Bar & Grill, see separate listing, entertainment. **Activities:** hot tub, exercise room. **Guest Services:** valet laundry, area transportation. *(See ad p. 190.)*

[SAVE] [🍴] [🛎] [🍸] [🛖] [BIZ] [📶] [✕] [🔌] [💻]

WYOMING INN OF JACKSON HOLE   307/734-0035   **32**
◆◆◆ Hotel. **Address:** 930 W Broadway Ave 83001

WHERE TO EAT

ATELIER ORTEGA   307/734-6400   **41**
◆◆ Desserts. Quick Serve. **Address:** 150 Scott Ln 83001

BIN22 WINE BAR & TAPAS   307/739-9463   **27**
◆◆◆ Small Plates. Fine Dining. **Address:** 200 W Broadway Ave 83001

THE BLUE LION   307/733-3912   **18**
◆◆◆ American. Fine Dining. **Address:** 160 N Millward St 83001

BON APPE THAI   307/734-0245   **35**
◆◆ Thai. Casual Dining. **Address:** 245 W Pearl St 83001

BUBBA'S BAR-B-QUE RESTAURANT   307/733-2288   **34**
◆◆ Barbecue. Casual Dining. **Address:** 100 Flat Creek Dr 83001

THE BUNNERY BAKERY & RESTAURANT   307/734-0075   **23**
◆◆ Breakfast Sandwiches. Casual Dining. **Address:** 130 N Cache St 83001

CAFE GENEVIEVE   307/732-1910   **31**
◆◆ Comfort Food Soul Food. Casual Dining. **Address:** 135 E Broadway 83001

EL ABUELITO   307/733-1207   **24**
◆◆ Mexican. Casual Dining. **Address:** 385 W Broadway 83001

E.LEAVEN RESTAURANT & BAKERY   307/733-5600   **19**
◆◆ Sandwiches Breads/Pastries. Quick Serve. **Address:** 175 W Center St 83001

FIGS RESTAURANT & BAR   307/733-2200   **22**
◆◆◆ Lebanese. Fine Dining. **Address:** 120 N Glenwood St 83001

GATHER   307/264-1820   **36**
◆◆◆ American. Casual Dining. **Address:** 72 S Glenwood St 83001

GRANARY RESTAURANT AT SPRING CREEK RANCH   307/733-8833   **16**
◆◆◆ Continental. Fine Dining. **Address:** 1800 Spirit Dance Rd 83001

GUN BARREL STEAK & GAME HOUSE   307/733-3287   **40**
◆◆ Regional Steak Wild Game. Casual Dining. **Address:** 862 W Broadway 83002

HATCH TAQUERIA & TEQUILAS   307/203-2780   **28**
◆◆ Traditional Mexican. Casual Dining. **Address:** 120 W Broadway Ave 83001

JACKSON HOLE ROASTERS RESTAURANT & COFFEEHOUSE   307/200-6099   **29**
◆ Sandwiches Breads/Pastries. Quick Serve. **Address:** 50 W Broadway Ave 83001

THE KITCHEN   307/734-1633   **21**
◆◆◆ New American. Casual Dining. **Address:** 155 N Glenwood St 83001

LOCAL RESTAURANT & BAR   307/201-1717   **26**
◆◆◆ Steak Seafood. Fine Dining. **Address:** 55 N Cache St 83001

MERRY PIGLETS MEXICAN GRILL   307/733-2966   **20**
◆◆◆ Tex-Mex. Casual Dining. **Address:** 160 N Cache St 83001

PEARL STREET BAGELS JACKSON   307/739-1218   **37**
◆ Coffee/Tea Sandwiches. Quick Serve. **Address:** 145 W Pearl Ave 83014

PEARL STREET MARKET   307/733-1300   **38**
◆ Specialty. Quick Serve. **Address:** 40 W Pearl Ave 83001

PERSEPHONE BAKERY & CAFE   307/200-6708   **32**
◆ Breads/Pastries Sandwiches. Quick Serve. **Address:** 145 E Broadway 83001

RENDEZVOUS BISTRO   307/739-1100   **42**
◆◆◆ Regional American. Casual Dining. **Address:** 380 S Broadway 83002

SILVER DOLLAR BAR & GRILL   307/733-2190   **25**

American Casual Dining
$10-$35

AAA Inspector Notes: This restaurant specializes in American-style chophouse cuisine, such as locally raised beef, wild game and seafood. Live music is offered every Tuesday through Saturday. **Features:** full bar, patio dining, happy hour. **Reservations:** suggested. **Address:** 50 N Glenwood St 83001 **Location:** Center of downtown; in The Wort Hotel. **Parking:** street only. [B] [L] [D] CALL [♿]

SNAKE RIVER BREWING   307/739-2337   **39**
◆◆ American. Brewpub. **Address:** 265 S Millward St 83001

SNAKE RIVER GRILL   307/733-0557   **30**
◆◆◆ Regional American. Fine Dining. **Address:** 84 E Broadway 83001

TRIO, AN AMERICAN BISTRO   307/734-8038   **33**
◆◆◆ Regional American. Casual Dining. **Address:** 45 S Glenwood St 83001

THE WILD SAGE   307/733-2000   **17**

Regional American Fine Dining
$28-$78

AAA Inspector Notes: This restaurant is a favorite for its upscale, intimate dining atmosphere and impeccable service. Through the open kitchen, diners can glimpse the chefs hard at work preparing their delectable meals. The seasonally changing menu might include lavender seared lamb loin, grilled bison short ribs, melt-in-your-mouth vanilla day-boat scallops or porcini-dusted elk short loin. The seasonal desserts are delicious and hard to resist. **Features:** full bar. **Reservations:** suggested. **Address:** 175 N Jackson St 83001 **Location:** Just nw from Town Square; in Rusty Parrot Lodge & Spa. **Parking:** on-site and valet. [B] [D] CALL [♿]

JACKSON HOLE INCLUDING GRAND TETON NATIONAL PARK

Visitors to the area often wonder exactly what "Jackson Hole" means. The "Hole" is actually a high mountain valley encompassed by the ranges of the Grand Tetons, bordered by the Teton Range on the west and the Gros Ventre Range on the east. Bisected by the Snake River, the valley is 80 miles long and 15 miles wide.

You'll rarely hear Jackson Hole Valley called anything other than Jackson Hole. Early trappers coined the term when they navigated the valley's steep slopes, which they likened to descending into an enormous hole. Although Jackson Hole, Wyoming, is home to the town of Jackson and the Jackson Hole Mountain Resort, you'll notice that folks refer to both of these places as Jackson Hole, too—don't get confused since this isn't technically correct. The valley also boasts the pristine wilderness of Grand Teton National Park (including Moose and Moran) along with the small communities of Kelly, Teton Village and Wilson.

Mountain men sporting beaver hats started to explore this remote and rugged frontier in the early 1800s, as they trekked through the territory now known as Jackson Hole and Yellowstone on a quest to trap animals—in fact, the valley was named for David Jackson, a partner in a fur-trapping company. The Homestead Act eventually drew pioneers willing to take a chance on improving a free plot of land—

Moran, Kelly and Wilson had a sprinkling of settlers by the 1890s. The harsh climate sent many packing, but those who stayed and toughed it out used the abandoned parcels to their advantage and developed large ranches.

By the late 1890s, the town of Jackson started to take root. A park, churches, bank, and shops sprang up, and ultimately a jail, saloons and rodeo added to the Old West intrigue. As the 20th century approached, residents made ends meet by hosting wealthy visitors at dude ranches and serving as guides for game-hunting and sport-fishing expeditions. The creation of Grand Teton National Park in 1929 launched Jackson Hole as a prime sightseeing destination and recreational paradise.

Outdoor enthusiasts flock to Grand Teton National Park to indulge in an all sorts of fun things to do, including high-altitude hiking, float trips, wildlife viewing, boating and cross-country skiing. The park offers a habitat for many large mammals, while the rare trumpeter swan is among the resident bird life. Teton Park Road leads to Jenny Lake Lodge, campgrounds, fishing sites and many of the park's trails. East of the Snake River, Jackson Hole Highway (US 26/89/191) runs parallel to Teton Park Road between Moran and Moose and affords superb views of the Teton Range.

The town of Jackson retains vestiges of the Old West, yet manages to please the discriminating traveler. The old town square, adorned with elk horn

This map shows cities in Jackson Hole where you will find attractions, hotels and restaurants. Cities are listed alphabetically in this book on the following pages.

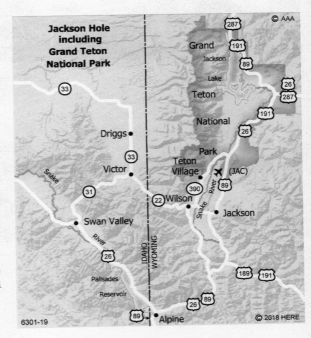

6301-19

© 2018 HERE

arches, is dotted with a mix of historic buildings, upscale places to eat and boutiques. You can see many of Jackson's historic structures on a walking tour sponsored by the Jackson Hole Historical Society & Museum. Teton Village serves as adventure hub to downhill skiers attempting the daring slopes of Jackson Hole Mountain Resort, or sightseers wishing to ride the gondola to lofty heights.

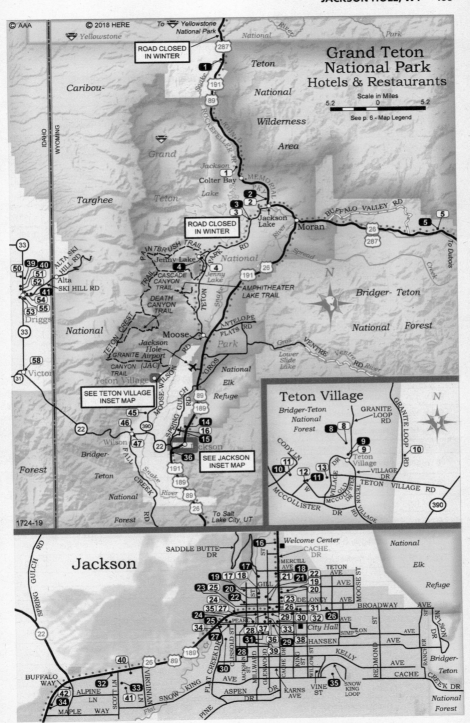

Grand Teton National Park

This index helps you "spot" where approved hotels and restaurants are located on the corresponding detailed maps. Hotel daily rate range is for comparison only. Restaurant price range is a combination of lunch and/or dinner. Turn to the listing page for more information and consult display ads for special promotions.

 For more details, rates and reservations: AAA.com/travelguides/hotels

GRAND TETON NATIONAL PARK

Map Page	Hotels	Diamond Rated	Rate Range	Page
1 p. 195	Headwaters Lodge & Cabins at Flagg Ranch	◈◈	Rates not provided	184
2 p. 195	Jackson Lake Lodge	◈◈◈	Rates not provided	184
3 p. 195	Signal Mountain Lodge	◈◈◈	Rates not provided	184
4 p. 195	Jenny Lake Lodge	◈◈◈◈	Rates not provided [SAVE]	184
5 p. 195	Togwotee Mountain Lodge & Cabins	◈◈	Rates not provided	184

Map Page	Restaurants	Diamond Rated	Cuisine	Price Range	Page
1 p. 195	Leek's Marina & Pizzeria	◈	Pizza Sandwiches	$10-$23	185
2 p. 195	The Mural Room	◈◈◈	Regional American	$12-$44	185
3 p. 195	Peaks Restaurant at Signal Mountain Lodge	◈◈◈	American	$19-$38	185
4 p. 195	Jenny Lake Lodge Dining Room	◈◈◈◈	Regional American	$10-$85	185
5 p. 195	Grizzly Grill & Red Fox Saloon at Togwotee Mountain Lodge	◈◈	American	$14-$28	185

TETON VILLAGE

Map Page	Hotels	Diamond Rated	Rate Range	Page
8 p. 195	**Four Seasons Resort & Residences Jackson Hole**	◈◈◈◈◈	$400-$1900 [SAVE]	209
9 p. 195	**Snake River Lodge & Spa**	◈◈◈◈	$129-$3300 [SAVE]	209
10 p. 195	**Teton Mountain Lodge & Spa**	◈◈◈◈	$169-$3899 [SAVE]	209
11 p. 195	**Hotel Terra Jackson Hole**	◈◈◈◈	$169-$3699 [SAVE]	209

Map Page	Restaurants	Diamond Rated	Cuisine	Price Range	Page
8 p. 195	**Westbank at Four Seasons**	◈◈◈◈	Regional American	$37-$80	209
9 p. 195	Gamefish Restaurant	◈◈◈	Regional American	$23-$45	209
10 p. 195	Teton Thai Teton Village	◈◈	Thai	$14-$28	209
11 p. 195	Spur Restaurant & Bar	◈◈◈	Regional American	$14-$52	209
12 p. 195	IL Villaggio Osteria	◈◈◈	Italian	$17-$38	209
13 p. 195	Mangy Moose Restaurant & Saloon	◈◈	New American	$7-$47	209

JACKSON

Map Page	Hotels	Diamond Rated	Rate Range	Page
14 p. 195	Flat Creek Inn	◈◈	Rates not provided	188
15 p. 195	**Spring Creek Ranch**	◈◈◈	Rates not provided [SAVE]	191
16 p. 195	**Rustic Inn Creekside Resort & Spa at Jackson Hole**	◈◈◈	Rates not provided [SAVE]	190
17 p. 195	Homewood Suites by Hilton Jackson Hole	◈◈◈	Rates not provided	188
18 p. 195	Lexington at Jackson Hole Hotel & Suites	◈◈◈	$109-$359	190
19 p. 195	**Rusty Parrot Lodge & Spa**	◈◈◈◈	$230-$580 [SAVE]	191

JACKSON (cont'd)

Map Page	Hotels (cont'd)	Diamond Rated	Rate Range	Page
20 p. 195	4 Winds Motel	◈	Rates not provided	187
21 p. 195	**Hotel Jackson**	◈◈◈◈	Rates not provided SAVE	188
22 p. 195	**Parkway Inn of Jackson Hole**	◈◈◈	$129-$339 SAVE	190
23 p. 195	**The Wort Hotel** (See ad p. 190.)	◈◈◈◈	$229-$479 SAVE	192
24 p. 195	**Jackson Hole Lodge** (See ad p. 191.)	◈◈	$89-$459 SAVE	190
25 p. 195	Mountain Modern Motel	◈◈	$89-$399	190
26 p. 195	Golden Eagle Inn	◈	Rates not provided	188
27 p. 195	**Elk Country Inn** (See ad p. 189, opposite inside front cover.)	◈◈	Rates not provided SAVE	188
28 p. 195	**49'er Inn & Suites** (See ad p. 189, opposite inside front cover.)	◈◈	Rates not provided SAVE	187
29 p. 195	**Antler Inn** (See ad p. 189, opposite inside front cover.)	◈◈	$100-$400 SAVE	187
30 p. 195	**Cowboy Village Resort** (See ad p. 189, opposite inside front cover.)	◈◈	$99-$314 SAVE	187
31 p. 195	SpringHill Suites by Marriott Jackson Hole	◈◈◈	$59-$466	191
32 p. 195	Wyoming Inn of Jackson Hole	◈◈◈	Rates not provided	192
33 p. 195	**The Lodge at Jackson Hole Hotel & Conference Center**	◈◈◈	Rates not provided SAVE	190
34 p. 195	**Hampton Inn by Hilton Jackson Hole** (See ad p. 188.)	◈◈◈	$123-$462 SAVE	188
35 p. 195	Snow King Resort Hotel	◈◈◈	$99-$499	191
36 p. 195	Super 8 Jackson	◈◈	$60-$229	191

Map Page	Restaurants	Diamond Rated	Cuisine	Price Range	Page
16 p. 195	Granary Restaurant at Spring Creek Ranch	◈◈◈	Continental	$14-$46	192
17 p. 195	**The Wild Sage**	◈◈◈◈	Regional American	$28-$78	192
18 p. 195	The Blue Lion	◈◈◈	American	$23-$50	192
19 p. 195	E.Leaven Restaurant & Bakery	◈◈	Sandwiches Breads/Pastries	$11-$15	192
20 p. 195	Merry Piglets Mexican Grill	◈◈	Tex-Mex	$12-$28	192
21 p. 195	The Kitchen	◈◈◈	New American	$18-$38	192
22 p. 195	Figs Restaurant & Bar	◈◈◈	Lebanese	$12-$36	192
23 p. 195	The Bunnery Bakery & Restaurant	◈◈	Breakfast Sandwiches	$12-$17	192
24 p. 195	El Abuelito	◈◈	Mexican	$8-$18	192
25 p. 195	**Silver Dollar Bar & Grill**	◈◈◈	American	$10-$35	192
26 p. 195	Local Restaurant & Bar	◈◈◈	Steak Seafood	$12-$122	192
27 p. 195	Bin22 Wine Bar & Tapas	◈◈◈	Small Plates	$9-$29	192
28 p. 195	Hatch Taqueria & Tequilas	◈◈	Traditional Mexican	$12-$23	192
29 p. 195	Jackson Hole Roasters Restaurant & Coffeehouse	◈◈	Sandwiches Breads/Pastries	$10-$14	192
30 p. 195	Snake River Grill	◈◈◈	Regional American	$21-$66	192
31 p. 195	Cafe Genevieve	◈◈	Comfort Food Soul Food	$9-$38	192
32 p. 195	Persephone Bakery & Cafe	◈	Breads/Pastries Sandwiches	$9-$13	192

Map Page	Restaurants (cont'd)	Diamond Rated	Cuisine	Price Range	Page
㉝ p. 195	Trio, An American Bistro	◆◆◆	Regional American	$18-$52	192
㉞ p. 195	Bubba's Bar-B-Que Restaurant	◆◆	Barbecue	$7-$28	192
㉟ p. 195	Bon Appe Thai	◆◆	Thai	$12-$25	192
㊱ p. 195	Gather	◆◆◆	American	$17-$41	192
㊲ p. 195	Pearl Street Bagels Jackson	◆	Coffee/Tea Sandwiches	$3-$8	192
㊳ p. 195	Pearl Street Market	◆	Specialty	$9-$12	192
㊴ p. 195	Snake River Brewing	◆◆	American	$9-$16	192
㊵ p. 195	Gun Barrel Steak & Game House	◆◆	Regional Steak Wild Game	$19-$47	192
㊶ p. 195	Atelier Ortega	◆◆	Desserts	$5-$15	192
㊷ p. 195	Rendezvous Bistro	◆◆◆	Regional American	$18-$38	192

DRIGGS, ID

Map Page	Hotels	Diamond Rated	Rate Range	Page
㊴ p. 195	**Super 8 Teton West**	◆◆	$65-$118 SAVE	42
㊵ p. 195	**Teton West Motel**	◆◆	Rates not provided SAVE	42
㊶ p. 195	Teton Valley Cabins	◆◆	Rates not provided	42

Map Page	Restaurants	Diamond Rated	Cuisine	Price Range	Page
㊿ p. 195	Seoul Restaurant - Korean Cuisine & Sushi	◆◆	Korean Sushi	$9-$22	42
(51) p. 195	Agave Mexican Restaurant	◆◆	Mexican	$7-$18	42
(52) p. 195	Big Hole Bagel & Bistro	◆	Breakfast Deli	$6-$10	42
(53) p. 195	Teton Thai	◆◆	Thai	$13-$22	42
(54) p. 195	Forage Bistro & Lounge	◆◆◆	Regional American	$11-$38	42
(55) p. 195	Provisions Local Kitchen	◆◆	American	$7-$14	42

WILSON

Map Page	Restaurants	Diamond Rated	Cuisine	Price Range	Page
㊺ p. 195	Sudachi Sushi Restaurant	◆◆◆	Japanese Sushi	$10-$35	211
㊻ p. 195	StreetFood at the Stagecoach	◆	Mexican	$11-$15	211
㊼ p. 195	Pearl Street Bagels Wilson	◆	Coffee/Tea Sandwiches	$5-$8	211

VICTOR, ID

Map Page	Restaurant	Diamond Rated	Cuisine	Price Range	Page
(58) p. 195	Knotty Pine Supper Club	◆◆	American	$13-$27	69

KEMMERER (E-1) pop. 2,656, elev. 6,908'

One feature of the boom that followed the discovery of coal near Kemmerer in 1897 was the saloon of "Preaching Lime" Huggins, who maintained that he never sold a drink to a man already under the influence. Over the bar mirror hung such mottos as "Don't buy a drink before seeing that your baby has shoes." One of his patrons liked the establishment because he could do his repenting during his sinning and "get the whole thing over at once."

A nationwide retail chain originated in Kemmerer when James Cash Penney opened his first store, the Golden Rule, in 1902 with an initial investment of $500. The original home of the founder is now a museum at 107 JC Penney Dr.

Native fossils and historical artifacts are displayed at the visitor center in Herschler Triangle Park.

Kemmerer/Diamondville Area Chamber of Commerce: 1601 N. Sunlight Dr., Kemmerer, WY 83101. **Phone:** (702) 239-6001.

BEST WESTERN PLUS FOSSIL COUNTRY INN & SUITES
(307)877-3388

Hotel
$109-$179

AAA Benefit: Members save up to 15% and earn bonus points!

Address: 760 US 30/189 83101 **Location:** Jct US 30 and 189. **Facility:** 80 units. 3 stories, interior corridors. **Parking:** winter plug-ins. **Terms:** cancellation fee imposed. **Pool:** heated indoor. **Activities:** hot tub, picnic facilities, exercise room. **Guest Services:** coin laundry.

LANDER (D-3) pop. 7,487, elev. 5,372'

Lander began around 1869 when Camp Augur was built to protect the settlers and Shoshone Native Americans. In 1884 Lander became the seat of newly created Fremont County, which is as large as some Eastern states. The county covers 5,861,120 acres and is an important wildlife habitat for moose, elk, bighorn sheep, deer and pronghorn antelopes.

North of Lander is the vast Wind River Mountain Range. Part of this range is now the Wind River Indian Reservation. Farther northwest near Dubois is an area that was the site of a horse ranch operated by George Parker, alias Butch Cassidy. Cassidy frequently sold his stock in Lander, whose citizens maintained he always had more to sell than he raised.

SR 131 follows the middle fork of the Popo Agie River southwest of Lander to Sinks Canyon State Park *(see attraction listing)* and Shoshone National Forest *(see place listing p. 208).* Lander contains the trailhead for the Continental Divide Snowmobile Trail.

Lander Area Chamber of Commerce: 160 N. 1st St., Lander, WY 82520. **Phone:** (307) 332-3892 or (800) 433-0662.

SINKS CANYON STATE PARK is 7.5 mi. s.w. on SR 131. Moose, bighorn sheep and other wild game often can be sighted. The Popo Agie River disappears into the sinks of the Madison Limestone and reappears in a rise one-quarter of a mile down the canyon in a large trout pool.

The Sinks Canyon State Park Visitor Center provides information about natural features and recreational opportunities. *See Recreation Areas Chart.* **Hours:** Park open daily dawn-dusk. Visitor center daily 9-6, Memorial Day-Labor Day. Campground daily, May-Oct. **Cost:** Day use free. Camping $11. **Phone:** (307) 332-6333, or (307) 332-3077 (visitor center).

HOLIDAY INN EXPRESS & SUITES LANDER   307/332-4005
Hotel. **Address:** 1002 11th St 82520

THE INN AT LANDER
307/332-2847

Hotel
Rates not provided

Address: 260 Grand View Dr 82520 **Location:** Jct US 287 and SR 789. **Facility:** 101 units. 2 stories (no elevator), interior corridors. **Parking:** winter plug-ins. **Pool:** heated outdoor. **Activities:** hot tub, exercise room. **Guest Services:** coin laundry. **Featured Amenity:** full hot breakfast.

RODEWAY INN & SUITES PRONGHORN LODGE
(307)332-3940

Motel
$70-$110

Address: 150 E Main St 82520 **Location:** Waterfront. Just n of jct US 287 and SR 789. **Facility:** 56 units, some efficiencies. 1-2 stories (no elevator), exterior corridors. **Parking:** winter plug-ins. **Dining:** The Oxbow Restaurant, see separate listing. **Activities:** hot tub, limited exercise equipment. **Guest Services:** coin laundry. **Featured Amenity:** continental breakfast.

WHERE TO EAT

COWFISH RESTAURANT & BREWERY   307/332-8227
American. Brewpub. **Address:** 126 Main St 82520

EL SOL DE MEXICO   307/332-9298
Mexican. Casual Dining. **Address:** 453 Main St 82520

THE MIDDLE FORK   307/335-5035
American. Casual Dining. **Address:** 351 Main St 82520

THE OXBOW RESTAURANT   307/332-0233
American. Casual Dining. **Address:** 170 E Main St 82520

LARAMIE (E-5) pop. 30,816, elev. 7,171'
• Hotels p. 201 • Restaurants p. 201

Although Native Americans roamed the Laramie Plains as early as 8000 B.C., Laramie's recorded history began in the early 19th century with the arrival of the area's first white man, Jacques LaRamie, a trapper for American Fur Co. In his steps followed mountain men, trappers, emigrants, soldiers and explorers, many tracing the old Cherokee Trail.

Fort Sanders, a short distance south, provided protection for the Overland Stage Line and for the Union Pacific. The railroad brought the bulk of Laramie's citizenry—including a sizable population of lawless riffraff who finally left town at the prompting of self-appointed vigilance committees. The first woman juror, Eliza Stewart, served in Laramie in March 1870. In the fall "Grandma" Louisa Swain became the first woman to vote in a general election.

Recreational opportunities abound nearby. Cross-country skiing is available east of Laramie, and downhill skiing and snowmobiling can be found in the Snowy Range of the Medicine Bow Mountains, west of the city on SR 130. Both regions are equally attractive to vacationers during the summer, with many camping and picnic areas.

Of geological interest is Sand Creek, a 6,000-acre natural landmark about 20 miles southwest of Laramie. Some of North America's finest examples of cross-bedded sandstone and "topple blocks" can be seen.

Laramie serves as the eastern end of a scenic portion of I-80, which runs 99 miles northwest to Walcott. Snowy Range Scenic Byway (SR 130), off the I-80 Snowy Range exit, offers a view of mountains, lakes and forests. At the summit, the Libby Flats Observatory and a viewing platform offer a panorama of the area.

Laramie Area Visitor Center: 210 E. Custer St., Laramie, WY 82070. **Phone:** (307) 745-4195 or (800) 445-5303.

Self-guiding tours: Brochures describing downtown and architectural walking tours are available at the Laramie Area Visitor Center.

ABRAHAM LINCOLN MEMORIAL MONUMENT is 10 mi. s.e. on I-80 exit 323, at the edge of a rest area. The 48.5-foot-tall monument, sculpted by Robert I. Russin, stands at an 8,640-foot summit off I-80 near Sherman Hill. The monument marks the highest point on this transcontinental route. I-80 follows the path of the first transcontinental railroad line.

[SAVE] **LARAMIE PLAINS MUSEUM** is 1 blk. n. of I-80 and US 30 Business Loop at 603 E. Ivinson St. The museum is the restored 1892 Victorian mansion of Edward Ivinson, one of the city's original settlers. Period furnishings and thousands of artifacts from the area are displayed. The grounds include a carriage house and a one-room log schoolhouse. **Hours:** Guided tours are given Tues.-Sat. 1-4. **Cost:** $10; $7 (senior citizens); $5 (students and military with ID); free (ages 0-5); $25 (family). **Phone:** (307) 742-4448. [GT]

UNIVERSITY OF WYOMING is between 9th and 30th sts. and Lewis and Grand aves. The university opened its doors in 1887. The 785-acre campus contains buildings of native sandstone. **Hours:** Cultural and fine arts programs and concerts are held year-round. **Phone:** (307) 766-4075.

American Heritage Center, 2111 Willett Dr. in the Centennial Complex of the University of Wyoming, is a repository for manuscripts, special collections, rare books and the university's archives as well as a site for lectures, concerts, symposiums and exhibits. The center features changing displays from its collections including the art of Henry Farny, Alfred Jacob Miller and Frederic Remington. **Hours:** Mon. 8-7, Tues.-Fri. 8-5. Closed major holidays. **Cost:** Free. **Phone:** (307) 766-4114.

Anthropology Museum is at 12th and Lewis sts. on the north side of the University of Wyoming campus. It chronicles the state's cultural history, including information about Northwest Plains Native Americans and other Native Americans of the U.S. and Canada. Collections include archeological and ethnological materials. **Hours:** Mon.-Fri. 8-5, Sept.-May; 7:30-4:30, rest of year. Closed major holidays. **Cost:** Free. **Phone:** (307) 766-5136.

Art Museum is at 2111 Willett Dr. in the Centennial Complex of the University of Wyoming. The museum contains more than 7,000 sculptures, prints, paintings and artifacts from many cultures and periods. Exhibitions focus on contemporary pieces, art of the American West and works from various countries that have influenced American artists. Artworks by established artists as well as traveling exhibitions are displayed. **Hours:** Mon.-Sat. 10-5 (also Mon. 5-9 when school is in session). Closed major holidays. **Cost:** Free. **Phone:** (307) 766-6622.

Geological Museum is in the e. wing of the S.H. Knight Building at the University of Wyoming. The museum interprets the physical and historical geology of the state through displays of rocks, minerals and fossils. Of interest is a mounted skeleton of a brontosaurus, purported to be one of only five exhibited in the world. Other dinosaur displays include an allosaurus, tyrannosaurus and triceratops. **Hours:** Mon.-Sat. 10-4. Closed major holidays. **Cost:** Free. **Phone:** (307) 766-2646.

[GEM] **WYOMING TERRITORIAL PRISON STATE HISTORIC SITE** is at 975 Snowy Range Rd. at jct. I-80 exit 311. The site features a restored 19th-century prison, a warden's house, a prison industries building, a homestead ranch display, museum exhibits, a nature trail and special events. The 1872 prison is said to be the only prison in which outlaw Butch Cassidy was incarcerated and an exhibit marks his time there.

Self-guiding museum and prison tours are available. **Hours:** Daily 8-7, May-Sept.; Wed.-Sat. 10-3, rest of year. Last admission 1 hour before closing. Closed day before Thanksgiving, Thanksgiving, Christmas and day after Christmas. **Cost:** $5; $2.50 (ages 12-17). **Phone:** (307) 745-3733.

AMERICINN LODGE & SUITES BY WYNDHAM LARAMIE
(307)745-0777
▼▼▼ Hotel. **Address:** 4712 E Grand Ave 82070

COMFORT INN LARAMIE   (307)742-6665
▼▼ Hotel. **Address:** 1655 Centennial Dr 82070

DAYS INN LARAMIE   (307)745-5678
▼▼ Hotel. **Address:** 1368 N McCue St 82072

FAIRFIELD INN & SUITES BY MARRIOTT LARAMIE
(307)460-2100
▼▼▼ Contemporary Hotel. **Ad-dress:** 1673 Centennial Dr 82070

AAA Benefit: Members save 5% or more!

HAMPTON INN BY HILTON LARAMIE   307/742-0125
▼▼▼ Contemporary Hotel. **Ad-dress:** 3715 E Grand Ave 82070

AAA Benefit: Members save 5% or more!

HILTON GARDEN INN LARAMIE   307/745-5500
▼▼▼ Hotel. **Address:** 2229 E Grand Ave 82070

AAA Benefit: Members save 5% or more!

HOLIDAY INN UNIVERSITY AREA   307/721-9000
▼▼▼ Hotel. **Address:** 204 S 30th St 82070

QUALITY INN & SUITES UNIVERSITY   (307)721-8856
▼▼ Hotel. **Address:** 3420 E Grand Ave 82070

WHERE TO EAT

ALTITUDE CHOPHOUSE & BREWERY   307/721-4031
▼▼ American. Casual Dining. **Address:** 320 S 2nd St 82070

ANONG'S THAI CUISINE   307/745-6262
▼▼ Thai. Casual Dining. **Address:** 101 E Ivinson St 82070

JEFFREY'S BISTRO   307/742-7046
▼▼ New World. Casual Dining. **Address:** 123 E Ivinson Ave 82070

NEW MANDARIN RESTAURANT   307/742-8822
▼▼ Mandarin. Casual Dining. **Address:** 1254 N 3rd St 82072

PRAIRIE ROSE CAFE   307/745-8140
▼▼ American. Casual Dining. **Address:** 410 S 2nd St 82070

SWEET MELISSA VEGETARIAN CAFE & FRONT STREET TAVERN   307/742-9607
▼▼ Small Plates Vegetarian. Casual Dining. **Address:** 213 S 1st St 82070

LITTLE AMERICA pop. 68

LITTLE AMERICA HOTEL   307/875-2400

▼▼
Motel
Rates not provided

Address: I-80, exit 68 82929 **Location:** I-80 exit 68, just n. **Facility:** 140 units, some two bedrooms. 1-2 stories (no elevator), - interior/exterior corridors. **Parking:** winter plug-ins. **Amenities:** *Some:* safes. **Pool:** heated outdoor. **Activities:** playground, exercise room. **Guest Services:** coin laundry.

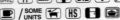

WHERE TO EAT

TRAVEL CENTER GRILL & DELI   307/872-2675
▼ Burgers Sandwiches. Quick Serve. **Address:** I-80, Exit 68 82929

LOVELL (B-3) pop. 2,360, elev. 3,837'

Lovell, founded by Mormons in 1900, serves as the southern gateway to Bighorn Canyon National Recreation Area *(see place listing p. 95)*. A recreation area visitor center offering interpretive displays and movies is at the junction of US 310 and scenic US 14A. Lovell is said to be the "Rose City" of Wyoming due to the exceptional climate for growing these flowers. Area recreational pursuits include camping, fishing, hunting, water sports, hiking, snowmobiling and trail riding.

Next to Bighorn Canyon is Pryor Mountain Wild Horse Range, a 38,000-acre refuge for wild horses and bighorn sheep.

Lovell Area Chamber of Commerce: 287 E. Main St., Lovell, WY 82431. **Phone:** (307) 548-7552.

HIDDEN TREASURE CHARTERS AND WYOMING ECO-TOURS departs from the Horseshoe Bend Marina, 1200 SR 37. Narrated boat rides on Bighorn Lake afford views of Bighorn Canyon National Recreation Area's wildlife and spectacular cliffs. Keep your eyes peeled for bighorn sheep and such birds as falcons, eagles, osprey, terns and swallows. Sunset dinner cruises also are available.

Time: Allow 2 hours minimum. **Hours:** Trips depart Tues.-Sat. and holidays at 10 and 2, Memorial Day-Labor Day. Sunset dinner cruises depart Fri.-Sat. at 6:30 p.m. Guests should arrive 15 minutes before boarding. **Cost:** $40; $26.25 (ages 1-12). Sunset dinner cruise $51.45. Recreation area admission $5 per private vehicle. Reservations are required. **Phone:** (307) 899-1401, or (307) 548-7230 for the marina. GT 🅰 🍴 🛉

LUSK (D-6) pop. 1,567, elev. 5,014'
• Hotels p. 202 • Restaurants p. 202

Named for an early settler, Lusk is a trading center for a ranching and dry-farming district that also is involved in some oil production. To the west are red-colored cliffs from which Native Americans obtained material for paint. Through this area ran the Cheyenne and Black Hills Stage Line, whose route is marked by two rows of white posts. Three miles east on US 20, a marker indicates the location of a segment of the Texas Trail. The trail was used to herd cattle from Texas to the open ranges of Wyoming, Montana and the Dakotas.

Niobrara Chamber of Commerce: 224 S. Main St., P.O. Box 457, Lusk, WY 82225. **Phone:** (307) 334-2950.

AMERICAS BEST VALUE INN COVERED WAGON LUSK
307/334-2836

Motel
Rates not provided

Address: 730 S Main St 82225 **Location:** Just n of jct US 20/85. **Facility:** 51 units. 1-2 stories (no elevator), interior/exterior corridors. **Parking:** winter plug-ins. **Pool:** heated indoor. **Activities:** sauna, hot tub, playground, picnic facilities. **Guest Services:** coin laundry. **Featured Amenity: breakfast buffet.**

BEST WESTERN PIONEER LUSK   (307)334-2640

Motel
$99–$199

AAA Benefit: Members save up to 15% and earn bonus points!

Address: 731 S Main St 82225 **Location:** Just n of jct US 20/85. **Facility:** 40 units. 1 story, exterior corridors. **Parking:** winter plug-ins. **Terms:** cancellation fee imposed. **Pool:** heated outdoor. **Activities:** bicycles, picnic facilities, exercise room. **Guest Services:** coin laundry.

WHERE TO EAT

THE PIZZA PLACE   307/334-3000
Pizza. Quick Serve. **Address:** 218 S Main St 82225

ROUGH 'N REFINED   307/334-0145
Coffee/Tea Sandwiches. Quick Serve. **Address:** 120 E 3rd St 82225

MEDICINE BOW NATIONAL FOREST
(D-5)

Elevations in the forest range from 5,000 ft. north of the Laramie River to 12,013 ft. at Medicine Bow Peak. Refer to AAA maps for additional elevation information.

In southeastern Wyoming, Medicine Bow-Routt National Forest consists of three separate districts that together cover 1,093,618 acres. Scenic SR 130 (closed in winter) crosses the Laramie and Brush Creek/Hayden districts, which extend northward from Colorado along the Snowy Range.

The Brush Creek/Hayden District spans the Continental Divide in the Sierra Madre Mountains west of Encampment. Douglas District, the northernmost section, is high in the rugged Laramie Mountains south of Douglas. Between Cheyenne and Laramie I-80 crosses the Pole Mountain Unit, noted for its unusual rock formations.

The Thunder Basin National Grassland *(see place listing p. 210)* lies in the energy-rich Powder River Basin north of Douglas. There also are four wilderness areas with 79,135 acres of forested land west of Laramie.

Opportunities for such winter sports as cross-country skiing and snowmobiling abound in the area. Camping, fishing, hiking and hunting also are available. For additional information contact the Forest Supervisor, 2468 Jackson St., Laramie, WY 82070. Phone (307) 745-2300. *See Recreation Areas Chart.*

MEETEETSE (B-2) pop. 327, elev. 5,798'
• Part of Yellowstone National Park area — see map p. 214

Meeteetse has retained so much of its original western flavor that you might feel like you've stepped onto a John Wayne movie set, but this is the real McCoy. Downtown's turn-of-the-20th-century buildings house 21st-century cafés and antique shops fronted by awning-covered wooden sidewalks. Horse-watering troughs and hitching posts complete the Old West feel.

Established in 1880, this is a town where Butch Cassidy once lived and Amelia Earhart and Will Rogers once visited, staying at a local dude ranch. Lying along the scenic portion of SR 120, which runs 83 miles between Cody and Thermopolis, Meeteetse is located in the midst of mountains, rivers and valleys. Grizzly bears, deer, bighorn sheep, elk, moose and mountain lions consider this area the perfect home, presenting great opportunities for wildlife photography. The picturesque surroundings also suit humans who enjoy boating, camping, fishing, water skiing, snowmobiling, cross-country skiing and hunting.

NEWCASTLE (C-6) pop. 3,532, elev. 4,321'

Founded in 1889 when coal was discovered in the area, Newcastle was named after its sister community in England, Newcastle-Upon-Tyne. Mining is a continuing industry, along with ranching, lumbering and petroleum exploration. The yield of Newcastle's oil field is processed by its own refinery.

Newcastle Area Chamber of Commerce: 1323 Washington Blvd., Newcastle, WY 82701. **Phone:** (307) 746-2739 or (800) 835-0157.

Self-guiding tours: Brochures about driving tours are available from the visitor center at the junction of US 85 and US 16.

NEWCASTLE LODGE & CONVENTION CENTER
307/746-2600
Hotel. **Address:** 22918 Hwy 85 82701

PINES MOTEL NEWCASTLE   (307)746-4334
Motel. **Address:** 248 E Wentworth St 82701

SAGE MOTEL   307/746-2724
Motel. **Address:** 1227 S Summit Ave 82701

WHERE TO EAT

GRAZERS BURGERS & BEERS   307/746-2255
American. Casual Dining. **Address:** 22918A Hwy 85 82701

PAINTER
- Hotels & Restaurants map & index p. 220
- Part of Yellowstone National Park area — see map p. 214

HUNTER PEAK RANCH   307/587-3711 **5**
♦♦ Ranch. **Address:** 4027 Crandall Rd 82414

PINEDALE (D-2) pop. 2,030, elev. 7,176'

With the majestic Wind River Range as a backdrop, Pinedale serves as an outfitting point for recreation in the Bridger-Teton National Forest *(see place listing p. 164)*. Outdoor activities in the area include trout fishing and various water sports on nearby Fremont Lake, the second largest natural lake in Wyoming *(see Recreation Areas Chart)*. Fishing float trips originate on the Green River, while camping, climbing, backpacking and cross-country and downhill skiing also are available.

Eleven miles southwest of town, Father DeSmet Monument designates the site where the first Catholic Mass in Wyoming was held in 1840.

Upper Green River Rendezvous National Historic Landmark is 6 miles west of Pinedale on US 191. Native Americans from throughout the West and such legendary mountain men as Jim Bridger and William Sublette gathered each year during the 1830s to meet the supply caravans from St. Louis and barter, trade for furs and cavort.

Sublette County Chamber of Commerce/Visitors' Center: 19 E. Pine St., P.O. Box 176, Pinedale, WY 82941. **Phone:** (307) 367-2242 or (888) 285-7282.

Self-guiding tours: Information about the Pinedale Walking Tour and day trips in the area is available at the visitor center.

MUSEUM OF THE MOUNTAIN MAN is at 700 E. Hennick St. The museum contains exhibits relating to the rugged individuals—Jim Bridger, Kit Carson, Thomas Fitzpatrick and William Sublette, to name a few—who opened the West to settlers. Displays focus on exploration, the fur trade, the Plains Native Americans and early settlement. Items of interest include Jim Bridger's rifle, a Shoshone sheep-horn bow and a collection of Rocky Mountain fur trade journals.

Time: Allow 30 minutes minimum. **Hours:** Daily 9-5, May-Oct. **Cost:** $10; $8 (ages 61+); free (ages 0-12). **Phone:** (307) 367-4101 or (877) 686-6266.

BAYMONT INN & SUITES   (307)367-8300
♦♦ Hotel. **Address:** 1424 W Pine St 82941

🔗 AAA.com/hertz—

When your ideal road trip
includes a comfortable ride

BEST WESTERN PINEDALE INN   (307)367-6869

♦♦ ♦♦
Hotel
$89-$169

Best Western. **AAA Benefit:** Members save up to 15% and earn bonus points!

Address: 864 W Pine St 82941 **Location:** On US 191 (W Pine St), 0.5 mi w of downtown. **Facility:** 84 units. 2 stories (no elevator), interior corridors. **Parking:** winter plug-ins. **Pool:** heated indoor. **Activities:** hot tub. **Guest Services:** coin laundry.

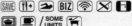

HAMPTON INN & SUITES BY HILTON PINEDALE
                                      (307)367-6700
♦♦♦ Hotel. **Address:** 55 Bloomfield Ave 82941

AAA Benefit: Members save 5% or more!

WHERE TO EAT

LAKESIDE LODGE BAR & GRILL   307/367-3555
♦♦ American. Casual Dining. **Address:** 99 Forest Service Rd 111 82941

STOCKMAN'S MOUNTAIN MAN TAVERN   307/367-4563
♦♦ American. Casual Dining. **Address:** 117 W Pine St 82941

WIND RIVER BREWING COMPANY   307/367-2337
♦♦ American. Casual Dining. **Address:** 402 W Pine St 82941

POWELL (B-3) pop. 6,314, elev. 4,365'
- Part of Yellowstone National Park area — see map p. 214

Native Americans from the Blackfoot, Crow and Shoshone tribes inhabited the area exclusively until explorer John Colter arrived in 1807. Following his arrival came a stream of explorers, trappers and miners. Powell, located about 75 miles from Yellowstone National Park's east entrance, was named after Mayor John Wesley Powell, an early-day explorer. The town's proximity to the Bighorn, Pryor and Absaroka mountain ranges makes it a recreational hot spot. A variety of wildlife inhabits the area, and historic walking tours of the city are available.

Powell Valley Chamber of Commerce: 111 S. Day St., Powell, WY 82435. **Phone:** (307) 754-3494 or (800) 325-4278.

HEART MOUNTAIN INTERPRETIVE CENTER, 1539 Rd. 19, provides a glimpse into the lives of Japanese-Americans interned at the Heart Mountain Relocation Center following the Pearl Harbor bombing. Designed to look like tar paper barracks, the museum building features artifacts and interactive displays, a reflection room and a theater. A short interpretive trail on the grounds offers eight stopping points.

Hours: Grounds daily 24 hours. Interpretive Learning Center daily 10-5, Memorial Day weekend-Oct. 1; Wed.-Sat. 10-5 or by appointment, rest of year. **Cost:** Grounds free. Interpretive Learning

Center $9; $7 (ages 62+ and students with ID); free (ages 0-12). **Phone:** (307) 754-8000. 🏧

RAWLINS (E-4) pop. 9,259, elev. 6,758'

In traditionally wool- and hay-producing Carbon County, Rawlins was a departure point for the Union Pacific Railroad and for miners bound for the gold-rich Black Hills. Nearby mines produced the "Rawlins Red" pigment that was used on the Brooklyn Bridge in 1874. The ruins of Fort Fred Steele, built in 1868 to protect early railroads and settlers, are 13 miles east of town off I-80.

During the 1870s Rawlins was a wild town with more than its share of outlaw activity. However, it came to an abrupt halt by the end of the decade when exasperated citizens employed vigilante tactics against two of the region's most notorious outlaws, Butch Cassidy and the Sundance Kid. After the lynching of "Big Nose" George Parrot, warnings were sent out to 24 other known outlaws, who left town the next morning.

On the southern edge of the Sweetwater jade fields and the eastern edge of the gem-riddled Red Desert, Rawlins is noteworthy for its geological features.

Carbon County Visitors Council: 214 4th St., Office 10, Rawlins, WY 82301. **Phone:** (307) 324-3020 or (800) 228-3547.

BEST WESTERN COTTONTREE INN RAWLINS
(307)324-2737

🏨
Hotel
$110-$150

AAA Benefit: Members save up to 15% and earn bonus points!

Address: 2221 W Spruce St 82301 **Location:** I-80 exit 211, just n. **Facility:** 122 units. 2 stories (no elevator), interior/exterior corridors. **Parking:** winter plug-ins. **Terms:** check-in 4 pm, cancellation fee imposed. **Pool:** heated indoor. **Activities:** hot tub, exercise room. **Guest Services:** coin laundry.

/ SOME / UNITS 🐾

COMFORT INN & SUITES
(307)324-3663
🔸🔸 Hotel. **Address:** 2366 E Cedar St 82301

FAIRFIELD INN & SUITES BY MARRIOTT RAWLINS
(307)328-5991
🔸🔸🔸 Contemporary Hotel. **Address:** 2370 E Cedar St 82301

AAA Benefit: Members save 5% or more!

HAMPTON INN BY HILTON RAWLINS
307/324-2320
🔸🔸 Hotel. **Address:** 406 Airport Rd 82301

AAA Benefit: Members save 5% or more!

MICROTEL INN & SUITES BY WYNDHAM RAWLINS
(307)324-5588
🔸🔸 Hotel. **Address:** 812 Locust St 82301

ANONG'S THAI CUISINE   307/324-6262
🔸🔸 Thai. Casual Dining. **Address:** 210 5th St 82301

ASPEN HOUSE RESTAURANT   307/324-4787
🔸🔸 American. Casual Dining. **Address:** 318 5th St 82301

BUCK'S SPORTS GRILL   307/328-5581
🔸 American. Casual Dining. **Address:** 401 W Cedar St 82301

SHOGUNZ PIZZERIA & BAR   307/328-5550
🔸🔸 Pizza Sandwiches. Casual Dining. **Address:** 309 W Cedar St 82301

RIVERTON (C-3) pop. 10,615, elev. 4,956'

Once part of Wind River Indian Reservation, the lower Wind River Basin now supports 130,000 acres of farmland surrounding Riverton. Castle Gardens, a state historical monument 45 miles east, is a formation of knobs, pinnacles and spires rising abruptly 10 to 100 feet above the prairie. Petroglyphs depicting warriors, hunters and animals decorate the soft sandstone formations.

Riverton Area Chamber of Commerce: 213 W. Main St., Suite C, Riverton, WY 82501. **Phone:** (307) 856-4801 or (800) 325-2732.

GAMBLING ESTABLISHMENTS
• **Wind River Casino** is at 10269 SR 789. **Hours:** Daily 24 hours. **Phone:** (307) 856-3964. *(See ad p. 205.)*

COMFORT INN & SUITES RIVERTON   (307)856-8900
🔸🔸 Hotel. **Address:** 2020 N Federal Blvd (US 26) 82501

HAMPTON INN & SUITES BY HILTON RIVERTON   307/856-3500
🔸🔸🔸 Hotel. **Address:** 2500 N Federal Blvd (US 26) 82501

AAA Benefit: Members save 5% or more!

HOLIDAY INN RIVERTON CONVENTION CENTER   307/856-8100
🔸🔸 Hotel. **Address:** 900 E Sunset Dr 82501

WIND RIVER HOTEL & CASINO   307/856-3964

🔸🔸🔸
Hotel
Rates not provided

Address: 10269 Hwy 789 82501 **Location:** 3 mi s from jct US 26. **Facility:** A colorful exterior depicts patterns from the Arapaho culture. A highlight of the lobby is the Discovery Room, a walk-through area describing native history using pictures, artifacts and movies. 90 units. 4 stories, interior corridors. **Parking:** winter plug-ins. **Terms:** check-in 4 pm. **Amenities:** safes. **Dining:** 3 restaurants, also, Red Willow, see separate listing. **Activities:** exercise room. **Guest Services:** coin laundry, area transportation. *(See ad p. 205.)*

/ SOME / UNITS 🐾

PERRETT'S   307/857-7306
🔸🔸 Italian. Casual Dining. **Address:** 519 W Main St (US 26) 82501

RED WILLOW   307/856-3964
♥♥ American. Casual Dining. **Address:** 10269 Hwy 789 82501 *(See ad p. 205.)*

ROCK SPRINGS (E-2) pop. 23,036, elev. 6,261'

Rock Springs began in 1862 as a way station along the Overland Stage route. The Union Pacific also chose this route because of the area's rich coal deposits that fueled the railroad's locomotives. Mining and refining are still major industries, with resources expanding to include trona and natural gas. Some of the world's largest deposits of trona, used in the manufacture of glass, phosphates, silicates and soaps, lie 30 miles west of the city.

To the north and stretching more than 70 miles between the town of Eden and the Green Mountains is the Red Desert, an area of moving sand dunes second in size only to the Sahara Desert. Of archeological and geological interest, the Sands, as the region is known, has produced evidence of human habitation as far back as 5000 B.C.

Petroglyphs and pictographs adorn the walls of rock outcrops in Cedar, Pine and Killpecker canyons and White Mountain. Visitors also can see evidence of prehistoric Wyoming at Western Wyoming Community College, which maintains a collection of fossils.

Boars Tusk, a volcanic monolith, rises 400 feet above Killpecker Valley at the edge of the Sands. The rock tower, 28 miles north of Rock Springs, is visible from US 191.

The Red Desert is home to one of the nation's largest herds of wild horses. To control the size of the herds, the Bureau of Land Management (BLM) conducts roundups; Mustangs captured by the BLM are kept at Rock Springs' Wild Horse Holding Facility, which conducts an Adopt-a-Horse program; phone (307) 352-0292. The Pilot Butte Wild Horse Scenic Loop provides views of these creatures; the dirt road has markers and covers some 23 miles.

Note: When traveling in desert areas, be sure to start with a full tank of gas and plenty of food and water. Off-road vehicles and cellphones are recommended for travel in remote areas.

Rock Springs Chamber of Commerce: 1897 Dewar Dr., P.O. Box 398, Rock Springs, WY 82901. **Phone:** (307) 362-3771.

Self-guiding tours: A self-guiding walking tour of downtown Rock Springs covers sites related to the community's coal mining history. Brochures are available at the chamber of commerce.

BEST WESTERN OUTLAW INN   (307)362-6623

Hotel
$109-$225

Best Western.

AAA Benefit: Members save up to 15% and earn bonus points!

Address: 1630 Elk St 82901 **Location:** I-80 exit 104 (Elk St), 0.3 mi n. Next to gas stations and truck stop. **Facility:** 100 units. 1-2 stories, interior/exterior corridors. **Parking:** winter plug-ins. **Terms:** cancellation fee imposed. **Dining:** Open Range Restaurant, see separate listing. **Pool:** heated indoor. **Activities:** exercise room. **Guest Services:** valet laundry, area transportation. **Featured Amenity: full hot breakfast.**

🖫 ✈ 🍴 ⟲ 🍸 CALL ♿ 🌊 👪 BIZ 📶 ✖ 🛏 💻 /SOME UNITS HS 🍳

HAMPTON INN BY HILTON ROCK SPRINGS   307/382-9222
♥♥♥ Hotel. **Address:** 1901 Dewar Dr 82901
AAA Benefit: Members save 5% or more!

HOLIDAY INN EXPRESS & SUITES ROCK SPRINGS
307/362-9200
♥♥♥ Hotel. **Address:** 1660 Sunset Dr 82901

HOLIDAY INN ROCK SPRINGS   (307)382-9200
♥♥♥ Hotel. **Address:** 1675 Sunset Dr 82901

HOMEWOOD SUITES BY HILTON ROCK SPRINGS
307/382-0764
♥♥♥ Extended Stay Hotel. **Address:** 60 Winston Dr 82901
AAA Benefit: Members save 5% or more!

MY PLACE HOTEL ROCK SPRINGS   307/362-5977
♥♥ Extended Stay Hotel. **Address:** 700 Gateway Blvd 82901

WHERE TO EAT

9 IRON ITALIAN GRILL & STEAKHOUSE   307/362-2561
♥♥ American. Casual Dining. **Address:** 1501 Clubhouse Dr 82901

BITTER CREEK BREWING   307/362-4782
♥♥ American. Casual Dining. **Address:** 604 Broadway St 82901

BONSAI   307/362-1888
♥♥ Asian Sushi. Casual Dining. **Address:** 1996 Dewar Dr 82901

COYOTE CREEK STEAKHOUSE & SALOON   307/382-4100
♥♥ American. Casual Dining. **Address:** 404 N St 82901

FIESTA GUADALAJARA   307/382-7147
♥♥ Mexican. Casual Dining. **Address:** 19 Elk St 82901

LEW'S   307/382-9894
♥♥ Chinese. Casual Dining. **Address:** 1506 9th St 82901

OPEN RANGE RESTAURANT   307/362-6623
♥♥
American Casual Dining
$8-$25

AAA Inspector Notes: Locals and travelers come together for choices that range from sandwiches, burgers and seafood to Angus beef, chops and cutlets, with prime rib and seafood specials offered every evening. Adventurous diners can appreciate the Rocky Mountain oysters appetizer, a great opportunity to prove power of the palate. For dessert, order the grilled carrot cake. **Features:** full bar. **Address:** 1630 Elk St 82901 **Location:** I-80 exit 104 (Elk St), 0.3 mi n; in Best Western Outlaw Inn.
B L D

SHERIDAN (B-4) pop. 17,444, elev. 3,724'
• Restaurants p. 208

Sheridan is located halfway between the Mount Rushmore National Monument and Yellowstone National Park in the valley of the Little and Big Goose. Access through the Bighorn Mountains via US 14 (Bighorn Scenic Byway) or US 14A (Medicine Wheel Passage) offers spectacular sightseeing opportunities. The majestic Bighorn Mountains rise to the west and rolling plains slope to the east.

Sheridan is rich in Western history. In 1866 the area was part of unreserved Native American territory that was home for the Sioux, Cheyenne and Arapaho. Native American chiefs such as Dull Knife, Red Cloud and Crazy Horse fought battles to keep the white man from their precious hunting grounds.

The Bozeman Trail, a shortcut scouted by John Bozeman through eastern Wyoming, cut across Native American hunting grounds to the rich gold fields of Montana. The trail, which ran south of Sheridan along part of what is now US 87, was the scene of so many battles that it became known as the Bloody Bozeman. The U.S. Cavalry forbade trains of fewer than 100 wagons to take this trail.

The discovery of gold in the Black Hills brought a new influx of fortune seekers and further confrontations, culminating in the Battle of the Little Bighorn just north of Sheridan in southern Montana *(see Little Bighorn Battlefield National Monument in Montana p. 128)*.

Many battle sites are in the area, including those of the Wagon Box Fight and the Fetterman Massacre, near Fort Phil Kearny State Historic Site in Story; Dull Knife Battle, south of town; the Sawyer Fight, 20 miles north near Dayton; Rosebud Battle, north in Montana; and the Connor Battlefield in Ranchester, 15 miles north of Sheridan.

After the wars ended, Sheridan was incorporated and built up by the profitable businesses of cattle ranching, farming and coal mining. For today's outdoor enthusiast, recreational activities are nearly unlimited in the nearby Bighorn National Forest *(see place listing p. 163)* and include wildlife viewing, hiking, fishing, hunting, snowmobiling and cross-country and downhill skiing.

The town recaptures the flavor of the Old West during the Sheridan WYO Rodeo in mid-July; phone (307) 672-9715 for ticket information. In addition to several PRCA rodeo performances, highlights include a pancake breakfast, a carnival, concerts, parades and a golf tournament.

Sheridan Travel and Tourism: 1517 E. 5th St., P.O. Box 7155, Sheridan, WY 82801. **Phone:** (307) 673-7120.

Self-guiding tours: A walking tour of the city's historic Main Street District covers many original buildings from the late 1800s and early 1990s. A map is available from Sheridan Travel and Tourism.

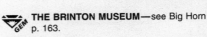 **THE BRINTON MUSEUM**—see Big Horn p. 163.

WYO THEATER is at 42 N. Main St. The theater is an Art Deco structure built in 1923 and renovated in 1989. It is said to be the oldest operating vaudeville theater in the state. Musical entertainment, ballets and stage presentations are featured year-round. **Hours:** Box office open Tues.-Fri. noon-4 (also Sat. on day of shows). **Cost:** Varies depending on event. **Phone:** (307) 672-9084.

BAYMONT INN & SUITES SHERIDAN   307/673-9500
Hotel. **Address:** 911 Sibley Cir 82801

BEST WESTERN SHERIDAN CENTER   (307)674-7421

Motel
$99-$500

 AAA Benefit: Members save up to 15% and earn bonus points!

Address: 612 N Main St 82801 **Location:** I-90 exit 23 (5th St), 1 mi w, then just s. **Facility:** 139 units. 2 stories (no elevator), interior/exterior corridors. **Parking:** winter plug-ins. **Terms:** cancellation fee imposed. **Pool:** heated indoor. **Guest Services:** valet and coin laundry, area transportation. **Featured Amenity:** breakfast buffet.

CANDLEWOOD SUITES   (307)675-2100
Extended Stay Hotel. **Address:** 1709 Sugarland Dr 82801

COMFORT INN & SUITES   (307)675-1101
Hotel. **Address:** 1950 E 5th St 82801

FAIRFIELD INN & SUITES BY MARRIOTT SHERIDAN
          (307)675-1280

Hotel
$64-$214

Fairfield **AAA Benefit:** Members save 5% or more!

Address: 2105 Sugarland Dr 82801 **Location:** I-90 exit 25, just w on E Brundage Ln, then just n. **Facility:** 72 units. 3 stories, interior corridors. **Terms:** cancellation fee imposed. **Pool:** heated indoor. **Activities:** exercise room. **Guest Services:** valet and coin laundry. **Featured Amenity:** full hot breakfast.

HAMPTON INN BY HILTON SHERIDAN   307/673-2734
Hotel. **Address:** 980 Sibley Cir 82801

AAA Benefit: Members save 5% or more!

HOLIDAY INN ATRIUM & CONVENTION CENTER
          307/672-8931
Hotel. **Address:** 1809 Sugarland Dr 82801

SUPER 8 SHERIDAN   (307)672-9725
Motel. **Address:** 2435 N Main St 82801

FRACKELTON'S 307/675-6055

♦♦♦♦ American. Casual Dining. **Address:** 55 N Main St 82801

JAVA MOON 307/673-5991

♦ Coffee/Tea. Casual Dining. **Address:** 170 N Main St 82801

MIDTOWN CAFE 307/674-0800

♦♦ Sandwiches Coffee/Tea. Casual Dining. **Address:** 137 N Main St 82801

RED VELVET BAKERY & BISTRO 307/763-7926

♦ Breads/Pastries. Casual Dining. **Address:** 35 N Main St 82801

WYOMING'S RIB & CHOPHOUSE 307/673-4700

♦♦ American. Casual Dining. **Address:** 847 N Main St 82801

SHOSHONE NATIONAL FOREST (C-2)

Elevations in the forest range from 4,600 ft. at Clarks Fork Canyon to 13,804 ft. at Gannett Peak. Refer to AAA maps for additional elevation information.

In northwestern Wyoming, the Shoshone National Forest was established by presidential proclamation in 1891 as the nation's first forest reserve. It occupies nearly 2.5 million acres. Its boundaries extend south from Montana and include parts of the Beartooth, Absaroka and Wind River mountains. The forest includes the state's highest mountain, Gannett Peak.

Forest watersheds and glacial runoff feed several rivers of the Missouri River Basin and serve as a major water source for many communities and ranches within or near the forest.

Scenic drives include Buffalo Bill Cody Scenic Byway (US 14/16/20) through the North Fork of the Shoshone River canyon en route to the east entrance of Yellowstone National Park *(see place listing p. 214)*; the Wyoming Centennial Scenic Byway over Togwotee Pass on US 287/26 between Dubois and Moran Junction; the Beartooth Scenic Highway (US 212) over the Beartooth Plateau; and the Chief Joseph Scenic Highway (SR 296) from its junction with SR 120 to the junction of US 212. SRs 296, 291 and 131 also travel past spectacular mountain scenery.

Backcountry hiking, trail riding, fishing and primitive camping are available in the Fitzpatrick Wilderness, which has two of Wyoming's highest peaks and some of the nation's largest glaciers; the Popo Agie Wilderness, dotted by more than 200 lakes; the Absaroka-Beartooth Wilderness, containing many lakes and granite peaks; and the North Absaroka Wilderness, scored by steep canyons. Cross-country skiing also is available.

Information and maps (a fee is charged) can be obtained by writing the Forest Supervisor, 808 Meadow Ln., Cody, WY 82414-4516. Phone (307) 527-6241. *See Recreation Areas Chart.*

SUNDANCE (B-6) pop. 1,182, elev. 4,750'

Sundance lies at the foot of Sundance Mountain, so named because the Sioux Native Americans held their councils and religious ceremonies at a place called Wi Wacippi Paha, or Temple of the Sioux. It is believed that Harry Longabaugh, better known as "The Sundance Kid," assumed his nickname in Sundance during his 18-month sentence in the Crook County jail for horse stealing.

Sundance is a convenient departure point for trips to nearby Devils Tower National Monument *(see place listing p. 175)* and Black Hills National Forest *(see place listing p. 164)*. An 82-mile circle tour via US 14, SRs 24 and 111 and I-90 circles a portion of the national forest and offers opportunities to see the volcanic core of Devils Tower as well as pronghorns, wild turkeys and white-tailed deer.

Sundance Area Chamber of Commerce: P.O. Box 1004, Sundance, WY 82729. **Phone:** (307) 283-1000 or (800) 477-9340.

BEST WESTERN INN AT SUNDANCE (307)283-2800

♦♦ ♦
Hotel
$128-$235

 Best Western. **AAA Benefit:** Members save up to 15% and earn bonus points!

Address: 2719 E Cleveland St 82729 **Location:** I-90 exit 189, just nw; 1.5 mi ne of SR 585. **Facility:** 44 units. 2 stories (no elevator), interior corridors. **Parking:** winter plug-ins. **Terms:** cancellation fee imposed. **Pool:** heated indoor. **Activities:** hot tub. **Guest Services:** coin laundry. **Featured Amenity:** breakfast buffet.

TETON VILLAGE (C-1) pop. 330, elev. 6,329'

• Hotels & Restaurants map & index p. 195
• Part of Jackson Hole Including Grand Teton National Park area — see map p. 193

Situated at the base of Jackson Hole Mountain Resort, Teton Village serves as a hub of activity during ski season. It is the site of many area lodgings and restaurants, and offers visitors the opportunity to browse in an assortment of specialty shops. An aerial tram in the village lifts passengers to the mountaintop, boasting one of North America's steepest and longest vertical drops.

Celebrate the joys of music at the Grand Teton Music Festival, which brings orchestra and chamber concerts in summer and winter months; phone (307) 733-1128 for ticket information.

Make the Connection

Find this symbol for places to look, book and save on AAA.com.

(See map & index p. 195.)

FOUR SEASONS RESORT & RESIDENCES JACKSON HOLE
(307)732-5000 **8**

Resort Hotel
$400-$1900

Address: 7680 Granite Loop Rd 83025 **Location:** At base of Jackson Hole Mountain Resort. **Facility:** A ski concierge is along for every step at this ski-in/ski-out resort, where fine Western décor epitomizes rustic elegance. The luxurious guest rooms feature a gas fireplace. 158 units, some two bedrooms, three bedrooms and condominiums. 10 stories, interior corridors. **Parking:** valet only. **Terms:** closed 4/9-5/4 & 10/30-11/22, check-in 4 pm, 30 day cancellation notice-fee imposed, resort fee. **Amenities:** video games, safes. **Dining:** 3 restaurants, also, Westbank at Four Seasons, see separate listing. **Pool:** heated outdoor. **Activities:** hot tub, steamroom, downhill skiing, snowboarding, recreation programs in season, game room, lawn sports, trails, health club, spa. **Guest Services:** valet laundry, boarding pass kiosk, area transportation.

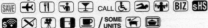

HOTEL TERRA JACKSON HOLE
(307)739-4000 **11**

Boutique Hotel
$169-$3699

Address: 3335 W Village Dr 83025 **Location:** At base of Jackson Hole Mountain Resort; Mid Village. **Facility:** "Upscale" and "eco luxury" best describe this full-service, ski-in/walk-out condominium hotel featuring upscale furnishings and luxurious 100 percent organic cotton sheets. 132 units, some condominiums. 5 stories, interior corridors. **Parking:** on-site and valet. **Terms:** closed 4/8-5/3, check-in 4 pm, 30 day cancellation notice-fee imposed, resort fee. **Amenities:** safes. **Dining:** IL Villaggio Osteria, see separate listing. **Pool:** heated outdoor. **Activities:** hot tub, steamroom, downhill skiing, snowboarding, bicycles, trails, exercise room, spa. **Guest Services:** complimentary and valet laundry, area transportation.

SNAKE RIVER LODGE & SPA
(307)732-6000 **9**

Resort Hotel
$129-$3300

Address: 7710 Granite Loop Rd 83025 **Location:** At base of Jackson Hole Mountain Resort. **Facility:** Set alongside the slopes for easy ski-in access, this resort offers endless recreational activities. A variety of guest rooms and condominiums is available; a few rooms have restricted floor space. 149 units, some two bedrooms, three bedrooms and condominiums. 5 stories, interior corridors. **Parking:** on-site and valet. **Terms:** closed 4/7-5/9 and 10/13-11/30, check-in 4 pm, 21 day cancellation notice-fee imposed, resort fee. **Amenities:** safes. **Dining:** Gamefish Restaurant, see separate listing. **Pool:** heated outdoor, heated indoor. **Activities:** sauna, hot tub, steamroom, downhill skiing, snowboarding, bicycles, trails, health club, spa. **Guest Services:** valet and coin laundry, area transportation.

TETON MOUNTAIN LODGE & SPA
(307)734-7111 **10**

Resort Condominium
$169-$3899

Address: 3385 Cody Ln 83025 **Location:** Slope side at the base of Jackson Hole Mountain Resort; Upper Village. **Facility:** Nestled among the majestic Tetons, this slope-side resort features an upscale leading-edge lobby with the coziest of seating arrangements and mesmerizing appointments and artwork. 145 units, some condominiums. 5 stories, interior corridors. **Parking:** on-site and valet, winter plug-ins. **Terms:** closed 4/8-5/3, check-in 4 pm, 30 day cancellation notice-fee imposed, resort fee. **Amenities:** safes. **Dining:** Spur Restaurant & Bar, see separate listing. **Pool:** heated outdoor, heated indoor. **Activities:** sauna, hot tub, steamroom, downhill skiing, snowboarding, ice skating, recreation programs, bicycles, trails, exercise room, spa. **Guest Services:** valet and coin laundry, area transportation.

WHERE TO EAT

GAMEFISH RESTAURANT   307-732-6040 **9**
Regional American. Casual Dining. **Address:** 7710 Granite Loop Rd 83025

IL VILLAGGIO OSTERIA   307-739-4100 **12**
Italian. Fine Dining. **Address:** 3335 W Village Dr 83025

MANGY MOOSE RESTAURANT & SALOON
307-733-4913 **13**
New American. Casual Dining. **Address:** 1 McCollister Dr 83025

SPUR RESTAURANT & BAR   307-734-7111 **11**
Regional American. Fine Dining. **Address:** 3385 Cody Ln 83025

TETON THAI TETON VILLAGE   307-733-0022 **10**
Thai. Casual Dining. **Address:** 7342 Granite Loop Rd 83025

WESTBANK AT FOUR SEASONS   307-732-5000 **8**

Regional American Fine Dining
$37-$80

AAA Inspector Notes: After a day skiing or white-water rafting, guests can savor a creatively presented, regionally influenced meal made all the more enjoyable by warmth from a massive stone fireplace. The grand dining room continues the resort's elegant rustic theme featuring floor-to-ceiling windows which offer panoramic views of the slopes and the mountains. **Features:** full bar. **Reservations:** suggested. **Address:** 7680 Granite Loop Rd 83025 **Location:** At base of Jackson Hole Mountain Resort; in Four Seasons Resort & Residences Jackson Hole. **Parking:** on-site (fee) and valet.

THERMOPOLIS (C-3) pop. 3,009, elev. 4,326'
• Hotels p. 210 • Restaurants p. 210

A treaty between the Shoshone and Arapaho nations and the United States specified that the waters of the hot mineral springs at Thermopolis would be available to everyone free of charge. The agreement continues to be honored at the State Bath House in Hot Springs State Park. Petroglyphs, 30 miles northwest of Thermopolis and about 8 miles off SR 120, are etched on a south-facing cliff at Legend Rock State Petroglyph Site.

Thermopolis is a favorite destination for hunters in search of pronghorn antelopes, game birds, elk and deer. South of Thermopolis on US 20 is Boysen

Reservoir, with developed recreational facilities at Boysen State Park *(see Recreation Areas Chart).*

Thermopolis provides access to two scenic highways—US 20 along Wind River Canyon and SR 120 traveling north to Cody.

Thermopolis-Hot Springs Chamber of Commerce: 220 Park St., P.O. Box 768, Thermopolis, WY 82443. **Phone:** (307) 864-3192.

THE WYOMING DINOSAUR CENTER AND DIG SITES is at 110 Carter Ranch Rd. on the e. side of town. The 16,000-square-foot complex houses interpretive displays, dioramas and more than 30 full-size skeletons. Visitors may view the preparation lab, where bones are prepared for display, and take a 1-hour tour of the paleontological dig site.

Hours: Daily 8-6, mid-May to mid-Sept.; 10-5, rest of year. **Cost:** Museum $10; $8 (ages 4-12, ages 60+ and military veterans with ID). Dig site $12.50; $10.50 (ages 4-13, ages 65+ and military veterans with ID). Combination museum and dig site $18.50; $14.50 (ages 4-13, ages 60+ and military veterans with ID). **Phone:** (307) 864-2997 or (800) 455-3466. GT

BEST WESTERN PLUS PLAZA HOTEL   (307)864-2939

Historic Hotel
$119-$180

Best Western PLUS

AAA Benefit: Members save up to 15% and earn bonus points!

Address: 116 E Park St 82443 **Location:** In Hot Springs State Park. **Facility:** There is an outdoor hot springs spa that is open year round in the courtyard of this hotel. A few highlights include nicely appointed rooms, enhanced personal care products and an upscale shower head. 36 units. 2 stories (no elevator), interior corridors. **Parking:** winter plug-ins. **Terms:** cancellation fee imposed. **Pool:** heated outdoor. **Activities:** hot tub.

SAVE ♦† CALL ⓑ ≋ BIZ 🛜 ✕ 🖥 🖼 🖳 / SOME UNITS HS

DAYS INN HOT SPRINGS CONVENTION CENTER
                                        (307)864-3131

♦♦ Hotel. **Address:** 115 E Park St 82443

WHERE TO EAT

THE FRONT PORCH   307/864-3494
♦♦ American. Casual Dining. **Address:** 536 Arapahoe St 82443

THE SAFARI CLUB RESTAURANT & LOUNGE   307/864-3131
♦♦ American. Casual Dining. **Address:** 115 E Park St 82443

THUNDER BASIN NATIONAL GRASSLAND (C-5)

Thunder Basin National Grassland is in Campbell, Converse, Crook, Niobrara and Weston counties. Covering 1,800,339 acres, the national grassland was once a dust bowl. Settlers from the East, familiar only with the homesteading methods for a humid climate, met with disaster when they tried to establish farms in Wyoming's semiarid plains. Poor soil and recurrent droughts foiled attempts to cultivate the land, which soon deteriorated into dust bowls.

The grassland serves as an example of the regenerative use of land deemed unsuitable for cultivation. Sheep and cattle graze on the grassland's vast acreage, which also supports one of the world's largest herds of pronghorns. The Bozeman and Texas trails traverse a portion of the grassland.

The grassland lies within the Powder River Basin and contains a wealth of natural resources for energy development, including oil, gas and coal. The Black Thunder Mine, 9 miles from SR 59 on east SR 450, is one of the largest coal mines in the country. It operates on the grassland under a special state permit with forest service consent and produces more than 30 million tons of coal per year. For further information phone (307) 358-4690, or contact the Forest Supervisor's Office at 2468 Jackson St., Laramie, WY 82070; phone (307) 745-2300.

TORRINGTON (D-6) pop. 6,501, elev. 4,098'

Traversed by the Oregon, Mormon and California trails and the Overland Stage, Pony Express and overland telegraph lines, Torrington served as a Western gateway for pioneers. Named after settler William Curtis' hometown in Connecticut, Torrington is primarily a livestock exchange center, with cattle raising and agriculture as its main economic contributors.

Goshen County Chamber of Commerce: 2042 Main St., Torrington, WY 82240. **Phone:** (307) 532-3879.

AMERICAS BEST VALUE INN TORRINGTON   307/532-7118
♦ Motel. **Address:** 1548 S Main St 82240

HOLIDAY INN EXPRESS & SUITES TORRINGTON
                                        307/532-7600

Hotel
Rates not provided

Address: 1700 E Valley Rd 82240 **Location:** On US 26 (E Valley Rd), 1.1 mi e of US 85 (Main St). Across from train tracks. **Facility:** 67 units. 2 stories, interior corridors. **Parking:** winter plug-ins. **Pool:** heated indoor. **Activities:** hot tub, exercise room. **Guest Services:** coin laundry. **Featured Amenity:** continental breakfast.

SAVE ⬅ ♦† CALL ⓑ ≋ 📶 BIZ 🛜 ✕ 🖥 🖼 🖳 / SOME UNITS 🐾 HS

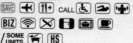

WAPITI (B-2) elev. 5,641'

• Hotels & Restaurants map & index p. 220
• Part of Yellowstone National Park area — see map p. 214

The Wapiti Valley was popularized by William F. "Buffalo Bill" Cody. He brought guests to the area to enjoy the beauty of the valley and Yellowstone National Park. Wapiti Valley provides a scenic byway into or out of Yellowstone National Park *(see place listing p. 214).* Among wildlife inhabiting the valley are elk, deer, buffalo, moose, bighorn sheep, bears, coyotes, bald and golden eagles, and even mountain lions.

Characterized by historic resorts, the valley also offers abundant recreational activities, including hiking, horseback riding, fishing, windsurfing, snowmobiling and skiing.

(See map & index p. 220.)

BILL CODY RANCH   307/587-2097 **20**
▼▼ Cabin. **Address:** 2604 N Fork Hwy 82414

WHEATLAND (D-6) pop. 3,627, elev. 4,738'

Attracted by the cheap land and irrigation water that were made available by the Carey Act of 1894, settlers streamed into Platte County and transformed its dry landscape into productive farmland, dotted with such aptly named towns as Wheatland.

Wheat continues to be the region's principal crop, sustained in part by the Wheatland Irrigation Project, one of the largest privately owned enterprises of its type in the country. Wheatland also is the home of a white marble quarrying business and Laramie River Power Station, which supplies electric power to Wyoming and six neighboring states.

Recreational opportunities include camping and winter sports in nearby Medicine Bow National Forest (see place listing p. 202). Grayrocks Reservoir, 16 miles northeast, is stocked with game fish and offers boating.

Platte County Chamber of Commerce: 65 16th St., Wheatland, WY 82201. **Phone:** (307) 322-2322.

BEST WESTERN TORCHLITE WHEATLAND
(307)322-4070

Motel
$109-$149

Best Western. **AAA Benefit:** Members save up to 15% and earn bonus points!

Address: 1809 N 16th St 82201 **Location:** I-25 exit 80, just e on Swanson Rd, then 0.6 mi s. **Facility:** 50 units. 2 stories (no elevator), exterior corridors. **Parking:** winter plug-ins. **Terms:** check-in 4 pm, cancellation fee imposed. **Pool:** heated outdoor. **Activities:** hot tub, picnic facilities. **Featured Amenity:** full hot breakfast.

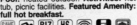

HEARTLAND INN & SUITES WHEATLAND   (307)322-9891
▼▼▼ Hotel. **Address:** 1556 Sherard Rd 82201

SUPER 8 BY WYNDHAM WHEATLAND   (307)322-2224
▼▼ Hotel. **Address:** 2401 16th St 82201

WILSON (C-1) pop. 1,482, elev. 6,152'
• Hotels & Restaurants map & index p. 195
• Part of Jackson Hole Including Grand Teton National Park area — see map p. 193

BAR J CHUCKWAGON SUPPER & WESTERN MUSIC SHOW, 1 mi. e. on SR 390 to 4200 W. Bar J Chuckwagon Rd., offers a chuck wagon supper and a live Western-style stage show. The Bar J Wranglers entertain guests with songs, stories and biscuit-baking and steak-grilling demonstrations. **Time:** Allow 4 hours minimum. **Hours:** Daily 5:30-10, Memorial Day-last Sat. in Sept. **Cost:** (Includes dinner and show) $25-$35; $12 (ages 4-12). Reservations are recommended. **Phone:** (307) 733-3370. **[TI]**

PEARL STREET BAGELS WILSON   307/739-1261 **47**
▼ Coffee/Tea Sandwiches. Quick Serve. **Address:** 1230 Ida Ln 83014

STREETFOOD AT THE STAGECOACH   307/200-6633 **46**
▼ Mexican. Quick Serve. **Address:** 5755 W SR 22 83014

SUDACHI SUSHI RESTAURANT   307/734-7832 **45**
▼▼▼ Japanese Sushi. Casual Dining. **Address:** 3465 N Pines Way, Suite 103 83014

WIND RIVER INDIAN RESERVATION (C-2)

Wind River Indian Reservation spans 2.2 million acres in western Wyoming; the tribal information office is at 15 North Fork Rd. in Fort Washakie. Of different linguistic stock and cultural background, the Shoshone and Arapaho tribes occupy different sections of the reservation. The graves of Chief Washakie and of Sacajawea, as well as the Shoshone Cultural Center, which offers displays and tours, are in Fort Washakie. Arapaho artifacts are displayed in the Arapaho Cultural Museum in Ethete.

Sun Dances are performed near Fort Washakie and Ethete for 3 days in July and August. Photography is prohibited. Powwows and rodeos are held throughout the summer. Christmas dances are performed Christmas Eve through Jan. 1.

The information office is open Mon.-Fri. 8-4:45. Phone (307) 332-3040.

WORLAND (B-3) pop. 5,487, elev. 4,061'

Worland is in a rich farming and stock-feeding area in the center of Wyoming's Big Horn Basin. Sugar beets, beans, malt barley and hay are harvested on irrigated lands; local industries produce aluminum cans, soft drinks, beet sugar and cat litter.

On the grounds of the county courthouse is a 260-year-old Douglas fir that has been carved into a monument honoring Native Americans, part of sculptor Peter Toth's "Trail of the Whispering Giants." Among the city's nine parks is Pioneer Square, which has statues honoring the area's early settlers. A nearby drinking fountain offers artesian mineral water from the Bighorn Mountains.

The Bighorn Mountains are popular with campers, hikers, hunters, skiers and snowmobilers. Passing through the city is Bighorn River, offering abundant fishing opportunities.

Vestiges of a far earlier time are the Gooseberry Formations and Painted Desert west on SR 431. In this area of dramatically eroded formations were found the remains of eohippus (dawn horse), the earliest known equine. Wild horses still can be viewed north of town.

Worland-Ten Sleep Chamber of Commerce: 111 S. 7th St., Worland, WY 82401. **Phone:** (307) 347-3226.

WASHAKIE MUSEUM & CULTURAL CENTER is at 2200 Big Horn Ave.; a 25-foot-tall bronze mam-

moth greets visitors at the entrance. Fossils, mammoth bones and rock art are on display in The Ancient Basin, an exhibit that explores the archeology, geology and paleontology of the Big Horn Basin. The Last West exhibit chronicles area history, highlighting events like the Johnson County War, the Spring Creek Raid and the harsh winter of 1886-87.

Visitors can watch movies about cattle barons and global climate change, hear stories about the Old West and the railroad era, and use a touch screen to design their own cattle brand. Changing exhibits, special events and educational programs are offered throughout the year.

Time: Allow 1 hour minimum. **Hours:** Mon.-Fri. 9-5:30, Sat. 9-5, Sun. noon-4, mid-May to mid-Sept.; Tues.-Sat. 9-4, rest of year. Closed Jan. 1, Presidents Day, Easter, Thanksgiving and Christmas. **Cost:** $8; $7 (ages 62+); $6 (ages 7-12); $25 (family). **Phone:** (307) 347-4102.

COMFORT INN WORLAND   (307)347-9898
▽▽ Hotel. **Address:** 100 N Road 11 82401

DAYS INN WORLAND   (307)347-4251
▽▽ Motel. **Address:** 500 N 10th St 82401

YELLOWSTONE NATIONAL PARK (B-1)

- Hotels p. 225 • Restaurants p. 225
- Attractions map p. 218
- Hotels & Restaurants map & index p. 220

Elevations in the park range from 5,314 ft. at the north entrance in Gardiner, Mont., to 11,358 ft. at Eagle Peak in the southeastern side of the park. Refer to AAA maps for additional elevation information.

Yellowstone National Park has five entrances: Gardiner, Mont. (north); West Yellowstone, Mont. (west); Jackson Hole via Grand Teton National Park (about 60 miles south); Cody (about 53 miles east); and Cooke City, Mont. (northeast).

The first national park, Yellowstone was established by an act of Congress in 1872. The region took its name from the dramatic gold-hued cliffs lining the river canyon, known by the Minnetaree Native Americans as *mi tse a-da-zi* (Yellow Rock River).

Though its mountain forests and meadows are beautiful in their own right, Yellowstone is unique for its geysers, hot springs, mud pools and fumaroles—the largest concentration of geothermal features in the world. The park sits atop one of the largest active volcanoes on earth, a "hot spot" that last erupted some 640,000 years ago, carving out a caldera 30 miles wide and 45 miles long. Heated by this vast subterranean magma chamber, the Yellowstone valley continues to steam and vent.

Fountains of scalding water burst high into the air from some geysers, while others bubble and spit in murky depths. Hot springs gleam in shades of emerald green and blue. Algae and bacteria withstand boiling temperatures to create these vivid colors; vigorous steam vents emit uncanny sounds and smells.

Miles of boardwalks, paved trails and driving loops allow visitors to come within close proximity of these active volcanic formations. Despite their cool

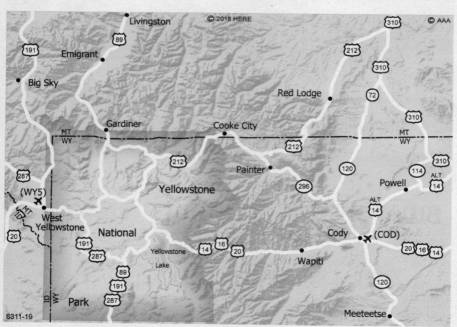

This map shows cities in Yellowstone National Park where you will find attractions, hotels and restaurants. Cities are listed alphabetically in this book on the following pages.

(See map & index p. 220.)

colors, mineral springs are boiling hot, and the solid-looking crusts around geyser formations can be remarkably fragile—keep a close watch over children while in these areas, and be sure to stay on boardwalks or formal paths.

In addition to its geologic wonders, Yellowstone National Park is also one of the most successful wildlife sanctuaries in the world. Grizzly and black bears can be sighted occasionally in the backcountry and sometimes from park roadways (a traffic situation known as a "bear jam"). The park also has several thousand elk; many mule deer, pronghorn antelopes and moose; bands of bighorn sheep; and about 4,600 bison. Gray wolves were reintroduced to Yellowstone 1995-97, and several packs now roam the park and surrounding areas; the wolf population is estimated to be between 80 and 110.

General Information

Most park roads are open to automobile travel from May through October (weather permitting). The 60-mile road between the north entrance at Gardiner, Mont., and the northeast entrance at Cooke City, Mont., is open all year. During the off-season this road is accessible only from the north entrance near Gardiner, Mont.; the northeast entrance via Red Lodge, Mont., is usually open from Memorial Day weekend through September 30. The east entrance from Cody usually opens in mid-May and remains open as weather permits.

The approach to Cooke City, Mont., from Red Lodge, Mont., via the Beartooth Scenic Highway (US 212) negotiates Beartooth Pass at an elevation of almost 11,000 feet. From Cody the approach to Sylvan Pass follows US 14/16/20 through the carved red walls of Wapiti Valley.

The road between Canyon and Tower-Roosevelt runs over Dunraven Pass and along Mount Washburn and passes Tower Fall, where things to see include the gorge, the falls on Tower Creek and the palisades of rock high above the Yellowstone River.

Although most of the park's 3,472 square miles lie in northwestern Wyoming, they also extend into Montana and Idaho. The central portion of the park is essentially a broad, elevated volcanic plateau that lies between 6,500 and 8,500 feet above sea level. On the south, east, north and northwest are mountain ranges with peaks and ridges rising between 2,000 and 4,000 feet above the enclosed tableland.

Most park facilities are open mid-May to mid-October, but food and lodging facilities are limited after October 1. During the off-season manned gas stations are available only at Gardiner and Cooke City, Mont. Unstaffed, credit card-only gas stations are available at developed locations when the roads are open. Interior park roads are open to guided

The most scenic route to Yellowstone

(See map & index p. 220.)

snowcoach and snowmobile tours from mid-December through the first week in March. During the summer, rental cars are available at Cody and Jackson as well as at Billings, Bozeman, Livingston and West Yellowstone, Mont.

The roads through the park make many of the most prominent attractions readily accessible. During the summer travel season visitors may encounter slow traffic. Be especially alert for others stopped in the road to watch wildlife; if you must stop, pull well off the highway onto a marked wayside.

Note: According to National Park Service figures, about 80 percent of the park roads are "in a structurally deficient state...including narrow shoulders and rough surfaces." The roads are being gradually repaired under a 20-year program. For up-to-date road information phone (307) 344-2117.

The park headquarters is at Mammoth Hot Springs, 5 miles from the north entrance. The main post office is at Mammoth; ranger stations are at Old Faithful, Grant Village, Tower-Roosevelt, Mammoth Hot Springs, Lake, Madison, Bechler, Canyon and the south entrance. The Mammoth ranger station, open all year, is accessible by car in winter via the north entrance. West Thumb Information Center is located at junction Grand Loop and South Entrance roads.

Park information can be received by tuning radios to 1610 AM. Low-powered transmitters broadcast from entrance stations.

From Memorial Day through Labor Day ranger-naturalists conduct geyser walks, natural- and living-history talks, photographic workshops and children's programs at Bridge Bay, Canyon, Fishing Bridge, Grant Village, Lake, Madison, Mammoth Hot Springs, Norris Geyser Basin, Old Faithful, West Thumb Geyser Basin and West Yellowstone. Free evening programs offer fun things to do with kids and are given at most park campgrounds during the summer season.

ADMISSION to the park is by private vehicle permit ($35), motorcycle permit ($30) and nonmotorized entry ($20), valid for 7 days. Park Annual Pass ($70) or America the Beautiful interagency annual pass ($80 for entrance to most federal sites) also is available. An Interagency Lifetime Senior Pass for U.S. citizens ages 62+ is $80; an Interagency Access Passport for physically impaired U.S. citizens provides free admission.

PETS are permitted in the park only if they are on a leash, crated or otherwise physically restricted at all times. They are not permitted more than 100 feet from the roads and parking areas, and are not permitted on trails, boardwalks, in the backcountry or in hydrothermal areas. It is illegal to leave pets unattended.

ADDRESS inquiries to the Superintendent, Yellowstone National Park, P.O. Box 168, Yellowstone National Park, WY 82190; phone (307) 344-7381. For Yellowstone lodging and guest service information phone (307) 344-7311 or (866) 439-7375. For road and weather information phone (307) 344-2117.

Activities

Not all of Yellowstone's grandeur can be seen from the boardwalks. More than 1,000 miles of backcountry trails lead to many of the park's less accessible attractions. A free backcountry use permit, available from any area ranger station, is required for those who wish to camp in the backcountry. The permit can be obtained in person and no more than 48 hours in advance. Advance backcountry reservations for a limited number of campsites can be obtained by mail or at a backcountry office for a $25 fee.

There is no better way to explore the park than a trip on horseback over the trails. Private stock can be ridden, or 1- or 2-hour guided rides are available at Tower-Roosevelt and Canyon from Xanterra Parks & Resorts. Horses cannot be rented without a guide.

Motorboats and rowboats can be rented from Xanterra Parks & Resorts at the Bridge Bay Marina on Yellowstone Lake. Guided fishing trips also are available. A permit is required for all vessels (motorized and nonmotorized, including float tubes) and

▼ See AAA listing p. 172 ▼

(See map & index p. 220.)

must be obtained in person. The fee is $10 for motorized vessels and $5 for nonmotorized vessels; the permits are valid for 7 days. Private boats launched in Yellowstone require an AIS (Aquatic Invasive Species) inspection in addition to a boat permit.

Jet skis, airboats, submersibles and similar watercraft are prohibited in Yellowstone National Park. All vessels are prohibited on park rivers and streams except the channel between Lewis and Shoshone lakes, where only hand-propelled vessels are permitted.

Most of the streams and lakes below the timberline contain one or more species of trout. Roadside streams and Yellowstone Lake offer some of the best fishing in the park and are fun places to go. Fishing tackle is sold by Delaware North general stores located throughout the park.

Anglers ages 16+ are required to purchase a Yellowstone National Park fishing permit. A 3-day permit costs $18; a 7-day permit is $25; a season permit is $40. Children under 16 may fish without a permit under the direct supervision of an adult who has a valid park fishing permit, or they may obtain a free permit signed by an adult. For further information phone (307) 344-2107. Fishing regulations and permits can be obtained at any ranger station, visitor center or Yellowstone Park General Stores. Fishing permits also are available at many businesses in the greater Yellowstone area. No state fishing license is required in Yellowstone National Park. The opening of the season varies from the Saturday of Memorial Day weekend to July 15 for different lakes and streams; it closes the first Sunday in November.

Check at visitor centers or ranger stations for season variations and legal limits. *See Recreation Areas Chart.*

Guided snowcoach tours by Xanterra Parks & Resorts to the interior of the park are available mid-December to early March from Mammoth Hot Springs, the south and north entrances to Yellowstone and Old Faithful Snow Lodge. Guided cross-country ski trips also are offered.

Note: It is not only against park regulations but also dangerous to feed, touch or tease any wildlife. Animals in the park are wild and should be viewed only from a safe distance. According to park regulations, you must stay at least 100 yards (the length of a football field) away from bears and wolves and at least 25 yards away from all other animals. The following items (whether new, used, clean, dirty, empty or full) may not be left unattended on picnic tables, in tents or tent trailers, in the back of pickups or in any other outdoor location at any time: food, beverage containers, cooking and eating utensils, stoves and grills, coolers and ice chests, cosmetics and toiletries, pet food and bowls, buckets and washbasins. All trash should be disposed of in bear-proof garbage cans.

ALBRIGHT VISITOR CENTER & MUSEUM is at Mammoth Hot Springs. Housed in one of the original U.S. Cavalry buildings, the headquarters museum focuses on those who shaped the history of Yellowstone, including Native Americans, mountain men, early explorers, the U.S. Army and the National Park Service. An art gallery displays the works of photographer William Henry Jackson and painter and explorer Thomas Moran. Films chronicle Moran's life and the park's development. An orientation area has interactive displays to help with trip planning, and park rangers offer talks and tours.

Hours: Daily 8-7, Memorial Day weekend-Sept. 30; 9-5, rest of year. Closed Thanksgiving and Veterans Day. Phone ahead to confirm schedule. **Cost:** Free. **Phone:** (307) 344-2263. GT

CANYON VISITOR EDUCATION CENTER is at Canyon Village. A room-size relief map illustrates Yellowstone's volcanic activity, and a variety of interactive exhibits describe the formation of geysers, hot springs and other geologic features here and around the world. A giant lava lamp demonstrates how magma rises with heat convection. Murals, dioramas and panoramas show how glaciers and volcanic eruptions have shaped the landscape.

A 20-minute film explores the connection between the park's geological origins and its wildlife. **Hours:** Daily 8-8, Memorial Day weekend-Labor Day; 8-6, day after Labor Day-Sept. 30; 9-5, May 1-day before Memorial Day and Oct. 1-10. **Cost:** Free. **Phone:** (307) 344-2550.

FISHING BRIDGE VISITOR CENTER is 1 mi. off the main park road on the east entrance road. The 1931 stone-and-log building houses exhibits about biological life in the park. Mounted specimens include a regional collection of birds, as well as a grizzly sow and cubs and a family of river otters. **Hours:** Daily 8-7, Memorial Day weekend-Sept. 30; 9-5, Oct. 1-10. **Cost:** Free. **Phone:** (307) 344-2450.

GRAND CANYON OF THE YELLOWSTONE is a section along the Yellowstone River between Canyon and Tower-Roosevelt. Noted for its spectacular yellow coloring, the deep river canyon offers striking views of the Yellowstone falls. Among the best vistas are Artist's Point on the south rim and Inspiration Point on the north rim. Lookout Point provides the best view of the Lower Falls. Uncle Tom's Trail descends about halfway and ends at the base of the Lower Falls on the south side. The Upper Falls are visible from several trails and lookouts.

GRANT VISITOR CENTER is on the shore of the West Thumb of Yellowstone Lake. Exhibits depict fire's role in shaping the environment. The film "Ten Years After Fire" recounts the 1988 blaze that

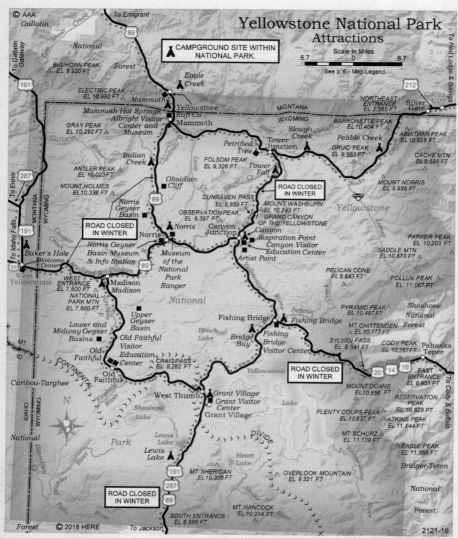

© AAA
Gallatin

To Emigrant

Yellowstone National Park
Attractions

Scale in Miles
6.7   0   6.7

See p. 6 - Map Legend

CAMPGROUND SITE WITHIN NATIONAL PARK.

National

Forest

BIG HORN PEAK
EL 9,930 FT

Eagle
Creek

To Gallatin
Gateway

ELECTRIC PEAK
EL 10,992 FT

Gardiner
Mammoth

Yellowstone
Mammoth

MONTANA

WYOMING

NORTHEAST
ENTRANCE
EL 7,365 FT

Silver
Gate

Cooke
City

To Red Lodge & Billings

Mammoth Hot Springs,
Albright Visitor
Center and
Museum

Raft Co
Mammoth

Slough
Creek

BARRONETTE PEAK
EL 10,404 FT

GRAY PEAK
EL 10,292 FT

Petrified
Tree

Tower
Junction

Pebble
Creek

DRUID PEAK
EL 9,583 FT

ABIATHAR PEAK
EL 10,928 FT

CACHE MTN
EL 9,596 FT

Indian
Creek

FOLSOM PEAK
EL 9,326 FT

Tower
Fall

ANTLER PEAK
EL 10,023 FT

Obsidian
Cliff

Yellowstone

MOUNT NORRIS
EL 9,936 FT

MOUNT HOLMES
EL 10,336 FT

Norris
Geyser
Basin

DUNRAVEN PASS
EL 8,859 FT

ROAD CLOSED
IN WINTER

MOUNT WASHBURN
EL 10,243 FT

OBSERVATION PEAK
EL 9,397 FT

GRAND CANYON
OF THE YELLOWSTONE

PARKER PEAK
EL 10,203 FT

ROAD CLOSED IN WINTER

Norris

Norris

Canyon
Junction

Canyon

Inspiration Point

Canyon Visitor
Education Center

SADDLE MTN
EL 10,670 FT

Norris Geyser
Basin Museum
& Info Station

Museum
of the
National
Park
Ranger

Artist Point

PELICAN CONE
EL 9,643 FT

POLLUX PEAK
EL 11,067 FT

Baker's Hole
Welcome
Center

PYRAMID PEAK
EL 10,497 FT

Shoshone

West
Yellowstone

WEST
ENTRANCE
EL 7,500 FT

Madison
Madison

National

MT CHITTENDEN
EL 10,177 FT

National

Forest

NATIONAL
PARK MTN
EL 7,500 FT

Upper
Geyser
Basin

Fishing Bridge

Fishing Bridge

SYLVAN PASS
EL 8,541 FT

CODY PEAK
EL 10,267 FT

Pahaska
Tepee

Lower and
Midway Geyser
Basins

Old Faithful
Visitor
Education
Center

Beach
Lake

Bridge
Bay

Fishing
Bridge
Visitor Center

Old
Faithful

CRAIG PASS
EL 8,262 FT

ROAD CLOSED IN WINTER

EAST
ENTRANCE
EL 6,951 FT

To Cody & Buffalo

Old
Faithful

Yellowstone

West Thumb

Grant Village
Grant Visitor
Center
Grant Village

Lake

MOUNT DOANE
EL 10,656 FT

RESERVATION
PEAK
EL 10,629 FT

Caribou-Targhee

Shoshone
Lake

Lewis
Lake

DIVIDE

PLENTY COUPS PEAK
EL 10,937 FT

ATKINS PEAK
EL 11,044 FT

National

Lewis
Lake

Heart
Lake

OVERLOOK MOUNTAIN
EL 9,321 FT

MT SCHURZ
EL 11,139 FT

EAGLE PEAK
EL 11,358 FT

Bridger-Teton

Park

MT SHERIDAN
EL 10,308 FT

ROAD CLOSED
IN WINTER

MT HANCOCK
EL 10,214 FT

National

Forest

Forest

© 2018 HERE

SOUTH ENTRANCE
EL 6,886 FT

To Jackson

2121-19

ROAD CLOSED
IN WINTER

ROAD CLOSED
IN WINTER

To Ennis

To Idaho Falls

MONTANA

WYOMING

IDAHO

WYOMING

(See map & index p. 220.)

scorched 1.2 million acres. **Hours:** Daily 8-7, Memorial Day weekend-Sept. 30; 9-5, Oct. 1-10. **Cost:** Free. **Phone:** (307) 344-2650.

LOWER AND MIDWAY GEYSER BASINS are n. of the Old Faithful area on the main park road. Covering 12 square miles, this area features clusters of thermal features including the Fountain Paint Pots. These boiling pools of red, yellow and brown mud change with the seasons and the water table. The 3-mile Firehole Lake Drive leads to Great Fountain Geyser, which erupts about twice a day from a beautiful travertine terrace. Excelsior Geyser, one of the largest features in the Midway Basin, discharges

thousands of gallons of water per minute into the Firehole River.

MAMMOTH HOT SPRINGS is near the park headquarters at the north entrance. The springs are characterized by terrace-like formations created by limestone deposits. Well-marked trails and boardwalks allow the safe viewing of the formations at close range. **Note:** Visitors must stay on the marked trails and boardwalks at all times, since in many places the thin crust is dangerous.

MUSEUM OF THE NATIONAL PARK RANGER is at the entrance to the Norris Campground. Housed in a 1908 soldier station, this small museum chronicles the role of national park rangers, from

(See map & index p. 220.)

early military roots to today's specialized profession. A 25-minute film, "An American Legacy," traces the history of the National Park Service. **Hours:** Daily 9-5, Memorial Day weekend-late Sept. **Cost:** Free. **Phone:** (307) 344-7353.

NORRIS GEYSER BASIN is just n. of Norris Junction on the main park road. Boardwalks and trails lead across this barren valley of steam vents and rainbow-colored pools. This is the oldest and hottest geothermal area in the park, with water temperatures above 200 degrees.

Steamboat Geyser, the world's tallest geyser, has reached heights of 300-400 feet but often remains quiet for months or years between major eruptions. Echinus Geyser was long considered the only predictable geyser at Norris, though its performance has fluctuated in the past decade. **Note:** Due to new seismic activity, some trails in this area may be closed.

NORRIS GEYSER BASIN MUSEUM & INFORMATION STATION is just off the main park road at Norris Junction. Exhibits describe the park's geothermal features, particularly in the active Norris area. **Hours:** Daily 9-6, mid-May through Sept. 30; 9-5, Oct. 1-10. **Cost:** Free. **Phone:** (307) 344-2812.

OLD FAITHFUL is on the main park road between Madison and West Thumb, just beyond the Old Faithful Inn. Though not quite as predictable as its name suggests, this 120-foot waterspout erupts every 80-90 minutes. A paved walkway and benches surround the cone geyser, keeping visitors about 300 feet away from the massive spray. Daily geyser predictions are posted at the Old Faithful Visitor Education Center and the lodge.

OLD FAITHFUL VISITOR EDUCATION CENTER is off the main park road between Madison and West Thumb, just beyond the Old Faithful Inn. Visitors can view Old Faithful through the center's massive front windows. Exhibits describe the park's geyser activity and Yellowstone history. Predictions are posted daily for eruptions throughout the park. **Hours:** Daily 8-8, Memorial Day weekend-Sept. 30; 9-5, mid-Apr. to Memorial Day weekend and Oct. 1-early Nov. **Cost:** Free. **Phone:** (307) 344-2751.

UPPER GEYSER BASIN is on the main park road between Madison and West Thumb. The area surrounding Old Faithful Lodge contains the world's largest concentration of geysers, including the star of the show, Old Faithful. Other geysers such as Grand and Riverside are less frequent but equally spectacular. Boardwalks and paved trails allow visitors to walk within safe distance of geysers, fumaroles, hot springs and mud pots across the basin. **Time:** Allow 2 hours minimum.

YELLOWSTONE LAKE is e. and s. of the park road between West Thumb and Fishing Bridge. Covering 132 square miles at 7,733 feet above sea level, this lake is the largest body of water in North America at so high an altitude. It is also home to the continent's largest population of wild cutthroat trout. The mountain lake has 110 miles of shoreline and a maximum depth of more than 400 feet. Boating and fishing are popular summer sports, but because the water stays so cold, swimming is not advised; the lake freezes over completely in winter.

RECREATIONAL ACTIVITIES

Hiking

- **Adventure Yellowstone** picks up at area hotels. Other activities are offered. **Hours:** Trips depart daily. **Phone:** (406) 585-9041.

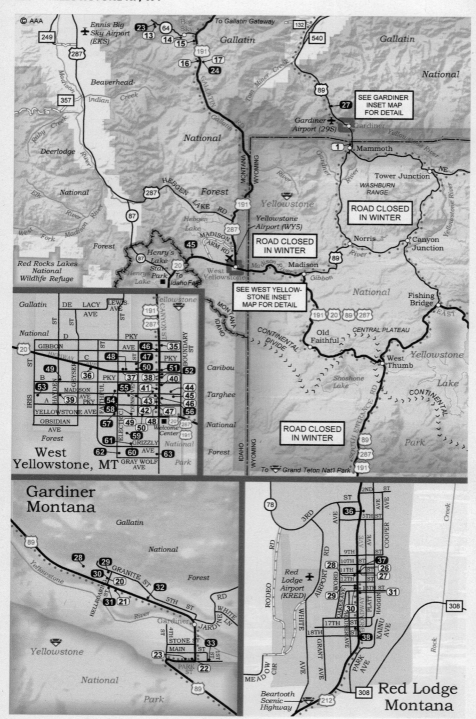

© AAA

Ennis Big Sky Airport (EKS)

To Gallatin Gateway

Gallatin

Gallatin

National

SEE GARDINER INSET MAP FOR DETAIL

Gardiner Airport (29S) Gardiner

Mammoth

Beaverhead-

Indian Creek

National

Tower Junction NE

WASHBURN RANGE

ROAD CLOSED IN WINTER

Norris Canyon Junction

Hebgen Lake

Yellowstone Airport (WY5)

ROAD CLOSED IN WINTER

Forest

Yellowstone

Madison

Fishing Bridge

EAST

National

SEE WEST YELLOW-STONE INSET MAP FOR DETAIL

West Yellowstone

To Idaho Falls

Henry's Lake State Park

Henry's Lake

Red Rocks Lakes National Wildlife Refuge

Old Faithful CENTRAL PLATEAU

CONTINENTAL DIVIDE

West Thumb

Yellowstone

Shoshone Lake

Lake

CONTINENTAL

ROAD CLOSED IN WINTER

Park

To Grand Teton Nat'l Park

West Yellowstone, MT

Gallatin

National

DE LACY AVE

LEWIS AVE

Yellowstone

GIBBON AVE

CANYON ST

BOUNDARY ST

PKY

Caribou

Targhee

National

Forest

OBSIDIAN AVE

Forest

GRIZZLY AVE

GRAY WOLF AVE

Welcome Center

Madison

YELLOWSTONE AVE

Gardiner Montana

Gallatin

National

Forest

Yellowstone River

GRANITE ST

5TH ST

Gardiner

STONE ST

MAIN ST

PARK ST

Yellowstone

National

Park

Beartooth Scenic Highway

Red Lodge Airport (KRED)

RODEO RD

MEADOW CIR

WHITE

Red Lodge Montana

Red Lodge Montana

Rock Creek

COOPER AVE

KAINU AVE

PARK AVE

GRANT AVE

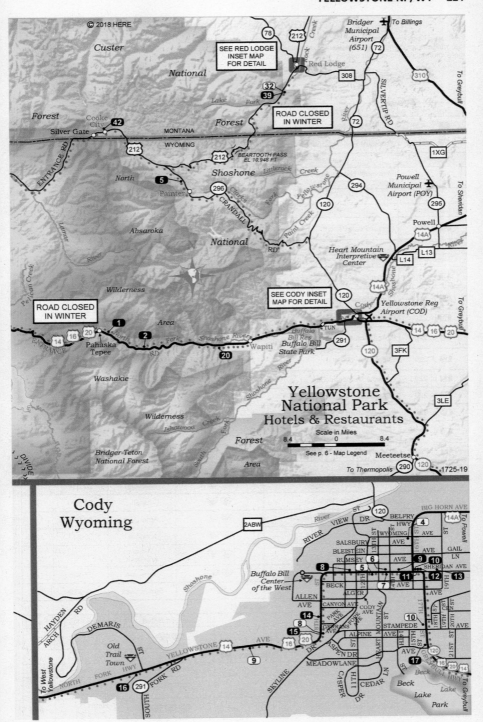

© 2018 HERE

Custer

National

SEE RED LODGE
INSET MAP
FOR DETAIL

78 · 212 · Red Lodge · 308 · To Billings · 72

Bridger
Municipal
Airport
(651)

310 · To Greybull

Forest

32
39

ROAD CLOSED
IN WINTER

Lake · Fork

72 · SILVERTIP RD · To Sheridan

Forest

Silver Gate · Cooke City · 42

National

MONTANA
WYOMING

212 · BEARTOOTH PASS EL 10,948 FT

1XG

North · 5

212 · Shoshone · Littlerock · Creek

294 · Powell
Municipal
Airport (POY)

295 · To Sheridan

ENTRANCE RD

Painter · 296 · CRANDALL RD

Clarks · Fork · Yellowstone

120

Powell · 14A

Absaroka

Paint Creek

Heart Mountain
Interpretive
Center

L14 · L13

National

Wilderness · *Area*

SEE CODY INSET
MAP FOR DETAIL

14A

ROAD CLOSED
IN WINTER

Shoshone River

1 · 14 · 18 · 20 · 2 · 20

Pahaska
Tepee

North · Fork · RD · Wapiti · Buffalo
Bill Res
Buffalo Bill
State Park

Cody

120

Yellowstone Reg
Airport (COD)

To Greybull

291

14 · 16 · 20

120 · 3FK

Washakie

ENTRANCE

Shoshone · River

3LE

Wilderness

Ishawooa · Creek

South · Fork

Yellowstone
National Park
Hotels & Restaurants

Scale in Miles
8.4 · 0 · 8.4
See p. 6 - Map Legend

3LE

DIVIDE

*Bridger-Teton
National Forest*

Forest

Area

Meeteetse

To Thermopolis · 290 · 120

1725-19

Cody
Wyoming

2ABW

River · VIEW · ST · DR · 120 · BIG HORN AVE

BELFRY
HWY
to
WYOMING

4 · 14A

To Powell

SALSBURY · AVE · AVE · GAIL LN

BLEISTEIN · AVE
RUMSEY · 6 · AVE · 9 · SHERIDAN AVE

Buffalo Bill
Center
of the West

8 · 5 · 10 · 11 · 12 · 13

HAYDEN · ARCH · RD

BECK · 7 · AVE · AVE

DEMARIS

ALLEN
AVE · ALGER · CODY · AVE

CANYON · AVE · AVE

14 · PARK · 10 · STAMPEDE

8 · AVE · AVE

15 · 20 · ALPINE · AVE

16 · ASPEN · AVE · 17 · 120

Old
Trail
Town

YELLOWSTONE · AVE · 14

9 · SKYLINE · MEADOWLANE · CEDAR

NORTH · FORK · HWY

16 · 291

SOUTH FORK RD

To West
Yellowstone

Beck
Lake
Park

To Greybull

16 · 20 · 14

Yellowstone National Park

This index helps you "spot" where approved hotels and restaurants are located on the corresponding detailed maps. Hotel daily rate range is for comparison only. Restaurant price range is a combination of lunch and/or dinner. Turn to the listing page for more information and consult display ads for special promotions.

 For more details, rates and reservations: AAA.com/travelguides/hotels

YELLOWSTONE NATIONAL PARK

Map Page	Hotels	Diamond Rated	Rate Range	Page
1 p. 220	Shoshone Lodge & Guest Ranch	◆◆	$150-$340	225
2 p. 220	Elephant Head Lodge (See ad p. 225.)	◆◆	$158-$370 [SAVE]	225

Map Page	Restaurant	Diamond Rated	Cuisine	Price Range	Page
① p. 220	Mammoth Hot Springs Hotel Dining Room	◆◆	Regional American	$8-$28	225

PAINTER

Map Page	Hotel	Diamond Rated	Rate Range	Page
5 p. 220	Hunter Peak Ranch	◆◆	Rates not provided	203

CODY

Map Page	Hotels	Diamond Rated	Rate Range	Page
8 p. 220	Moose Creek Lodge & Suites	◆◆	Rates not provided	175
9 p. 220	Cody Motor Lodge	◆	Rates not provided [SAVE]	175
10 p. 220	Comfort Inn at Buffalo Bill Village Resort	◆◆◆	$110-$215	175
11 p. 220	Holiday Inn at Buffalo Bill Village Resort	◆◆◆	Rates not provided	175
12 p. 220	Buffalo Bill Village	◆	Rates not provided	175
13 p. 220	A Western Rose Motel	◆	$85-$199	175
14 p. 220	Best Western Sunset Inn	◆◆	$151-$250 [SAVE]	175
15 p. 220	Best Western Premier Ivy Inn & Suites	◆◆◆	$125-$315 [SAVE]	175
16 p. 220	The Cody	◆◆◆	Rates not provided	175
17 p. 220	Rodeway Inn	◆	$75-$162 [SAVE]	175

Map Page	Restaurants	Diamond Rated	Cuisine	Price Range	Page
④ p. 220	Heritage Bakery & Bistro	◆◆	American	$9-$14	175
⑤ p. 220	Adriano's Italian Restaurant	◆◆	Italian	$9-$26	175
⑥ p. 220	Wyoming's Rib & Chop House	◆◆	American	$8-$32	175
⑦ p. 220	Zapata's	◆◆	Mexican	$9-$18	175
⑧ p. 220	8th Street at the Ivy	◆◆	Western American	$13-$29	175
⑨ p. 220	Bubba's Bar-B-Que Restaurant	◆◆	Barbecue	$7-$25	175
⑩ p. 220	The Breadboard	◆	Sandwiches	$4-$15	175

WAPITI

Map Page	Hotel	Diamond Rated	Rate Range	Page
20 p. 220	Bill Cody Ranch	◆◆	Rates not provided	211

BIG SKY, MT

Map Page	Hotels	Diamond Rated	Rate Range	Page
23 p. 220	The Lodge at Big Sky	◆◆◆	Rates not provided	96
24 p. 220	Rainbow Ranch Lodge	◆◆◆	Rates not provided	96

Map Page	Restaurants	Diamond Rated	Cuisine	Price Range	Page
13 p. 220	The Cabin Bar & Grill	◆◆	Regional American	$10-$38	96
14 p. 220	Lotus Pad	◆◆	Thai	$14-$24	96
15 p. 220	Buck's T-4	◆◆◆	Regional American	$13-$39	96
16 p. 220	**The Corral Steakhouse**	◆◆	Steak	$9-$35	96
17 p. 220	Rainbow Ranch Lodge	◆◆◆	Regional American	$30-$60	96

GARDINER, MT

Map Page	Hotels	Diamond Rated	Rate Range	Page
27 p. 220	Yellowstone Basin Inn	◆◆	$100-$535	110
28 p. 220	Yellowstone Village Inn	◆◆	Rates not provided	110
29 p. 220	Travelodge Gardiner at Yellowstone Park North Entrance	◆◆		110
30 p. 220	Comfort Inn Yellowstone North	◆◆	$186-$277	110
31 p. 220	**Best Western By Mammoth Hot Springs**	◆◆	$139-$269 SAVE	109
32 p. 220	Yellowstone Super 8-Gardiner	◆◆	$50-$222	110
33 p. 220	**Yellowstone River Motel**	◆	$78-$199 SAVE	110

Map Page	Restaurants	Diamond Rated	Cuisine	Price Range	Page
20 p. 220	The Antler Pub & Grill	◆◆	American	$9-$28	110
21 p. 220	**Yellowstone Mine Restaurant**	◆◆	American	$9-$22	110
22 p. 220	Rosie's Bistro	◆	American	$10-$17	110
23 p. 220	The Raven Grill	◆◆	American	$9-$26	110

RED LODGE, MT

Map Page	Hotels	Diamond Rated	Rate Range	Page
36 p. 220	Comfort Inn by Choice Hotels of Red Lodge	◆◆	$110-$198	134
37 p. 220	The Pollard	◆◆	Rates not provided	134
38 p. 220	Yodeler Motel	◆◆	Rates not provided	134
39 p. 220	Rock Creek Resort	◆◆	Rates not provided	134

Map Page	Restaurants	Diamond Rated	Cuisine	Price Range	Page
26 p. 220	The Pub at the Pollard	◆◆	American	$7-$20	135
27 p. 220	The Dining Room at The Pollard	◆◆◆	Regional American	$10-$36	135
28 p. 220	Bogart's	◆◆	American	$9-$24	134
29 p. 220	Red Lodge Pizza Co.	◆◆	Pizza	$9-$25	135
30 p. 220	Carbon County Steakhouse	◆◆◆	Steak	$12-$36	134
31 p. 220	China Garden	◆◆	Chinese	$8-$17	135
32 p. 220	Old Piney Dell	◆◆◆	American	$16-$32	135

COOKE CITY, MT

Map Page	Hotel	Diamond Rated	Rate Range	Page
42 p. 220	Elk Horn Lodge	◆	$160-$180	104

WEST YELLOWSTONE, MT

Map Page	Hotels	Diamond Rated	Rate Range	Page
45 p. 220	**Super 8 West Yellowstone**	◆◆	$113-$325 SAVE	140
46 p. 220	**Best Western Weston Inn**	◆◆	$139-$329 SAVE	138

WEST YELLOWSTONE, MT (cont'd)

Map Page	Hotels (cont'd)	Diamond Rated	Rate Range	Page
47 p. 220	**One Horse Motel**	◈	$122-$148 [SAVE]	140
48 p. 220	Evergreen Motel	◈	Rates not provided	139
49 p. 220	**Lazy G Motel**	◈	$119 [SAVE]	140
50 p. 220	**Crosswinds Inn**	◈◈	Rates not provided [SAVE]	138
51 p. 220	**Brandin' Iron Inn**	◈◈	$79-$239 [SAVE]	138
52 p. 220	**Best Western Desert Inn**	◈◈◈	$105-$320 [SAVE]	138
53 p. 220	Yellowstone West Gate Hotel	◈◈	Rates not provided	140
54 p. 220	**Days Inn West Yellowstone**	◈◈	$100-$278 [SAVE]	139
55 p. 220	West Yellowstone City Center Motel	◈	Rates not provided	140
56 p. 220	**Alpine Motel**	◈◈	$109-$199 [SAVE]	138
57 p. 220	**Holiday Inn West Yellowstone Conference Hotel** *(See ad p. 139.)*	◈◈◈	Rates not provided [SAVE]	139
58 p. 220	Three Bear Lodge	◈◈	Rates not provided	140
59 p. 220	ClubHouse Inn	◈◈	$189-$349	138
60 p. 220	**Explorer Cabins at Yellowstone** *(See ad p. 139.)*	◈◈◈	Rates not provided [SAVE]	139
61 p. 220	**Yellowstone Park Hotel** *(See ad p. 139.)*	◈◈◈	$89-$329 [SAVE]	140
62 p. 220	Yellowstone Lodge	◈◈	Rates not provided	140
63 p. 220	**Gray Wolf Inn & Suites** *(See ad p. 139.)*	◈◈◈	$89-$329 [SAVE]	139

Map Page	Restaurants	Diamond Rated	Cuisine	Price Range	Page
㉟ p. 220	Cafe Madriz	◈◈	Spanish Small Plates	$8-$30	140
㊱ p. 220	Ernie's Bakery, Sandwich Shop & Deli	◈	Breakfast Sandwiches	$7-$19	140
㊲ p. 220	Euro Cafe	◈◈	Breakfast Sandwiches	$9-$13	140
㊳ p. 220	Slippery Otter Pub & Eatery	◈◈	American	$10-$31	140
㊴ p. 220	Running Bear Pancake House	◈◈	Breakfast Sandwiches	$7-$15	140
㊵ p. 220	Bullwinkle's Saloon & Eatery	◈◈	American	$10-$49	140
㊶ p. 220	Pete's Rocky Mountain Pizza & Pasta	◈◈	Pizza Sandwiches	$8-$20	140
㊷ p. 220	Gusher Pizza and Sandwich Shoppe	◈◈	American	$8-$16	140
㊸ p. 220	Madison Crossing Lounge	◈◈◈	American	$14-$25	140
㊹ p. 220	Red Lotus	◈◈	Chinese	$9-$28	140
㊺ p. 220	Wild West Pizzeria & Saloon	◈◈	Pizza Sandwiches	$9-$24	140
㊻ p. 220	Arrowleaf Ice Cream Parlor & Grill	◈	Burgers	$6-$9	140
㊼ p. 220	Canyon Street Grill	◈◈	Burgers Sandwiches	$8-$17	140
㊽ p. 220	Serenity Bistro	◈◈	New French	$12-$38	140
㊾ p. 220	**Three Bear Restaurant**	◈◈	American	$8-$25	140
㊿ p. 220	Timberline Cafe	◈◈	American	$8-$19	140

(See map & index p. 220.)

ELEPHANT HEAD LODGE　　(307)587-3980　**2**

◆◆◆◆
Historic Cabin
$158-$370

Address: 1170 N Fork Hwy 82414 **Location:** 11.7 mi e of Yellowstone National Park east gate on US 14/16/20. **Facility:** Located just minutes from the park entrance, this small mountain lodge features cozy wilderness cabins, including three with lofts. All have spectacular views and decks for watching wildlife. 15 cabins. 1 story, exterior corridors. **Terms:** closed 10/1-5/14, 30 day cancellation notice-fee imposed. **Activities:** fishing, recreation programs in season, playground, picnic facilities, trails. (See ad this page.)

[SAVE] [🍴] [🍷] [BIZ] [📶] [✕] [🚭] [🅆] [☎] [▣]
/ [SOME UNITS] [🐾] [🛄] [💼]

SHOSHONE LODGE & GUEST RANCH　(307)587-4044　**1**
◆◆◆◆ Cabin. **Address:** 349 North Fork Hwy 82190

WHERE TO EAT

MAMMOTH HOT SPRINGS HOTEL DINING ROOM
　　　　　　　　307/344-7901　**1**
◆◆◆◆ Regional American. Casual Dining. **Address:** Mammoth Hot Springs 82190

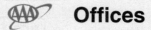 **Offices**

Main office listings are shown in **BOLD TYPE** and toll-free member service numbers appear in *ITALIC TYPE*.
All are closed Saturdays, Sundays and holidays unless otherwise indicated.
The addresses, phone numbers and hours for any AAA/CAA office are subject to change.
The type of service provided is designated below the name of the city where the office is located:

✛ Auto travel services, including books and maps, and on-demand TripTik® routings.
● Auto travel services, including selected books and maps, and on-demand TripTik® routings.
■ Books/maps only, no marked maps or on-demand TripTik® routings.
▲ Travel Agency Services, cruise, tour, air, car and rail reservations; domestic and international hotel reservations; passport photo services; international and domestic travel guides and maps; travel money products; and International Driving Permits. In addition, assistance with travel related insurance products including trip cancellation, travel accident, lost luggage, trip delay and assistance products.
✪ Insurance services provided. If only this icon appears, only insurance services are provided at that office.
🅲 Car Care Plus Facility provides car care services.
🅲🅳 Electric vehicle charging station on premises.

AAA NATIONAL OFFICE: 1000 AAA DRIVE, HEATHROW, FLORIDA 32746-5063, (407) 444-7000

IDAHO

BOISE—AAA OREGON/IDAHO, 7155 W DENTON ST, 83704. WEEKDAYS (M-F) 8:00-5:30, WED 8:00-6:30. (208) 342-9391, *(800) 999-9391.* ✛ ▲ ✪

COEUR D'ALENE—AAA WASHINGTON, 296 W SUNSET AVE #33, 83815. WEEKDAYS (M-F) 8:30-5:30. (208) 664-5868, *(800) 407-2020.* ● ▲ ✪

IDAHO FALLS—AAA OREGON/IDAHO, 3418 S 25TH EAST, 83404. WEEKDAYS (M-F) 8:30-5:30. ✛ ▲ ✪

LEWISTON—AAA WASHINGTON, 802 BRYDEN AVE, 83501. WEEKDAYS (M-F) 8:30-5:30. (208) 798-5555 ✪

MERIDIAN—AAA OREGON/IDAHO, 2310 E OVERLAND STE 110, 83642. WEEKDAYS (M-F) 8:30-5:30. (208) 884-4222 ✛ ▲ ✪

POCATELLO—AAA OREGON/IDAHO, 1000 POCATELLO CRK RD #E5, 83201. WEEKDAYS (M-F) 8:30-5:30, WED 8:30-6:30. (208) 237-2225, *(800) 574-4222.* ✛ ▲ ✪

TWIN FALLS—AAA OREGON/IDAHO, 1239 POLE LINE RD E #315, 83301. WEEKDAYS (M-F) 8:30-5:30. (208) 734-6441, *(800) 999-6441.* ✛ ▲ ✪

MONTANA

BILLINGS—AAA MOUNTAINWEST, 1111 MAIN ST #12, 59105. WEEKDAYS (M-F) 9:00-5:00 (OR CALL FOR AN APPOINTMENT). (406) 969-2277 ✪

BILLINGS—AAA MOUNTAINWEST, 3220 4TH AVE N, 59101. WEEKDAYS (M-F) 8:30-5:30. (406) 248-7738, *(800) 391-4222.* ✛ ▲ ✪

BOZEMAN—AAA MOUNTAINWEST, 1530 N 19TH AVE STE B, 59718. WEEKDAYS (M-F) 8:30-5:30. (406) 586-6156, *(800) 391-4222.* ✛ ▲ ✪

BOZEMAN—AAA MOUNTAINWEST, 3508 LARAMIE DR STE 1, 59718. WEEKDAYS (M-F) 9:00-5:00. (406) 586-4334 ■

GREAT FALLS—AAA MOUNTAINWEST, 1520 3RD ST NW STE G, 59404. WEEKDAYS (M-F) 8:30-5:30. (406) 727-2900, *(800) 391-4222.* ✛ ▲ ✪

HELENA—AAA MOUNTAINWEST, 2100 11TH AVE, 59601. WEEKDAYS (M-F) 8:30-5:30. (406) 447-8100, *(800) 332-6119.* ✛ ▲ ✪

KALISPELL—AAA MOUNTAINWEST, 135 HUTTON RANCH RD #106, 59901. WEEKDAYS (M-F) 8:30-5:30. (406) 758-6980, *(800) 391-4222.* ✛ ▲ ✪

MISSOULA—AAA MOUNTAINWEST, 1200 S RESERVE STE B, 59801. WEEKDAYS (M-F) 8:30-5:30. (406) 829-5500, *(800) 391-4222.* ✛ ▲ ✪

MISSOULA—AAA MOUNTAINWEST, 2704 BROOKS STE 1, 59801. WEEKDAYS (M-F) 9:00-5:00. (406) 926-1282 ✪

WYOMING

CHEYENNE—AAA MOUNTAINWEST, 2316 DELL RANGE BLVD #B, 82009. WEEKDAYS (M-F) 8:30-5:30. (307) 634-8861, *(800) 391-4222.* ✛ ▲ ✪

ROCK SPRINGS—AAA MOUNTAINWEST, 157 K ST, 82901. WEEKDAYS (M-F) 9:00-5:00. (307) 362-1222 ✪

Border Information

U.S. Residents Traveling to Canada

Border crossing requirements: Travelers are required to present proper travel documents in order to enter Canada and return to the U.S.

Air travel: A U.S. passport is required.

Land or sea travel: Proof of citizenship and proof of identity are required. Approved documents include a passport or passport card, Enhanced Driver's License or NEXUS trusted traveler program card. Visit the U.S. Department of State website travel.state.gov for the most current information on these requirements. Canadian citizens should refer to the Canada Border Services Agency website www.cbsa-asfc.gc.ca.

U.S. resident aliens: An Alien Registration Receipt Card (Green Card) as well as a passport from the country of citizenship is required.

Children: All children must provide their own travel documents. In lieu of a U.S. passport or passport card, children under 16 traveling to Canada by land or sea may present an original or copy of their birth certificate, a Report of Birth Abroad obtained from a U.S. Consulate or a Naturalization Certificate. Minors must be accompanied by both parents; if one parent is absent, a notarized letter of consent from the absent parent giving permission to go on the trip is required.

Legal Issues: Persons with felony convictions, DUI convictions or other offenses may be denied entry into Canada.

Firearms: Canada has strict laws regarding the importing, exporting, possession, use, storage, display and transportation of firearms. These are federal laws that apply across the country. Firearms are divided into classes: non-restricted (most ordinary rifles and shotguns); restricted (mainly handguns) and prohibited (full and converted automatics and certain handguns, among others).

To bring a non-restricted or restricted firearm into Canada you must:
- Be 18 years of age or older
- Declare firearm(s) in writing at the first point of entry
- Obtain an Authorization to Transport (ATT) from a provincial or territorial Chief Firearms Officer prior to arrival at the point of entry; contact the Canadian Firearms Centre at (800) 731-4000 for additional details.

Hunters may bring in, duty-free, 200 rounds of ammunition; a valid license or declaration to purchase ammunition is required. Those planning to hunt in multiple provinces or territories must obtain a hunting license from each one.

Firearms are forbidden in many of Canada's national and provincial parks, game reserves and adjacent areas. For additional information regarding the temporary importation and use of firearms consult the Canada Border Services Agency website.

Personal items: Clothing, personal items, sports and recreational equipment, automobiles, snowmobiles, cameras, personal computers and food products appropriate for the purpose and duration of the visit may be brought into Canada duty and tax-free. Customs may require a refundable security deposit at the time of entry.

Tobacco products: Those meeting age requirements (18 years in Alberta, Manitoba, Northwest Territories, Nunavut, Saskatchewan, Quebec and Yukon; 19 years in other provinces) may bring in up to 50

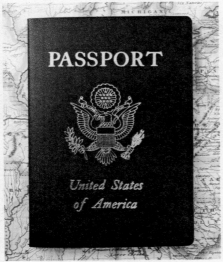

cigars, 200 cigarettes, 200 grams of tobacco and 200 tobacco sticks.

Alcohol: Those meeting age requirements (18 years in Alberta, Manitoba and Quebec; 19 years in other provinces and territories) may bring in limited alcoholic beverages: 40 fluid ounces (1.14 litres) of liquor, 53 fluid ounces (1.5 litres) of wine (about two 750-ml bottles) or 287 fluid ounces (8.5 litres) of beer or ale (the equivalent of 24 12-ounce bottles or cans).

- Amounts exceeding the allowable quantities are subject to federal duty and taxes, and provincial/territorial liquor fees.
- Provincial fees are paid at customs at the time of entry in all provinces and Yukon.
- It is illegal to bring more than the allowable alcohol quantity into the Northwest Territories or Nunavut.

Purchases: Articles purchased at Canadian duty-free shops are subject to U.S. Customs exemptions and restrictions; those purchased at U.S. duty-free shops before entering Canada are subject to duty if brought back into the United States.

Prescription drugs: Persons requiring medication while visiting Canada are permitted to bring it for their own use. Medication should be in the original packaging with a label listing the drug and its intended use. Bring a copy of the prescription and the prescribing doctor's phone number.

Gifts: Items not exceeding $60 (CAN) in value (excluding tobacco, alcoholic beverages and advertising matter) taken into or mailed to Canada are allowed free entry. Gifts valued at more than $60 are subject to regular duty and taxes on the excess amount.

Pets: You must have a certificate for a dog or cat 3 months and older. It must clearly describe the animal, declare that the animal is currently vaccinated against rabies and include a licensed veterinarian signature.

- Collar tags are not sufficient proof of immunization.
- Be sure the vaccination does not expire while traveling in Canada.
- The certificate is also required to bring the animal back into the U.S.

Exemptions: Service animals; healthy puppies and kittens under 3 months old with a health certificate signed by a licensed

veterinarian indicating that the animal is too young to vaccinate.

Vehicles
- Vehicles entering Canada for leisure travel, including trailers not exceeding 8 feet 6 inches (2.6 m) in width, are generally subject to quick and routine entry procedures.
- To temporarily leave or store a car, trailer or other goods in Canada if you must leave the country, you must pay an import duty and taxes or present a valid permit. Canadian Customs officials issue vehicle permits at the point of entry.
- You are required to carry your vehicle registration document when traveling in Canada.
- If driving a car other than your own, you must have written permission from the owner.
- If driving a rented car, you must provide a copy of the rental contract.
- A valid U.S. driver's license is valid in Canada.
- In all Canadian provinces and territories except Alberta, British Columbia and Saskatchewan, it is illegal to use radar detectors, even if unplugged.
- Seat belt use is required for the driver and all passengers.

Financial Responsibility Laws in Canada: When an accident involves death, injury or property damage, Canadian provinces and territories require evidence of financial responsibility.

U.S. motorists should check with their insurance company regarding whether they are required to obtain and carry a yellow Non-Resident Inter-Province Motor Vehicle Liability Insurance Card (accepted as evidence of financial responsibility throughout Canada). Those not carrying proper proof may be subject to a substantial fine. If renting a vehicle, check with the rental car company.

U.S. Residents Returning to the U.S.

U.S. citizens returning to the U.S. from Canada by air must have a valid passport. Those returning by land or sea are required to present the appropriate travel documents outlined above.

Every individual seeking entry into the United States—foreign visitors, U.S. citizens or lawful permanent residents—must be inspected at the point of entry and each family (persons living in the same household related by blood, marriage, domestic partnership or adoption) must complete a declarations form. Random searches may be conducted by U.S. Customs and Border Protection agents.

U.S. Exemptions for a Stay in Canada of 48 Hours or More

- Each individual may bring back tax- and duty-free articles not exceeding $800 in retail value.
- Any amount over the $800 exemption is subject to duty.
- The exemption is allowed once every 31 days.
- A family may combine purchases to avoid exceeding individual exemption limits.
- Exemptions are based on fair retail value (keep receipts of all purchases as proof).
- Exemptions apply to articles acquired only for personal or household use or as gifts and not intended for sale.
- The exemption may include 100 cigars, 200 cigarettes and 1 litre (33.8 fluid ounces) of liquor per person over age 21. Customs enforces state liquor laws.
- All articles must accompany you on your return.

U.S. Exemptions for a Stay in Canada Less Than 48 Hours

- Each individual may bring back tax- and duty-free articles not exceeding $200 in retail value.
- The exemption may include no more than 10 cigars, 50 cigarettes, 150 millilitres (5 fluid ounces) of alcohol or 150 millilitres of perfume containing alcohol.
- A family may not combine purchases.
- If purchases exceed the $200 exemption, you forfeit the exemption and all purchases become subject to duty.
- All articles must be declared and accompany you upon return.

Gifts

- Gifts up to $100 fair retail value may be sent to friends or relatives in the United States provided no recipient receives more than one gift per day (gifts do not have to be included in the $800 exemption).
- Gifts of tobacco products, alcoholic beverages or perfume containing alcohol valued at more than $5 retail are excluded from this provision.

- Mark the contents, retail value and "Unsolicited Gift" on the outside of the package.

Prohibited: Narcotics and dangerous drugs, drug paraphernalia, obscene articles and publications, seditious or treasonable matter, lottery tickets, hazardous items (fireworks, dangerous toys, toxic or poisonous substances) citrus products and switchblade knives. Also prohibited are any goods originating in embargoed countries.

Canadian Residents Traveling to the U.S.

Canadian citizens entering the U.S. by air must have a valid passport. Canadian citizens entering the U.S. by land or sea are required to present the appropriate travel documents; refer to the Canada Border Services Agency website www.cbsa-asfc.gc.ca or travel.state.gov for the most current information on these requirements.

If traveling to the United States with a minor 15 years or younger, carry documentation proving your custodial rights. A person under age 18 traveling to the United States alone or with only one parent or another adult must carry certified documentation proving that the trip is permitted by both parents.

U.S. Customs permits Canadian residents to bring—duty-free for personal use and not intended for sale—the following: clothing, personal items and equipment appropriate to

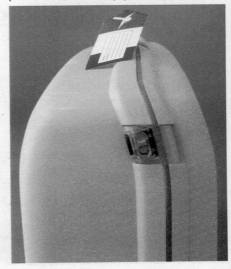

the trip, up to 200 cigarettes, 50 cigars or 2 kilograms of tobacco, and 1 litre of liquor.

Canadian Residents Returning to Canada

There are no exemptions for same-day cross-border shoppers.

Canadian residents may claim a $200 (CAN) exemption on goods, excluding alcoholic beverages and tobacco products, if returning after less than 48 hours and not using any other exemption. This exemption may apply any number of times in a year. No tobacco or alcohol may be brought back if returning from a visit of less than 48 hours.

For each absence of 48 hours or more (but fewer than seven days), residents may bring back, free of duty and taxes, goods valued up to $800 (CAN) any number of times a year, provided the visit to the United States is 48 hours or more and all goods accompany the purchaser (a written declaration may be required).

If returning after 7 days or more (not counting the departure day from Canada) you may claim up to a $800 (CAN) exemption, but goods other than alcohol and tobacco products need not accompany you (a written declaration may be required).

Permitted within the $200 and $800 exemptions: up to 50 cigars, 200 cigarettes, 200 tobacco sticks and 200 grams of tobacco; and up to 1.14 litres (40 fluid ounces) of liquor, 1.5 litres (53 fluid ounces) of wine (about two 750-ml bottles) or 8.5 litres (287 fluid ounces) of beer or ale (the equivalent of 24 12-ounce bottles or cans). You must meet the minimum age requirement of the province or territory entered to claim alcohol or tobacco products.

While AAA makes every effort to provide accurate and complete information, AAA makes no warranty, express or implied, and assumes no legal liability or responsibility for the accuracy or completeness of any information contained herein.

Photo Credits

Page numbers are in bold type. Picture credit abbreviations are as follows:
- (i) numeric sequence from top to bottom, left to right ▪ (AAA) AAA Travel library.

- (Cover) Glacier National Park, MT / © iStockphoto.com / stellalevi

- **2** (i) © iStockphoto.com / norme

- **2** (ii) © iStockphoto.com/ magmarcz

- **2** (iii) © iStockphoto.com / powerofforever

- **8** (i) © iStockphoto.com / Ron_Thomas

- **8** (ii) © iStockphoto.com / zrfphoto

- **9** © iStockphoto.com / christiannafzger

- **10** (i) Courtesy of Wikimedia Commons

- **10** (ii) Courtesy of Wikimedia Commons

- **13** (i) © iStockphoto.com / Riishede

- **13** (ii) © iStockphoto.com / Silvrshootr

- **13** (iii) © iStockphoto.com / vkbhat

- **13** (iv) © iStockphoto.com / NikonShutterman

- **13** (v) © iStockphoto.com / DIGIcal

- **14** (i) © iStockphoto.com / norme

- **14** (ii) © iStockphoto.com / Pierdelune

- **14** (iii) © Wolfgang Kaehler / age fotostock

- **14** (iv) © Jcarr29 / Wikimedia Commons / CC BY SA

- **72** (i) © iStockphoto.com / Dean_Fikar

- **72** (ii) © iStockphoto.com / RiverNorthPhotography

- **73** © iStockphoto.com / ANDY_BOWLIN

- **74** (i) Courtesy of Wikimedia Commons

- **74** (ii) © Jeremy Blakeslee / Wikimedia Commons / CC BY SA

- **77** (i) © iStockphoto.com / tonda

- **77** (ii) © iStockphoto.com / ChrisBoswell

- **77** (iii) © iStockphoto.com / mlharing

- **77** (iv) © iStockphoto.com / Dean_Fikar

- **77** (v) © iStockphoto.com/ magmarcz

- **78** (i) Stephen Saks Photography / Alamy Stock Photo

- **78** (ii) © SuperStock / age fotostock

- **78** (iii) © Yunner / Wikimedia Commons / CC BY SA

- **78** (iv) Patti McConville / Alamy Stock Photo

- **144** (i) © iStockphoto.com / SeanXu

- **144** (ii) © iStockphoto.com / lightpix

- **145** © iStockphoto.com / RiverNorthPhotography

- **146** (i) Courtesy of Wikimedia Commons

- **146** (ii) Courtesy of Wikimedia Commons

- **149** (i) © iStockphoto.com / James Brey

- **149** (ii) © iStockphoto.com / Juanmonino

- **149** (iii) © iStockphoto.com / Ron_Thomas

- **149** (iv) © iStockphoto.com / VirtualVV

- **149** (v) © iStockphoto.com / stellalevi

- **150** (i) Ian Dagnall Commercial Collection / Alamy Stock Photo

- **150** (ii) © iStockphoto.com / powerofforever

- **150** (iii) © SuperStock / age fotostock

- **150** (iv) © iStockphoto.com / pawel.gaul

- **225** Garry Gay / Alamy Stock Photo

- **227** © image100 / age fotostock

Use the free travel planning tools at AAA.com/maps

Hit the Road with Identity Theft Protection

Identity thieves don't take vacations. Ensure you're protected before you leave.

Visit your local AAA/CAA office or online at

AAA.com/IDTheft • CAA.ca

All products not available at all locations.

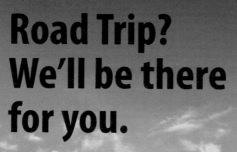

LET'S GET SOCIAL

Stay connected with AAA and CAA

Visit with us on your favorite social media sites for the latest updates on hot discounts, cool destinations and handy automotive know-how. *Talk with us!*

 AAA.com/Facebook

 AAA.com/Twitter

 Instagram.com/aaa_national

 AAA.com/Googleplus

 YouTube.com/AAA

CAA Social Media:
CAA.ca/social

Bring It Home

You always want the best for those you care about. Extend the same benefits you enjoy with a **AAA/CAA Associate Membership.** With roadside assistance, vacation planning, travel guides, exclusive savings, and much more, they can rely on AAA/CAA.

To purchase an Associate Membership, contact your local club office, visit **AAA.com** or **CAA.ca**, or call **800-Join-AAA** (564-6222).

The **FREEDOM** to Get Where You Want to Go

Take advantage of valuable resources from the leading authority on senior driver safety and mobility.

Before you hit the open road, make the AAA or CAA senior driving site the first stop on your journey.

SeniorDriving.AAA.com
SeniorsDriving.CAA.ca

We're here to get you there.

AAA members get more with Hertz.*

- Up to 20% savings on the base rate of all rentals
- Additional driver fee waived for AAA members
- Complimentary use of one child safety seat
- Young Renter fee waived for AAA members ages 20-24
- Free Hertz Gold Plus Rewards® membership with exclusive bonus points
- Discounted NeverLost® navigation system and satellite radio
- 10% off prepay fuel option

Click: AAA.com/hertz
Call: 1-800-654-3080
Visit: Your local AAA branch or Hertz neighborhood location.